CONTENTS

Directory of Maps

ABOUT THE AUTHOR

Eric Lindberg is a Denver-based travel writer and photographer specializing in adventure travel, culture, the outdoors, and offbeat, far-flung destinations. A member of the Society of American Travel Writers (SATW), he has won numerous photography and writing awards for work published nationally and abroad. Eric is the 2013 and 2011 Photographer of the Year, SATW. For more information, visit ericlindberg.com.

ACKNOWLEDGMENTS

Thanks to Rich Grant, Katie Converse, and Deborah Park from Visit Denver for sharing their expertise and familiarity with the many attractions, activities, and events that make the city such a wonderful place to live and play. Thanks to Dan Rabin for his expert advice on Denver's ever-expanding beer culture.

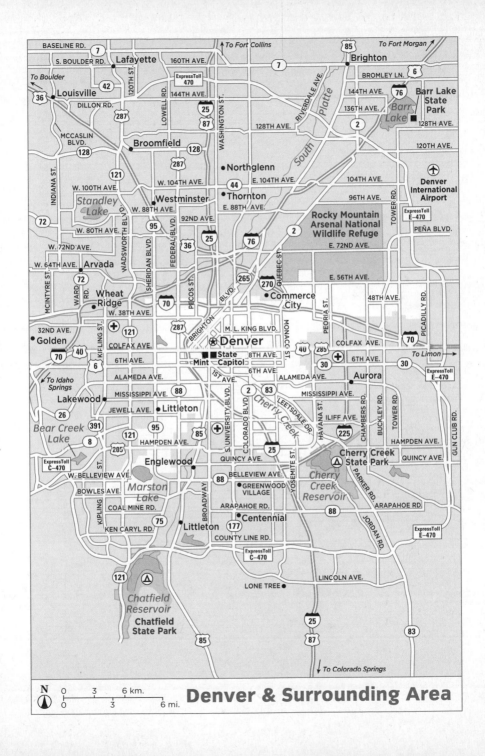

Denver & Surrounding Area

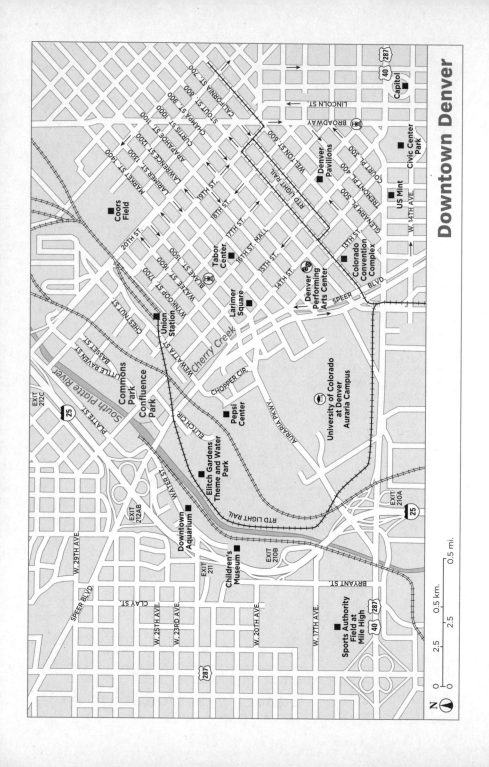

Downtown Denver

INTRODUCTION

Welcome to the Mile High City. Whether you're relocating or just visiting, I'm sure you'll love it here. With sweeping Rocky Mountain vistas and casual hospitality, Denver is a place rich in history, beauty, and excitement. *Insiders' Guide to Denver* is designed to help you make the most of your time here.

For starters, chances are good that if you're already in Denver reading this book, the sky will be a startling shade of blue for at least part of the day. The sun shines 300 days a year here, and sunglasses are highly recommended. In fact, bad weather is perhaps the biggest misconception about Denver. Put simply, snowcapped peaks in the Rockies don't mean snow-covered streets in Denver. We do get the occasional blizzard, but most snows melt within a day or two, leaving fresh, clean air and sunny weather in their wake.

Beyond the great climate, Denver is a vibrant, growing city. It's no surprise that Democrats chose it as the site of their 2008 National Convention; nor did all that national attention hurt Denver's reputation as a great place to stage a mammoth party. Regardless of why you're visiting, one of the first landmarks many visitors see is Denver International Airport (DIA), Denver's gateway to the rest of the world. In addition to its spectacular tented terminal building, DIA is known for its beautiful stonework, whimsical artwork, great views of both mountains and open plains, and a location that provides easy access to Colorado's interstate system.

Even die-hard Denver lovers find new things to treasure about our city. For instance, our city parks are vast expanses of green space with walking trails and flower beds. Denver has more than 850 miles of paved off-road bike trails. If what you really want is great shopping, you're in luck there too. The Cherry Creek Shopping Center stands as the area's top attraction, surpassing even the Mint, Coors Brewery, and the Denver museums in tourist draw, but it shares the retail arena with other regional shopping centers strewn throughout the Metro Denver area.

Denver is also a sports town, with modern venues for all its professional teams. Coors Field in Lower Downtown houses the Colorado Rockies baseball team. The glass and steel Pepsi Center, also in Lower Downtown, is shared by the Colorado Avalanche hockey team and Denver's basketball team, the Nuggets. The Denver Broncos play nearby at Sports Authority Field at Mile High, and the stadium is also the venue for the Denver Outlaws professional lacrosse team. The Colorado Rapids, a professional soccer team, plays its games at the new Dick's Sporting Goods Park in Commerce City. A new facility called the Broomfield Events Center was built on the northwestern edge of Metro Denver for two minor league clubs—the Rocky Mountain Rage hockey team and the Colorado 14ers basketball team.

There are so many things to do in or near downtown these days that boredom is out of the question. Elitch Gardens Theme & Water Park is located in the once-abandoned Platte Valley area just west of downtown. Brewpubs are a way of life—in or out of baseball season.

And the 16th Street Mall and Larimer Square (Larimer Street between 14th and 15th Streets downtown) are year-round destinations where visitors can experience Denver's flavor and appreciation for historical buildings and the lore that accompanies them.

And more development is yet to come. Denver's Union Station is set to become a regional transit/retail/housing center similar to Union Station in Washington, DC, and the Ferry Building in San Francisco. Commons Park continues to grow on the western edge of the transit site, and the metropolitan governments continue the expansion of one of the best urban trail systems in the country. If cultural experiences are also your interest, the Denver Art Museum opened the Frederic C. Hamilton Building in 2006, completing its seven-year, $90.5-million expansion project. The newly inaugurated Clyfford Still Museum houses the work of one of America's leading abstract expressionist painters.

While no book can ever capture everything great about a metropolitan area as diverse as Denver, this one attempts to distill the best of everything into a format that will give newcomers the inside scoop, offer visitors a guide on what to see and experience, and bring even more information to longtime Denverites. So go forth and tour, buy a pair of cowboy boots, picnic in the park, and gaze at the mountains from the middle of the city while savoring the beauty.

HOW TO USE THIS BOOK

Insiders' Guide to Denver is designed to let you flip easily through the pages, either looking for something specific or simply finding something that catches your eye. For overall subject areas, such as nightlife or shopping, go to the Contents. To find information on specific places, such as the name of a restaurant or a ski resort, consult the Index.

This book is a guide, not a directory. So while I've made sure to include all the leading tourist attractions, restaurants, hotels, and natural wonders in Metro Denver, to a great extent my choices are personal. But that's one of this guide's strong points—honest, knowledgeable insider-based information on Denver and five of the six surrounding counties. Boulder County has enough of its own attractions to warrant a separate book, *Insiders' Guide to Boulder and Rocky Mountain National Park.*

Nor is this book a novel. It's designed to be read selectively, on a need-to-know or want-to-know basis, rather than all in one sitting. Each chapter stands alone and has its own introduction. If you are new to the area, you'll want to start by reading through the Area Overview and Getting Here, Getting Around chapters. Then carry the book in your backpack as you explore, or tuck it in the glove box of your car. When you want to know where to stop for lunch, or whether the Denver Zoo is open on Sunday (it is), you'll be glad you have it nearby.

If you're moving to the Denver area or already live here, be sure to check out the blue-tabbed pages at the back of the book. There you will find the **Living Here** appendix that offers sections on relocation, education, health care, retirement, and media.

In each chapter, you'll find **Insiders' Tips** (represented by an **i**), which offer up useful information you might not find elsewhere. Sprinkled throughout the book are **Close-ups,** which offer insight into some of the most intriguing—and often idiosyncratic yet endearing—aspects of Denver.

You'll also find listings accompanied by the ✳ symbol—these are our top picks for attractions, restaurants, accommodations, and everything in between that you shouldn't miss while you're in the area. You want the best this region has to offer? Go with our **Insiders' Choice.**

Enjoy your stay, whether it be for a few hours or a lifetime.

AREA OVERVIEW

Denver is, today, as it has been for more than 100 years, the largest metropolis between California and Missouri. An expansive self-regard still comes easily to the present inhabitants of Metro Denver, just as it did when the town was being established in the mid-1800s.

Most are proud of its agricultural roots, and many keep a pair of cowboy boots in the closet for times when hootin' and hollerin' are just what the doctor ordered. Even so, residents are well aware that Metro Denver is an economic powerhouse with a thriving cultural community, strong recreational offerings, and the best shopping in a seven-state region. The metropolitan area is defined by the city and county of Denver and its five suburban counties: Adams, Arapahoe, Broomfield, Douglas, and Jefferson. Boulder County is close by but regarded as having its own identity. Only about 40 percent of Greater Denver's present citizens were born here. Natives and newcomers alike are uneasy about recent growth, and its threats to their quality of life, but boosterism runs rampant.

Because of its geographic location near the nation's center, Denver is already a major hub of the railroad, airline, and highway systems. Denver International Airport helped secure the city's potential as a focus of worldwide trade and transportation, playing on its location midway between Munich and Tokyo, Canada and Mexico.

Geography also has much to do with the city's self-image. No matter where you are in Denver, you have only to look west to see the Rocky Mountains running north and south like a wall dividing west from east. Yet as the "Queen City of the Plains," Denver has an urban fabric that extends into the mountains on the west and overlays the first swells of the Great Plains to the east.

HISTORY

Settling the Land

European settlers first came from the south, beginning with Spanish explorers and soldiers in the 1600s. During the next two centuries, a slow movement of mostly agrarian colonists from Mexico and New Mexico gave a distinctly Hispanic culture to the southern part of the state. The city of Pueblo, less than a two-hour drive south of Denver, and all points south were Mexican territory until the US grabbed them after the 1848 war with Mexico. As Colorado grew, the ancestors of today's Hispanic citizens generated much of the sweat that built the state's mining, railroads, and agriculture.

Invaders from the east came faster and hit harder. In 1858, little more than 50 years after the first mountain men began trapping furs in the Rockies, a party of prospectors panned gold from the Platte River in what is now the city of Englewood on Denver's southern edge. Their discovery earned each man no more than about $10 a day, but it was enough to start the rush.

The history of modern Denver began at the confluence of the South Platte River with tiny Cherry Creek, where cottonwood groves sheltered the camps of Indians and early explorers such as John C. Frémont. By the beginning of 1859, the city of Denver had been established there by friends of James W. Denver, then governor of the Kansas Territory. Within months, the cottonwood groves had been axed into oblivion and replaced by some 400 cabins and a lot of bare dirt and mud. Today, new life has been breathed into that area as a new breed of pioneer reclaims the industrial wasteland for use as an elegant creekside neighborhood.

Striking Gold

Gold strikes in the mountains brought not just a growing swarm of fortune seekers from the east but also merchants, industrial entrepreneurs, and other citizens of a real city, including the bad elements. Denver had "more brawls, more pistol shots with criminal intent … than in any community with equal numbers on Earth," according to Horace Greeley. "Uncle Dick" Wootton, an early merchant, later recalled that "stealing was the only occupation of a considerable portion of the population, who would take anything from a pet calf, or a counterfeit gold dollar, up to a saw mill."

As Denver matured, it acquired a certain air of refinement, becoming the capital of the new Colorado Territory in 1867 and capital of the state of Colorado in 1876. "A shooting affray in the street is as rare as in Liverpool," noted British traveler Isabella Bird in 1872, "and one no longer sees men dangling to the lamp posts when one looks out in the morning." Still, she noted, Denver was not a very pretty sight. It was a city that "lay spread out, brown and treeless, upon the brown and treeless plain, which seemed to nourish nothing but wormwood and the Spanish bayonet."

The kind of money needed to polish the city's rough edges was soon to come from Colorado's growing cattle, mining, railroad, steel, banking, and other industries. Journalistic accounts of the time were filled with news about gambling houses and painted ladies, but a new class of aristocrat began decorating Denver's Capitol Hill neighborhood with mansions that have now become tourist destinations. Silver strikes in the mountains in the late 1870s caused another mining boom that poured money into the city until the silver market collapsed in 1893 and threw Denver into a depression. Yet more gold strikes in the mountains, along with the growth of Colorado's agriculture and manufacturing industries, brought Denver citizens into the 20th century, making them more prone to creating parks than cavorting in bawdy houses.

Still, the Queen City of the Plains was more plain than queenly, as one visitor put it. Major credit for developing her assets generally goes to Mayor Robert Speer, who pursued his dream of a "City Beautiful" during the first two decades of the 20th century. He created parks both in the city and the mountains, planted thousands of trees, and is credited with laying hundreds of miles of sewers and paving streets that turned Cherry Creek from a garbage dump into the centerpiece

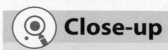 **Close-up**

A 19th-Century Perspective of Denver

In 1873, British traveler Isabella Bird spent time in Denver and other areas of Colorado. *A Lady's Life in the Rocky Mountains,* her account of those travels, is still in print and can easily be found at Denver bookstores and libraries.

An intrepid traveler and keen observer, Isabella came to town after spending a summer in Estes Park that included a dramatic climb up 14,255-foot-high Longs Peak in what is now Rocky Mountain National Park. The peak had been scaled for the first time only five years before a true character named Rocky Mountain Jim hauled Isabella to the summit. If she had gone three weeks earlier, Isabella could have been the first woman to stand there, but she was beaten by American writer and orator Anna Dickinson.

Isabella was surprised by Denver, which she called a "great, braggart city." Here, as recounted with permission from the biography *Amazing Traveler: Isabella Bird,* is her description of the streets of Denver: "Hunters and trappers in buckskin clothing; men of the Plains with belts and revolvers, in great blue cloaks, relics of the war; horsemen in fur coats and caps and buffalo-hide boots with the hair outside; Broadway dandies in light kid gloves; rich English sporting tourists, clean, comely and supercilious-looking; and hundreds of Indians on their small ponies, the men wearing buckskin suits sewn with beads, and red blankets, with faces painted vermilion, and hair hanging lank and straight, and squaws much bundled up riding astride with furs over their saddles."

Readers interested in learning more about Isabella Bird and her adventures are directed to *Amazing Traveler: Isabella Bird* by Boulder author Evelyn Kaye (Blue Panda Publications, 1999).

of what is today Speer Boulevard. The Denver Civic Center is the culmination of his planning, a popular downtown park located between the capitol and city and county buildings that was completed nearly two decades after his 1918 death.

War Spurs Growth

Despite the Great Depression, Denver's population grew by more than 50 percent between 1910 and 1940. World War II initiated the area's greatest surge when fear of attack on the nation's coasts transformed the area into a center of military and other government functions. Within a year after Pearl Harbor, major employment bases appeared in facilities such as the Denver Federal Center, the Rocky Mountain Arsenal, and the Fitzsimons Army Medical Center. Those who came for war-related opportunities stayed on when the war was done, and Metro Denver now contains some 50 percent of Colorado's population.

Optimism & Diversification

Since World War II the local economy has had its ups and downs, but Metro Denver has never lost that growth momentum. The city's economy endured the aftereffects of an oil bust in the 1980s as well as the dotcom bust in 2002, but in each case the recessions were short-lived. They were followed by unprecedented spending on transportation infrastructure, including Denver International Airport, a major expansion and installation of light-rail lanes along Interstate 25, and a transportation project named FasTracks that will result in a comprehensive commuter-rail and light-rail system by 2018.

Perhaps nowhere is revitalization more evident than in the area known as the Central Platte Valley, the city's birthplace at the confluence of the South Platte River and Cherry Creek. As Denver grew up and outward in the 1870s, the Central Platte Valley became the rail and warehousing district; by the 1970s it had become an urban wasteland best known for the trash-strewn vacant fields that were crisscrossed by railroad tracks. The area is now rebounding as the focal point of the new Denver, a planned community of green spaces and residential, retail, office, and entertainment developments. Much of the vision is already under way, led by the early developments of anchor projects that included Coors Field, the 50,000-seat home to Denver's major league Colorado Rockies; Elitch Gardens, a 60-acre amusement and water park; and high-rise residential projects clustered around Commons Park.

Lower Downtown, a warehouse district along the valley's edge that is best known for its turn-of-the-20th-century redbrick buildings, was the first to rebound. Since Coors Field opened in 1995, it has become a hotbed of restaurants, brewpubs, prestigious offices, condominiums, and lofts around Denver's historic railroad terminal, Union Station.

Big City Pains

Of course, not everything is perfect about Metro Denver.

Tourists strolling amid the stately buildings and flower gardens of Denver's Civic Center might well be asked for money by transients who lounge in the shade. While crime is no more prevalent in Denver than in any midsize city, it pays to stay alert when visiting downtown and fringe neighborhoods. Rush hour traffic can also be annoying, especially on I-25 and I-70. Special carpool lanes and light-rail lines do help to ease the pain.

Denver also is plagued by seasonal weather patterns that trap visible layers of yellow-brown haze in the air. Warm summer breezes carry them away, but during the months when a crackling fire would be most welcome, wood-burning bans are often in effect.

Even without air pollution, visitors may temporarily find it a bit more difficult to breathe at a mile above sea level. They may also feel headachy and strangely out of sorts, but at higher elevations the symptoms of altitude sickness can become acute, signaling a collapse of the body's ability to take in and metabolize oxygen. Those who plan to exert themselves in the mountains should take a few days to acclimate and drink an abnormally large amount of water.

It's also important to distinguish between weather patterns in Denver and in the nearby mountains. Snow can be piling up on ski slopes in Vail or Aspen at the same time golfers and joggers are enjoying 70-degree weather in Denver. Periodic cold spells do set in between November to February, and Denver does get some whopping winter snowstorms. But within a few days, most of the snow has melted and people are back out walking their dogs and working in their yards. Snow melts particularly fast during the late winter and early spring when chinook winds come roaring down from the mountains at speeds that have been clocked as high as 143 miles per hour. These warm, dry "snow-eaters" suck moisture out of the snow and have been known to raise Front Range temperatures by as much as 36 degrees within two hours. They've also been known to tear the roofs off houses, topple trees, and blow semitrailers right off the interstate.

The National Center for Atmospheric Research studies those weather extremes from its mountainside campus in nearby Boulder, and meteorologists joke that the area is an ideal place to be stationed because they can golf in the morning and chase thunderstorms in the afternoon. Both play into the common observation: "If you don't like the weather, just wait five minutes."

DENVER SUBURBS

Much of what we've already said about Metro Denver has focused on the city itself, but the suburban counties have their own lives and characters. While Metro Denver was home to about 2.9 million people in 2012, only around 620,000 of them lived in the city and county of Denver. The rest are settled in suburban counties that ring the core city.

Jefferson County, West of Denver

Among Metro Denver counties, Jefferson is the third largest, with approximately 540,000 residents. It serves as Metro Denver's gateway to the mountains, wrapping around the western end of the metropolitan area and including the mountain communities of Evergreen and Conifer. Jefferson tends to attract residents motivated by quality of life who can afford to locate in or near the mountains. Not surprisingly, its population is highly educated and includes a high percentage of dual-income families. Skiers, sightseers, mountaineers, and other motorists travel west through Jefferson County on I-70 or US 6 through scenic Clear Creek Canyon, the historic main thoroughfare to the gold and silver meccas of the 1800s. Many of these passersby notice little more than the city of Golden to the north or the upscale homes that dot the hills alongside the road.

But "Jeffco," in the local slang, is also an urban county in which cities such as Arvada, Edgewater, Westminster, Wheat Ridge, and Lakewood represent a continuum of the urban fabric that reaches out from Denver.

Jefferson County is highly industrialized, with an emphasis on high technology. Golden, the county seat, claims Metro Denver's highest percentage of technology PhDs, and up to a third of Colorado School of Mines' graduates stay in the county. The region's geotechnology, materials, mining, and energy businesses are clustered in Jefferson County. The federal government is its largest employer, with the mammoth Denver Federal Center in Lakewood and the National Renewable Energy Laboratory in Golden.

i If you're a low-altitude person like many new arrivals in Denver, you may wonder why you have a nagging slight headache. Don't worry; it's just the altitude. Drink lots of water and your physiology should be Denverized within a week.

Arapahoe County, East & South of Denver

The Arapahoe County of the Kansas Territory once covered nearly half the present state of Colorado, but nowadays the county covers only about 800 square miles. Reaching halfway from Denver to the Kansas border, Arapahoe County claims more than 580,000 residents in cities that include Englewood, Greenwood Village, Centennial, and Littleton, the county seat.

Arapahoe contains most of the city of Aurora, the state's biggest city by area and its third-largest in population. Since World War II, Aurora has been heavily influenced by the military. The sites of two former military bases are here: Fitzsimons Army Medical Center, which is being redeveloped into a new research center and campus for the University of Colorado's Health Sciences Center; and Lowry Air Force Base, which has been redeveloped into a residential neighborhood. Buckley Air Force Base (the city's largest employer) is still in use to the east.

The county's second- and third-largest cities are Englewood and Littleton. Littleton still has something of a small-town feel, but its school system has produced Scholastic Aptitude Test scores that rank among Metro Denver's highest. Englewood was a prairie when Colorado's first gold was discovered there in 1858. By the late 1800s, its fruit orchards gave the city its modern name, derived from the Old English words for "wooded place." Denver's ladies and gentlemen often made it their destination for Sunday carriage drives and picnics. Today Englewood boasts more jobs and businesses per square mile than any other city in the Rocky Mountains. The small communities of Glendale and Sheridan also are part of Arapahoe County.

Adams County, Northeast of Denver

Adams County, population just over 450,000, ceded 53 of its approximately 1,200 square miles to the city of Denver in the 1990s for the construction of a new airport. But Adams is still Metro Denver's largest county by area. Lying north of Arapahoe County, Adams County is perhaps Greater Denver's most economically diverse county, hosting agriculture, heavy industry, transportation, and high-tech companies. It does have an image as Metro Denver's big-shouldered, blue-collar county, thanks to the spread of warehouses, smokestack industries, and oil refineries that can be seen along I-70 and I-270. At the same time, it has its share of communications, biopharmaceutical, and computer software and hardware companies in the urbanized eastern region. The county seat is in Brighton. Other cities and towns in the county include Northglenn, Thornton, Bennett, Federal Heights, and parts of Arvada and Westminster.

Anyone who looks at a map will see a large blank space east of Commerce City with a scattering of lakes and the words "Rocky Mountain Arsenal (Restricted Area)." During World War II the Rocky Mountain Arsenal was located on 17,000 acres of land 10 miles northeast of downtown Denver, where the US Army manufactured chemical weapons such as mustard gas, white phosphorus, and napalm. Contaminated groundwater began to cause crop damage in the mid-1950s, so production stopped and cleanup began. Cleanup was completed

Metro Denver Vital Statistics

Denver was named for James W. Denver, governor of the Kansas Territory when the city was founded.

Denver became the capital of the new Colorado Territory in 1867 and capital of the state of Colorado in 1876.

Population: As of 2011, the US Census Bureau estimated the population of the City and County of Denver at 619,968, Adams County at 451,443, Arapahoe County at 584,948, Broomfield County at 57,352, Douglas County at 292,167, and Jefferson County at 539,884.

Location: The city sits at the base of the Rocky Mountains, about a third of the way between Wyoming and New Mexico.

Terrain: Rocky Mountain foothills on the west, rolling plains on the east.

Altitude: A bronze disk embedded on one of the western steps of the State Capitol building proclaims, Elevation 5,280 Feet. The words One Mile Above Sea Level are chiseled just above.

Climate: Mild. Dry heat in summer makes days bearable and nights pleasantly cool. Snow seldom stays long on the ground during winter. Average maximum temperature in the summer is 85 degrees; minimum is 56. Average maximum winter temperature is 45 degrees; minimum is 18. Average annual rainfall is 11 inches. Average annual snowfall is 60 inches. Average number of days with snow, ice pellets, or hail of 1 inch or more in depth is 18. Clear days: 115. Partly cloudy days: 130. Cloudy days: 120.

Denver government consists of a mayor and a city council. The current mayor is Michael Hancock.

in 2010. The majority of the site is now the Rocky Mountain Arsenal National Wildlife Refuge, the most impressive wildlife refuge in Metro Denver. A continuous flow of weekend visitors and weekday school groups visit to view eagles, elk, and other wildlife that call the arsenal home.

While dealing gracefully with its past, Adams County is well positioned for its future. In exchange for land on which DIA was built, Adams was promised economic growth as it developed around the airport. It has been a primary beneficiary of economic spin-offs. Thanks to residential and commercial development on the county's western side, Adams is also home to some of the Denver metro area's best new golf courses (see the Parks and Recreation chapter for details) and an entertainment complex at Church Ranch Road and US 35 that rivals any in the area. More growth continues between Brighton and DIA, bringing housing, retail, and industrial parks.

Adams County's own Front Range Airport is just 3 miles southeast of Denver International Airport, having begun operations in 1983. The abundance of air transportation has enhanced basic industries such as metalworking, food processing, and wood products in Adams County's southwestern corner, as well as high-technology companies along the 120th Avenue corridor in the county's northwestern corner.

Broomfield County, Northeast of Denver

Incorporated in 1961, the suburb of Broomfield became a county in 2001, making it the 64th and newest county in Colorado. Its name comes from broomcorn, a type of sorghum used for making brooms that was grown in the area. With a population of 58,000, it's the smallest county in the state. The US 36/Boulder Turnpike passes through the southern part of the county, offering a 20-minute drive to either Denver or Boulder during non-rush hours. The eastern part of the county is bordered by I–25. The drive to Denver International Airport takes around 40 minutes.

The Broomfield area grew quickly in the 1990s along with the state's overall explosive economic growth. A number of companies are based here, including Vail Resorts, Level 3 Communications, White Wave Foods, and Ball. With quality school systems, a low crime rate, and an extensive system of trails, open space, and 63 parks, the area is popular with families. Housing options range from affordable rentals, upscale apartments, and high-end condos and townhomes to starter homes, mid-level homes, and mansions.

Although Broomfield County can seem far removed from the urban attractions of Denver, several entertainment centers entice residents from here and from neighboring counties. 1STBANK Center offers a full calendar of music, sports, and events. Flatiron Crossing is a large regional mall with flagship stores such as Macy's, Nordstrom, and Dick's Sporting Goods, plus dozens of other retailers. Omni Interlocken Resort is a luxury resort hotel with a 27-hole championship golf course, spa, and Meritage, an excellent restaurant.

Douglas County, South of Denver

Flowing through the Pike National Forest southwest of Denver, the South Platte River has some of the most celebrated trout fishing on Colorado's Front Range, once described by *Time* magazine as "the St. Peter's Basilica of trout fishing." That distinction is just one of the things that make Douglas County such an attractive place that nearly 300,000 people call it home.

Many are housed in Highlands Ranch, one of Metro Denver's most popular planned communities because of its mountain views, abundant parks, and looping pedestrian trail system. The unincorporated community's population is expected to reach 100,000 by the year 2015. The county also includes Castle Rock, Lone Tree, Larkspur, and Parker as well as a piece of Littleton. Although Douglas County is the only metro county that does not share a boundary with the city and county of Denver (it is separated by a slice of Arapahoe County that wraps under the city's south side), it serves as Metro Denver's southern frontier. Douglas is the only Metro Denver county in which the vast majority of the population lives in unincorporated communities such as Castle Pines. It also is one of the area's prestigious ZIP codes, with the region's highest median income and home prices, and by far the highest ratio of people commuting outside the county to reach their jobs.

As the focus of what local planners call the Denver/Colorado Springs Development Corridor, Douglas also took a turn as

Colorado's fastest-growing county, with a population that grew 191 percent between 1990 and 2000. That rate has slowed considerably in recent years, but with 29 planned communities and 319 subdivisions covering nearly 18 percent of the county, Douglas anticipates a half-million new residents by 2030.

Meanwhile, the county plans to protect as much as 70 percent of its 841 square miles as open space, in the form of ranches, greenbelts, and public parks. Its county seat of Castle Rock, so named for the monolith-capped hill that towers above it, is just short of halfway to Colorado Springs, and most of its workers commute to one metropolis or the other.

GETTING HERE, GETTING AROUND

If you get lost, look at the mountains. That's the mantra when it comes to getting your bearings in Denver. The mountains to the west can orient even the most turned-around traveler, so take advantage of them as you're navigating the region. The second vital fact about Denver is that its historic core parallels Cherry Creek, while the rest of its streets were laid out in north-south and east-west grids. At times that can make downtown's diagonal streets feel like a confounding mistake in the midst of otherwise neatly planned neighborhoods.

Cherry Creek cuts through the town from northwest to southeast, and that's where the city's founders planted their roots. Later generations corrected the slapdash planning, orienting their streets to match more traditional compass points. It helps to look at a Denver map to understand the lay of the land. In general, from downtown Denver, Aurora is to the east; the Denver Tech Center, Englewood, and Greenwood Village are to the south; Littleton is southwest; Lakewood, Wheat Ridge, and Golden are to the west; Arvada, Broomfield, and Westminster are to the northwest; and Commerce City, Northglenn, and Thornton are to the north.

"Downtown" refers to the area that is roughly bounded by 13th Avenue on the south, Speer Boulevard (which follows Cherry Creek) on the west, the South Platte River on the north, and Grant Street on the southeast. Most downtown streets run one way. Seventeenth Street, where most of the banks and big office buildings are located, is in many ways the heart of downtown. The 16th Street Mall is a popular walking and shopping street.

Somewhere around Market Street, downtown becomes Lower Downtown, or "LoDo" (say "low-dough"). This is roughly the area from Larimer and Market Streets west to Union Station and the Platte River, and from 20th Street to Cherry Creek. Capitol Hill is the name given to the area just east of downtown. LoHi is the district just west of LoDo and the Platte River extending to the area around 32nd Avenue and Tejon Street. Immediately northwest of Denver and next to LoHi, Highland is the neighborhood bordered by W. 38th Avenue to the north, Speer Boulevard and W. 29th Avenue to the south, and Federal Boulevard to the west. Many residents consider LoHi part of Highland. RiNo, or River North, is the area north of downtown bounded by I-70 to the north, I-25 to the west, Park Avenue West to the south, and Lawrence to the east.

Our Area Overview chapter, which talks about the different counties that make up Metro Denver, should help you orient yourself. For descriptions of neighborhoods, see our Relocation chapter.

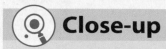 **Close-up**

Art at the Airport

When Denver International Airport (DIA) was built in the mid-1990s, funding for art was part of the construction budget. That's because Denver, like many other cities, has a percent-for-art ordinance that requires developers of city projects to set aside prescribed monies for the commissioning of art at the site. At DIA, art funding was divided among 26 projects.

That sounds like a lot of art, but it isn't always easy to find. The public artworks were often integrated with the architecture, becoming one with the overall experience of the soaring tent roof and airy concourses. The main areas to look for art are in the center of each concourse, along the underground train passages, and throughout Jeppesen Terminal.

Here are a few of our favorite pieces:

The 30-foot-high fiberglass blue horse, known as *Mustang*, is perhaps the most dramatic, and certainly the bluest, piece of art people see as they come into the airport via Peña Boulevard. Created by well-known New Mexico artist Luis Jiménez, the rearing horse has eyes reminiscent of red neon lights. Completed posthumously, *Mustang* has become known as the masterpiece of an artist who is cherished among America's most important 20th-century sculptors.

Near the carousels in the baggage claim area, check out the two whimsical suitcase gargoyles by Terry Allen. They go by the name *Notre Denver*.

Close to baggage claim areas are two colorful murals painted by Denver artist Leo Tanguma, a Chicano activist/artist who likes to involve the community in creating his work. He calls the murals *In Peace and Harmony with Nature* and *Children of the World Dream of Peace*.

Across the terminal atrium from one of Tanguma's murals is Gary Sweeney's *America, Why I Love Her*, two mixed-media murals of the US with the artist's small framed snapshots of odd Americana tourism destinations tacked onto the appropriate locations (ever seen the Frog Fantasies Museum in Eureka Springs, Arkansas?).

LOGISTICS: FINDING AN ADDRESS

In central Denver, the streets are laid out on a sort of grid: Broadway runs north-south and serves as the dividing line between east and west addresses. Ellsworth Avenue runs east-west and serves as the dividing line between north and south streets and addresses. Broadway and Ellsworth Avenue are the "zero hundred blocks." As streets travel away from them, address numbers go up.

AAA Colorado, with offices in Denver, Littleton, Westminster, and Wheat Ridge, has excellent Metro Denver area maps.

MAIN THOROUGHFARES

I-25 runs north-south through Denver in a line from Cheyenne to Colorado Springs (and farther in each direction, of course). Just north of downtown, it intersects I-70, the major route to the mountains that runs east-west through the northern edge of the city. I-225 cuts diagonally across Aurora, running

Sweeney, who used to work as a baggage handler for Continental Airlines, included arrows that point to Denver on his maps and little signs underneath that say: "You are here . . . but your luggage is in Spokane." Not everybody was amused in the early 1990s, when glitches in the automated baggage system caused multiple delays in the airport's opening date.

In the terminal atrium, on Level 6 bridges connecting the building's east and west sides, adjacent to escalators, are 28 glossy, vibrant, ceramic vases by internationally known ceramicist Betty Woodman. She titled her work *Balustrade*, because she envisioned the vases as components of balustrades for the bridges. This was Woodman's first public commission, and she has since gone on to exhibit widely in the US and Europe.

Another favorite piece is *Untitled (Garden)*, an installation created by Michael Singer in Concourse C. His mossy ruins are visible above the train station, and you can look down on them from the concourse gate level.

Artists have transformed DIA's floors in several places, including the terminal (*Great Hall Floor* by Jaune Quick-to-See Smith and Ken Iwamasa) and Concourse B (*21st Century Artifacts* by Carolyn Braaksma and Mark Villareal). So if you watch where you're walking, you'll see pictographs and fossils inlaid in the terrazzo floors. In the food court areas in Concourse A, you'll notice colorful mosaics that appear at ground level to be abstract. But go up one floor and take a look from above and you'll see that the tiles form foreshortened figures of people. Denver artists Barb McKee and Darrell Anderson collaborated on this project.

Finally, on the way out of the airport, you may notice a line of rusted farm implements. It's not that there wasn't time to clean up this equipment before DIA construction started; rather, this collection of artifacts is an art installation called *Fenceline Artifact*, created by Sherry Wiggins and Buster Simpson to acknowledge that agriculture was historically one of the primary uses of the land on which DIA was built.

northeast to southwest and connecting with I-70 just west of Peoria Street and with I-25 near the Denver Tech Center.

The so-called Denver Beltway is comprised of three separate highways (with a fourth segment planned) that form a loop around the city. The Northwest Parkway is a toll road that cuts across the north between US 36 at Broomfield and I-25.

The second segment, a toll road called E-470, runs east from I-25 to I-76. There it turns south, passes Denver International Airport (take the Peña Boulevard exit to reach DIA), and rejoins I-25 near Park Meadows Mall. The final section begins there. Called C-470, it's the only piece that doesn't charge a toll. It serves the metro area's south and west sections, stretching from I-25 at the Arapahoe County/Douglas County border west past Littleton, then north to I-70. The final segment—intended to connect C-470 at I-70 with the Northwest Parkway—is the subject of a hotly contested debate in the northwest communities of Golden and Arvada. For now those plans are on hold.

FasTracks Transportation Expansion Project

If you're visiting or new to Denver, you might hear people talking about FasTracks, a 12-year plan that will add 120 miles of new light-rail lines, 18 new miles of express bus service, 21,000 new parking spaces at rail and bus stations, and expanded bus service throughout Denver. Construction began in 2008 and is expected to take about a decade to complete. It was originally expected to cost $4.7 billion, part of which will come from a 0.4 percent sales tax increase approved by voters that began in 2005.

Other major thoroughfares are 6th Avenue (US 6), which joins up with I-70 at Golden; Santa Fe Drive (US 85), a north-south route that can be a good alternative to I-25; and Broadway. Colfax Avenue (Highway 40) is an east-west route but, like Broadway, it has a lot of traffic and can be a slow pathway from one side of town to another. Speer Boulevard runs parallel to Cherry Creek and connects Downtown Denver with the Cherry Creek shopping area.

Rush hour comes early in Denver. Assuming all goes well, the highways will usually have cleared in the mornings by 9 a.m., but the evening rush hour starts as early as 3:30 p.m.

HOV (high-occupancy vehicle) lanes encourage carpooling on several of Denver's major commuter routes, including South Santa Fe Drive, eastbound US 36, and I-25 north of downtown. Watch for them and use them; they'll save you 15 to 20 minutes of stop-and-go in rush hours. To use these lanes, you must have at least two occupants per vehicle.

Downtown parking is tight but not impossible and is much cheaper than in other big cities. Options for drivers are on-street meters and parking lots. Bring coins and small bills; you'll need to spend anywhere from $6 to $15 for an afternoon shopping spree.

PUBLIC TRANSPORTATION

REGIONAL TRANSPORTATION DISTRICT
1600 Blake St.
(303) 299-6000
rtd-denver.com

The Regional Transportation District (RTD) provides bus and light-rail service throughout the city and suburbs.

Light-Rail—RTD operates six light-rail routes in Denver and its southern suburbs, five of which begin in the downtown core and run north and south along a central corridor that roughly parallels I-25. The sixth provides spur service on the southeastern edges of the system, between Lincoln Avenue and the Nine Mile station. Light-rail lines serve the Five Points neighborhood, downtown Denver, the Auraria campus, the University of Denver, Golden, Jefferson County, Englewood, Littleton, Aurora, Greenwood Village, Centennial, Lone Tree, and Parker. Feeder buses serve all stations, providing mass transit from the central corridor into suburbs on either side of I-25. Fares range from $2.25 to $5 each way, depending on how far you travel on the train. Seniors 65 and over, people with disabilities,

Medicare recipients, and students ages 6 to 19 pay roughly half price. For more info visit rtd-fastracks.com.

Buses—RTD runs local, express, and regional bus service. Local buses operate on many routes downtown and cost $2.25. Express routes travel longer distances without as many stops; the basic fare is $4. Regional routes run to Boulder and other outlying areas; the fare is $5. The regional buses are comfortably upholstered, with reclining seats and air-conditioning. In all cases, exact change is required. Tokens, ticket books, and monthly passes are available at RTD stations and supermarkets, and many discounts apply (for senior citizens, students, and the disabled). RTD also provides transportation to and from the airport (for more information, see the Airports section later in this chapter), as well as to and from professional football and baseball games (details are provided in our Spectator Sports chapter). Information about routes, schedules, and fares is available at (303) 299-6000, rtd-denver.com, and all RTD stations.

> **i** Ski traffic on I-70 is a major problem during winter months. Prepare for a long, slow trip through the Eisenhower Tunnel, especially on weekends and during holidays. Leaving early for the slopes and returning later in the day to miss peak travel hours can help avoid congestion. A trip from Denver to Breckenridge can take three or more hours on heavy traffic days.

TAXIS

Generally you don't just wave down a cruising taxi on Metro Denver streets, although it is sometimes possible downtown. Plan to call ahead when you need a ride, usually about 30 minutes before you need to leave. All taxi companies are allowed to take you out of the city if you wish, but it gets expensive. Rides to and from Denver International Airport cost around $55.

All companies have similar rate structures: $2.60 entry fee and $2.20 a mile: Metro Taxi, (303) 333-3333 or metrotaxidenver.com; Yellow Cab of Denver, (303) 777-7777 or denveryellowcab.com; Freedom Cab, (303) 444-4444 or freedomcabs.com.

LEAVING TOWN: PLANES, TRAINS & BUSES

Airports

DENVER INTERNATIONAL AIRPORT
8500 Peña Blvd.
(303) 342-2000
flydenver.com
Denver residents are fond of their airport, even if it is 24 miles from downtown, and based on passenger traffic, they aren't the only ones. DIA served a record 52 million passengers in 2011, making it the nation's fifth and the world's eleventh busiest airport. Its six runways can land three aircraft at once using state-of-the-art radar, and with 53 square miles of land, it is large enough to hold several more if air traffic demands them. DIA is situated to the north and east of Denver and is bisected by Peña Boulevard. To reach it, take I-70 to exit 284 or, from the north, take 104th Avenue to Tower Road, and then drive south to Peña Boulevard. Two toll roads, the Northwest Parkway and E-470, also serve DIA. Take the Peña Boulevard exits off either road.

Charges for short-term parking run $1–3 an hour, depending on location, up to a 24-hour maximum of between $11 and $21. Long-term parking costs $7 a day.

You could let RTD do the driving. Sky-Ride operates seven major routes to DIA from stations throughout Metro Denver. One-way fare for the suburban routes is $13; from downtown, $11; and from the Stapleton Park-n-Ride, which is just north of the old Stapleton airport and offers $1 per day parking to SkyRide passengers, is $9. SkyRide information is available at (303) 299-6000 or rtd-denver.com/skyride.shtml.

DIA's unique terminal has a dramatic tented roof of Teflon-coated fiberglass that has been fashioned into 34 peaks that symbolize the Rocky Mountains. From a distance, the roof also looks like an encampment of tepees, a nod to the Native Americans who regularly used the site for temporary residence. Inside, many surfaces are brushed steel, and $7.5 million worth of commissioned art adorns the floors, walls, and ceilings. (See our Close-up in this chapter for a more complete description of the art at DIA.)

DIA has three concourses and a main terminal, all of which are connected by underground trains. A pedestrian bridge also connects Concourse A with the main terminal, offering passengers a close-up view of the airfield and artwork, as well as a soothing soundtrack of authentic Native American chants.

Travelers appreciate the well-planned variety of retail shops and restaurants within the terminal. Airport administrators work hard to attract local businesses that add color to the more typical national chain stores.

Ground transportation from DIA into Metro Denver is plentiful. Taxis can be hailed outside the baggage claim area and cost approximately $55 to downtown, more if you're going farther (see the Taxis section in this chapter). Shuttle buses are provided by many major hotels, so check with yours. Otherwise, a number of other shuttle companies provide service from DIA to Metro Denver locations as well as major mountain ski towns. More information about ground transportation is available at (303) 342-4059. You must have a destination in order to get a price quote, but shuttle service to downtown Denver will cost around $22 per person. Out of Colorado, you can call (800) AIR-2-DEN to make arrangements ahead of time.

The 16th Street Mall

One of Denver's major attractions, the 16th Street Mall is a fun place to stroll, browse, shop, and eat any time of the year. Although it's a pedestrian-only thoroughfare, free MallRide shuttle buses run up and down its 1-mile length, connecting the two RTD (Regional Transportation District) bus terminals on Broadway and Market Street. The shuttle buses operate between about 5 a.m. and 1:30 a.m. on weekdays, from about 5:30 a.m. to 1:30 a.m. on Saturdays, and from about 6 a.m. to 1:30 a.m. on Sundays and holidays. Frequency depends on the time of day and ranges from one every 10 minutes to almost one a minute during the morning and afternoon rush hours.

All major rental car companies service DIA, with customer service counters located near the baggage claim carousels. Rental agents recommend making arrangements before you arrive, as many run out of cars during peak times.

ADVANTAGE RENT-A-CAR
(800) 777-5500

ALAMO RENT A CAR
(800) GO ALAMO

AVIS RENT A CAR
(800) 331-1212

BUDGET CAR AND TRUCK RENTAL
(800) 527-0700

DOLLAR RENT A CAR
(800) 800-4000

ENTERPRISE RENT-A-CAR
(800) RENT A CAR

HERTZ RENT A CAR
(800) 654-3131

NATIONAL CAR RENTAL
(800) 227-7368

PAYLESS CAR RENTAL
(800) PAY LESS

THRIFTY CAR RENTAL
(800) 367-2277

CENTENNIAL AIRPORT
7800 S. Peoria St., Englewood
(303) 790-0598
centennialairport.com
This suburban airport southeast of Denver is among the busiest general aviation airports in the country. It features three lighted runways and an instrument-landing system for bad weather. Two full-service fixed-base operators are on hand for fueling. Private, corporate, and charter planes are welcomed at this airport, although no commercial carriers provide service. Ground transportation is limited to taxis, rental cars, and crew cars for corporate pilots.

COLORADO SPRINGS AIRPORT
7770 Milton E. Proby Pkwy., Colorado Springs
(719) 550-1972
flycos.com
This small airport is about 90 miles south of Denver and provides service to and from 10 major US cities as well as Denver. Travelers whose end destination is located in Denver's southern suburbs may find it handier to use this airport, although many of its flights also land in Denver. Shuttle and van service is available to a variety of locations in the Denver area at rates that start at about $40 per person.

Trains

DENVER UNION STATION
1701 Wynkoop St.
(303) 534-2812
denverunionstation.org
Like many cities in the West and Midwest, Denver has a Union Station that dates from the 19th century and fell upon hard times once planes and interstates provided other ways to travel. A consortium of planners, politicians, and developers are in the process of bringing the old dame back to life. Once the redevelopment is completed, Union Station will be the hub for ingoing and outgoing buses and light-rail trains. Restaurants and retail shops will fill its cavernous terminal, and mixed use high-rises will surround it with housing, office, and retail units. The completion date depends on several variables, not the least of which is an improvement in economic conditions that will free up construction funding. During construction, Amtrak has temporarily relocated its station to 1800 21st St. west of Coors Field. Amtrak will return to Denver Union Station in spring of 2014. Until then, Amtrak continues

to offer services on a regular basis. The famous *California Zephyr* still runs through Denver on its east-west route between Chicago and the San Francisco Bay. It travels an amazingly scenic route across the Continental Divide and through Glenwood Canyon on its way to Salt Lake City and, eventually, Oakland, California. Union Station is in Lower Downtown at Wynkoop and 17th Streets. For Amtrak information call (800) 872-7245. For recorded information about Amtrak departures and arrivals in Denver, call the Denver Amtrak ticket office at (303) 825-2583.

Buses

GREYHOUND BUS TERMINAL
1055 19th St.
(303) 293-6555, (800) 231-2222
greyhound.com
The Denver terminus for Greyhound and other private bus lines is at 20th and Curtis Streets, only a few blocks away from RTD's Market Street Station. Generally, RTD provides bus service to points less than an hour away, such as Boulder and Longmont, while Greyhound passengers travel longer distances. Buses to such places as Fort Collins and the mountains originate at this 20th and Curtis station. For online fare and schedule information, visit Greyhound's website at greyhound.com, then click on station locator and follow the prompts to Colorado and Denver.

ACCOMMODATIONS

Greater Denver is a community of travelers: those who made their way here to live, those who come for vacations, and, increasingly, those who are sent here on business or for conventions. It's one of those places residents seldom have trouble convincing friends and relatives from other states to come and visit. More than 12 million overnight visitors came to Denver in 2012, spending more than $2.7 billion in the process. The city's tourism bureau marked that as a record year and expects the upward trend to continue.

The appetites of travelers for good accommodations are well matched by more than 45,000 hotel and motel rooms in the Denver area. Whether your tastes tend toward the magnificent or the humble, you'll find plenty of choices.

OVERVIEW

One good general source of hotel information is Visit Denver, the city's convention and visitors bureau. Its website is the region's best for one-stop shopping, with information about lodging options throughout Metro Denver as well as an online booking engine. It also compiles deals and seasonal specials.

Denver hotels tend to be less vacation-driven and more commerce-oriented, but there is still some price variation from month to month. They do tend to give much better rates on weekends than during the week—a boon for the working person who wants a weekend getaway. Some offer special package deals that might include such things as tickets and a limousine ride to a show, carriage rides, or dinner at a local fine restaurant. Ask about discounts and specials when making reservations.

In general, downtown is the preferred location to stay while seeing the sights of Denver. The near-east side of Denver is the most convenient place to stay for those visiting the Denver Museum of Nature and Science. Lodgings on the west side of Denver provide the best access to Golden, home of the Coors Brewery. The west side also allows fast access to downtown and makes for a speedy mountain getaway via I-70. Sporting events are another big attraction, and downtown or the near-west side are prime lodging locations for ready access to the Colorado Rockies at Coors Field or the Denver Broncos at Sports Authority Field at Mile High. Business travelers tend to gravitate toward hotels near the airport, in downtown Denver, and around the Denver Tech Center to the southeast.

Many hotels offer free continental breakfasts, transportation, newspapers, attached parking, and free or discounted access to nearby athletic clubs. In most of our listings, we haven't detailed all the freebies, so make a point of asking when you check in.

Price Code

Our listings rate hotels according to a three-symbol price key, representing average room cost per night during the week for a double occupancy.

$.................less than $100

$$ ....$100 to $150

$$$ .... more than $150

HOTELS

Denver

ALOFT DENVER INTERNATIONAL AIRPORT $$
16470 E. 40th Circle, Aurora
(303) 371-9500
aloftdia.com

One of the closest hotels to DIA, the Aloft hotel chain is known for contemporary design and comfortable rooms. This 144-room site near Denver International Airport doesn't disappoint, with reasonably priced loftlike rooms that offer, among more standard features, plug-and-play stations for charging electronics and linking them to LCD televisions. Internet access is available throughout the hotel, including at the check-in desk, where kiosks allow guests to serve themselves if they prefer. Pets and kids have programs of their own, and food is available round the clock at re:fuel, a self-service eatery.

BEST INN & SUITES AT STAPLETON $
4950 Quebec St.
(303) 320-0260, (877) 813-9355
bestinndenver.com

Well located in east Denver near the Stapleton neighborhood and Denver International Airport, this former Days Inn is a good bet

for air travelers on a budget, business travelers on extended stays, and anyone who is relocating and needs a weekly or monthly rental. All rooms come with full kitchens and access to an outdoor pool and exercise room. Parking is free.

BEST WESTERN PLUS DIA INN & SUITES $$
7020 Tower Rd.
(303) 373-1600
bestwesterndia.com

This completely renovated Best Western is popular for its proximity to the airport just 15 minutes away. All rooms include free hot breakfast, a free business center, and access to indoor pool and hot tub. A free airport shuttle runs every half hour 24/7. Pets are allowed for a daily $20 fee.

Ancient Secrets of the Brown Palace Hotel

The Navarre Building, 1727 Tremont Place, across the street from the Brown Palace, was built in 1890 as the Brinker Collegiate Institution, the first coeducational college west of the Missouri River. Nine years later it was converted into the Hotel Richelieu, the city's most elegant gambling house and brothel. In its basement you can still see rails disappearing into the wall where rail carts once traveled a tunnel beneath Tremont Place, delivering fine foods from the Brown Palace kitchens. Legend has it that these carts also delivered Brown Palace patrons too discreet to be seen entering and leaving the Hotel Richelieu.

✳BROWN PALACE HOTEL $$$
321 17th St.
(303) 297-3111, (800) 321-2599
brownpalace.com
This is Denver's most famous hotel, and deservedly so. If you want a central downtown location, prestigious accommodations, and a historic experience all in one, you can't do better than the Brown Palace. The list of celebs and potentates who have stayed here since Henry C. Brown opened the doors in 1892 includes the Beatles, Elvis Presley, Snoop Dogg, British royalty, kings from Sweden and Romania, Japan's emperor, US presidents that stretch back to Teddy Roosevelt, and entertainment industry names ranging from Lionel Barrymore to Bruce Willis. Flo Ziegfeld wanted to stay here, but stormed off in a huff once he was told he couldn't bring in his dog.

When the Brown Palace opened, it represented the state of the art in Italian Renaissance hotel design, with a sunlit eight-story atrium lobby and tiers of balconies above white onyx walls. Today, it has earned Mobil's four star and AAA's four diamond ratings, and is a member of the National Trust Historic Hotels of America. Its 241 rooms and suites feature all the modern conveniences required by business and pleasure travelers alike, as well as pure artesian water from the deep spring that flows beneath the hotel. The hotel offers more than 13,000 square feet of meeting space that can accommodate groups of up to 800; three elegant restaurants and a cigar bar (Palace Arms, Ship Tavern, and Ellyngton's are reviewed in our Restaurants chapter; the cigar bar is described in the Nightlife chapter); a full-service 5,200-square-foot spa; and traditional afternoon tea, served daily in the atrium lobby much as it was a century ago. Valet parking is available for $26 a night.

COMFORT INN & SUITES $
4685 Quebec St.
(303) 388-8100
comfortnortheast.com
This Comfort Inn offers 138 rooms near the new Stapleton neighborhood, just 17 miles south of Denver International Airport. While full development of the former airport site will take years to complete, Stapleton already boasts a full complement of shopping and dining destinations. It also is close to Northfield Stapleton, an outdoor shopping center built on land that once was used as landing strips. Guests of this hotel have access to a fitness center, wireless high-speed Internet service, and a free continental breakfast.

COMFORT INN DOWNTOWN $$
401 17th St.
(303) 296-0400
denvercomfortinn.com
Although it's an economy accommodation, this 231-room downtown hotel is connected by a skywalk across Tremont Place to the Brown Palace Hotel, one of Denver's luxury inns. That means guests have access to many of the same amenities, including 24-hour room service, valet parking ($25 a day), and close proximity to the Brown's elegant restaurants, lounges, meeting spaces, and lobby. The Comfort Inn is pet-friendly and provides its guests with free high-speed Internet service and full American breakfasts. The State Capitol, Civic Center, Denver Art Museum, and 16th Street Mall are a short walk away.

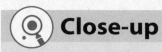

Close-up

Denver's Most Famous Hotel

Quite simply, the **Brown Palace**—known locally as "The Brown"—is Denver's most famous hotel. Opened on August 12, 1892, it has conducted business every day since—never stopping to catch its breath during any of its many renovations.

The hotel was the brainchild of Henry Brown, a real estate mogul from Ohio who came to Denver in 1860 and purchased acres of land, including the triangular plot at the corner of Broadway, Tremont, and 17th Street where the hotel stands today. (Not surprisingly, the building also is triangular.)

The hotel opened with 400 guest rooms that rented for between $1 and $4 a night. The lobby boasted the country's first atrium, with balconies rising eight floors above ground. Cast-iron railings with ornate grillwork surround each floor. It had no restaurants, but it did have at least 18 stores (most have been replaced by the two-story spa). The Brown has always had its own water supply, using deep artesian wells that provide water to every faucet in the hotel. The hotel also produces its own baked goods in a carousel oven that is one of only three in the world.

Over the years The Brown has housed its share of famous guests. President Dwight Eisenhower left a dent in the fireplace mantle when his erratic golf ball hit the wall. When the Beatles stayed in 1964, the hotel received a slew of applications from young girls wanting to work as housekeepers. Even the singer once-again-known-as Prince spent a few days at The Brown. He requested that the bed be stripped to the frame so that he could install his own water-filled mattress pad.

The hotel is still the palace that Henry Brown envisioned. But even those without deep pockets can enjoy it. The sophisticated afternoon tea served daily in the lobby is open to anyone willing to pay for the tea, pastries, sandwiches, champagne, and wines. One-hour tours ($10 per person) are offered every Wednesday and Saturday at 3 p.m.

COURTYARD DENVER AIRPORT $$
6901 Tower Rd.
(303) 371-0300, (800) 228-9290
marriott.com

Billing itself as one of the hotels closest to Denver International Airport, this Courtyard property has 196 rooms and six suites, 2,900 square feet of meeting space, an indoor pool and fitness center, a full-service restaurant and bar, and complimentary parking and airport shuttle service. It also offers long-term park and fly packages.

COURTYARD DENVER DOWNTOWN $$
934 16th St.
(303) 571-1114, (888) 249-1810
courtyarddenver.com

Located on Denver's downtown 16th Street Mall, this elegant Courtyard gets extra points for its proximity to just about everything, including the Colorado Convention Center, federal buildings, and the University of Colorado Denver. It has 166 rooms and 11 suites on six floors that overlook the city's lively pedestrian mall. Amenities include 3,200 square feet of meeting space, valet parking

($26 a day), a fitness center, and the popular Rialto Cafe.

COURTYARD DENVER STAPLETON $$
7415 E. 41st Ave.
(303) 333-3303, (888) 238-8240
marriott.com

Positioned off I-70 on Denver's northeast side, this Courtyard is adjacent to the new Stapleton neighborhood and 17 miles from Denver International Airport. It offers 134 rooms, 12 suites, 1,274 square feet of meeting space, and free on-site parking. Pets are welcome. Guests have access to an indoor pool, a fitness center, free parking, and a cafe that is open only for breakfast.

CROWNE PLAZA—DENVER
   INTERNATIONAL AIRPORT $$
15500 E. 40th Ave.
(303) 371-9494
cpdenverairport.com

Renovated in 2008, this airy hotel has 255 rooms and three suites on six floors. Meals are served in The Terrace, a full-service restaurant, and at the Mountain Terrace, the lobby lounge. Located north of the Chambers Avenue exit from I-70, it also has nearly 80,000 square feet of meeting and exhibit space, an indoor pool, whirlpool, sauna, and fitness room. Free parking is provided, as is free shuttle service to DIA and Stapleton shops. Pets are allowed.

CROWNE PLAZA HOTEL DENVER $$$
1450 Glenarm Place
(303) 573-1450
hoteldenver.net

This centrally located downtown hotel was fully renovated in 2007, leaving it with 364 guest rooms and 32 suites on 16 floors. It's within easy walking distance to the Denver Art Museum, the Denver Center for the Performing Arts, Lower Downtown, and the State Capitol. Amenities include an outdoor pool, fitness center, Off Sixteenth Restaurant, a lobby bar called The Place, and 7,387 square feet of meeting space. Self-parking is available for $10 a day.

THE CURTIS $$$
1405 Curtis St.
(303) 571-0300, (800) 525-6651
thecurtis.com

The underlying theme at the trendy Curtis is pop culture. This whimsical boutique hotel in the heart of downtown has 13 themed floors, each devoted to a specific time in American pop culture. The 336 contemporary guest rooms have flat-screen TVs and iPod docks. Dine at the hotel's The Corner Office and enjoy a drink at the upscale, urban Martini Bar. The staff is friendly and knowledgeable about nearby entertainment options.

DENVER MARRIOTT CITY CENTER $$$
1701 California St.
(303) 297-1300, (800) 228-9290
marriott.com

Marriott's flagship hotel in the city, the Denver Marriott City Center lies in the heart of Denver's financial district, but also is less than two blocks from the city's pedestrian mall and less than four blocks from the Colorado Convention Center. It is among the city's largest hotels, with 601 rooms and 14 suites on 20 floors and 27,000 square feet of meeting space, which often is booked with high-profile fund-raisers, galas, and national conferences. Allie's American Grille is open for breakfast and lunch; the subterranean D-Spot Lounge serves lunch, dinner, and cocktails. The Marriott also offers its guests a fitness center, an indoor pool, and valet parking ($29 a day).

DENVER MARRIOTT TECH CENTER $$$
4900 S. Syracuse St.
(303) 779-1100, (800) 228-9290
marriott.com

Alongside I-25 and on the edge of the city of Denver's farthest southeast corner, this hotel provides excellent access to businesses located in the Denver Tech Center. With 616 rooms and 12 suites spread across 11 floors, this hotel offers its guests breathtaking views of the mountains to the west, the plains to the east, and Denver's skyline to the northwest. Guests can choose from traditional and regional cuisine at The Lift and deli foods at the Front Range Trading Post. Recreational facilities include a workout room, indoor pool, outdoor pool whirlpool and spa, steam room, and racquetball and handball courts. Valet parking is $15 a day.

DOUBLETREE HOTEL DENVER $$
3203 Quebec St.
(303) 321-3333
denver.doubletree.com

Located 20 minutes from DIA and one of the finer "airport hotels," the Doubletree is just off I-70 near the developing Stapleton neighborhood and offers free shuttle service to Denver International Airport as well as the Northfield Stapleton shopping center. It has an outdoor hot tub, an indoor pool, and exercise equipment for the guests in its 561 rooms. Facilities include The Café, two lounges, an indoor pool, and a renovated fitness center.

DRURY INN DENVER EAST $
4380 Peoria St.
(303) 373-1983
druryhotels.com

A well-situated inn for the price-conscious traveler, the Drury Inn is off I-70 near Denver International Airport. A free breakfast bar and evening cocktails and snacks are available in the lobby. The hotel also has a heated indoor-outdoor pool and meeting rooms.

EMBASSY SUITES DENVER— AURORA $$
4444 N. Havana St., Aurora
(303) 375-0400
embassysuites.com

Ten miles from Denver International Airport and around 10 minutes from downtown, this property offers full-service accommodations with quick access to I-70 and I-225. It has 210 two-room suites, Northfield's restaurant and lounge, indoor pool and whirlpool, a fitness center, and complimentary shuttle service within 5 miles. Guests also enjoy free cooked-to-order breakfasts, complimentary evening cocktails and nonalcoholic beverages, parking, and airport shuttles.

EMBASSY SUITES DENVER DOWNTOWN $$$
1420 Stout St.
(303) 592-1000
embassysuites.com

Within easy walking distance of Denver's downtown scene, Embassy Suites Denver Downtown is an all-suites hotel across the street from the Convention Center. Living areas are spacious and furnished with amenities that provide a homey atmosphere. A hot breakfast buffet and evening manager's reception with complimentary beverages and snacks are included for all guests.

EMBASSY SUITES DENVER SOUTHEAST $$
7525 E. Hampden Ave.
(303) 696-6644
embassysuites.com

Of the Embassy Suites hotels in Metro Denver, this one is nearest the Denver Tech Center, with fast access to Cherry Creek and downtown. Each of its 206 suites has a living room and bedroom, with food service available at the Creekside Bar & Grille. Guests also can enjoy exercise facilities, an indoor pool, free cooked-to-order breakfast, and complimentary evening cocktails and nonalcoholic beverages.

*FOUR SEASONS HOTEL DENVER $$$
1111 14th St.
(303) 389-3000
fourseasons.com/denver

One of the newest additions to the Denver skyline, the 45-story Four Seasons Hotel offers the hospitality, accommodations, and amenities for which this world-class chain is known. Located in the heart of downtown, the hotel features 239 spacious guest rooms and suites, a luxury spa and fitness center, and a rooftop outdoor pool. The hotel's Edge Restaurant is a popular steak house that emphasizes farm-to-table cuisine. It's open for breakfast, lunch, and dinner daily.

GRAND HYATT DENVER $$$
1750 Welton St.
(303) 295-1234
granddenver.hyatt.com

Denver's first Hyatt is still among the city's nicest downtown hotels, earning the AAA Four-Diamond rating. In addition to 516 elegant rooms, all with city views, the hotel often hosts civic gatherings and fund-raising galas. All rooms have large flat-screen TVs, stereos with iPod docks, and wired workstations. Meals and 24-hour room service are available from 1876 Restaurant. For cozy drinks and socializing, Fireside Terrace provides the perfect venue. The Grand Hyatt outdoor jogging track, tennis court, and swimming pool let guests sample Denver's famous sunshine from within the privacy of its rooftop setting.

HILTON GARDEN INN $$$
1400 Welton St.
(303) 603-8000
hgidenverdowntown.com

Centrally located next to the Convention Center, this Hilton Garden Inn is within walking distance of all downtown attractions. Offering clean, comfortable, and spacious rooms with somewhat generic decor, the hotel is a good midrange choice. Other nice features include a DazBog coffee shop and Pi Kitchen + Bar, serving contemporary fusion cuisine.

HILTON GARDEN INN DENVER/ CHERRY CREEK $$
600 S. Colorado Blvd.
(303) 754-9800
hgicherrycreek.com

On Colorado Boulevard in the heart of the Cherry Creek shopping district, this hotel offers fast access to downtown as well as the district's upscale shops, restaurants, and movie theaters. Guests in its 210 rooms have access to a 24-hour fitness center, beauty salon, outdoor swimming pool, business center, meals service at the Boulevard Bistro, and complimentary parking. The hotel also can accommodate groups of up to 300 in its 12,000-square-foot meeting space.

HOLIDAY INN DENVER EAST $$
3333 Quebec St.
(303) 321-3500
histapletonhotel.com

The hotel's 300 guest rooms overlook a striking 11-story atrium lobby, and many rooms have views of the Rockies and downtown. The hotel offers a free airport shuttle and has a restaurant and lounge. The health club includes a year-round heated outdoor pool and whirlpool. Restaurants and shops are within walking distance.

HOLIDAY INN SELECT—
DENVER/CHERRY CREEK $–$$
455 S. Colorado Blvd.
(303) 388-5561
cherrycreekhoteldenver.com

Four miles from downtown and a mile from the Cherry Creek shopping district, this hotel is newly renovated in most areas. It offers 275 rooms, food service from The Front Range Grill, a martini bar, a fitness center, free access to a nearby Bally's Total Fitness, and an attractive indoor pool with skylights.

✳HOTEL MONACO $$$
1717 Champa St.
(303) 296-1717, (800) 990-1303
monaco-denver.com

Offering guests a "world of hip, high style luxury," Hotel Monaco is located in the renovated 1917 Railway Exchange and 1937 Moderne Title buildings. This Kimpton Hotel property offers 189 rooms and suites decked out in plush interiors designed to create a residential feeling. Fourteen of the 32 suites contain whirlpool spas. On-site exercise facilities and the Renaissance Aveda Spa & Salon continue the pampering. Can't travel without your beloved pet? No problem. Or if you need a temporary pet, the hotel will provide a pet goldfish during your stay.

✳HOTEL TEATRO $$$
1100 14th St.
(303) 228-1100
hotelteatro.com

The boutique Hotel Teatro has made grandeur out of the historic downtown Tramway Tower, which was built in 1911. It now caters to the luxury business and upscale leisure markets from a prime downtown spot across from the Denver Center for the Performing Arts. The hotel offers 111 well-appointed rooms that don't scrimp on anything. The hotel also houses Restaurant Kevin Taylor, a nationally known venue for elegant French cuisine, and Chef Taylor's modern Italian fare at Prima Ristorante. A fitness center and 24-hour room service are available. Complimentary transportation is offered to guests traveling within a 3-mile radius of the hotel. Valet parking is $29 a day. Pets stay free.

HOTEL VQ AT MILE HIGH $
1975 Mile High Stadium Circle
(303) 433-8331, (800) 388-5381
hotelvq.com

If you live and breathe football and consider yourself a Broncos fan, this is the hotel for you. It sits in the northeast corner of the Sports Authority Field parking lot and provides close-up comfortable views of the stadium from many of the guest rooms. A 14-story circular tower holds 169 rooms and a penthouse restaurant called the Skybox Grill and Sports Bar, also providing great views of downtown Denver, located across I-25 from the hotel. Parking is free, as is courtesy transportation to downtown destinations.

HYATT REGENCY DENVER AT COLORADO CONVENTION CENTER $$$
650 15th St.
(303) 436-1234
denverregency.hyatt.com

Offering 1,100 rooms, this elegant new hotel across from the Convention Center consists of two towers that sit side by side, with the Peaks Lounge topping the shorter of the two. Its 27th-floor windows provide one of the best panoramic views of the city, with drinks around $10–12 apiece. Guest rooms in the taller tower include 72 suites, several of which have 3,000 square feet of space and/or outside patio decks. Breakfast, lunch, and dinner are served at the Altitude restaurant, and the Strata Bar often has live entertainment. For snacks around the clock, visit Perks coffee bar and gift shop. Also on-site: a full-service health club, an outdoor lap pool, a spa, and a 24-hour business lounge.

HYATT REGENCY TECH CENTER $$$
7800 E. Tufts Ave.
(303) 779-1234
techcenter.hyatt.com

The Tech Center Hyatt is surrounded by enough open space that you have great views of the Rockies even if you're standing in the parking lot. A majestic facility with 451 rooms, it's a short walk from here to easy light-rail access to downtown Denver. The free shuttle takes guests to Park Meadows Mall and the nearby Landmark Entertainment District. For a scenic dining spot, visit the rooftop restaurant and lounge, or rejuvenate yourself at the indoor pool, dry sauna, sundeck, hot tub, and exercise room.

LA QUINTA INN—DENVER CENTRAL $
3500 Park Ave. West
(303) 458-1222
lq.com

Just north of downtown Denver, this newly renovated La Quinta Inn is a 3-story, 106-room hotel with an outdoor swimming pool. A continental breakfast is offered. It's close to Coors Field and the Elitch Gardens Theme & Water Park, and is also convenient to downtown, the west side, and the sports complexes of Sports Authority Field at Mile High and the Pepsi Center.

LA QUINTA INN—DENVER CHERRY CREEK $
1975 S. Colorado Blvd.
(303) 758-8886
lq.com

This inexpensive but pleasant hotel is located midway between downtown Denver and the Denver Tech Center. The inn offers quiet, comfortable rooms, free high-speed Internet access, an outdoor heated pool, a continental breakfast, and a guest laundry facility. Many midrange and chain restaurants are nearby.

LA QUINTA INN & SUITES—DIA $
6801 Tower Rd.
(303) 371-0888
lq.com

For those early-morning departures (or late-night arrivals), this La Quinta is a convenient place to stay. It has 169 rooms and a 24-hour fitness center with indoor pool. Airport shuttle and free continental breakfast are available.

LOEWS DENVER HOTEL $$
4150 E. Mississippi Ave.
(303) 782-9300
loewshotels.com/Denver-Hotel

An Italian-inspired decor of plush furnishings, marble, murals, frescoes, and continental antiques fill the Loews Denver Hotel from lobby and library to the guest rooms. Well located near Cherry Creek, this exclusive hotel offers 183 guest rooms, including 17 suites. Meals are available at the award-winning Tuscany Restaurant and during happy hour at T-Bar lounge. Complimentary car service is available within a 6-mile radius.

*MAGNOLIA HOTEL $$-$$$
818 17th St.
(303) 607-9000, (888) 915-1110
magnoliahoteldenver.com

One of downtown Denver's historic boutique hotels, the 244-room Magnolia Hotel building once housed the American National Bank. Guests have access to a health club, a free continental breakfast, and on-site dining at Harry's Bar, a hip, retro-designed lounge. The Magnolia is located just off 16th Street Mall with its many attractions.

*OXFORD HOTEL $$$
1600 17th St.
(303) 628-5400, (800) 228-5838
theoxfordhotel.com

One of the city's top boutique hotels, the historic Oxford Hotel is in the heart of Lower Downtown, one of the city's liveliest urban neighborhoods. Reminders of its 1891 origins remain, including an extensive art collection, the piano of legendary gold rush queen Baby Doe Tabor, and the Cruise Room bar, which is an art deco jewel of a nightspot. The Oxford's prime location places guests within walking distance of some of the city's best restaurants and nightclubs, as well as Union Station, Coors Field, the Pepsi Center, and Elitch Gardens. Guests have access to The Oxford Club, a full-service health club located next door; complimentary morning coffee on each level; town car service within a 2-mile radius; and the services of a dedicated bath butler. Pets are allowed.

QUALITY INN $
3975 Peoria Way
(303) 371-5640
choicehotels.com

This moderately priced hotel benefits from close proximity to DIA. Located on I-70, west of the intersection with I-225, it's also convenient to the Denver Coliseum and the city of Aurora. The 112 rooms are attractive but basic. Complimentary airport shuttle service is available, as is a free continental breakfast. Pets are welcome for a small fee.

RAMADA INN DOWNTOWN $
1150 E. Colfax Ave.
(303) 831-7700
ramada.com

East Colfax is not the most scenic street in Denver, but on this part of it you are still within the trendy urban Capitol Hill neighborhood. Some fine restaurants, pubs, and concert venues are located within a few blocks, as are the Denver Botanic Gardens, City Park, the Denver Zoo, and the Denver Museum of Nature and Science. The Ramada has 143 rooms at very reasonable prices, with a heated outdoor pool and hot tub. A free shuttle is available within a 3-mile radius.

RAMADA PLAZA DENVER CENTRAL
HOTEL $
4849 Bannock St.
(303) 292-9500
ramada.com
While not in the most scenic area of the city, this Ramada Hotel is well located at the dead center of Metro Denver. It's affordable and convenient for visits to the Denver Merchandise Mart, the National Western Stock Show, and other areas around Metro Denver. In addition to 200 rooms and 6 two-bedroom suites, the hotel has an outdoor heated pool, a full-service dining room, a deli, and Teddy's Lounge, a tavern that heats up whenever cowboys come to town.

RED LION HOTEL—
DENVER CENTRAL $
4040 Quebec St.
(303) 321-6666
redlion.com
The Red Lion is one of many hotels that serve the airport and the west side of Denver. It's located near the Stapleton neighborhood off I-70, which guarantees fast access to downtown Denver and points west. It boasts 298 guest rooms, two ballrooms, a restaurant and lounge, and a renovated fitness center.

RENAISSANCE DENVER HOTEL $$$
3801 Quebec St.
(303) 399-7500
denverrenaissance.com
The Renaissance offers high-end accommodations on the east side of Metro Denver. Just south of I-70, it has 400 guest rooms, Vivace! Ristorante for traditional Italian cuisine, a health club with spas, and indoor and outdoor pools. The airport shuttle is complimentary.

RESIDENCE INN BY MARRIOTT—
DENVER DOWNTOWN $$$
2777 N. Zuni St.
(303) 458-5318
marriott.com
Residence Inns are equipped as extended-stay accommodations, with per-night prices dropping substantially if you're there more than a week. Each of the 159 suites has a fully equipped kitchen and living room area. Either one-bed studio suites or two-bed, loft-style penthouse suites are available. The inn offers a complimentary hot breakfast, heated outdoor swimming pool, hot tub, and exercise room. Just across I-25 from downtown, the hotel has a free shuttle to major sports venues and the LoDo area.

RESIDENCE INN DENVER
CITY CENTER $$$
1725 Champa St.
(303) 296-3444
marriott.com
This all-suite, extended-stay hotel has 14 floors and 229 suites. Suites range from studios to two-bedrooms and come with full kitchens, flat-screen televisions, and wireless Internet. Amenities include a small fitness center, eighth-floor patio with hot tub, and complimentary breakfast buffet and cocktails. The hotel's biggest selling point is its location—within walking distance of the 16th Street pedestrian mall and the heart of downtown.

*RITZ-CARLTON, DENVER $$$
1881 Curtis St.
(303) 312-3800
ritzcarlton.com
This fine, big beauty of a hotel is little more than two blocks from the 16th Street Mall and all its attractions, but is also close to the

pubs, shops, and galleries of Lower Downtown. Each of the hotel's 202 luxurious guest rooms is more than 550 square feet. The hotel has 47 suites, 32 Club Level rooms, and one Ritz-Carlton suite. Elway's Downtown is the signature restaurant, named for retired Broncos quarterback John Elway. The property also includes a full-service spa and free access to the nearby FORZA Fitness Club. Overnight valet parking is available for $31. Pets are allowed, but you'll pay a steep price for the privilege.

SHERATON DENVER DOWNTOWN HOTEL $$–$$$
1550 Court Place
(303) 893-3333, (800) 444-2326
sheratondenverdowntown.com

This downtown hotel property is among the nation's largest with 1,231 rooms and 82 suites, the highest of which offer stunning panoramic views of the city. It also houses the 15/Fifty Restaurant and Lounge; a fitness center with sauna; an outdoor heated pool; and a sundeck. It's just off the 16th Street Mall and close to the many attractions of downtown Denver.

*WARWICK HOTEL $$$
1776 Grant St.
(303) 861-2000
warwickdenver.com

The accommodations shine in this tony, newly renovated Uptown hotel, thanks to features such as leather mahogany desk chairs, 32-inch flat-screen TVs, Serta Eurotop mattresses, and Italian window treatments. Most of the 219 rooms have private balconies that overlook the downtown cityscape. The heated rooftop pool is exceptional, as are the 24-hour health club and Randolph's, the hotel's signature restaurant. The Warwick

is known for its romantic and night-on-the-town weekend packages.

WESTIN DENVER DOWNTOWN $$$
1672 Lawrence St.
(303) 572-9100
westindenverdowntown.com

Although the alphabet places this downtown hotel at the bottom of our list, it really deserves to be near the top. Located just off the 16th Street Mall, the four-diamond Westin is central to the best shopping, restaurants, entertainment, and nightlife of downtown Denver. The hotel itself is palatial, with 430 rooms and two good restaurants. There's a health club, racquetball courts, an indoor/outdoor pool, a sauna, and a nice hot tub on the western sundeck by the outdoor pool.

Adams County

COMFORT INN CENTRAL $
401 E. 58th Ave., Denver
(303) 297-1717
comfortinn-central.com

This Comfort Inn, adjacent to the Merchandise Mart, is located along I-25 just north of I-70, with easy access to downtown Denver. It has 161 newly renovated rooms, complimentary continental breakfast, a restaurant, a balcony on every room above the second floor, an outdoor heated pool, and an exercise facility. The inn is pet-friendly.

DOUBLETREE BY HILTON HOTEL DENVER—THORNTON $$–$$$
83 E. 120th Ave., Thornton
(303) 451-1002
denverthornton.doubletree.com

Located 20 minutes north of Denver up I-25, this Doubletree offers easy access to DIA. You can't miss this place because it is, in fact, a gray stone castle. The medieval theme is carried out in some of the interior decoration, but it's a modern hotel with close to 5,000 square feet of meeting space and 133 rooms. Enjoy spacious rooms, a restaurant and lounge, indoor heated pool and whirlpool, an outdoor space with fire pits, and nice views of the Rockies.

LA QUINTA INN—NORTHGLENN $
345 W. 120th Ave., Westminster
(303) 252-9800
lq.com
Northglenn is among the northernmost suburbs in Metro Denver, which makes this hotel attractive to visitors arriving from the north or planning trips that include visits to Rocky Mountain National Park, Loveland, or Fort Collins. The 130 rooms are basic but tidy. This is the only La Quinta in Metro Denver with privileges at a nearby health club; it also has a heated outdoor pool, free continental breakfast, and guest laundry facility.

Arapahoe County

COURTYARD BY MARRIOTT— DENVER TECH CENTER $–$$$
6565 S. Boston St., Greenwood Village
(303) 721-0300
marriott.com
The Courtyard by Marriott is in Greenwood Village's southeastern tip, near the intersection of I-25 and Arapahoe Road. Set in the Denver Tech Center area, it's a good choice for visitors doing business in the area. The hotel has 143 large rooms, most with king-size or double beds, and suites with living room areas. It also offers a mini gym, indoor pool and Jacuzzi, the Bistro cafe, and a lounge bar. Free shuttle rides are offered within a 5-mile radius.

DENVER MARRIOTT SOUTH $$
10345 Park Meadows Dr., Littleton
(303) 925-0004
marriott.com
This 279-room, newly renovated hotel is just 1 mile from Park Meadows Mall and near the Denver Tech Center and other south Denver business hubs. Its decor is inspired by the Arts and Crafts architecture popularized at the turn of the 20th century, and its main floor is anchored by a two-sided stone fireplace. Rooms come equipped for business with a desk, ergonomic chair, two-line phones with voice mail, and high-speed Internet access. Many rooms have mountain views. The hotel is adjacent to the RTD light-rail station, providing easy access to downtown Denver.

DOUBLETREE BY HILTON HOTEL DENVER—AURORA $$
13696 E. Iliff Place, Aurora
(303) 337-2800
doubletree.com
This Doubletree Hotel is strategically situated alongside I-225, 10 minutes from the Denver Tech Center and 20 minutes from the airport. The hotel has 248 recently renovated rooms, a heated indoor pool, and a 24-hour fitness center. All-day food service is provided by Fitzgerald's Restaurant.

EMBASSY SUITES DENVER TECH CENTER $$
10250 E. Costilla Ave., Centennial
(303) 792-0433
embassysuites.hilton.com
Close to the Denver Tech Center, Inverness Business Park, and I-25, this Embassy Suites has 246 two-room suites that provide a separate living room with sofabed and table. Free transportation is provided within a 6-mile radius. Hot breakfast and a nightly manager's

reception are complimentary. The restaurant has Southwestern and traditional cuisine, and you can work your meal off at the fitness center, indoor pool, and whirlpool.

HAMPTON INN DENVER— SOUTHEAST $-$$
9231 E. Arapahoe Rd., Greenwood Village
(303) 792-9999
hamptoninn.hilton.com

This Hampton Inn is one of several hotels clustered on the southeastern tip of Greenwood Village, adjacent to the intersection of Arapahoe Road and I-25. It has 150 rooms, an outdoor swimming pool, workout facilities, and a free continental buffet breakfast. It offers easy access to stores in the Park Meadows shopping center.

THE INVERNESS HOTEL AND CONFERENCE CENTER $$$
200 Inverness Dr. West, Englewood
(303) 799-5800, (800) 832-9053
invernesshotel.com

Located west of Centennial Airport at the intersection of I-25 and County Line Road, the Inverness provides easy access to visitors traveling on to Castle Rock, Colorado Springs, and other destinations south of Denver. The hotel's attractive, high-style exterior reflects the luxurious guest rooms inside. Guests can play the adjoining 18-hole Inverness Golf Course. The hotel also has a billiards room, three lighted tennis courts, indoor and outdoor pools, saunas, indoor and outdoor whirlpool baths, a full-service spa, and a health club with aerobics studio, exercise circuit, and exercise equipment. Guests can also enjoy five distinctive restaurants, including contemporary Colorado fusion cuisine at Baca restaurant.

LA QUINTA INN—AURORA $
1011 S. Abilene St., Aurora
(303) 337-0206
lq.com

Located right off I-225, this La Quinta Inn provides quick access north to the airport and south to the Denver Tech Center and Douglas County. It has a heated outdoor pool and laundry facilities and includes a free breakfast and free cable TV. There are plenty of nearby restaurants. Its 121 rooms are basic but tidy and attractive. Pets are welcome.

RESIDENCE INN BY MARRIOTT— DENVER TECH CENTER $-$$
6565 S. Yosemite St., Englewood
(303) 740-7177
marriott.com

Don't let the Englewood mailing address fool you. This 128-suite property is an extended-stay hotel that serves Greenwood Village and the Denver Tech Center area. All suites include a fully equipped kitchen, complimentary breakfast, and an evening social from Monday through Thursday. The hotel has an outdoor swimming pool, heated spa, and fitness center. Nearby strip mall shopping includes coffee and bagel shops. Pets are welcome for a fee.

SHERATON DENVER TECH CENTER $-$$
7007 S. Clinton St., Englewood
(303) 799-6200
sheratondenvertech.com

This Sheraton is situated at the far southeastern tip of Greenwood Village between the Denver Tech Center and Centennial Airport. Guests can enjoy great views of the mountains, especially from the club levels on the 9th and 10th floors, which offer concierge service, complimentary breakfasts, and cocktails and hors d'oeuvres in the evening. The hotel has undergone a recent multimillion-dollar renovation, including all 263 rooms. Amenities include a restaurant, lounge, 24-hour exercise facility, outdoor heated pool, and whirlpool.

Jefferson County

DAYS INN & SUITES GOLDEN/WEST DENVER $
15059 W. Colfax Ave., Golden
(303) 277-0200
daysinn.com
Another cost-conscious alternative on the west side, this Days Inn sits at a major node of the west side's transportation web. You can go straight west to Golden, hop on I-70 west or east, or jog south to catch US 6 for a fast no-stoplight run to downtown Denver. The hotel has 157 recently renovated rooms, a restaurant, heated outdoor swimming pool, hot tub, sauna, and exercise area.

DENVER MARRIOTT WEST $$
1717 Denver West Blvd., Golden
(303) 279-9100
marriott.com
Denver Marriott West is set in the Denver West Office Park just off I-70 in Golden. Guests in its 305 rooms are 20 minutes from downtown Denver and 10 minutes from the foothills via I-70 West. It has indoor and outdoor pools, exercise equipment, saunas, and a restaurant and lounge.

DENVER WEST INN $
7150 W. Colfax Ave., Lakewood
(303) 238-1251
denverwestinn.com
Denver West is an inexpensive choice for business and vacation travelers, with 122 rooms. It's well located near two major east-west thoroughfares (West Colfax Avenue

and US 6) and less than 5 miles east of I-70, which provides easy access to both downtown Denver and the mountains. There's an on-site laundry, a seasonal outdoor pool, and free coffee 24 hours a day in the lobby.

DOUBLETREE HOTEL DENVER NORTH $$
8773 Yates Dr., Westminster
(303) 427-4000
doubletreehilton.com
Visitors seeking ready access to Boulder County as well as Metro Denver will appreciate this Doubletree Hotel, located just north of US 36 in Westminster. It has 180 rooms, including "Jacuzzi suites," as well as 8,400 square feet of meeting space, a restaurant, a lounge, and a very nice fitness area with whirlpool, sauna, indoor swimming pool, and exercise room. Complimentary shuttle service within a 6-mile radius is available.

HAMPTON INN DENVER— SOUTHWEST $
3605 S. Wadsworth Blvd., Lakewood
(303) 989-6900
hamptoninn.hilton.com
Convenient to the mountains, the city, and Jefferson County's largest businesses, the Hampton Inn has 150 rooms, an outdoor swimming pool, free continental breakfast, meeting rooms, quiet neighborhood surroundings, and the Foothills Golf Course nearby.

HILLTOP INN & SUITES $$–$$$
9009 Metro Airport Ave., Broomfield
(303) 469-3900
hilltopandwildflowers.com
The Hilltop Inn could almost be listed in our Bed-and-Breakfast Inns section because of its quiet, British country inn ambience,

complimentary breakfast, and the comfortable great room with fireplace and books. Amenities include gas fireplaces, satellite TV, Internet access, and laundry room. The great room and patio are good places for wedding-related events as well as cocktail parties. Each suite has its own private entrance and fireplace, kitchenette, private bath, and king-size bed. Some have whirlpool baths and separate sitting rooms.

LA QUINTA INN—GOLDEN $
3301 Youngfield Service Rd., Golden
(303) 279-5565
lq.com
Located near the Adolph Coors Co. brewery and the city of Golden, this hotel has 129 rooms on 3 floors and a heated outdoor pool. This affordable hotel has easy access to I-70 and the mountains. Pets are welcome.

LA QUINTA INN—
WESTMINSTER MALL $
8701 Turnpike Dr., Westminster
(303) 425-9099
lq.com
Located just off of I-70, this hotel provides easy access to Denver and Boulder. It has 129 rooms, a heated outdoor pool, free continental breakfast, and guest laundry facilities. Rooms are basic but tidy and comfortable. Pets are welcome.

OMNI INTERLOCKEN RESORT $$$
500 Interlocken Blvd., Broomfield
(303) 438-6600
omnihotels.com
This 390-room, four-diamond resort provides luxury accommodations in a rather unlikely spot along the four-lane turnpike between Boulder and Denver. The hotel boasts a 27-hole golf course, a full-service spa, two outdoor pools, a whirlpool, an outdoor pavilion suitable for weddings and other large gatherings, and a business center. The Tap Room offers pub fare, microbrews, foosball, and pool tables. The Meritage restaurant is open for breakfast, lunch, and dinner.

SHERATON DENVER WEST
HOTEL $$–$$$
360 Union Blvd., Lakewood
(303) 987-2000
sheratondenverwest.com
Aimed at the business traveler, with a full-service business center and more than 18,000 square feet of meeting space, this 242-room hotel is also one of the nicest places in Denver Metro's western quadrant. Right off US 6, it's a great staging point for trips to the mountains and business trips that involve the Denver Federal Center. It's surrounded by a thriving business and commercial area. The Sheraton has a restaurant and lounge, the full-service Massage and Bodyworks Spa, and a 10,000-square-foot health club with heated lap pool, hot tub, and state-of-the-art cardio equipment. Pets are allowed.

TABLE MOUNTAIN INN $$$
1310 Washington Ave., Golden
(303) 277-9898
tablemountaininn.com
Table Mountain is a charming 74-room Santa Fe–style inn. Its main street location puts guests in the midst of the neighborly, small-town Golden atmosphere. It's within walking distance of the Coors Brewery and the Colorado School of Mines, yet a 20-minute drive on 6th Avenue will take you to downtown Denver. Its Southwestern-cuisine restaurant is a west-side culinary treasure.

WESTIN WESTMINSTER   **$$$**
10600 Westminster Blvd., Westminster
(303) 410-5000
westindenverboulder.com

Conveniently located between Denver and Boulder, this four-diamond hotel has 369 elegantly designed guest rooms, a heated indoor pool, a whirlpool, and a pleasant outdoor terrace area. Dining is available at Kachina Southwestern Grill, offering breakfast, lunch, and dinner. The Westin's location along the Boulder-Denver turnpike is across the boulevard from the Promenade, with a 3-rink ice rink, bowling alley, a dozen restaurants, a 24-screen theater, and the not-to-be-missed Butterfly Pavilion. The hotel is pet-friendly.

BED-AND-BREAKFAST INNS

Some travelers prefer the charm, intimacy, and often historic surroundings of a bed-and-breakfast inn over the impersonal hotel/restaurant/gift shop experience. Metro Denver offers them a selection of inns that compare with the best anywhere.

In the use of our price-key symbols ($, $$, or $$$), representing double occupancy during the week, we've tried to represent the average price of accommodations for each bed-and-breakfast inn, but remember that the inns often have a limited number of rooms and have widely varying price ranges. All the inns in our listing are located in or near downtown Denver. All accept credit cards, and none accept pets. None will turn away people with children, but in some cases, as indicated, children may be difficult to accommodate due to limits on room size and capacity.

CAPITOL HILL MANSION   **$$$**
1207 Pennsylvania St.
(303) 839-5221, (800) 839-9329
capitolhillmansion.com

All the fineries you expect from a bed-and-breakfast inn can be found in this 1891 mansion of ruby sandstone. The mansion is on the National Register of Historic Places, having been built in 1891 as one of the last great mansions raised before the silver crash put a temporary damper on local development. Located near the State Capitol, it's surrounded by ornate historic homes built when Capitol Hill was known as "snob knob." The exterior is a turreted, balconied affair with a grand curved porch. The interior lives up to even the most aristocratic expectations, with crafted, patterned plaster and golden oak paneling opening to a dramatic sweeping staircase with stained- and beveled-glass windows. Each room is individually decorated with such touches as brass beds, claw-foot tubs, private balconies, curved-glass windows, high ceilings, fireplaces, and oak floors. Soothing music, soft lighting, and jetted tubs are among the other attractions. There are eight guest rooms, each with a private bath and some with whirlpools.

CASTLE MARNE   **$$$**
1572 Race St.
(303) 331-0621, (800) 926-2763
castlemarne.com

Victorian architecture with an eccentric flair is the charm of this bed-and-breakfast on Denver's near-east side, 20 blocks from downtown and an easier and more scenic walk from the Denver Zoo, the Denver Museum of Nature and Science, and the Denver Botanic Gardens. Built in 1889, Castle Marne really looks like a small castle. Its designer was the eclectic architect William Lang, who also designed Denver's famous "Unsinkable" Molly Brown House, now a major landmark and tourist attraction.

Some of the 9 guest rooms have their own Jacuzzi tubs for two. Three of the rooms have private balconies with hot tubs for two. All have furnishings chosen to bring together authentic period antiques, family heirlooms, and exacting reproductions to create a mood of tranquil and elegant charm. You can find that same mood in the parlor, a serene retreat of high ceilings and glowing dark woods, and the cherry-paneled dining room. The castle's big visual treasure is what they call their Peacock Window, a circular stained-glass beauty partway up the grand staircase. The castle also has a gift shop, a game room, a Victorian garden, an airy veranda, and a guest office for the business traveler, including computer. Generally, only well-behaved children older than age 10 are allowed. Most rooms are subject to a maximum occupancy of two persons.

HOLIDAY CHALET $$
1820 E. Colfax Ave.
(303) 437-8245, (800) 626-4497
holidaychalet.net
Though each of the 10 rooms has its own kitchen, Holiday Chalet serves a full breakfast. This Victorian-charm hotel is a restored 3-story brownstone mansion built in 1896 for a prominent Denver jeweler. It's situated within easy walking to the Denver Zoo, the Denver Museum of Nature and Science, and the Denver Botanic Gardens. It's about 10 blocks from downtown.

LUMBER BARON INN & GARDENS $$$
2555 W. 37th Ave.
(303) 477-8205
lumberbaron.com
One of Denver's newer bed-and-breakfast inns, the Lumber Baron offers Victorian-era furnishings, gourmet breakfasts, and pleasant gardens. The first 2 floors have 12-foot ceilings and are divided among 5 suites, all with Jacuzzis large enough to hold two. The inn is also known for the Murder Mystery Dinners it stages.

QUEEN ANNE BED & BREAKFAST INN $$
2147 Tremont Place
(303) 296-6666
queenannebnb.com
The Queen Anne Bed & Breakfast Inn is in the Clements Historic District, a restored area on the edge of downtown that is Denver's oldest continuously occupied residential neighborhood. The inn consists of two adjacent Victorian buildings in the Queen Anne style of architecture, of 1879 and 1886 vintage, both of which are on the National Register of Historic Places. They offer elegantly restored interiors, period furnishings, and 14 quaintly homey rooms featuring individual baths, writing desks, piped-in chamber music, and fresh flowers. Coors Field is 15 minutes away on foot.

HOSTELS

Hostels are for the truly cost-conscious traveler who is not looking for frills and is comfortable sharing a bathroom with other guests. In exchange, they provide opportunities for special camaraderie and locations that often are extremely convenient. We've listed only downtown Denver options, prices for which can be as low as $19 per night. There are no age restrictions on occupants, except that people younger than age 18 cannot check in without a parent or guardian.

DENVER INTERNATIONAL HOSTEL $
630 E. 16th Ave.
(303) 832-9996
youthhostels.com/denver

The Denver International Hostel is on the edge of downtown, just 6 blocks from the State Capitol. All lodging is dormitory style, which means guests share bedrooms that are separated by gender. How many people share a room? It depends on the night. Bathrooms with showers are down the hall. The hostel has a communal kitchen a common room with a TV, library, and stereo, balconies, storage, and sports equipment. The office is open for check in 8–10 a.m. and 5–10:30 p.m. There is no curfew; guests get keys to come and go as they please.

MELBOURNE HOTEL & HOSTEL $
607 22nd St.
(303) 292-6386
denverhostel.com

This historic downtown hotel is located in Denver's Ballpark neighborhood, within easy walking distance of the Greyhound bus terminal, the Amtrak train station, and Lower Downtown. Rooms have refrigerators, a full kitchen, and free wireless Internet. Coin-operated laundry facilities are available. Bathrooms are off the hall. Travelers can choose from a dormitory-style room or private hotel rooms. The Melbourne is Denver's most child-accommodating hostel. Family rooms have a double bed, a set of bunk beds, and a lavatory.

RESTAURANTS

etro Denver residents love to dine out, and a host of innovative restaurateurs love to keep them fed. Lots of hot young chefs are busy in their kitchens creating menus that have their own distinctive Rocky Mountain charm. They emphasize game meats, trout, lamb, and other locally raised crops. Southwestern influences abound; many of the new chefs are liberal in their use of chilies, cilantro, tomatillos, and black beans. Pacific Coast seafood and fish are flown in daily, and fresh sushi and sashimi are easy to find.

Reflecting the international appetites of its locals, Metro Denver counts among its blessings a wide variety of global cuisines, including top-notch Vietnamese, Thai, Japanese, Korean, Italian, French, Mexican, Peruvian, Ethiopian, and Brazilian restaurants. There are also plenty of California-influenced bistros, vegetarian specialists, and one-of-a-kind properties that reflect the talents of their chef/owners.

OVERVIEW

In this section we've left out chain restaurants such as Chili's and Pizza Hut, not because we have anything against them, but on the assumption that readers already know what to expect at these places. In the case of exceptional merit, we've bent our rules on chains. Locally owned chains that operate only within the Metro Denver area are included.

As you can imagine, no one book could ever describe all of Metro Denver's restaurants. We've picked out the best and the brightest, as is our mandate throughout this guide. Some are special-occasion places; others are neighborhood joints. Some are widely known local institutions, others much less so. It can be the food, the ambience, the crowd, the service, or all of the above that make a place worth a visit. Obviously

we don't expect everyone to agree with all our choices, and restaurants are notoriously mutable creatures, apt to change or go out of business without warning. Hours and days of operation change, too, so we suggest you call before you go. Also, while some restaurants serve continuously, others close between lunch and dinner, so if you're looking for a mid-afternoon bite, definitely call first. For dining out with children, take a look at our Kidstuff chapter, where we have described restaurants that cater to kids or places where the entertainment is at least as memorable as the food. If you're looking to combine eating with music, or if you're more in the mood for a bar than a restaurant, check our Nightlife chapter.

We've listed restaurants alphabetically by category. Listing by category has its own set of problems, of course. In Denver, it seems that every third restaurant has at least a few Mexican-inspired items on the menu, and steak houses and seafood restaurants usually cross over into each other's territory. Each restaurant is in Denver unless otherwise noted.

Denver is very casual, and the suburbs even more so. It's possible to eat a $100 dinner in shorts and sandals and not feel out of place. But Denverites generally do dress up for a nice meal, especially at trendy bistros. In general, price is a good guide to how formal the clientele will be. Unless noted otherwise, all restaurants are open for lunch and dinner. Many downtown restaurants serve lunch on weekdays only.

Price Code

To give an idea of price, we've used the following symbols. These price codes are based on the average price of two dinner entrees, excluding alcohol, dessert, tax, and tip. Lunch menus are often less expensive.

$................... less than $17
$$ .... $17 to $26
$$$ .... $26 to $35
$$$$ .... more than $35

AFRICAN

THE ETHIOPIAN RESTAURANT $-$$
2816 E. Colfax Ave.
(303) 322-5939
The small, homey Ethiopian Restaurant has a warm pink dining room and serves lunch and dinner daily at reasonable prices, plus an exceptional Ethiopian honey wine.

MATAAM FEZ MOROCCAN
   RESTAURANT $$$$
4609 E. Colfax Ave.
(303) 399-9282
mataamfez-denver.com
A meal at Mataam Fez is more than a meal; it's an experience. A 5-course Moroccan feast is served in sumptuous tented surroundings with entertainment on the weekends. Patrons sit on the floor with their shoes off and eat with their fingers. This restaurant is open for dinner only. There also is a location in Boulder.

QUEEN OF SHEBA ETHIOPIAN
   RESTAURANT $-$$
7225 E. Colfax Ave., at Quebec Street
(303) 399-9442
This small, casual spot has become a Denver favorite for Ethiopian cuisine. Prices at Queen of Sheba are rock bottom. A favorite with meat eaters is the shish kebab. Beer and wine are the only alcohol served. Queen of Sheba serves lunch and dinner and is closed on Monday.

AMERICAN

AVENUE GRILL $$-$$$
630 E. 17th Ave.
(303) 861-2820
avenuegrill.com
Denver's movers and shakers gather at the long bar here and do business at the banquettes with their cellular phones. This is not a place to hide out in a dark corner, as there are none. So what's to eat? Salads, sandwiches, burgers, a few Southwestern dishes, a tasty cioppino, and some killer desserts. It's a great people-watching spot. Lunch and dinner are served daily, except Sunday when it's open for dinner only.

BANG! $$
3472 W. 32nd Ave.
(303) 455-1117
bangdenver.com

This popular Highland spot seats about 40 inside and more when the outside patio is open. It can be noisy and crowded, but that's part of the charm. Down-home specialties include meat loaf and catfish, and there are less traditional offerings as well. Beer and wine are served. Open for lunch and dinner Tuesday through Saturday, as well as brunch on Saturday; closed on Sunday and Monday.

THE BROKER $$$–$$$$
821 17th St.
(303) 292-5065
thebrokerrestaurant.com

The downtown Broker is situated in what was once a bank and seats some diners at tables in the old vault. It serves classic and contemporary American entrees and is known for its steaks, ice-cold peeled shrimp, good wine lists, and excellent desserts. This downtown restaurant is a popular place for a business lunch and is open for dinner 7 days a week, and for lunch weekdays only. This is one of the rare Denver dining spots where the attire tends to be somewhat dressy, though it's not required.

i Denver has always been a town whose inhabitants enjoy dining out. In fact, restaurants are often filled all week long. If a restaurant takes reservations, make them to avoid a possible long wait. Otherwise, plan to dine early or late.

THE CHERRY CRICKET $
2641 E. 2nd Ave.
(303) 322-7666
cherrycricket.com

The Cherry Cricket is known for famously juicy burgers and an extensive roster of microbrews. The salads are substantial, fresh, and quite good. This is a loud neighborhood joint that goes crazy on St. Patrick's Day. Once just a blue-collar dive, it has gained a substantial following among the monied shoppers and Cherry Creek residents who enjoy its comfortable simplicity.

CROC'S MEXICAN GRILL $$
1630 Market St.
(303) 436-1144
crocsmexicangrill.com

A high-energy restaurant with brick walls, a big bar, and a 20-foot-long crocodile suspended from the ceiling, Croc's serves mainly Mexican food at reasonable prices. There are also burgers, seafood, and a wall-to-wall happy hour. Croc's offers a weekend brunch of Mexican omelets, huevos rancheros, and breakfast burritos.

EL RANCHO RESTAURANT $$$
Exit 252 off I-70, El Rancho
(303) 526-0661

Located about 18 miles west of Denver near Genesee, El Rancho has a rustic log cabin atmosphere and seven fireplaces. The main dining room has a view of the Rocky Mountains, serves such regional specialties as buffalo, elk, and trout, and uses the freshest ingredients and Colorado products when available. Open since 1948, El Rancho serves dinner on Wednesday and Thursday, lunch and dinner on Friday, Saturday, and Sunday, and a Sunday breakfast buffet; closed

Monday and Tuesday. The outdoor patio with its great views makes a meal special.

EUCLID HALL BAR & KITCHEN $$
1327 14th St.
(303) 595-4255
euclidhall.com

Based in an 1883 building that once housed the infamous Soapy Smith's bar, Euclid Hall offers high-quality pub food from around the world in a fun atmosphere. It's also a popular spot to sample more than 40 craft beers from Colorado and beyond. Stop in for the Study Hall happy hour from 3 to 6 p.m. daily. The proprietors also own Rioja and Bistro Vendôme, both reviewed elsewhere in this guide.

FRESHCRAFT $$
1530 Blake St.
(303) 758-9608
freshcraft.com

Nearly all the food at this contemporary American restaurant is made from scratch using fresh ingredients, and its late-night hours make this a popular place for after-hours dining in LoDo. Freshcraft offers a wide selection of craft beers, including more than two dozen beers on tap, that pair well with their menu. Beer lovers and anyone who enjoys comfort food with a twist will be happy here.

FRUITION RESTAURANT $$$$
1313 E. 6th Ave.
(303) 831-1962
fruitionrestaurant.com

Open every night for dinner, Fruition is a celebrated neighborhood bistro that consistently makes local and national best-of lists. Serving sophisticated American-style comfort food made with ingredients that are locally grown or raised whenever possible, Fruition is one of the bright stars in the city's expanding cultural scene. The chef owns a farm in Larkspur that is the source for some of the restaurant's fruits, vegetables, and eggs.

GIGGLING GRIZZLY $$
1320 20th St.
(303) 297-8300
giggling-grizzly.com

You can tell from the big grizzly (yes, giggling) painted outside that this is a fun place to be. It's really more of a bar than a restaurant, but you can get burgers, sandwiches, and other comfort food snacks. The crowd tends to be young, with music best described as rockin' and on the loud side. It's a good place to sample LoDo fever and, well, drink lots of alcohol. The Grizzly serves dinner nightly.

GOVNR'S PARK $$
672 Logan St.
(303) 831-8605
govnrspark.com

Named for its proximity to the governor's mansion across the street, this is a popular spot with the Friday-night crowd looking for the relaxed after-work scene. Govnr's Park has been a big, boisterous neighborhood restaurant and tavern since it opened in 1976, with a massive beer list and a menu full of sandwiches, burgers, and tavern dishes. The front patio, shaded by a large awning, is especially nice for an informal Sunday brunch.

GUNTHER TOODY'S $
4500 E. Alameda Ave., Glendale
(303) 399-1959

You'll feel like you're in a scene in the movie *Grease* at this '50s-concept diner with gum-chewing waiters and waitresses. The food is classic American fare, and the milk shakes will bring out the kid in you. We highly recommend it for children. Breakfast, lunch, and dinner are served every day. Additional locations include: 9220 E. Arapahoe Rd., Englewood (303-799-1958); 7355 Ralston Rd., Arvada (303-422-1954); 8266 W. Bowles Ave., Littleton (303-932-1957); and 301 W. 104th St., Northglenn (303-453-1956).

HBURGER CO $$
1555 Blake St.
(303) 901-7005
hburger.com
Although this place celebrates the hamburger with 8 different variations, it offers an abundance of other selections. Several creative sandwiches, a delicious veggie burger, salads, and sides ensure that no one leaves hungry. Try the liquid nitrogen–fueled milk shake, voted the best in Denver.

IGNITE! $$
2124 Larimer St.
(303) 296-2600
ignite-denver.com
Located in the Ballpark district, this gastropub adds deliciously creative twists to standard tavern fare. Offering a selection of soups, salads, casserole dishes, Neapolitan pizzas, and sharing plates, Ignite! is popular for its cast-iron cooking and wood-roasted entrees. Alfresco dining during the warm months and cozy indoor dining during the winter make this a popular urban retreat.

JONESY'S EAT BAR $$–$$$
400 E. 20th Ave.
(303) 863-7473
jeatbar.com
Located in a row of once-dilapidated storefronts, Jonesy's is a key player in the gentrification process of an urban area now known as Uptown. Jonesy's serves upscale gastropub fare, with beers and wines as prominent on the menu as salads, sliders, appetizers, and entrees such as shredded lamb and green onion gnocchi. Open daily for dinner and on Saturday and Sunday for brunch.

LINGER $$$
2030 W. 30th Ave.
(303) 993-3120
lingerdenver.com
Linger celebrates the culinary art of street food—freshly prepared regional cuisine served from street carts throughout Asia and the Americas. Here, the cuisine is offered as small plates perfect for sampling and sharing with friends. Diners enjoy an excellent view of the Denver skyline. Linger is a sister restaurant of Root Down (reviewed later in this section). Closed Sunday and Monday.

LODO'S BAR & GRILL $$
1946 Market St.
(303) 293-8555
lodosbarandgrill.com
The rooftop deck of the original downtown location near the home-plate entrance to Coors Field is legendary, letting you drink in the view while enjoying your meal. Meanwhile, the Highlands Ranch south location (8545 S. Quebec St.; 303-346-2930) offers its own rooftop deck with stunning views of the Denver skyline and the mountains, including Pikes Peak. The newest location in Westminster (3053 W. 104h Ave.; 303-635-8025) is perched on a bluff that overlooks the northern suburbs and has western views of Longs Peak. All three properties have big-screen TVs for watching sports, 24 beers on tap, and eats that include fish-and-chips, shrimp,

fajitas, pasta, sandwiches, and salads. Lunch and dinner are served daily at all locations.

MARLOWE'S $$$
501 16th St.
(303) 595-3700
marlowesdenver.com

First opened in the 1980s, Marlowe's remains a popular gathering spot for lunch, dinner, or after work. The restaurant serves steaks, chops, seafood, salads, pasta, and fresh Maine lobster. Marlowe's features an extensive martini list as well as daily happy hour specials. Located across from Denver Pavilions, it boasts a nice patio on the 16th Street Mall with prime people-watching. Lunch and dinner are served daily, and breakfast is served Saturday and Sunday.

MERCURY CAFE $-$$
2199 California St.
(303) 294-9281
mercurycafe.com

In addition to hosting one of the best and most eclectic performing arts scenes in town, the funky, friendly Mercury Cafe serves local, natural, or organic meals in its bohemian Ballpark space. It's open for breakfast and lunch on Saturday and Sunday, and for dinner Tuesday through Sunday. The menu is as varied as the entertainment lineup; a meal here might include vegetable, garlic, or striped bass linguine; marinated and breaded tofu; or grilled elk or chicken shish kebabs. Save room for the homemade desserts. Its owners are as green as they come, powering the place with wind and solar energy, and filling their gas tanks with recycled cooking oil. Two performance areas offer dance parties, poetry slams, live music, open mic nights, and a wide range of other diverse entertainment. Closed Monday, and they do not accept credit cards.

MUSTARD'S LAST STAND II $
2081 S. University Blvd.
(303) 722-7936

You can't get more American than hot dogs, french fries, and root beer floats, all of which this plain little joint does to perfection. Its location near the University of Denver guarantees a steady clientele, but older folks sneak over for the Polish sausage, too. The original Mustard's Last Stand is at 1719 Broadway in Boulder (303-444-5841). It's open daily; credit cards not accepted.

MY BROTHER'S BAR $
2376 15th St.
(303) 455-9991

The entrance to this corner tavern looks less than inviting, but everyone is welcome behind the inauspicious doors. An eclectic crowd gathers in this historic watering hole for burgers (a tasty vegetarian version is available) and beers. The pleasantly shaded patio out back is a hidden delight. It's a good place to keep in mind when you're hungry late at night, as they serve past midnight. It's closed on Sunday.

PALACE ARMS $$$$
321 17th Ave., at the Brown Palace Hotel
(303) 297-3111
brownpalace.com

The poshest of the Brown Palace's four restaurants, the Palace Arms is one of the very few places in Denver where jackets are suggested (although optional) for gentlemen. The setting and service are superb, holdovers from a more formal era. The room is decorated with antiques dating from the 18th century, including a pair of dueling pistols said to have belonged to Napoleon. The fare is contemporary regional cuisine, and the award-winning wine list features close to 1,000 options. Reservations are recommended. Open Tuesday through Saturday for dinner.

THE PALM $$$$
1201 16th St.
(303) 825-7256
thepalm.com
The downtown Westin provides the backdrop for this top-notch restaurant, where Denver's business set devours thick slabs of dry-aged beef, lobster, and Italian cuisine while discussing mergers and acquisitions. Caricatures of Denver's noted and notorious hang on the wall. Serves lunch and dinner Monday through Friday; dinner only on weekends. Reservations are recommended.

PARAMOUNT CAFE $$
519 16th St.
(303) 893-2000
paramountcafe.com
A favorite for people-watching, the Paramount's outdoor seating area extends into the 16th Street pedestrian mall. This casual lunch or dinner spot serves burgers, sandwiches, and Tex-Mex food at low prices in a setting reminiscent of a '50s diner. Happy hour after work is a lively scene. Lunch and dinner are served daily.

POTAGER RESTAURANT AND WINE
BAR $$$
1109 Ogden St.
(303) 832-5788
potagerrestaurant.com
Potager is everything a great restaurant should be: intimate, friendly, and unpretentious, plus the food is sublime. Potager

opened in 1997 in the heart of Capitol Hill and draws raves from everyone who discovers its elegant yet cozy space. Chef Teri Rippeto is creative and bold in her choices. She specializes in fresh, local, seasonal food and changes the menu monthly. The decor is stark yet soft, with natural wood and nearly bare walls. Dinner is served Tuesday through Saturday. Checks are not accepted.

RACINES $$
650 Sherman St.
(303) 595-0418
racinesrestaurant.com
Racines is a large, laid-back Golden Triangle landmark that is busy from breakfast through the last dinner, which on weekends is nearly 11 p.m. People love it for the urbane decor, the hip staff, and the variety of entrees. The menu has something for everyone, from sandwiches to pastas to a selection of Mexican entrees. An in-house bakery makes carrot cake, muffins, and Racines's locally famous brownies—all ready to be packaged up and taken home. The weekend late-night scene can be colorful.

i In 1944, Louis Ballast dropped a slice of cheese onto a hamburger at his Denver drive-in restaurant and patented the invention as "the Cheeseburger." Other claimants can take up their case with the Denver Metro Convention & Visitors Bureau, which stands by this bit of trivia.

REIVER'S $$
1085 S. Gaylord St.
(303) 733-8856
reiversbarandgrill.com
A popular watering hole in the Washington Park neighborhood, Reiver's is best known

for its burgers and casual atmosphere. Among the house specialties are shepherd's pie and chicken-fried steak, although the appetizer and salad menus are deep and varied. After your meal, stroll around the neighborhood and window-shop. Lunch and dinner are served every day. Free valet parking is offered Tuesday through Saturday after 5 p.m.

RIALTO CAFE $$$
934 16th St.
(303) 893-2233
rialtocafe.com

Housed on the ground floor of a Courtyard by Marriott on Denver's busy 16th Street pedestrian mall, this great-looking restaurant features dark woods, a pressed-tin ceiling, and motifs from the '20s and '30s. The food is New American cuisine and includes Colorado-inspired dishes such as buffalo meat loaf and Colorado bison burger. Friday and Saturday evenings are good for martinis and people-watching. Breakfast, lunch, and dinner served daily.

*ROOT DOWN $$$
1600 W. 33rd Ave.
(303) 993-4200
rootdowndenver.com

Embracing the farm-to-table concept of eating, Root Down uses local ingredients whenever possible, resulting in one of the city's best dining experiences. Entrees are inspired by global cuisine, and the menu changes seasonally. The wait can be long, especially on weekends, but most diners concur the food is worth it. This is the sister restaurant to Linger (reviewed earlier in this section).

SHIP TAVERN $$$
321 17th St., at the Brown Palace Hotel
(303) 297-3111
brownpalace.com

In the Brown Palace Hotel (but accessible through its own entrance off Tremont Place), the Ship Tavern is modeled after a classic English pub and is crammed with replicas of actual ships from America's clipper period. The food is classic, too: prime rib, Rocky Mountain trout, chicken, lamb, and sandwiches. Lunch and dinner are served daily; live entertainment is booked Wednesday through Saturday evenings.

*THE SQUEAKY BEAN $$$–$$$$
1500 Wynkoop St.
(303) 623-2665
thesqueakybean.com

One of the new stars on the Denver culinary scene, the Bean earned a four-star review from the *Denver Post* within months of opening. The small menu of meat, fish, and vegetables rotates monthly to offer seasonal foods, and the vegetable dishes are exceptional. The bar serves a variety of innovative craft cocktails.

STEUBEN'S $$–$$$
523 E. 17th Ave.
(303) 830-1001
steubens.com

Once a run-down auto shop, Steuben's is in one of the hottest areas of town. A trace of the old garage decor lingers in the renovated space, although there's nothing run-down about it now. Don't expect diner prices for dishes that mix nostalgia—tomato soup, deviled eggs, iceberg wedge with blue cheese dressing, milk shakes, grilled cheese, butterscotch pudding—with new takes on regional specialties—cayenne étouffée,

Maine lobster roll, spicy pinto bean sloppy joe. The chocolate cake is epic. Open daily for lunch and dinner, with Sunday brunch. Its kitchen stays open until 11 p.m. on Sunday and weekdays, and until midnight on weekends.

STRINGS $$$$
1700 Humboldt St.
(303) 831-7310
stringsrestaurant.com
Diners rate this classy spot as one of Denver's best. They like its distinctively eclectic California-Italian menu of pasta, seafood, warm salads, and grilled dishes; appreciate the artistic presentation; and enjoy its extensive wine list. The place is a perfect example of Denver's vibrant restaurant spirit. It's open for lunch on weekdays, and daily for dinner.

TOM'S URBAN 24 $$
1460 Larimer St.
(720) 214-0516
tomsurban24.com
Tom's Urban 24 brings quality comfort food to LoDo with round-the-clock dining. Sourced from more than 30 Colorado farmers, Tom's menu satisfies appetites with cuisine ranging from Mexican-influenced plates and Asian fusion to tasty salads, char-grilled burgers, artisan pizza, and a host of comforting side dishes.

TRILLIUM $$$-$$$$
2134 Larimer St.
(303) 379-9759
trilliumdenver.com
This casual urban bistro near Coors Field offers cuisine that blends American and Scandinavian culinary traditions. The menu changes seasonally and uses fresh ingredients whenever available. Choose from small

plates, smorgasbord, and large plates. Dinner and happy hour service is offered Tuesday through Sunday.

TRINITY GRILLE $$$$
1801 Broadway
(303) 293-2288
trinitygrille.com
A popular spot for lunching businesspeople, the Trinity Grille is brisk and shiny with polished wood, brass railings, and a black-and-white tile floor. Steaks, soups, salads, sandwiches, and fish are the mainstay of the menu. The crab cakes, in particular, are highly recommended. It serves dinner Monday through Saturday and lunches on weekdays only. Closed Sunday.

VESTA DIPPING GRILL $$$-$$$$
1822 Blake St.
(303) 296-1970
vestagrill.com
One of the city's longtime favorites, Vesta offers Denver diners relaxed yet upscale dining in a renovated warehouse with exposed brick walls, high-backed booths, and funky lighting. Guests start off with a variety of appetizers, and move on to either skewered dinners or more traditional entrees, all served with a choice of three homemade sauces that give the meal spice, pizzazz, and variety. Sharing is encouraged. Dinner is served nightly, with the kitchen open until 10 p.m. Sunday through Thursday and 11 p.m. weekends.

WAZEE LOUNGE & SUPPER CLUB $
1600 15th St.
(303) 623-9518
wazeesupperclub.com
It's back to the '40s, or some other unspecified prior decade, at this laid-back

pizza-and-burgers joint that has been open since the 1970s. A LoDo favorite for years, it's hard to say just what makes this place so cool. The diverse crowd? The bohemian ambience? The pizza? Regardless, it remains popular year after year. Lunch and dinner served daily, with late-night until 2 a.m. Monday through Saturday.

ASIAN

BA LE SANDWICH $
1044 S. Federal Blvd.
(303) 922-2129
Denver Post restaurant critics love Ba Le for a number of reasons. First, it's located in the heart of the city's largest Asian neighborhood, which means its diners know what they're looking for. Second, it specializes in the classic Banh Mi sandwich, a Southeast Asian staple made of french bread, pork pâté, carrots, cabbage, and chili. Third, prices are reasonable—just a few dollars for the sandwich, which is best when washed down with a sugarcane soda.

BD'S MONGOLIAN BARBECUE $$$
1620 Wazee St.
(303) 571-1824
Once you choose your meats, vegetables, and sauce, the cook stir-fries it while you watch. BD's is a no-frills way to dine when you're tired of all the upscale joints around town. Lunch and dinner daily.

✳CHOLON BISTRO $$
1555 Blake St.
(303) 353-5223
cholon.com
ChoLon translates to "big market" in Vietnamese, and this popular bistro offers delicious twists on traditional Asian fare. Much of

the menu is based on street food, including wok dishes, dumplings, spring rolls, and pot stickers. Start with the small bites menu, then move on to small plates, and finish with a large plate or wok dish. Sharing is encouraged.

✳DOMO RESTAURANT $$$
1365 Osage St.
(303) 595-3666
domorestaurant.com
No sushi. No upscale see-and-be-seen surroundings. Domo is all about an authentic Japanese country food experience. Teriyaki meats and fish, for example, are flavored like the real thing, not layered in gooey sauce. Reservations are accepted only for parties of six or more; everyone else is seated on a walk-in basis.

IMPERIAL CHINESE RESTAURANT & LOUNGE $$
431 S. Broadway
(303) 698-2800
imperialchinese.com
Imperial does indeed live up to its name, with opulent decor that resembles the set of *The Last Emperor*. And better, the food matches the quality decor. The restaurant specializes in seafood, but don't pass up the sesame chicken or, if you're in the mood for the royal treatment, the fabulous Peking duck. Lunch and dinner are served daily except Sunday, which is dinner only.

J'S NOODLES STAR THAI $
945 S. Federal Blvd.
(303) 922-5495
jsnoodlesstarthai.blogspot.com
A standout among the many Asian restaurants along South Federal, J's Noodles has been successful for many years. For many

Thai aficionados, this plain storefront restaurant in the heart of Metro Denver's Asian restaurant area tops the list for its combination of outstanding food and low prices. Try a noodle bowl at lunch or a curry for dinner.

✳LITTLE OLLIE'S ASIAN CAFE $$
2364 E. 3rd Ave.
(303) 316-8888
littleolliescherrycreek.com
Long one of Denver's best Asian restaurants, Little Ollie's puts a new twist on old favorites, with dishes such as stir-fried lobster, Shanghai shrimp, and steamed sea bass. Vegetarians will be pleased with the variety of nonmeat entrees. With a patio that's open year-round (heated in winter), you can always indulge in some sidewalk dining. Lunch and dinner are served daily, with rotating daily lunch specials offered as well.

NEW ORIENT $$
10203 E. Iliff Ave., Aurora
(303) 751-1288
neworientdining.com
A small, simply decorated restaurant, New Orient serves Vietnamese, Chinese, and "Amerasian" cuisine, updating traditional recipes with creative touches. This means that you can have roast-duck soup and pineapple-paprika shrimp for lunch with cappuccino mud torte for dessert. Seafood is a specialty. It's closed on Monday.

✳NEW SAIGON $$
630 S. Federal Blvd.
(303) 936-4954
newsaigon.com
Yet another Federal Boulevard Asian restaurant, New Saigon is a perennial winner in *Westword*'s "Best Vietnamese Restaurant" category. One of Denver's first Vietnamese restaurants, it has been in business since 1987. Despite tons of competition, its loyal fans can't be lured away from the spicy beef, noodle bowls, and acclaimed fish dishes. New Saigon offers great food in slightly more upscale surroundings than its Federal Boulevard counterparts.

PARALLEL SEVENTEEN $$$–$$$$
1600 E. 17th Ave.
(303) 399-0988
parallelseventeen.com
For small plates served in a small, cosmopolitan space, Parallel Seventeen is unparalleled. The food is fancy even though the prices aren't, and most cocktails on the large drink menu come with lychee fruit garnishes. Family recipes have been modernized, and the owners urge their guests to eat family style. Try the sticky Vietnamese barbecued ribs or the calamari fried with lemons and limes and served with mango on a bed of greens.

P.F. CHANG'S CHINA BISTRO $$
1415 15th St.
(303) 260-7222
pfchangs.com
Don't expect the usual sweet-and-sour chicken at Chang's. In fact, don't expect the usual Chinese fare at all; Chang's does it with a stylish twist. From crab wontons to melt-in-your-mouth flourless chocolate cake, P.F. Chang's serves flavorful meals to the LoDo crowd. Our only gripe: Entrees can be a bit sweet. Enlist the excellent waitstaff to help ensure the best combination of items. For appetizers, try the shrimp dumplings and lettuce cups stuffed with chicken. And don't forget the garlic snap peas, a P.F. Chang signature side dish. Other area locations are at 8315 S. Park Meadows Center Dr., Littleton

(303-790-7744); and 1 W. Flatirons Circle, Broomfield (720-887-6200).

SONODA'S $$$
1620 Market St.
(303) 595-9500
sonodassushi.com

Proprietor Kenny Sonoda calls his casual restaurants "Japanese seafood houses and sushi bars," and, indeed, the menu features changing seafood specials depending on what's fresh and available. Additional area locations are at Park Meadows Mall, Littleton (303-708-8800); and 3108 S. Parker Rd., Aurora (303-337-3800).

*SUSHI DEN $$$
1487 S. Pearl St.
(303) 777-0026
sushiden.net

A chic, modern restaurant that just happens to be a sushi bar, Sushi Den does a superb job with cooked fish, too. The standout is the steamed fresh fish in a bamboo basket. The sushi bar is a visual feast, and the dining room is modern with lots of black, granite, and concrete. Presentation here is artful, from decor to plate. It's open weekdays for lunch and daily for dinner, with service until 11:30 p.m. on weekends. Expect crowds during peak hours.

THAI BASIL $$
1422 E. 18th Ave.
(303) 861-1226
thaibasil.co

With six locations in the greater Denver area, this popular Asian bistro chain offers an extensive menu of Chinese, Thai, and Vietnamese entrees at affordable prices. Choose from a variety of soups, noodle and rice dishes, Thai curries, and main dishes. Sauces sometimes tend toward the sweet side. Additional Denver locations are at 540 E. Alameda Ave. (303-715-1188) and 3301 W. 38th Ave. (303-433-2888).

THAI BISTRO $$
5924 S. Kipling St., Littleton
(720) 981-7700
thaibistro.net

Thai Bistro offers a wide array of menu choices that range from pad thai to curries to Thai tapioca, all excellent picks. The Thai chefs focus on balancing sweet and sour, spicy and mild. Many dishes can be ordered vegetarian. Lunch and dinner are served Monday through Saturday; dinner only on Sunday.

TOMMY'S THAI $$
3410 E. Colfax Ave.
(303) 377-4244
tommysthaidenver.com

Tommy's has been a staple on Capitol Hill since 1988, but its popularity has grown as seedy Colfax Avenue gentrifies. Once a narrow one-room joint, Tommy's has expanded into a hip place for young and old. Although Chinese food is served, the best items on the menu are the Thai dishes. Those of note include the tom kha gai soup, fried tofu wedges, shu mai steamed pork dumplings, any of the curries, spring rolls, and the traditional pad thai with Thai iced coffee.

i Some of Denver's most unusual restaurants can be found in the small one- to five-shop shopping centers in Denver's older neighborhoods.

YOISHO RESTAURANT $–$$
7236 E. Colfax Ave.
(303) 322-6265

A tiny Japanese restaurant with a devoted East Denver following, Yoisho has a simple menu with fried Japanese dishes (no sushi here), noodle bowls, and notable gyoza dumplings. There is no liquor license.

BAKERIES

*DEVIL'S FOOD $
1020 S. Gaylord St.
(303) 733-7448
devilsfoodbakery.com

Devil's Food started as a Washington Park bakery whose motto was "Open Bright and Surly." Then came the breakfast and lunch crowds. The luscious homemade baked goods are present throughout the day, either over the counter for walk-ins or in the funky restaurant next door. The eggs Benedict is highly recommended. Servers are as artistic as the atmosphere. Open daily for breakfast and lunch; dinner Monday through Saturday. Expect a wait on weekend mornings.

OMONIA BAKERY $
2813 E. Colfax Ave.
(303) 394-9333

This authentic Greek bakery will satisfy a craving for baklava, koularakia, kataifi, or galataboureko. A napoleon is available, too, and, of course, there's strong coffee to go with whatever sweet your heart desires. It's open daily from 9 a.m. until 9 p.m. and doesn't accept credit cards.

RHEINLANDER BAKERY $
5721 Olde Wadsworth Blvd., Arvada
(303) 467-1810
rheinlanderbakery.com

Authentic German rye bread tops the list at this charming family-run old-world bakery in Arvada's historic Olde Town district, which has been operating since 1963. Coffee cakes, Danish pastries, European-style tortes, strudel, and cookies are available, too. Bakers also do a wide range of special interest items with no gluten, no wheat, and no sugar. The Rheinlander is open from 9 a.m. to 5 p.m. Sunday and Monday, and from 8:30 a.m. to 6 p.m. Tuesday through Saturday.

ROSALES MEXICAN BAKERY $
2636 W. 32nd Ave.
(303) 458-8420
rosalesbakery.com

This family-operated bakery carries 80 varieties of authentic Mexican pastries and bread baked fresh daily, as well as a selection of imported Mexican items. Neighbors know it as the place to go for Day of the Dead breads. Rosales also serves carnitas, tortas, and tamales, and is open daily from 6 a.m. to 10 p.m.

BARBECUE

BROTHERS BBQ $
6499 Leetsdale Dr.
(303) 322-3289
brothers-bbq.com

Brothers BBQ dishes up award-winning slow-smoked ribs either vinegary Memphis-style or sweet and smoky Kansas City–style at any of its Metro Denver locations. You might also try its smoky barbecued chicken or pulled-pork sandwich. Open for lunch and dinner daily, and takeout is a good option as well. Call ahead for pickup. Check out their website for additional area location information.

SAM TAYLOR'S BAR-B-Q $
435 S. Cherry St., Glendale
(303) 388-9300
samtaylorsbbq.com
Is Sam Taylor's smoky-sweet and spicy bar-becue the best in town? Lots of folks say it is. The atmosphere is ultracasual family style, with picnic tables on the patio. The amazing melt-in-your-mouth barbecue is served daily for lunch and dinner.

WINSTON HILL'S RIBS & STUFF $
5090 E. Arapahoe Rd., Centennial
(303) 843-6475
winstonhillsribsandstuff.com
For decades, Daddy Bruce Randolph was the revered king of barbecue, but after his death in 1994, relatives have vied for the honor. Winston Hill is a cousin, and he uses Daddy's Arkansas-based recipes and serves them to the world's smallest crowd (about eight can squeeze into the restaurant at any one time). A larger audience comes to the "rib shack" for takeout. Lunch and dinner Monday through Saturday; closed Sunday.

BREAKFAST

**BENNY'S RESTAURANT Y
   TEQUILA BAR** $
301 E. 7th Ave.
(303) 894-0788
bennysrestaurant.com
Benny's is actually a full-service Mexican joint with as much history as flavor in its food. But we've listed it under breakfast because it offers the best breakfast burrito known to humankind. Fat and filled with eggs, pota-toes, and a choice of menudo, sausage, or meat, it's served smothered in green chile with tender chunks of pork. It's no diet plate, mind you, but great comfort food. And while you wait you can munch chips and salsa (also among the best in Denver). There are other breakfast items, all with Benny's Mexican flair. Breakfast is served Saturday and Sunday; lunch and dinner are served 7 days a week.

DELECTABLE EGG $
1642 Market St.
(303) 572-8146
delectableegg.com
Traditional breakfast choices including omelets, eggs Benedict, waffles, french toast, and pancakes lure customers to this local spot. The original Delectable Egg is housed in an old warehouse in Lower Downtown, which makes it look a little like a greasy-diner-gone-chic (although the food isn't unusually greasy). Other locations are spiffed up to match the good, standard breakfast dishes. Breakfast and lunch are served daily. Additional area locations are at 1625 Court Place, Denver (303-892-5720); 200 Quebec St., Denver (720-859-9933); and 1005 W. 120th Ave., Westminster (303-451-7227).

DOZENS $
236 W. 13th Ave.
(303) 572-0066
dozensrestaurant.com
Want a breakfast that will stay with you, but don't want to ingest too much grease? Doz-ens is the place. With two locations, it serves a traditional American breakfast of wonder-ful omelets, griddle combinations, waffles, and pancakes. Homemade baked goods are available, too. Dozens bustles weekdays with the business crowd and on weekends with the more relaxed coffee-drinking, paper-reading crowd. It serves breakfast and lunch daily. A second location is in Aurora at 2180 S. Havana St. (303-337-6627).

ELLYNGTON'S $$$
321 17th St., at the Brown Palace Hotel
(303) 297-3111
brownpalace.com
Best known for its lavish champagne brunch (with Dom Perignon, if you've got the bucks for it), the classy and urbane Ellyngton's also serves a tasteful breakfast and lunch, but no dinner. Sunday brunch is an extravagant buffet with impressive displays of food.

HOT CAKES DINER $
1400 E. 18th Ave.
(303) 832-4351
If you're in the mood for pancakes (or any other home-cooked breakfast), head to Hot Cakes, a favorite of Uptown residents as well as employees from the surrounding hospitals. The cakes are so big that one is enough, and they come in a mind-boggling range of flavors. The lunch menu and environment are just as appealing as the flapjacks. The walls are filled with original works of art, and the waitstaff is young, friendly, and appealingly funky. Open daily for breakfast and lunch.

LE PEEP RESTAURANT $
999 18th St.
(303) 244-0360
lepeep.com
Le Peep is a local chain with a dozen different properties throughout Colorado's Front Range, but it's best known as a Metro Denver breakfast legend. There's a small selection of sandwiches, but Le Peep is all about breakfast. Omelets, pancakes, french toast—you get the picture. There's nothing gourmet here, but it's tasty. Coffee drinkers will like the self-serve pot left on the table. Breakfast and lunch daily. Additional Denver locations are at 1699 S. Colorado Blvd. (303-759-3388);

2456 S. Parker Rd. (303-369-5404); and 1875 York St. (303-399-7320).

PETE'S KITCHEN $–$$
1962 E. Colfax Ave.
(303) 321-3139
petesrestaurants.com/peteskitchen
One of the few places serving 24 hours a day, Pete's Kitchen is a longtime Denver tradition. The ambience is classic diner, the food tends toward Greek, and breakfast is available anytime. The lines tend to get long after the bars close and on weekend mornings. Great people-watching and reliable food day or night mark this colorful local joint.

Breakfast Burritos

Spend a few days in Denver and you should notice a fast food like none other, the hearty hold-in-one-hand breakfast burrito. Find it at vendors' stands throughout downtown and along major thoroughfares, or in neighborhood restaurants.

The favorites from a Best Breakfast Burrito reader's poll in *Westword* were Big Mama's Burritos, 9730 W. 44th, Wheat Ridge; Santiago's, 571 Santa Fe Dr. and 5701 Leetsdale Dr.; Taco Mex, 7840 E. Colfax; Senor Miguels, 14583 E. Alameda; El Valle, 2925 W. 38th; and Bow-Ree-Toe De-Lite, 5050 S. Federal Blvd.

SAM'S NO. 3 $
15th & Curtis
(303) 534-1927
samsno3.com

Although it also serves lunch and dinner, Sam's No. 3 is renowned for its breakfasts. Specialty omelets, breakfast burritos, skillet plates, a variety of egg dishes, and an espresso bar keep customers happy 7 days a week. They also serve Greek specialties for breakfast, lunch, and dinner. Regular customers keep coming back for the Colorado green chile. A second location is at 2580 S. Havana (303-751-0347).

✳SNOOZE $–$$
Park Avenue and Larimer Street
700 Colorado Blvd.
(303) 297-0700
snoozeeatery.com
Everything at this popular downtown daytime eatery is made from scratch using fresh, quality ingredients. The menu is creative and varied enough to warrant repeat visits. Favorites are the sweet potato pancakes, huevos rancheros, ham Benedict III, and french toast. Expect a line on weekends and during peak morning hours. Enjoy watching the local scene while you wait.

BREWPUBS

BRECKENRIDGE BREWERY $$–$$$
2220 Blake St.
(303) 297-3644
breckbrew.com
The emphasis here is on the microbrewed beers and ales, but no one need go hungry with a menu that includes hearty pub fare—burgers, chicken sandwiches, salads, soups—for lunch and dinner daily. The original location is close to Coors Field and is a great place for an after-game brew. The second location is at 471 Kalamath St. (303-573-0431).

FRESHCRAFT $$
1530 Blake St.
(303) 758-9608
freshcraft.com
Along with a full menu of contemporary American cuisine, Freshcraft offers a wide selection of craft beers that pair well with the menu. Offering comfort food with a few fun twists, most items at Freshcraft are made from scratch using fresh ingredients. The late-night hours make this a popular place for after-hours dining in LoDo. Vegan and gluten-free options are part of the menu.

ROCK BOTTOM RESTAURANT & BREWERY $$
1001 16th St.
(303) 534-7616
rockbottom.com
A huge brewpub with outdoor seating on the 16th Street Mall, the Rock Bottom is related to the Walnut Brewery in Boulder. It's popular from lunchtime well into the evening, and the extensive menu includes salads, pastas, barbecued meats, and sandwiches. It's an all-around favorite with locals, whether the action is on the patio or around the impressive bar. Open daily. Other locations are in Westminster and Englewood, with details on the website.

WYNKOOP BREWING COMPANY $–$$
1634 18th St., at Wynkoop Street
(303) 297-2700
wynkoop.com
Housed in the historic J. S. Brown Mercantile Building, the Wynkoop led the way in the resurgence of Lower Downtown. Before John Hickenlooper became mayor and eventually governor, he opened Denver's first brewpub in 1988. It still sizzles, serving a variety of handcrafted ales and pub fare,

such as potpies with quinoa crust, at reasonable prices for lunch and dinner. The main dining area is noisy and crowded. Upstairs is a classic pool hall that hops with the 20 to 30 set. Lunch and dinner are served daily.

COFFEE

✳COMMON GROUNDS $
3484 W. 32nd Ave.
(303) 458-5248
1550 17th St.
(303) 296-9248
commongroundscoffeehouse.com
A coffeehouse in the European tradition, Common Grounds doubles as a community center for the west Highland neighborhood and has a second location in LoDo. Lots of free reading material, board games, and a piano for would-be Liberaces make this a place to stop and sit a spell. Pastries, cakes, muffins, and bagels are available. It's open 7 days a week from sunrise until bedtime.

✳INK! COFFEE $
1200 17th St.
(303) 534-1235
inkcoffee.com
Cool, trendy, and urbane, this local chain has quickly become one of Denver's more popular caffeine stations. Their coffee beans are hand-roasted at 6,600 feet, allowing them to roast longer at lower temperatures for a smoother finish. Come here for gourmet sandwiches, fresh salads, pastries, and an exceptional cup of coffee. For information on their many area locations, please visit their website.

> ℹ **The Seattle-style coffee shop is alive and well in Denver, as in other big cities. Many of Denver's are great spots to take a break, experience a local neighborhood, and have a light meal. Most serve bagels, scones, desserts, and other treats as well as light sandwiches.**

PARIS ON THE PLATTE CAFE & BAR $
1553 Platte St.
(303) 455-2451
parisontheplattecafeandbar.com
Popular with neighborhood artists, Paris on the Platte is Denver's oldest coffeehouse, operating under several different names since 1972 and within a few buildings of the current site. The coffeehouse is now connected to a used bookstore and serves more than just coffee. Choose from sandwiches, pizzas, salads, soups, pastries, and bagels. They also have a full bar. It's open daily, until the wee hours on Friday and Saturday.

✳ROOSTER & MOON COFFEE PUB $
955 Bannock St.
(303) 993-2622
roosterandmoon.com
Good atmosphere, comfy surroundings, and great food from breakfast through dinner make Rooster & Moon much more than your standard coffeehouse. Abundant power outlets, free wireless Internet, and a solid cool factor make it a great neighborhood java joint. And in the evening, a full bar helps the transition into a neighborhood pub and gathering place. For a special treat, try Grandma Patsy's Banana Puddin'.

✱ST. MARK'S COFFEEHOUSE $
2019 E. 17th Ave.
(303) 322-8384
stmarkscoffeehouse.com
The bohemian alternative to the much more crowded Market at Larimer Square, St. Mark's serves coffee, cappuccino, and baked goods daily from sunrise until midnight. Patrons sit outside for people-watching or inside on folding chairs and former church pews.

STELLA'S COFFEHAUS $
1476 S. Pearl St.
(303) 777-1031
stellascoffee.com
Stella's is almost certainly the only Denver coffeehouse with a branch in Amsterdam— the owner's family runs a cafe by the same name in that European city. Stella's has lots of outdoor seating and scrumptious baked goods and desserts. It also serves a light lunch. The adjoining Amsterdam Room has live entertainment on weekends. It's open until 11:30 p.m. Sunday through Thursday and until midnight on Friday and Saturday.

TATTERED COVER COFFEE SHOP $
1628 16th St.
(303) 436-1070
tatteredcover.com
Located in Denver's finest bookstore, the coffee shop at the Tattered Cover Book Store offers a full menu of coffee drinks, pastries, and light snacks. Buy a book, grab a latte or chai, and enjoy the local bookstore scene. It's a great place to while away a rainy afternoon. A second location is at 2526 E. Colfax Ave. (303-322-7727).

CONTINENTAL

BRIARWOOD INN $$$$
1630 8th St., Golden
(303) 279-3121
thebriarwoodinn.com
The Briarwood Inn isn't that far from downtown, but it's a world away from the hustle-bustle. A romantic getaway, the formal, old-fashioned Briarwood Inn is Victorian in its decor and continental in its cuisine. Dinner is served nightly, and lunch is served Tuesday through Saturday, with afternoon tea on Saturday. It's especially nice when it's decorated for the winter holidays. Reservations are required.

DELICATESSENS

ECONOMY GREEK FOODS $
717 Lipan St.
(303) 861-3001
economygreekfoods.com
A Denver institution since 1901, the Economy stocks hard-to-find varieties of imported feta cheese and olives as well as other Greek and Mediterranean specialties. It's open weekdays for breakfast and lunch, featuring gyros and other deli items.

✱THE MARKET $
1445 Larimer St.
(303) 534-5140
themarketatlarimer.com
Come to The Market for great food and desserts or just a cup of coffee and amazing people-watching. You can make a meal out of the gourmet offerings, which include made-to-order deli sandwiches and a changing variety of soups and salads. It's not really a restaurant, so we've included it in this category. The baked goods, top-of-the-line

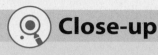

Close-up

Civic Center Eats Outdoor Cafe

Every Tuesday and Thursday during the summer months through September, more than 30 local food trucks roll into the main esplanade at Civic Center and diners select from hundreds of gourmet lunch items between 11 a.m. and 2 p.m. Cuisine ranges from Asian, barbecue, Greek, and Latin through American, pizza, sandwiches, wraps, desserts, and more. From here you're within sight of the Capitol building, Denver Art Museum, and Denver Public Library. Enjoy live music and great views while dining alfresco and connecting with the local lunchtime scene. There are even shaded tables and an ATM machine. Along with supporting Denver's growing gourmet food truck business, some of the proceeds benefit the Civic Center Conservancy, a nonprofit group committed to restoring and revitalizing Civic Center Park.

chocolates, and shelves of imported food items make this as much a shopping destination as a dining spot, and the espresso bar is always busy. Bring a cup of cappuccino and a plate of biscotti out to a table on the sidewalk and watch the world go by. It's open 7 days a week.

NEW YORK DELI NEWS $
7105 E. Hampden Ave.
(303) 759-4741
nydndenver.com

New York Deli News serves breakfast, lunch, and dinner daily. You'll enjoy great pumpernickel bread, pastrami, bagels, corned beef (all flown in from New York), and—loosen your belt—genuine New York–style cheesecake.

ZAIDY'S DELI $$
121 Adams St.
(303) 333-5336
zaidysdeli.com

Zaidy's may very well be the closest thing to an authentic New York Jewish deli that can be found in Metro Denver. This is a prime source for breakfast and lunches that range from potato latkes to smoked fish, and matzo ball soup just like your grandmother used to make. Open daily from breakfast until 7 p.m.

FRENCH

BISTRO VENDOME $$$$
1420 Larimer St.
(303) 825-3232
bistrovendome.com

This restaurant serving classic French bistro cuisine quickly became a star on the local culinary scene due to the authentic dishes featuring seasonal, local ingredients whenever possible. The extensive wine menu features wines representing all the major French wine regions. Open daily for dinner and brunch on weekends.

COOHILLS $$$$
1400 Wewatta St.
(303) 623-5700
coohills.com

Inspired by the local, farm-fresh menus found in casual restaurants across Europe, Coohills blends tradition with regional tastes through its seafood, grilled or smoked meats, pastas, salads. and local vegetables. Ingredients are Colorado-grown whenever possible, and while the food may be French-influenced, it's closer to contemporary American cuisine. Coohills is open every evening for dinner and for lunch Wednesday through Friday.

LE CENTRAL $$–$$$
112 E. 8th Ave.
(303) 863-8094
lecentral.com
Le Central styles itself as "the affordable French restaurant" and does a good job of living up to that claim without skimping on quality. The restaurant is a charming series of low-ceilinged rooms; the food is country French. Lunch and dinner are served daily in addition to brunch on Saturday and Sunday.

LE GRAND BISTRO & OYSTER BAR $$$$
1512 Curtis St.
(303) 534-1155
legranddenver.com
Dining at Le Grand Bistro is like traveling to a Paris brasserie from another era. Housed in a historic brick LoDo building, Le Grand Bistro serves up an authentic French bistro menu in an atmospheric Parisian setting. A well-rounded wine list provides excellent pairing possibilities.

FUSION

＊ZENGO $$$–$$$$
1610 Little Raven St.
(720) 904-0965
richardsandoval.com/zengodenver
Combining the flavors of Latin and Asian cuisine, Zengo's creative menu is a seductive journey into the culinary highlights of both regions. The small plates are perfect

for sharing with friends and the best way to sample artful dishes such as Thai chicken empanadas, duck tacos, pork arepas, and wagyu beef sushi rolls. Every few months the kitchen offers special dishes that unite the flavors of one Asian and one Latin country. Things get a bit loud when the place is crowded; relax with one of their superb specialty cocktails.

GREEK

YANNI'S $$
5425 Landmark Place, Greenwood Village
(303) 692-0404
This is a classic Greek family-run tavern, with a blue-and-white interior and outdoor tables with umbrellas. The menu leans heavily on traditional, hearty dishes such as moussaka and pastitsio. Everything here is fresh, including the homemade bread. Knock back a shot of ouzo and let the feasting begin. Lunch is served Tuesday through Saturday, dinner Tuesday through Sunday; closed Monday.

ICE CREAM

LIKS $
2039 E. 13th Ave.
(303) 321-2370
liksicecream.com
Take a number and get in line at this well-known Denver spot. The homemade ice creams at this old-fashioned parlor come in such tempting flavors as Almond Roca and Cheesman Park (a strawberry-cheesecake concoction named for the park a few blocks away). Don't fret if they're out of your favorite flavor; they'll put it on the request list and call you when it's available. It's open 7 days a week from noon until 9 p.m.

✳LITTLE MAN ICE CREAM $
2620 16th St.
(303) 455-3811
littlemanicecream.com

This shop in the Highland neighborhood is a community gathering place all summer as locals stop by for some of the best ice cream in town. Little Man makes gelato, ice cream, and sorbet in small batches, so the quality remains high. Look for the big steel milk jug towering above the shop. Open daily year-round from 11 a.m. until 10:30 p.m. (until 11 p.m. on Friday and Saturday).

✳SWEET ACTION ICE CREAM $
52 Broadway
(303) 282-4645
sweetactionicecream.com

Handmade with fresh, natural Colorado ingredients, the ice cream here is yet another Denver standout. Choose from exotic flavors such as Thai iced tea, pumpkin fudge ripple, Colorado peach, vegan Earl Grey, Vietnamese coffee, and chocolate Andes mint. Open every afternoon and evening except Monday.

INDIAN

INDIA'S $$–$$$
7400 E. Hampden
(303) 755-4284

India's is a feast for the senses, with tantalizing aromas, colorful cloth hangings, and hypnotic Indian music. Located in a strip shopping mall just behind Tamarac Square, India's is Denver's oldest Indian restaurant and one of its finest. The curries are hot and spicy, and the tandoori dishes are very popular. Reservations are recommended. Dinner is served nightly, lunch Monday through Saturday.

JEWEL OF INDIA $$$
10343 N. Federal Blvd., Westminster
(303) 469-7779
jewelofindia.com

Suburban Westminster may seem an unlikely place for one of the area's finest Indian restaurants, as may Jewel of India's location in a shopping center anchored by a King Soopers grocery store. But once you are inside the narrow door, the truth becomes evident. Jujhar Singh has transformed the storefront into a little slice of India, complete with lamb, chicken, seafood, and vegetarian dishes, all of which come with homemade naan. If you're unfamiliar with the dishes, try the Thalis, which includes a little bit of everything to serve one or two people. Singh uses family recipes from his home region of Punjab. Jewel of India serves lunch buffets and dinners 7 days a week.

✳LITTLE INDIA $$
330 E. 6th Ave.
(303) 871-9777
littleindiadenver.com

Consistent winners of the city's Best Indian Buffet and Best Indian Restaurant awards, Little India achieves the perfect blend of spices, heat, savory, and sweet that defines classic India cuisine. With a diverse selection of tandoori dishes, kormas, curries, vindaloos, masalas, and saags, this small chain of restaurants will satisfy lovers of Indian food as well as those jumping in for their first taste. The lunch buffet is excellent. Additional Denver locations are at 1533 Champa St. (303-629-5777) and 2390 S. Down St. (303-298-1939). An additional location is in Lakewood at 425 S. Teller St. (303-937-9777).

ITALIAN

BAROLO GRILL $$$
3030 E. 6th Ave.
(303) 393-1040
barologrilldenver.com
Since opening in 1992, Barolo has consistently ranked as one of the hottest of
the city's hot spots. The food in this chic
restaurant could be called "Cal-Ital," combining as it does northern Italian recipes with
California ingredients. Barolo does several
good fish dishes with great sauces. Wines
are an especially good value. It serves dinner
only, Tuesday through Saturday; reservations
strongly recommended.

CARMINE'S ON PENN $$$$
92 S. Pennsylvania St.
(303) 777-6443
carminescolorado.com
Make a reservation; this place is way too
popular to expect a table during the dinner
hour without one. And for good reason. A
selection of delicate, homemade pasta is
the base for spicy and flavorful sauces. The
portions are enough to feed two, plus lunch
the next day. The wine list is adequate, if not
expansive. The atmosphere bustles with an
eclectic neighborhood scene. Carmine's is
fast becoming a Denver institution. Dinner
only, Tuesday through Sunday.

✳CHERRY TOMATO $$$
4645 E. 23rd Ave.
(303) 377-1914
cherrytomatodenver.com
The Cherry Tomato is another Insiders'
favorite, best known as a neighborhood
restaurant for Park Hill dwellers. Its Italian
entrees are as filling as they are delicious,
so come with an empty stomach. Among

the specialties is Pasta Felese, made with
chicken, artichoke hearts, and sun-dried
tomatoes in a white-wine cream sauce. The
place fills up fast and doesn't take reservations for parties of fewer than six. You can
call ahead when you're leaving home to be
put on the waiting list. Open for dinner only,
Tuesday through Sunday; closed Monday.

CINZETTI'S ITALIAN MARKET $$$
281 W. 104th Ave., Northglenn
(303) 451-7300
cinzettis.com
Cinzetti's (pronounced Chin-ZEH-tees) is a
"concept" restaurant. It's designed around a
central Tuscan marketplace with 14 different
cooking stations, each serving something
different—pastas, pizzas, fish and meats, and
desserts, for example. All diners pay a flat
rate at the door and can sample anything
that strikes their fancies. The food is surprisingly tasty for mass-produced buffet fare,
and wine and soft drinks are included in
the price.

DINO'S $$
10040 W. Colfax Ave., Lakewood
(303) 238-7393
Denver Post restaurant critics rave about this
landmark Italian restaurant in Lakewood, a
suburb west of downtown Denver. Homemade pasta, sausage, meatballs, lasagna, and
spumoni are among the standouts on the
menu. Lots of regulars come for the authentic Italian food; on Sunday they come right
after church for a traditional family dinner.

IL FORNAIO $$$–$$$$
8000 E. Belleview Ave., Greenwood
Village
(303) 221-8400
ilfornaio.com

A deliciously elegant dining option, Il For-naio is a California-based restaurant chain whose specialty is breads and baked goods (*il fornaio* means "the baker"). Meals can be quite good, too, though not always up to par with the prices and surroundings. Ask the server what's good and fresh to make the best selection.

IL POSTO $$$–$$$$
2011 E. 17th Ave.
(303) 394-0100
ilpostodenver.com

This hip trattoria features innovative twists on classic northern Italian dishes. Pastas are homemade and produce is local when-ever possible. The gnocchi is their signature dish. Reservations are recommended. Open daily Tuesday through Sunday for lunch and dinner.

> **i** Both Mexican and Italian food are plentiful in Denver. One area of town where you're sure to find the best of both is northwest Denver, which was originally settled by Italian immigrants, welcomed a new wave of Hispanic immigrants, and is still known today for its authentic cuisine.

LUCA D'ITALIA $$$$
711 Grant St.
(303) 832-6600
lucadenver.com

Chef Frank Bonanno was a Denver legend before he opened this Tuscan place around the corner from his Mizuna restaurant. He quickly created buzz with the wild-boar ragu, the trio of rabbit (a confit of leg, tender-loin, and braised meat with leeks), and the classic Italian bread pudding (panzanella). It's open for dinner Tuesday through Saturday.

MAGGIANO'S LITTLE ITALY $$$$
500 16th St., Denver Pavilions
(303) 260-7707
7401 S. Clinton St., Denver Tech Center
(303) 858-1405
maggianos.com

Dark woods, brass, and red-checkered table-cloths give the feel of 1940s Little Italy at this family-style restaurant. Both places are friendly, and the large food portions are served with gusto. Salads are simple but fresh and crisp.

*PANZANO $$$$
909 17th St.
(303) 296-3525
panzano-denver.com

Housed in the Hotel Monaco Denver, Pan-zano is a trip into calming dark woods and earth tones. Chef Elise Wiggins is among Denver's finest, creating extraordinary north-ern Italian dishes and a strong local follow-ing. Two open kitchens fill the air with scents of baked goods. Reservations, especially at the bustling noontime, are recommended. Breakfast, lunch, and dinner served week-days; brunch and dinner served Saturday and Sunday.

LATIN

*CAFE BRAZIL $$$
4408 Lowell Blvd.
(303) 480-1877
cafebrazildenver.com

Cafe Brazil is a tiny, intimate restaurant in what used to be an old-world Italian neigh-borhood on Denver's west side. The colorful restaurant highlights cuisine from Bahia in the north of Brazil, providing hot, tropical cuisine at its authentic best. Try the feijoada completa, Brazil's national dish, a delicious combination of black beans, meat, fruit, and rice. Cafe Brazil is open for dinner only and is closed Sunday and Monday. Reservations are recommended.

CUBA CUBA $$$$
1173 Delaware St.
(303) 605-2822
cubacubacafe.com
Two tiny historic homes were joined together to make room for this Latin American restaurant in the Golden Triangle. Enter one and find yourself in the bar. Cross over into the other and you're in the dining room. The food is zesty and heavy on pork (Lechon Asado—or roasted pork, onions, and garlic—is its signature dish). Salads and coconut-lime rice make good vegetarian alternatives, and if cocktails are your thing, try the mojitos. They're among Denver's best. Open Monday through Saturday for dinner.

MEDITERRANEAN

✳RIOJA $$$$
1431 Larimer St.
(303) 820-2282
riojadenver.com
Rioja has been a consistent downtown hot spot since it opened years ago and for good reason. Serving creative Mediterranean cuisine with an emphasis on seasonal and local products, the restaurant offers well-crafted appetizers, handmade pastas, and flavorful entrees. Reservations are recommended. Open for dinner every day and lunch Wednesday through Friday.

MEXICAN/SOUTHWESTERN

THE BLUE BONNET CAFE & LOUNGE $
457 S. Broadway
(303) 778-0147
bluebonnetrestaurant.com
This Mexican joint was "discovered" by Denver yuppies in the 1980s and remains popular—prepare to wait a while for a table. There's nothing fancy here, but they serve large portions with great big margaritas to wash everything down. The refried beans are a standout.

EL NOA NOA $$
722 Santa Fe Dr.
(303) 623-9968
denvermexicanrestaurants.net
Santa Fe Drive anchors one of Denver's earliest Mexican-American neighborhoods, hence the authentic restaurants that line its streets. El Noa Noa is an elder statesman, with a series of small dining rooms inside and an exceptional outdoor patio, complete with fountain and wrought-iron chairs. The food is typical Tex-Mex with some home style Mexican favorites thrown in for good measure, but El Noa Noa likely is best known for the tasty enchiladas, burritos, tacos, and rellenos it dishes out.

EL TACO DE MEXICO $
714 Santa Fe Dr.
(303) 623-3926
This simple restaurant holds its own, despite stiff competition from larger and better-known El Noa Noa next door. It's more like a diner than an evening dinner destination, with ultracasual meals served at the bar or at a few tables. It's open daily for breakfast, lunch, and dinner. Credit cards not accepted.

JACK-N-GRILL $–$$
2524 N. Federal Blvd.
(303) 964-9544
jackngrill.com
New Mexican dishes have made this small chain of restaurants' reputation. With three locations, Jack-n-Grill serves a mean green chile, vaquero tacos moistened with barbecue sauce, and 7-pound burritos so big the servers will take your picture if you finish one. Open daily, but call ahead as each restaurant has its own hours. Additional locations are at 9310 Sheridan Blvd., Westminster (303-428-4788); and 2630 W. Bellevue Ave., Littleton (303-474-4242).

JULIA BLACKBIRD'S NEW MEXICAN CAFE $$
3434 W. 32nd Ave.
(303) 433-2688
juliablackbirds.com
This little jewel in the charming Highland neighborhood is quickly gaining in reputation, and the weekend lines prove it. The menu is true to its New Mexican roots with blue-corn tortillas, hearty posole, light and delicious sopapillas, and pine nut chocolate cake. Lunch and dinner are served daily, though you should call to verify seasonal hours.

LA LOMA RESTAURANT $$
2527 W. 26th Ave.
(303) 433-8300
lalomamexican.com
In the up-and-coming Diamond Hill neighborhood just west of I-25 at Speer Boulevard, La Loma is rather incongruously housed in an 1887 Victorian home that has been renovated into a series of sprawling dining rooms. The restaurant is known for its big margaritas and authentic food.

LAS DELICIAS $–$$
439 E. 19th Ave.
(303) 839-5675
lasdelicias.net
This family-run restaurant has five locations, and loyal customers still can't get enough of their Michoacán-style food. House specialties include carnitas and fajitas, carne adovada, taquitos, carne asada, and steak ranchero, as well as hearty Mexican breakfasts. Open daily for breakfast, lunch, and dinner. For additional area location information, check out their website.

LOLA DENVER $$
1575 Boulder St.
(720) 939-9277
loladenver.com
Serving both Mexican and Latin American cuisine with an emphasis on seafood, Lola is known for its creative menu and extensive, award-winning tequila bar. The menu changes frequently to take advantage of seasonal ingredients, and the ceviche bar is top-notch. Try the guacamole prepared table-side.

MEXICO CITY RESTAURANT & LOUNGE $
2115 Larimer St.
(303) 296-0563
Denverites make a big fuss about authenticity when discussing the comparative merits of restaurants, but there's no argument here. This is the real thing, served inside a well-worn building in a neglected inner-city neighborhood that only recently has begun to gentrify. The green chile and burritos are favorites, and breakfast is a real eye-opener. If you're a fan of menudo, this is the place to go. It's closed Monday, but serves breakfast and lunch on the other days of the week. No credit cards.

✳MEZCAL $$
3230 E. Colfax Ave.
(303) 322-5219
mezcalcolorado.com

This authentic taqueria/cantina serves homestyle regional cuisine from across Mexico. With an extensive menu ranging from red chile posole and mole rojo to fish tacos and tampiquena, Mezcal has won a devoted local following. The restaurant is warmly decorated with Mexican wrestling posters and Moroccan lamps, and the margaritas are excellent. More than 270 tequilas are available. Happy hour takes place 7 days a week 4–6 p.m.

MORRISON INN $–$$
301 Bear Creek Ave., Morrison
(303) 697-6650

This is a fun, Americanized restaurant in an 1885 building smack in the heart of the foothills town of Morrison. It's known for custom-made (not premixed) margaritas and for its designation as a beginning—or ending—spot for motorcycle riders, mountain bikers, and hikers. The fare is standard Mexican served for lunch and dinner daily.

✳PINCHE TACOS $
Civic Center Eats
Civic Center Park (Tues and Thurs, June through Sept)
pinchetacos.com

Serving Mexican comida de la calle (street food) from a trailer, Pinche Tacos offers a full menu of delicious breakfast, vegetarian, beef, pork, and chicken tacos. Tacos are served on locally made corn tortillas and everything is made fresh daily. Check the website for their Facebook page and additional street locations.

✳PINCHE TAQUERIA $
1514 York St.
(720) 475-1337
3300 W. 32nd Ave.
(720) 502-4608
pinchetacos.com

The food cart proved so popular that Pinche Tacos opened these brick-and-mortar restaurants. They add a contemporary twist to Mexican street food using authentic regional recipes and local products whenever possible. Their specialty? Street tacos, of course.

PLAYA DE ORO $
3551 W. 38th Ave.
(303) 433-5777

Playa de Oro is known for its crispy, golden brown chile rellenos—poblano chiles stuffed with Monterey Jack. They also serve a wide array of other Mexican dishes for breakfast, lunch, and dinner Monday through Saturday, and breakfast and lunch on Sunday. Prices are incredibly low to very reasonable.

ROSA LINDA'S MEXICAN CAFE $–$$
2005 W. 33rd Ave.
(303) 455-0608
rosalindasmexicancafe.com

You say you want a neighborhood restaurant? Check out this one. Run by the Aquirre family since 1985, Rosa Linda's is a small, plain place with great burritos, enchiladas, and soft chile rellenos. It wins awards for its shredded beef burritos, chile rellenos, and other specialties. There are a few tables on the sidewalk. Open Monday through Saturday 9 a.m. to 9 p.m.

TABLE MOUNTAIN GRILL & CANTINA $$–$$$
1310 Washington Ave., Golden
(303) 277-9898
tablemountaininn.com

Enter the restaurant at the modern adobe-style Table Mountain Inn for Southwestern dishes that range from prime rib of buffalo to cowboy chops and grilled salmon. For lunch, choose among buffalo burgers, chicken, salads, and daily specials—all spiced and prepared with Southwestern flair. Breakfast, lunch, and dinner served daily. Brunch is available Saturday and Sunday.

*TAMAYO $$
1400 Larimer St.
(720) 946-1433
richardsandoval.com/tamayo

A perennial downtown favorite, Tamayo merges Old Mexico flavors with a modern twist to create delicious contemporary Mexican cuisine. The patio is a nice place to relax and sip one of their more than 100 tequilas as the sun sets. Open for lunch Monday through Friday and for dinner every night.

TAQUERIA PATZCUARO $$
2616 W. 32nd Ave.
(303) 455-4389
patzcuaros.com

A casual restaurant in a Spanish-speaking pocket of the Highland area, Taqueria Patzcuaro draws fans from all over the city with traditional Michoacán dishes as well as its green chile and soft tacos.

MIDDLE EASTERN

*JERUSALEM RESTAURANT $$
1890 E. Evans Ave.
(303) 777-8828
jerusalemrestaurant.com

A tiny eight-table restaurant that does a bustling take-out business, Jerusalem is popular with students from the University of Denver campus nearby. Everything is good here, including the kebabs, hummus, baba ghanoush, and phyllo pastries. Students cramming for an exam no doubt also appreciate the fact that Jerusalem is open until 4 a.m. Sunday through Thursday and 5 a.m. on Friday and Saturday. The space crunch is eased during summer months by the outdoor patio. Alcohol is not served.

PIZZA

BEAU JO'S PIZZA $–$$
2710 S. Colorado Blvd.
(303) 758-1519
beaujos.com

The original Beau Jo's is still in Idaho Springs, a beloved stopping point for Denverites on their way home from skiing who crave thick-crusted pizza. Beau Jo's has two branches in southeast Denver and Arvada (7805 Wadsworth Blvd.; 303-420-8376), as well as locations in Boulder, Fort Collins, Evergreen, and Steamboat Springs.

BONNIE BRAE TAVERN $–$$
740 S. University Blvd.
(303) 777-2262
bonniebraetavern.com

The crowds! The noise! The pizza! This astoundingly popular neighborhood pizza joint was founded in 1934 and is always busy. It's a fun place, but don't come here if you're in a hurry. Bonnie Brae serves lunch and dinner daily except Monday. Takeout is available.

CAFE COLORE $-$$
1512 Larimer St.
(303) 534-6844
cafecoloredenver.com
Cafe Colore has a menu that's built around a clever gimmick: Pizzas come with sauces of red, green, or white, the three colors of the Italian flag. Other Italian entrees, plus calzones, are available. You can enjoy eating outside on the patio in good weather.

LUCKY PIE PIZZA & TAP HOUSE $
1610 16th St.
(303) 825-1021
luckypiepizza.com
Choose from a dozen innovative pizza entrees or create your own from a selection of meats, cheeses, and toppings. Offering traditional Neapolitan-style pizza with a twist, Lucky Pie combines old-world with top quality local and Italian ingredients. The menu includes a fine selection of cheeses, soups, salads, charcuterie, and other entrees. Beer aficionados will be happy with the 21 rotating taps of craft beer, both local and from around the world. Lucky Pie offers 25 wines by the glass and a full bar, including original, handcrafted cocktails.

MARCO'S PIZZERIA $
2129 Larimer St.
(303) 296-7000
marcoscoalfiredpizza.com
Naples is the birthplace of pizza, and Marco's serves authentic Neapolitan pizza, New York pizza pies, and a nice variety of salads. Combining Italian flour and cheeses with fresh local produce, this pizzeria turns out some

of the best pizza in Metro Denver. A second location is in Englewood at 10111 Inverness Main St. (303-790-9000).

PARISI $-$$$
4401 Tennyson St.
(303) 561-0234
parisidenver.com
Parisi is a combination grocery, Italian deli, trattoria, and pizzeria—and it excels in all areas. Simone Parisi, who grew up in Florence, makes pizza in the true Italian tradition, meaning you order a rustica or Margherita, not pepperoni and mushroom. The crust is medium-thick, the tomato sauce chunky, and the mozzarella fresh. Multicourse dishes from the more formal trattoria are equally fresh and delicious. Enjoy your meal in the recently renovated building or have your feast packed to go. You can also find authentic Italian groceries on the shelves in the shop. The deli and pizzeria side is open Monday through Saturday for lunch and dinner, and the trattoria is open Wednesday through Saturday for dinner.

PASQUINI'S PIZZERIA $-$$
1310 S. Broadway
(303) 744-0917
pasquinis.com
A nifty little pizzeria with an artsy interior and mosaic-topped tables, Pasquini's serves New York–style thin crust, sauceless bianca, and thick-crust Sicilian-style pizzas and individual pizzettas with interesting toppings. Also on the menu are calzones and subs. The original Pasquini's is nestled amid the antiques stores on South Broadway at Louisiana Avenue. The latest is a hipster-style neighborhood joint in the Highland neighborhood. Takeout and delivery are available. For area location information, check out their website.

*PROTO'S PIZZERIA NAPOLETANA $
2401 15th St.
(720) 855-9400
protospizza.com

Owners Pam Proto and Rayme Rossello developed their pizza tastes while on an extended trip to Italy. They returned to Colorado and started selling their thin-crusted pies layered with fresh ingredients. They now own six restaurants, including this one in Denver's Central Platte Valley. (The others are in Longmont, Lafayette, Boulder, Broomfield, and Boise, Idaho.) Legions of fans say they're the best in town. Proto's also serves cocktails and wine.

SEAFOOD

FRESH FISH COMPANY $$$
7800 E. Hampden Ave.
(303) 740-9556
thefreshfishco.com

The aquatic theme extends to the decor at this big restaurant, which consists of walls of beautiful tropical aquariums. Mesquite grilling is a specialty here, and the Sunday brunch, with all-you-can-eat crab legs and shrimp, is very popular. Lunch is served Monday through Friday, dinner nightly.

JAX FISH HOUSE $$$
1539 17th St.
(303) 292-5767
jaxfishhousedenver.com

Jax won't slip a skimpy slice of fish on your plate. Here you'll get a hearty slab of fresh fish, well seasoned and served with a nice variety of side dishes. The raw oysters, stone crab claws, and crawfish are all delicious and succulent. Non-fish eaters can opt for a burger or steak, but fish is truly the dish. The place is hopping, too, so don't expect to be seated right away. Just take your time and enjoy the buildup. Jax serves dinner only, every night.

MCCORMICK'S FISH HOUSE & BAR $$$
1659 Wazee St.
(303) 825-1107
mccormickandschmicks.com

In this elegant dining room can be found some of the freshest fish in Denver. If oysters are in season, you'll find them here, on the ground floor of the venerable Oxford Hotel. You'll also find steaks, poultry, and pasta dishes. Private dining rooms are available. It's open daily for breakfast, lunch, and dinner, with late night service until 1 a.m. on weekends.

*240 UNION $$$
240 Union Blvd., at 6th Avenue, Lakewood
(303) 989-3562
240union.com

The menu changes seasonally at this creative restaurant on Denver's western flanks. It specializes in seafood, but pastas and pizzas round out the offerings. A nice enclosed patio and wall-to-wall open grill complement the wooden half walls designed to represent "the city meeting the foothills." The lounge is popular for after-work drinks and appetizers. 240 Union serves lunch and dinner nightly and dinner only on Saturday.

STEAKS

AURORA SUMMIT $$–$$$$
2700 S. Havana St., Aurora
(303) 751-2112
aurorasummit.com

A classic steak house with a dark, woodsy, masculine ambience, Aurora Summit serves

USDA prime, aged, corn-fed beef. In the tradition of steak houses, the menu also includes seafood entrees. In the large front lounge, there's a small dance floor and piano bar that light up Wednesday through Saturday nights. Aurora Summit serves lunch and dinner daily except Saturday, which is dinner only. Reservations are preferred.

THE BUCKHORN EXCHANGE $$$$
1000 Osage St.
(303) 534-9505
buckhorn.com

The Buckhorn Exchange is an institution, proudly reminding patrons that it was Denver's original steak house (founded in 1893 by "Shorty Scout" Zietz) and is located in the city's oldest neighborhood, which is served by light-rail. It's famous for Shorty Scout's stuffed bird and animal collection, with more than 500 trophies that include moose, elk, buffalo, and bear. More than 500 of them are on display throughout the building. It's also famous for the traditional Western fare on its menu, with exotic options tucked in among the steaks and baby back ribs. Try alligator tail, rattlesnake, quail, game hen, or the house specialty, Rocky Mountain oysters. If you're vegetarian, call ahead to order a vegetarian plate made to order just for you. Dinner reservations are recommended. The Buckhorn is open for dinner daily, and for lunch on weekdays only.

THE DENVER CHOPHOUSE &
BREWERY $$$–$$$$
1735 19th St.
(303) 296-0800
denverchophouse.com

The Denver ChopHouse is housed in the old Union Pacific Railroad warehouse, a block away from Coors Field. Its biggest asset is the outdoor barbecue area, with a patio and rolling roof, but the interior is also inviting, with rich, dark wood and high booths. The food is inventive; try the portobello mushrooms dipped in Worcestershire and garlic then grilled. Lunch and dinner are served daily. Reservations are suggested for weekends.

EDGE RESTAURANT $$$$
1111 14th St.
(303) 389-3343
edgerestaurantdenver.com

Located in the Four Seasons Hotel, Edge is an upscale steak house that matches the elegance and service normally associated with the hotel chain. Along with wood-grilled steaks that are primarily Colorado-sourced, they get rave reviews for their seafood. The crab cakes are a favorite. The adjoining Edge bar offers a creative tapas menu. Open daily for breakfast, lunch, and dinner.

ELWAY'S $$$$
1881 Curtis St., at the Ritz-Carlton Hotel
(303) 312-3107
elways.com

Former Broncos quarterback John Elway is a Denver legend, and his two restaurants are local institutions. In addition to good steaks and sides, cold martinis, and prime locations at the Ritz-Carlton and alongside the tony Cherry Creek Shopping Center (2500 E. 1st Ave.; 303-399-5353), Elway's often serves up celebrities who got hungry while shopping at Neiman Marcus and decided to drop in for a meal. It's open weekdays for lunch and daily for dinner.

THE FORT $$$$
19192 Hwy. 8, Morrison
(303) 697-4771
thefort.com

The Fort is one of a kind, combining Wild West flair with classy fare; where else do waiters dressed in leather vests and beads open bottles of champagne with a tomahawk? Located in the foothills, with a panoramic view of the plains below, the restaurant is a full-size adobe replica of Bent's Fort, Colorado's first fur-trading post. Buffalo is among the more popular dishes; other unusual entrees include elk, quail, rattlesnake, and Rocky Mountain oysters (rolled in seasoned flour and deep-fried). More traditional preparations of trout and steak are available, and for those who wish to sample a little bit of everything, there's a game plate. Reservations are recommended. The Fort serves dinner nightly.

MORTON'S STEAKHOUSE $$$$
1710 Wynkoop St.
(303) 825-3353
mortons.com

Located in Lower Downtown across from Union Station, Morton's is a classic, classy steak house. It is always mentioned when people talk about where to get great steaks. Only USDA prime served here. If surf and turf is what you're after, Morton's has a good selection of seafood, and they fly live lobster in from Maine. It serves dinner nightly; reservations are recommended.

SULLIVAN'S STEAKHOUSE $$$$
1745 Wazee St.
(303) 295-2664
sullivansteakhouse.com

The interior of this LoDo favorite is as dark and rich as a medium-well steak. Live music from the bar drifts throughout as diners enjoy one of Denver's best steak dinners with all the trimmings. Open daily for dinner; reservations recommended; valet parking available.

VEGETARIAN

*CITY O' CITY $
206 E. 13th Ave.
(303) 831-6443
cityocitydenver.com

The sister restaurant to Watercourse Foods (see below), City O' City offers dozens of vegetarian and vegan dishes 7 a.m. to 2 a.m. every day. Cozy and friendly in a neighborhood-dive sort of way, this restaurant also has a full bar with craft cocktails and a nice selection of wines and microbrews. The Watercourse bakery next door ensures a steady stream of fresh baked goods to go with the lattes and cappuccinos made in the coffee bar area. A local favorite is the seitan wings with barbecue sauce.

*WATERCOURSE FOODS $$
837 E. 17th Ave.
(303) 832-7313
watercoursefoods.com

For more than 14 years this hip vegetarian restaurant and bakery has been serving meatless cuisine that even carnivores enjoy. The menu is extensive, the ingredients are fresh, and dishes are creatively prepared. They serve wine and beer. Open every day for breakfast, lunch, and dinner. Expect a wait during peak hours. It's worth it.

NIGHTLIFE

Denver nightlife extends into the wee hours but in different ways and with different types of people. Artists and bohemians are drawn to gallery openings along Santa Fe Drive, Tennyson Street, Navajo Street, and the River North district. Glitterati tend to congregate in Cherry Creek, Uptown, and certain downtown landmarks. The party-hearty group heads for Capitol Hill's funky urban clubs or to Lower Downtown, where the streets are so full of well-dressed singles on weekends that cars and limos can barely move. Bars, restaurants, dance clubs, and movie theaters all over town rock on weekends and lots of weeknights when warm weather draws people out for a leisurely walk, a bite to eat, and a little live music.

OVERVIEW

In this chapter, we survey Denver's nightlife, stopping in at a few of our favorite bars, brewpubs, live music venues, comedy clubs, and movie houses. This isn't meant to be a comprehensive listing; for that kind of inclusiveness, the best place to turn is *Westword,* Denver's free weekly. The Friday edition of the *Denver Post* carries weekend entertainment listings, as does the *Daily Camera* with Boulder's happenings. The newspaper *Out Front Colorado* is a good source of information about gay and lesbian nightlife, and it is free and widely distributed in many coffee and sandwich shops.

Because people interpret "nightlife" so broadly—including everything from a wine bar with live poetry readings to an outdoor rock concert at a stadium—there is some inevitable overlap with other chapters. A brewpub such as the Wynkoop serves dinner but also draws a late-night billiards crowd. Theater and dance performances and concerts, such as those at the Denver Performing Arts Complex, are covered in our chapter on The Arts. We also direct your attention to such popular in-town music venues as the Paramount Theatre, the Ogden Theatre, and the Swallow Hill Music Association.

Keep in mind that today's hot spot could be tomorrow's Siberia. No guidebook could ever hope to keep up with the strange twists of taste that make one place worth lining up for and another worth taking pains to avoid. And, of course, music and dance clubs change their format and hours frequently. Some clubs rotate nightly, offering, for example, hip-hop on Monday, electronica on Tuesday, karaoke on Wednesday, and DJs on Thursday. If you're looking for a specific kind of music, it's always best to call ahead.

The drinking age for any kind of alcoholic beverage is 21. Closing time at bars and nightclubs is generally 2 a.m., but most restaurants stop serving food earlier. The few that keep their kitchens open until midnight are noted in the Restaurants chapter.

Colorado is not a state that takes drunk driving lightly. Penalties are severe for driving under the influence or while impaired. If you've had too much to drink, any restaurant or bar will call a taxi for you. If you're headed into the mountain towns of Central City and Black Hawk for an evening of gambling, consider taking one of the shuttle services rather than driving your own car.

BARS & OTHER GATHERING SPOTS

BANNOCK STREET GARAGE
1015 Bannock St.
(303) 246-8275
This Golden Triangle watering hole is out of the way and sparkling, but its patrons still think of it as a dive bar. That may be because the walls are filled with motorcycle parts and logos, and the regulars tend to ride—and/or love—fast bikes. Owners took advantage of the building's roots as an auto garage when they did the renovation.

i Many of Denver's watering holes (or bars or gathering places) offer Happy Hour specials on drinks and appetizers. Call ahead to inquire about specials and times.

BROWN PALACE
321 17th St., at the Brown Palace Hotel
(303) 297-3111
brownpalace.com
The grande dame of Denver hotels, the Brown Palace has three dining rooms, including Ellyngton's and the formal Palace Arms. The Ship Tavern is the most casual, which makes a good place to stop for a drink or a bite to eat. It's more restaurant than bar, but with dark wood and nautical decor, it has the

feel of an English pub. Churchill Bar is tucked unobtrusively into a corner of the hotel lobby, which makes it an excellent place to slip away for a snifter of cognac, a cigar, or a quiet conversation. Its menu includes more than 60 cigars, single-malt scotches, small-batch bourbons, and other temptations. Thanks to a fancy ventilation system, even nonsmokers can enjoy the ambience. Lunch and hors d'oeuvres can also be ordered.

THE BUCKHORN EXCHANGE
1000 Osage St.
(303) 534-9505
buckhorn.com
The upstairs saloon at the Buckhorn Exchange has been a Denver institution for more than 100 years—Colorado's first liquor license is posted on the wall. The hand-carved, white-oak bar dates from 1857 and was brought over from Germany. Expect a daily happy hour and live country and folk music Wednesday through Saturday.

✳CRUISE ROOM
1600 17th St.
(303) 628-5400
The restored Oxford Hotel, a block away from Union Station, boasts a restaurant and bar complex that's among the city's best. The intimately sized Cruise Room was modeled after a lounge on the *Queen Mary* and has a wonderful art deco interior that dates from the lifting of Prohibition in 1933. A favorite with visiting authors, the Cruise Room is a great place for a late-night drink, especially if your taste runs to martinis. The bar doesn't have live music, but the jukebox is well stocked with jazz and Big Band music. Be forewarned: It can be tough to get a seat on the weekend unless you arrive early and stake out your spot. Also anchoring the

ground floor of the Oxford Hotel is McCormick's Fish House & Bar, with a roomy corner bar that attracts a big evening crowd for Guinness Stout on tap and other libations. Check out the well-priced happy hour appetizers after work or for a late-night snack.

CRU WINE BAR
1442 Larimer St.
(303) 893-9463
cruawinebar.com
Although they offer a nice lunch menu, artisan cheeses, and stone oven-fired pizza, the big draw here is the selection of more than 300 wines. It's a cozy LoDo spot to sample wines from around the world. The happy hour each weekday 4–6:30 p.m. includes small bite plates starting at $3 and $3 off wines by the glass.

FADÓ IRISH PUB
1735 19th St.
(303) 297-0066
fadoirishpub.com
A welcome departure from the LoDo brewpub scene, Fadó brings Ireland to Denver. Most of this authentic Irish pub really is authentic—built in Ireland and brought to Denver piece by piece. Relax in one of nearly a dozen cozy nooks, or be in the middle of the crowd that surrounds the large central bar. There's a full Irish menu, too, with appetizers served until midnight. On Monday nights, Irish bands provide the entertainment.

KATIE MULLEN'S
16th Street Mall at 1550 Court Place
(303) 573-0336
katiemullens.com
Popular both as a restaurant and bar, Katie Mullen's is artfully designed to feel like an authentic Irish pub. Decorated with furniture shipped directly from Ireland, the four bar areas provide distinct themes for enjoying a wide variety of Irish-oriented food and drink items. Happy hour is 4–7 p.m. every day.

PARIS ON THE PLATTE CAFE & BAR
1553 Platte St.
(303) 455-2451
parisontheplatte.com
The Central Platte Valley is filling with brownstones and pricey apartments, so what better place for the locals to relax than a warm and cozy bar? Wine lovers have a wide variety to choose from, and those in need of a light snack can order desserts or bread and cheese platters. DJs and live bands often shoehorn themselves into a corner of the bar, transforming what can be a quiet retreat into a rocking venue.

i If you like the nightlife but aren't into the skimpy miniskirt crowd, try Fadó Irish Pub at 19th and Wynkoop. You'll find cozy spots for conversation and enjoy the authentic decor, much of which was shipped over from Ireland.

✳PEAKS LOUNGE
650 15th St., at the Hyatt Regency Denver at Colorado Convention Center
(303) 436-1234
With one of the best mountain views in all of Denver, Peaks Lounge at the top of the Hyatt Regency Denver (27th floor) looks out across downtown and west to the Front Range. Choose from more than 40 wines by the glass and sample an enticing small plate and dessert menu. Prices aren't cheap, but the views are unmatched.

SANCHO'S BROKEN ARROW
741 E. Colfax Ave.
(303) 832-5288
quixotes.com

Sancho's is best described as a dive bar, but it's a very hip one devoted to the Grateful Dead and its fans. The decor, the music, the bands, and the crowd are as tie-dyed as they come. Sancho's is located across the street from the Fillmore Auditorium and on Monday night books jam bands.

BREWERIES

BRECKENRIDGE BREWERY
471 Kalamath St.
(303) 623-2739
breckenridgebrewery.com

First opening their doors in Breckenridge in 1990, Breckenridge Brewery relocated to Denver two years later and is now the largest brewery in town. They offer an enticing array of year-round, seasonal, small batch, and barrel-aged beers. Although they now ship to 32 states, the quality remains consistently high.

*DENVER BEER COMPANY
1695 Platte St.
(303) 433-2739
denverbeerco.com

With a sprawling outdoor patio area and a wide selection of seasonal ales and lagers, Denver Beer Company is one of the city's newer breweries. The rotating menu of beers, both traditional and experimental, ensures that there's always a new brew or two on tap.

GREAT DIVIDE BREWING COMPANY
2201 Arapahoe St.
(303) 296-9460
greatdivide.com

Brewing craft beer since 1994 when the local microbrew industry was just beginning, Great Divide has won numerous awards for its products. The Tap Room features 16 taps of seasonal and year-round beers. They offer tours daily. Be prepared for a noisy but friendly room when the place is busy.

MILLERCOORS BREWERY
13th & Ford Streets, Golden
(303) 277-2337 (tours)

It's not exactly in Denver, but we can't overlook the beer with a stronger Colorado connection than any other. Although Coors officially joined up with Miller in 2008, the same beer that made Golden famous is still brewed here. Located roughly 25 minutes from downtown, this is the world's largest single-site brewery. The tours are a popular activity for out-of-town visitors, and most people stop after the tour at the sampling room to taste some of the product made at this mammoth facility.

PROST BREWING COMPANY
2540 19th St.
(303) 729-1175
prostbrewing.com

If you like German beers, or you'd like to try some for the first time, this is the place for you. One of Denver's newer breweries, Prost focuses its brewing efforts on German-style beer: pilsners, bocks, dunkels, and other German lagers and wheat beers. The atmosphere is lively and fun, with large community tables similar to a traditional German biergarten.

RIVER NORTH BREWERY
2401 Blake St.
(303) 296-2617
rivernorthbrewery.com
Located a walkable distance just north of the ballpark at the edge of the up-and-coming River North Art District (RiNo), River North produces Belgian-style ales and American ales with a Belgian slant. The large garage door stays open during warm weather, making the tasting room even more inviting.

TRVE
227 Broadway, #101
(303) 351-1021
trvebrewing.com
Pronounced "TRUE," TRVE is one of the city's newer breweries and a hip addition to the Broadway/Baker neighborhood. Their 30-foot beer table is designed to encourage conversation and a friendly atmosphere where everyone is welcome. The owners are passionate about beer, and it shows in the creatively-crafted brews. Open Wednesday through Sunday.

BREWPUBS

BULL & BUSH
4700 Cherry Creek South Dr.
(303) 759-0333
bullandbush.com
Built in 1971, this popular neighborhood gathering place with its Tudor architecture and English interior decor is a re-creation of a famous London pub. Their brewery beer list includes eight year-round beers and more than two dozen seasonal beers, along with a variety of other American and European beers. The kitchen serves from an extensive pub menu, and they also offer hundreds of whiskeys.

ROCK BOTTOM RESTAURANT & BREWERY
1001 16th St.
(303) 534-7616
rockbottom.com
Yet another brewpub and pool hall, the huge, sunny Rock Bottom Brewery is popular with the young lawyers and bankers who work on 17th Street. Try the Red Rocks Red Ale and drink it on the patio for some of the best people-watching on the 16th Street Mall. The food's pretty good, too. And, of course, you can shop at the in-house boutique for T-shirts and the like.

WYNKOOP BREWING COMPANY
1634 18th St.
(303) 297-2700
wynkoop.com
After 5 p.m. is a busy time for the Wynkoop Brewing Company, Denver's first brewpub and also America's largest. Opened in 1988 by John Hickenlooper, now Colorado's governor, the Wynkoop offers comedy downstairs, dining on the first floor, and pool upstairs, all in the historic circa 1899 J. S. Brown Mercantile Building. Regulars like the Railyard Ale, but teetotalers swear by the house-brewed root beer. The billiards room has 22 pool tables, dart lanes, and two private pool rooms, as well as a full-service bar. Comedy is offered in the basement at the Impulse Theater. Details are provided in the Comedy Clubs section below.

TAP HOUSES

*ALE HOUSE AT AMATO'S
2501 16th St.
(303) 433-9734
alehousedenver.com
With 42 craft brews on tap, including a large selection of Colorado-brewed beers, and

great downtown views from their rooftop patio and open-air bar, Amato's is among the area's most popular brewpubs. The beer lineup changes daily, and they also offer 30+ wines and a selection of hand-crafted cocktails. Stay for lunch or dinner and enjoy casual, upscale pub entrees.

BRECKENRIDGE COLORADO CRAFT
2220 Blake St.
(303) 297-3644
breckbrew.com
The Breckenridge Colorado Craft, which originally opened in 1992 as Breckenridge Blake Street Pub, has beer drinking and billiards late into the evening (and early into the morning), with food available for those who need more. Sixteen taps offer a regular lineup of beer as well as rotating seasonal brews.

EUCLID HALL BAR & KITCHEN
1327 14th St.
(303) 595-4255
euclidhall.com
Based in an 1883 building that once housed the infamous Soapy Smith's bar, Euclid Hall offers high quality pub food from around the world in a fun atmosphere. It's also a popular spot to sample more than 40 craft beers from Colorado and beyond. Stop in for the Study Hall happy hour 3–6 p.m. daily. The proprietors also own Rioja and Bistro Vendôme.

FALLING ROCK TAP HOUSE
1919 Blake St.
(303) 293-8338
fallingrocktaphouse.com
Beer geeks will be in heaven with the huge selection of quality beers at this pub just down the street from Coors Field. Enjoy your brew inside or on the large outdoor patio on the street level. If crowds aren't your thing, avoid peak hours. Open until 2 a.m. daily.

✳FRESHCRAFT
1530 Blake St.
(303) 758-9608
freshcraft.com
We listed Freshcraft in the restaurant section, but it's worth another mention here. Along with a full menu of contemporary American cuisine, Freshcraft offers a wide selection of craft beers that pair well with their menu. Their late-night hours make this a popular place for after-hours dining in LoDo.

LUCKY PIE PIZZA & TAP HOUSE
1610 16th St.
(303) 825-1021
luckypiepizza.com
Choose from a dozen innovative pizza entrees or create your own from a selection of meats, cheeses, and toppings. Offering traditional Neapolitan-style pizza with a twist, Lucky Pie combines old-world with top quality local and Italian ingredients. The menu includes a fine section of cheeses, soups, salads, charcuterie, and other entrees. Beer aficionados will be happy with the 21 rotating taps of craft beer, both local and from around the world. Lucky Pie offers 25 wines by the glass and a full bar, including original, handcrafted cocktails.

LIVE MUSIC

BENDER'S 13TH AVENUE TAVERN
314 E. 13th Ave.
(303) 861-7070
The building at this location has been lots of things, but none of the businesses have been as successful as Bender's. It's known

for the mural that covers its eastern exterior, and also for the odd assortment of bands that climb onto its stage. Offerings include rock, punk, rockabilly, and alt country. Or, as one regular described it, "everything but jazz."

BLUEBIRD THEATER
3317 E. Colfax Ave.
(303) 322-2308
bluebirdtheater.net

For a diverse range of musical acts in a gritty neighborhood, try the Bluebird. Located on Denver's often-colorful East Colfax Avenue, the Bluebird opened as a movie house in 1913 and has since had several incarnations (including a stint as a porn house). Local bands as well as up-and-coming acts share the marquee. There's a balcony for the under-21 set, 550 seats on the main level, and several tables arranged to accommodate the evening's musical attraction (arrive early to secure a table). A dance floor sometimes serves as a mosh pit, depending on the act. Hours and ticket prices vary depending on who's playing.

✳DAZZLE
930 Lincoln St.
(303) 839-5100
dazzlejazz.com

Dazzle has become one of Denver's most respected jazz venues. Its location, along Lincoln Street in the Golden Triangle neighborhood, appeals to locals who are tired of fighting for parking in trendy LoDo. The venue features local, national, and international musicians. The crowd is mature—in their 30s to 60s—and the restaurant and bar menus reflect their tastes. Expect martinis and smooth sounds here. Open for music 7 nights a week.

✳EL CHAPULTEPEC
1962 Market St.
(303) 295-9126
thepeclodo.com

Once on the edge of gentrified Denver, El Chapultepec used to be a slightly dangerous place to drink beer, eat a burrito, and listen to jazz. It now finds itself in the rising shadow of Coors Field, encroached upon by brewpubs, art galleries, and designer tile shops. So far, the essential attraction—sizzling jazz—has remained the same. The "'Pec" is a landmark that often attracts touring musicians, who jam with other jazz greats on its tiny bandstand after leaving the stage at larger venues. El Chapultepec is open every night; there's no cover charge, and they don't take reservations.

FILLMORE AUDITORIUM
1510 Clarkson St.
(303) 837-0360
fillmoreauditorium.org

Originally built in 1905, the Fillmore is a restored concert hall and a prominent Denver music venue. Located on Clarkson Street at Colfax Avenue in the Capitol Hill neighborhood, it presents local and national acts throughout the year. Concerts are generally geared toward the younger crowd.

FUNKY BUDDHA
776 Lincoln St.
(303) 832-5075
coclubs.com/funky-buddha

Denver Post critic Ricardo Baca calls Funky Buddha "a happy-hour favorite," with cheap drinks and an hors d'oeuvres menu that includes stuffed mushrooms, hummus, red pepper dip, and lamb skewers. Denvercity search.com describes it as "La La Land without all the famous folk." With no dancing but

DJ music on the weekends, this chic urban bar is a hip place to meet and greet, located just south of downtown in the Golden Triangle neighborhood.

✳JAZZ@JACK'S
500 16th St.
(303) 433-1000
jazzatjacks.com

Since 1984, Stephen and Dave Watts have been playing their own blend of smooth and fusion jazz in a band called Dotsero. For many of those years, they played at their own club in the Central Platte Valley. In 2006, they moved their Jazz@Jack's venue to the heart of Denver's downtown, on the 3rd floor of the Denver Pavilions complex. Dotsero shares the stage with a broad range of guest artists and comedians. The room with a view can also be rented for private occasions.

✳LANNIE'S CLOCKTOWER CABARET
1601 Arapahoe St., Lower Level
(303) 293-0075
lannies.com

This is an old-style nightclub but with the hippest acts in town. Singer Lannie Garrett spent several decades performing at other people's clubs before starting her own in downtown's historic Daniels & Fisher Tower, and everything about the place is special. The underground room is intimate and romantic. When Lannie is onstage, expect anything from swing to torch songs, Hollywood tunes, disco hits, and the overripe country-and-western routine of her alter ego, Patsy DeCline. On other nights she fills the stage with burlesque, drag, R&B, soul, and traveling artists of all types. The kitchen is open until midnight, serving appetizers and desserts.

OGDEN THEATRE
935 E. Colfax Ave.
(303) 832-1874
ogdentheater.net

Another of Denver's famed former movie houses, the Ogden attracts a wide range of acts, from Offspring to the more sedate Stephen Stills. The Ogden often has the best ticket in town, aside from major concert venues. Hours and ticket prices vary.

DANCING

THE CHURCH
1160 Lincoln St.
(303) 832-3528
coclubs.com/the-church

Take an old cathedral and transform it into a dance club, complete with stained-glass windows and an elevated altar area, and you've got one of Denver's hottest clubs. The Church attracts dancers of all ages (of course, the weekends tend toward the younger set) mainly because it is large enough to offer a variety of music styles; we recommend it for ages 18 to 25. The weekends offer different music in different rooms. There is a sushi bar, a wine bar, and a cigar bar. Thursday is 18+ night, and there's no cover before 10 p.m. Friday and Saturday.

THE HI-DIVE
7 S. Broadway
(720) 733-0230
hi-dive.com

For live music, try the hi-dive for hip new bands, record-release parties, and DJs. It's well positioned in a string of small dives just a stone's throw from the galleries that line South Santa Drive. It seats 285 and has a killer sound system. Plan on occasional cover charges.

JACKSON'S LODO
1520 20th St.
(303) 298-7625
jacksonsdenver.com

A great place to drink while you listen to Top 40, hip-hop, and alternative music, Jackson's attracts a youngish crowd—ages 21 to 30. Located across the street from Coors Field, it boasts Denver's largest rooftop patio. It's open daily until the wee hours.

> **i** While locals and visitors still flock to LoDo nightclubs, hipsters prefer these grittier scenes: the warehouse district, on Larimer Street but centered around 27th and 29th Streets; upper downtown, between 20th and 22nd Streets on California, Welton, Stout, and Champa Streets; and Broadway and Lincoln Streets as they intersect 11th Street.

LA RUMBA
99 W. 9th Ave.
(303) 572-8006
larumba-denver.com

Catch the Latin, salsa, and swing craze at this neighborhood spot, which is open Thursday through Saturday. The 14-piece salsa band is popular, as are the salsa and swing lessons that begin at 9:30 p.m. Thursday and Saturday evenings. The decor is fun with comfy couches for resting between steps. The dress is classy. Cover is $5–10.

ZIGGIES SALOON
4923 W. 38th Ave.
(303) 455-9930
ziggieslivemusic.com

Denver's oldest blues club, Ziggies offers live music nightly in its Berkeley Heights barroom and a dance floor for those who rock.

On Sunday evenings, there's a no-cover-charge open-stage blues jam beginning at 7 p.m.

ROADHOUSES

BUFFALO ROSE SALOON
1119 Washington St., Golden
(303) 278-6800
buffalorose.net

Established in 1851, the Buffalo Rose is still going strong in its downtown Golden location. Three nights a week it presents musical acts that range from well-known rock groups to folk singers, with cover charges that start at around $3. During the summer, the outdoor patio bar is popular, and there's music 7 days a week.

HERMAN'S HIDEAWAY
1578 S. Broadway
(303) 777-5840
hermanshideaway.com

Herman's Hideaway is a live-music showcase with a large dance floor. The entertainment can vary from rock to Cajun. As you might expect of a funky South Broadway roadhouse, the decor is casual and the atmosphere laid-back. The crowd is 20s to 40s. Advance ticketing is advisable for special bookings of nationally known acts.

✳LINCOLN'S ROAD HOUSE
1201 S. Pearl St.
(303) 777-3700
lincolnsroadhouse.com

Live music on Friday and Saturday nights and on Sunday afternoons makes this small but soulful joint a popular place to hear blues and rock while enjoying New Orleans–style po'boys, crawfish étouffée, and cheeseburgers. Come here and rub shoulders with the locals in the place recently named best blues club in Denver.

i A few restaurants that are equally good spots for a predinner or late-night drink and a nosh are Marlowe's at 16th Street and Glenarm Place (303-595-3700); Paramount Cafe, next door to Marlowe's at 519 16th St. (303-893-2000); and Avenue Grill, 630 E. 17th Ave. (303-861-2820), the choice of Denver's uptown movers and shakers.

*LITTLE BEAR
28075 Hwy. 74 (Main Street), Evergreen
(303) 674-9991
littlebearsaloon.com

Even folks from the plains brave the narrow mountain roads to make the scene at the legendary Little Bear. Neither the route nor the rollicking roadhouse atmosphere is for the timid, but it's a fine place to listen to national and local rock, folk, and blues musicians. It's open daily, with live entertainment 6 days a week and a small cover charge on the weekends. Pizza and burgers are served daily from 11 a.m.

COUNTRY-AND-WESTERN NIGHTCLUBS

*GRIZZLY ROSE SALOON & DANCE EMPORIUM
5450 N. Valley Hwy.
(303) 295-1330
grizzlyrose.com

Grizzly Rose has been voted the nation's No. 1 country music dance hall by the Country Music Association, and it's where the big names come to play when they're in town.

With a 5,000-square-foot dance floor and headliners such as Willie Nelson, Merle Haggard, and Toby Keith, it's not hard to see why Grizzly Rose is the undisputed favorite in the live-music C&W category. Advance ticketing is recommended for national acts; call Grizzly Rose or Ticketmaster, (303) 830-TIXS. When no concert is scheduled, Tuesday and Wednesday are no-cover nights. Sunday night is family night, when all ages are welcome.

STAMPEDE MESQUITE GRILL & DANCE EMPORIUM
2430 S. Havana St., Aurora
(303) 696-7686
stampedeclub.com

Stampede Mesquite also bills itself as Denver's premier country bar and dance club, which tells you it all boils down to preference. The Stampede has a giant racetrack dance floor, line dancing and lessons, a yuppie clientele, and an antique bar. Call ahead for reservations at the restaurant, which is on a 2nd-floor balcony overlooking the nightclub and offers well-priced dinner specials.

TEDDY'S RESTAURANT AND LOUNGE
4849 Bannock St.
(303) 292-9500

Teddy's Restaurant and Lounge, located in the Ramada Plaza Denver Central Hotel near the intersection of I-70 and I-25, has a different musical format every night, but we love it best on country night. Genres vary from merengue, cumbia, and Latin rock to country, disco, oldies, and Top 40. Happy hour comes with free hors d'oeuvres; meals are available at the hotel's full-service restaurant.

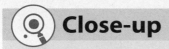

Close-up

Denver and Beer

Denver is a beer lover's paradise. Brewing more beer than any other city in the US, Denver has a wide selection of microbreweries, brewpubs, and beer cafes. The Great American Beer Festival held here each fall is the largest ticketed beer festival in the US. Along with the breweries, tap houses, and brewpubs we've listed in this section, here are a few more places to begin your own beer pilgrimage:

CAUTION: Brewing Co., 12445 E. 39th Ave., Unit 314; (970) 315-2739; cautionbrewingco.com

Cheeky Monk Belgian Beer Cafe, 543 Colfax Ave.; (303) 861-0347; thecheekymonk.com

Cherry Cricket, 2641 E. 2nd Ave.; (303) 327-7666; cherrycricket.com

Copper Kettle Brewing Company, 1338 S. Valentia St., #100; (720) 443-2522; copperkettledenver.com

Hogshead Brewery, 4460 W. 29th Ave.; (303) 495-3105; hogsheadbrewery.com

Our Mutual Friend Malt & Brew, 2810 Larimer St.; (720) 722-2810; omfmb .com

Pint's Pub, 221 W. 13th St.; (303) 534-7543; pintspub.com

Renegade Brewing Co., 925 W. 9th Ave; (720) 401-4089; renegadebrewing .com

Sandlot Brewpub at Coors Field (during Rockies games only), 2145 Blake St.; (303) 298-1587

Strange Brewing Co, 1330 Zuni St; (720) 985-2337; strangebrewingco.com

Vine Street Pub, 1700 Vine St.; (303) 388-2337; mountainsunpub.com

Wit's End Brewing, 2505 W. 2nd Ave.; (303) 459-4379; witsendbrewing.com

SPORTS BARS

BLAKE STREET TAVERN
2301 Blake St.
(303) 675-0505
blakestreettavern.com
This popular sports bar serves microbrews as well as a menu of quality salads, burgers, pizzas, calzones, and sandwiches plus pool tables and music. Just a block north of Coors Field, it's a good choice for Rockies fans. If you want to experience downtown at full volume, come here on a weekend night or during a Rockies game.

SPORTS COLUMN
1930 Blake St.
(303) 296-1930
denversportscolumn.com
Billing itself as "major league excitement," Sports Column joins the ranks of Lower Downtown sports bars with picturesque rooftop patios. It has the requisite pool tables, foosball, and food. It also features five big-screen TVs, plenty of video games, and a kitchen that stays open late.

ALL-AGES NIGHTLIFE

✳MERCURY CAFE
2199 California St.
(303) 294-9281
mercurycafe.com

The reincarnation of a legendary Denver nightclub of the '70s and early '80s, Mercury Cafe offers everything from swing dancing and Big Band music to performance art, comedy, twice-weekly poetry readings, theater, and lectures. Mercury also serves dinner Tuesday through Sunday and brunch on weekends. Credit cards are not accepted.

COMEDY CLUBS

COMEDY WORKS
1226 15th St.
(303) 595-3637
comedyworks.com

Roseanne (formerly Barr and Arnold) is among the many comics who made appearances at Comedy Works early in their careers. Tuesday night is new talent night; Wednesday through Sunday nights are for established performers. Ticket prices vary, but $18 is about the upper limit unless a headliner is on the bill, which could cost up to $40. Reservations are recommended, and it's for ages 21 and older only.

IMPULSE THEATER
1634 18th St.
(302) 297-2111
impulsetheater.com

This show opened in 1987 and is billed as Denver's longest-running comedy show. It occupies the lower level of the Wynkoop Brewing Company, with performances Thursday, Friday, and Saturday. Don't expect stand-up. This place does skits, scenes, and

ensemble comedy similar to *Saturday Night Live.* And customers feel like they're attending a sporting event since they decide which "team" is funniest. Reservations are recommended.

WITS END COMEDY CLUB
6080 W. 92nd Ave., Westminster
(303) 430-4242
witsendcomedyclub.com

Wits End Comedy Club offers the comic hijinks of local, national, and international jokemeisters. The humor tends toward the clean side, but you still have to be age 21 or older to attend. Comedians are booked Thursday through Sunday.

MOVIES

Denver offers an extensive array of neighborhood theaters, most like those in any other city. The theaters listed below will give you a more unusual experience.

✳FILM ON THE ROCKS
Red Rocks Amphitheatre
I-70 West to Morrison exit, Morrison
(866) 464-2626
redrocksonline.com

This summer series pairs performances by local bands with screenings of great movies, such as *Willy Wonka and the Chocolate Factory* with opening act The Flobots and headliner Buckner Funken Jazz. The outdoor setting makes it a magical movie experience. Bring something soft to sit on and rain gear, just in case.

*LANDMARK MAYAN
110 Broadway, between 1st and 2nd Avenues
(303) 352-1992
landmarktheatres.com

Denver's finest art-movie house is the Mayan. This 1930s-era theater is decorated on every inch of its wall and ceiling surface with wonderful Mayan figures and other designs. Everything is classy here: the decor, the audience, the films, even the espresso and pastries served in the 2nd-floor cafe. There's one large screen on the main level and two smaller ones above. The Landmark Chez Artiste Cinema at 2800 S. Colorado Blvd., the Esquire Theater at 590 Downing St., and the Landmark Theatre Greenwood Village at 5415 Landmark Place, are owned by the same company and offer similar independent and foreign film schedules. Discounted multiple admission tickets are available and can be used at all four locations. Be sure to buy popcorn at any of these theaters: They use real butter!

SIE FILMCENTER
2510 E. Colfax
(720) 381-0813

Located in the Lowenstein Cultureplex, the SIE FilmCenter brings to Denver the best of art house films with an excellent calendar of independent, classic, foreign, documentary, and retrospective movie offerings. This is also the home of the annual Starz Denver Film Festival held each November. The center is open 365 days a year.

SHOPPING

I n this chapter we focus on three major shopping areas that have a great concentration and variety of stores: Cherry Creek North; Downtown, LoDo, and Larimer Square; and South Broadway. The Cherry Creek and Larimer Square areas are small enough to view by foot, and that's how we've written those sections, with directions from one place to the next. South Broadway is more spread out—we survey the shops from north to south, but you'll want to travel by car or bus rather than walk the whole span.

To finish off your introduction to Denver shopping, we've included a roundup of where to go for arts and crafts, books, clothes, food and gourmet cooking supplies, furniture, gifts, and outlet and bargain stores.

Most stores are open daily and accept credit cards, but call ahead to be sure.

But first, the basics—department and grocery stores. Major department stores with one or more locations in Metro Denver include Macy's, Nordstrom, Dillard's, Sears, Neiman Marcus, and JCPenney. For Western wear, Rockmont, Miller Stockman, and Sheplers have locations throughout the metro area. Sports Authority, Recreational Equipment Inc. (REI), Dick's Sporting Goods, BassPro Shops, and Cabela's stores supply Denverites with gear for camping, hiking, biking, rafting, fishing, and other outdoor activities.

The big supermarket chains include King Soopers and Safeway. For natural foods, visit any of the Whole Foods, Sunflower, or Vitamin Cottage markets.

MAJOR SHOPPING AREAS

Cherry Creek North

The neighborhood directly to the north of the mall, Cherry Creek North, is a delightful mélange of interesting shops, galleries, clothing designers, cafes, and restaurants.

At the corner of Detroit Street and 2nd Avenue is **Room and Board,** a contemporary furniture store that consistently ranks high in local "best of" polls. If you're looking for something to hang above the sofa, **Saks Galleries,** 3019 E. 2nd Ave., specializes in 19th- and 20th-century representational art.

Pismo Contemporary Art Glass, 2770 E. 2nd Ave., stocks an unmatched selection of art glass by Coloradans Brian Maytum, Kit Karbler, and internationally known glass artist Dale Chihuly in its luxurious gallery. A great source for funky clothing and inexpensive jewelry for men and women is **Eccentricity,** 290 Fillmore St.

Gallery M, 180 Cook St., features contemporary fine art, photography, and sculpture by both national and international artists. **Show of Hands,** 210 Clayton St., on the other hand, showcases American crafts in clay, metal, wood, and fiber as well as stocking wall art and paintings.

Among the designer labels carried at **Lawrence Covell,** 225 Steele St., are Yohji Yamamoto, Kiton, and Luciano Barbera. This upscale men's and women's store is known for its first-class service.

Kids' stuff can be found at **The Wizard's Chest,** 230 Fillmore St., which in addition to children's toys carries grown-up games and an attic full of costumes and masks. **Kazoo & Company,** 2930 E. 2nd Ave., has educational games and toys.

Hermitage Bookshop, 290 Fillmore St., is a pleasant spot with neat library stacks of first editions and other rare and/or old books.

Downtown, LoDo & Larimer Square

Downtown Denver's mile-long main shopping thoroughfare, 16th Street, was transformed into a tree-lined pedestrian mall in 1980 and now boasts 25,000 flowers in the summer. Free shuttle buses run the length of the mall as often as every 90 seconds, connecting Lower Downtown with the Civic Center area. Many of the stores along 16th Street are touristy, but it's worth strolling the stretch to see what's here. With **TJMaxx** and **Ross,** the corner of 16th and California Streets has become a mini off-price mecca in downtown. Restaurants along the mall often have outdoor seating—great for people-watching—and there are shaded benches for those who've brought their own lunch or their laptops. The entire mall offers free wireless service to all outdoor visitors. If you haven't planned ahead, buy a to-go lunch from a street vendor or fast-food restaurant.

The heart of Larimer Square is Larimer Street between 15th and 14th Streets. From

Tabor Center, walk 1 block south through the cluster of stores and restaurants called **Writer Square,** and on the other side you'll find yourself standing on the spot where Denver got its start in 1858. Denver's first bank, bookstore, photographer, and dry-goods store were located on this block. The original buildings were made of wood and were destroyed in a fire in 1863; the brick structures that now line the street were erected for the most part in the 1870s to 1890s, and the entire area was renovated in the mid-1970s. Interested visitors can pick up a walking-tour brochure and information on the individual buildings at the kiosk on the east side of the street.

Larimer Square has a nice mix of shops and restaurants, including **Cry Baby Ranch,** which has Western furnishings and pricey trinkets. **The Market** has an exhaustive selection of gourmet goodies as well as coffee, deli, and bakery items to take out or eat on the premises. Also on the block: **John Atencio** jewelry; **Scarpaletto** shoes; and **Eve** women's clothing. At this point you're just a few blocks from the renowned **Tattered Cover Book Store** at 16th and Wynkoop Streets.

As you move into LoDo, check out **Bouquets,** 1525 15th St., for the most unusual flowers and flower arrangements in town. Stop at **Rockmont Ranch Wear,** at 1626 Wazee St., for a look back in time as well as an opportunity to buy authentic Western clothing. Rockmont founders invented the snap-front Western shirt, and for more than 60 years have been generating duds for rodeo cowboys, Hollywood stars, and city slickers alike. The building, open every day, includes a museum and a retail store.

The 1700 block of Wazee Street was once the heart of Denver's contemporary art district, and it still is, in a sense, although closures and additions have shifted the emphasis away from the avant-garde. We write more about that in our The Arts chapter.

A bit farther uptown, collectors of Native American crafts head for the **Mudhead Gallery** in the Hyatt Regency Hotel, 555 17th St. (mudheadgallery.net).

The **Native American Trading Company,** a fine source for pots, textiles, and Edward S. Curtis photogravures, is across from the Denver Art Museum at 1301 Bannock St. (nativeamericantradingco.com).

On the southern edge of downtown is one of Denver's most venerable stores. **Sports Authority** is at 10th Avenue and Broadway, in a wildly extravagant building known as the Sportscastle. This 6-level store, originally built as a car dealership, stocks everything, including tents, cameras, bicycles, and tennis shoes. It has dozens of other locations throughout the state (find them at sportsauthority.com), but none is as architecturally distinctive as this one.

South Broadway

South Broadway is an antiques lover's paradise. In fact, the area between Arizona and Iowa Streets is dubbed "Antiques Row." There are a few furniture stores tucked in as well. Your best bet is to just make your way south on Broadway (it's one-way north of the I-25 interchange). Many of the shops are listed in our Antiques category.

SHOPPING MALLS

ASPEN GROVE LIFESTYLE CENTER
7301 S. Santa Fe Dr., Littleton
(303) 794-0640
shopaspengrove.com

Built in 2001, Aspen Grove was one of Metro Denver's first "lifestyle centers," or outdoor shopping centers that allow for more than just mall shopping. It draws clients from throughout the area, but its primary customers come from Littleton and southwest Denver. Its stores include Bath & Body Works, Chico's, Eddie Bauer, Pottery Barn, Talbot's, Children's Place, Pier 1, and Williams-Sonoma. Dining choices include The Bistro, Noodles & Co., Ted's Montana Grill, Qdoba Mexican Grill, and Panera Bread Co.

BELMAR
408 S. Teller St., Lakewood
(303) 742-1520
belmarcolorado.com

The Belmar shopping area creates a new downtown for the first-tier Denver suburb of Lakewood. Fans of Belmar come here for the summer farmers' market, fall Italian festival, and winter holiday celebrations, including a winter ice-skating rink. They also know it as home to a Whole Foods Market, as well as chain stores and local restaurants strewn out along a network of new streets. In addition to national chains that are represented in most malls, Belmar boasts a Coldwater Creek that has a full-service spa, two dentists, five electronics and wireless phone stores, banks, bars, and restaurants that serve American, Asian, Indian, Italian, and Mexican food.

✳CHERRY CREEK NORTH
East of University Boulevard, between
1st and 3rd Streets
(303) 394-2904
cherrycreeknorth.com

One of Colorado's top visitor destinations, Cherry Creek North is Denver's high-end shopping district. Located across the street from Cherry Creek Shopping Center, these

16 blocks are home to more than 320 businesses, including galleries, boutiques, restaurants, professional services, spas, and two hotels. Come here to walk and browse, people-watch, and soak in the local atmosphere.

CHERRY CREEK SHOPPING CENTER
3000 E. 1st Ave.
(303) 388-3900
cherrycreekmall.com

Anchored by Nordstrom, Neiman Marcus, and Macy's, the Cherry Creek Shopping Center's 160 stores include high-end specialty stores such as Louis Vuitton, Abercrombie & Fitch, Banana Republic, and Ann Taylor. There is a dining area with quick food and several restaurants, such as Elway's, Brio Tuscan Grill, and Kona Grill. Retail tenants include Tiffany & Co., Apple, Coach, Ralph Lauren, Williams-Sonoma, Tommy Bahama, and Anthropologie.

Another attraction is an elaborate play area for kids, with seating for adults, near the mall entrance to Macy's. The area features super-size, colorful breakfast-food items for the kids to crawl on. Kids can't resist sliding down the bacon into an egg yolk.

COLORADO MILLS
14500 W. Colfax Ave., Lakewood
(303) 384-3000
coloradomills.com

Colorado Mills is one of the newer malls in the metro area. The stores in this snazzy center are all one-of-a-kind outlets, offering reduced prices on merchandise from such retailers as Ann Taylor, Neiman Marcus Last Call, Tommy Hilfiger, Off 5th Saks Fifth Avenue, Bath & Body Works, SKECHERS, Levi's, Kenneth Cole, Eddie Bauer, Gap, Guess, and Sports Authority. Off Broadway Shoe Warehouse is big enough to satisfy any shoe lover, carrying designs that range from sane to gotta-have-it crazy.

Located off I-70 on the west side of the metro area, Colorado Mills is a convenient stop for travelers on their way to and from the mountains, and residents from all parts of town find it worth the drive for the unique selection and bargain prices. The mall has a standard food court and a 16-screen theater complex.

DENVER PAVILIONS
On the 16th Street Mall between Tremont and Welton Streets
(303) 260-6000
denverpavilions.com

The Pavilions doesn't fit into traditional mall or shopping area categories because it offers more than retail. With 40 shops, restaurants, and entertainment venues, Pavilions bills itself as the new wave of shopping. You can browse Banana Republic, indulge in something decadent at the Corner Bakery, and then take in a flick at the United Artists theater (all high-backed stadium seating).

Denver Pavilions boasts several large attractions, including Maggiano's Little Italy, Coyote Ugly Saloon, Lucky Strike Lanes, Jazz@Jack's, and Hard Rock Cafe, along with more familiar shops such as Barnes & Noble, Bath & Body Works, Gap, and Victoria's Secret. Try Rocky Mountain Chocolate Factory for fine chocolates. I Heart Denver supports the city's creative economy by showcasing the work of more than 135 local artists and designers at this retail space. Mall crawlers used to the confines of suburban malls may be surprised at the Pavilions' open-air setting. But with a yearly average of 300 days of sunshine, outdoor shopping is rarely a problem in Denver.

FLATIRON CROSSING
US 36 at Interlocken or FlatIron Circle exits
(720) 887-9900
flatironcrossing.com
FlatIron Crossing is an indoor-outdoor center with 1.5 million square feet of shopping anchored by Nordstrom, Macy's, and Dillard's. Its 170 specialty retailers include well-known names such as Gap, Apple, and Ann Taylor as well as lesser-known shops in the Village. The center is located amid 30 acres of green space and parklike settings and offers access to local trails.

LOWENSTEIN CULTUREPLEX
2508–2526 E. Colfax Ave.
This small entertainment complex contains several local gems. Tattered Cover Book Store, Twist and Shout Records, and Denver Film Center are here, providing the community with some of the best selection of books, music, and cinema in the city. After browsing the aisles, go next door to Chipotle for fresh Mexican cuisine.

NORTHFIELD STAPLETON
8340 E. 49th Ave.
(303) 375-5464
northfieldstapleton.com
Northfield is one of Denver's newest outdoor-lifestyles centers, opening in 2006 with Harkins Theatre, Colorado's only Bass Pro Shop, SuperTarget, and Macy's as anchors. More than 60 tenants fill out the Main Street segment. Restaurants include Bar Louie, La Sandia Cantina, and Ling & Louie's Asian Bar and Grill. In addition to providing one of the region's roomiest parking lots, the center is located at what may be the best crossroad for out-of-state visitors. I-70 (which runs from Kansas to Utah) and I-270 (which veers north to Nebraska) intersect near the center's southwest corner.

ORCHARD TOWN CENTER
I-25 and 144th Avenue, Westminster
(303) 450-8600
theorchardtowncenter.com
Anchored by Macy's, JCPenney, SuperTarget, and REI, Orchard Town Center has more than 65 specialty shops and stores. Designed as an open-air retail and entertainment district with paths leading to a "town square," it offers a full calendar of events and various amenities for kids.

PARK MEADOWS
8401 Park Meadows Center Dr., Lone Tree
(303) 792-2999
parkmeadows.com
Park Meadows is anchored by Nordstrom, Dillard's, and Macy's. The dining hall is huge, and the restaurants are on the swanky side. Park Meadows grows larger each year with the addition of retail around its perimeter. It's a great mix of low-, mid-, and high-end retail.

SOUTHWEST PLAZA
Wadsworth Boulevard and West Bowles Avenue, Littleton
(303) 973-5300
southwestplaza.com
Once Denver's largest mall, Southwest Plaza serves Jefferson County's booming population. Anchored by Dillard's, Macy's, JCPenney, and Sears, it has almost every type of clothing, food, music, and shoe store, as well as a movie theater and a SuperTarget.

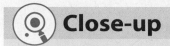 Close-up

Indoor-Outdoor FlatIron Crossing

FlatIron Crossing opened with a splash in August 2000 and continues to attract both stores and shoppers. Touted as reflecting the outdoor lifestyle of Coloradans, the center combines a 1.2-million-square-foot interior mall with a 240,000-square-foot outdoor, streetscaped shopping area. A 14-screen AMC theater anchors the southwestern corner.

The idea was to create more than just another shopping experience. According to Westcor Partners, the center's developer, the goal was to create a place that people think of as both a community showplace and a great place to spend a Saturday afternoon. With its 30 acres of green space and parks, access to local trail systems, and two parklike areas with lush landscapes and streams and fountains, FlatIron Crossing may do just that.

Inside the mall, natural materials and abundant sunlight were essential design elements. The interior makes generous use of wood beams, iron, patterned stone, and Colorado limestone. Some windows allow high-morning sun, while others are set to capture the glow of late afternoons.

The center's largest tenants are Nordstrom, Macy's, and Dillard's. The interior stores tend to be highly recognizable national chains such as Eddie Bauer, Banana Republic, Fossil, and Pottery Barn, while smaller and, in some cases, local stores populate the Village. All told, there are more than 200 specialty retailers and restaurants located throughout the mall's far-flung properties. In an effort to bring more people out of the mall and into the Village, the center hosts farmers' markets and Thursday-evening street fairs.

FlatIron Crossing launched the FlatIron Crossing Music & Art Foundation to help restore endangered music and arts programs in Colorado schools and communities. Guided by board members from the local arts and education communities, the foundation will benefit from many activities at FlatIron Crossing over the years as well as raise funds through community, business, and government sources.

Located off US 36, the center is conveniently situated along the growing Denver-Boulder corridor and draws residents of both cities.

THE STREETS AT SOUTHGLENN
South University Boulevard and East Arapahoe Road, Centennial
(303) 539-7141
shopsouthglenn.com
The Streets at SouthGlenn was created when the old SouthGlenn Mall was demolished in 2006. Anchored by Macy's and Sears, the new site offers more than 50 retail tenants, including Old Navy, Whole Foods, Best Buy, Staples, Dick's Sporting Goods, and a 14-screen movie theater. The shopping area also has 20 restaurants and a fitness club.

TOWN CENTER AT AURORA
I-225 at East Alameda Avenue and Sable Street, Aurora
(303) 344-4120
simon.com
This center has the look and feel of a fairly typical suburban mall. Anchored by Macy's, Dillard's, Sears, and JCPenney, it offers

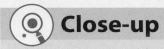 **Close-up**

Park Meadows Draws Shoppers from Afar

When Park Meadows opened in August 1996, it was hailed as a shopping center unlike any ever built. In fact, it was described as a "retail resort." We're not sure whether shoppers feel like they're on vacation, but they are certainly attracted to Park Meadows as if it were a vacation spot. About 13 million people came the first year to check out Greater Denver's largest shopping center—all 1.5 million square feet of it.

With three top-drawer anchors—Colorado's first Nordstrom, Denver's first Dillard's, and Colorado's largest Macy's—Park Meadows attracts visitors from a seven-state region and has become one of the area's premier shopping destinations.

While most malls are conglomerates of individual stores, Park Meadows was designed to feel like a mountain ski lodge (a very, very busy one!). Massive natural wood-beam cathedral ceilings soar above the second level, the shopping center is bathed in natural light, and large stone fireplaces are located throughout. Shoppers can rest in overstuffed leather chairs and couches. Hahn Company, the developer of Park Meadows, also commissioned eight Colorado artists to create $2 million worth of artwork.

The shopping center is home to 160 stores, many of which were new to Colorado when they opened, including Crate & Barrel, Restoration Hardware, and Nordstrom. While the obligatory dining area is located near the center, Park Meadows also houses "better" restaurants, including California Pizza Kitchen, Red Robin, Yard House, and P.F. Chang's China Bistro. Even the 12-screen movie theater here is a little bigger and a little glitzier.

recognizable stores such as the Disney Store, Bath & Body Works, and Old Navy, as well as 150 smaller, more boutique-type shops.

ANTIQUES

The South Broadway area has the greatest concentration of antiques stores in the Metro Denver area. In addition to the store listed below, you're sure to find more, especially continuing farther south on Broadway. And if you're willing to travel out of Denver 30 to 40 minutes, you might want to check out the town of Niwot and its 2-block main street filled with antiques shops. Auctions are sometimes held on Sunday. To get to Niwot, take I-25 north to Highway 52 west to connect with Highway 119. Niwot is about 1 mile north of the intersection of Highways 52 and 119.

The town of Lyons, which lies at the mouth of St. Vrain Canyon on the way to Estes Park, about 45 minutes from downtown Denver, is another great antiques lover's mecca. Antiques stores dot both sides of the old-fashioned Main Street. You'll find a few that specialize in Western memorabilia. To get there from central Denver, take I-25 north to the Highway 66 exit, then go west about 17 miles.

Closer to town, check out the following shop.

DECADE
56 S. Broadway
(303) 733-2288
Voted "Best Store Anywhere on Broadway" by the readers and editors of *Westword,* this little shop mixes vintage and new. They have a constantly changing array of furniture that spans the decades and a good selection of home accessories as well. They also have a small clothing boutique in the back that offers mostly new men's and women's clothing, jewelry, and such. The shop tends to carry more vintage options in the fall than earlier in the year.

ARTS & CRAFTS

For arts and crafts, make Cherry Creek North your first stop (see Major Shopping Areas at the beginning of this chapter). Additional sources include the following.

AKENTE EXPRESS
919 Park Ave. West
(303) 297-8817
Akente Express is an African-American heritage shop that stocks original fabrics from Africa, handmade clothing, jewelry, artwork, sculpture, and all-natural, alcohol-free essential oils.

I HEART DENVER
Level 2 of Denver Pavilions
500 16th St., #264
(720) 317-2328
iheartdenver.info
This unique store features local artwork, with 70 percent of each sale going back to the artist or designer. Offering a wide range of items from hand-printed T-shirts and stationery to original art, the store's stock changes frequently, making I Heart Denver a popular

place to find gifts and home-decorating items.

OLD SANTA FE POTTERY
2485 S. Santa Fe Dr.
(303) 871-9434
oldsantafepottery.com
Old Santa Fe Pottery houses two rows of shops filled with Southwestern decorative items, Oaxacan wood carvings, painted Talavera ceramics, furniture, rugs, and all sorts of pottery. You'll enjoy a pretty central courtyard reminiscent of a Mexican village.

BOOKS

The behemoth Tattered Cover Book Store dominates Metro Denver's literary scene, but Denver's readers are avid enough to support more than one general-interest bookstore. Large chains such as Barnes & Noble have branches in many regional shopping malls. Another good all-around bookstore for new and used books is the **Book Rack,** 2382 S. Colorado Blvd. (303-756-9891; thebookrack .com).

THE BOOKIES
4315 E. Mississippi Ave.
(303) 759-1117
netnewsdesk.com/thebookies
Though The Bookies is primarily known for its great children's selection, it also carries most best-seller titles, too. Better yet, every book is sold at a discount of at least 15 percent. (The discount does not apply to educational and teacher resource books.)

GALLAGHER BOOKS
1498 S. Broadway
(303) 756-5821
gcbooks.com

Located on Denver's famed antiques row, Gallagher Books is a member of the Rocky Mountain Antiquarian Booksellers Association. The shop features rare and out-of-print books, books and posters on WWI and WWII, fine binding, and other specialty items.

MURDER BY THE BOOK
1574 S. Pearl St.
(303) 871-9401
murderbythebook.com
Murder by the Book, a cozy store in a former home, specializes in new and used mystery novels and crime fiction. If your kids love mysteries, check out the children's selections.

✴TATTERED COVER (THREE LOCATIONS)
2526 E. Colfax Ave.
(303) 322-7727
tatteredcover.com
The Tattered Cover is truly one of the country's finest independent bookstores—and for book lovers, one of Denver's finest attractions. Built on the philosophy of comfort and personal service, the store provides readers and browsers a place to while away an afternoon (or full day) amid shelf after shelf of books, cozy corners, and overstuffed chairs and couches. Opened more than 35 years ago, the original Cherry Creek store expanded a number of times before moving into the renovated Lowenstein Theater, on the corner of Colfax Avenue and Elizabeth Street, in 2006. A second location followed in historic LoDo (1628 16th St.; 303-436-1070), just blocks from Coors Field. In 2004 a third location sprang up in suburban Highlands Ranch (9315 Dorchester St.; 303-470-7050), a 21,754-square-foot addition to the suburban neighborhood. Tattered Cover now houses more than half a million books—150,000 titles—in its three locations. In addition to this expansive book selection, all locations offer a coffee shop, newsstand, and extensive calendar of signings and literary events. You can sign up for the online mailing list to receive an online newsletter and announcements of special events and promotions.

TOO GOOD TO MISS

Like any city, Denver has a few unique places that don't fit into other categories but are worth checking out just for the novelty. We've included a few below.

BOYER'S COFFEE COMPANY
7295 N. Washington St.
(303) 289-3345, (800) 452-5282
boyerscoffee.com
Boyer's, a Denver-based coffee roaster and packager, offers its coffee and related items at lower-than-supermarket prices. Its warehouse store is open to the public weekdays only.

DJUNA
899 N. Broadway
(303) 355-3500
djuna.com
This locally owned furniture store offers an eclectic collection of vintage-inspired furnishings, fine art, antiques, elegant linens and fabrics, and much more. It's a big place and worth spending an hour or two browsing.

EUROPEAN MART
5225 Leetsdale Dr.
(303) 321-7144
When you're in the mood for Hungarian salami, smoked fish, Danish cheeses, or hearty sausage, the European Mart is the

place to stop. Filled with eastern European delicacies—meats, fish, candies, cookies—this shop is the real thing. The Russian owners are helpful and eager to please, and the food is great.

FOR HEAVEN'S SAKE
4383 Tennyson St.
(303) 964-9339
forheavensake.com
This New Age gift and book shop in the Berkeley neighborhood area offers a wide array of products such as candles, crystals, books, music, and the increasingly popular "lucky bamboo." The store also sponsors in-house events and classes, including a monthly Psychic Fair, which features palm and tarot readings among other events.

IKEA
9800 E. IKEA Way, Centennial
(303) 768-9164
ikea.com
Although it's a chain, we're including IKEA here because there are few locations in the middle of the country. Wildly popular for its inexpensive, functional furnishings, IKEA has something for every room in the home.

OUTLETS

THE OUTLETS AT CASTLE ROCK
Exit 184, Meadow Parkway (off I-25 South), Castle Rock
(303) 688-4494
outletsatcastlerock.com
The largest outlet mall in the Front Range, Castle Rock has 110 stores—everything from designer clothes to electronics. Open 7 days a week, the outlet has an easy and convenient layout and a central food court with the usual fast-food offerings.

THE OUTLETS AT LOVELAND
I-25 North to exit 257B, Loveland
(970) 663-1717
outletsatloveland.com
With 82 stores, The Outlets at Loveland include the standard offering of clothes and kitchenware. Though there is no food court on-site, several restaurants are within walking distance.

TOURS & ATTRACTIONS

In this chapter we've rounded up our favorite museums, gardens, and historic houses. What Metro Denver has to offer in this category may surprise newcomers: The Museum of Nature and Science is the fifth largest of its kind in the country, and the newly expanded Denver Art Museum is the largest such institution between Kansas City and the West Coast. Denver's Zoo and its Botanic Gardens are both highly respected, and the city is full of special-interest museums devoted to such diverse subjects as firefighters, railroads, African Americans in the West, dolls, and the English painter J. M. W. Turner. The new Clyfford Still Museum is home to the works of one of the greatest abstract expressionist artists of the 20th century. Among the most popular tourist attractions in the area are the tours at the US Mint in Denver and Coors Brewery in Golden.

We've organized this chapter by category: museums, historic houses and other historic sites, and parks and gardens. Readers with a particular interest in the arts may also want to check out The Arts chapter, as community art centers and galleries are listed there. At the end of the chapter, we suggest ways to combine visits to different sites that are near each other or that tie in thematically (for example, if you want to spend a day immersing yourself in Western history).

Because hours and admission prices are subject to change, we have included only the basics, with phone numbers and web addresses for you to check once you're ready to visit.

MUSEUMS

✳AMERICAN MUSEUM OF WESTERN ART
1727 Tremont Place
(303) 293-2000
anschutzcollection.org
This museum is the permanent home of the Anschutz Collection, a major group of paintings depicting the American West from the early 19th century to the present. Among the more than 650 paintings and drawings are works by Remington, Bierstadt, Russell, Catlin, O'Keeffe, and Blumenschein. The

museum is open for scheduled tours every Monday and Wednesday. Tours last from 1.5 to 2 hours. Children under 8 are not allowed due to the fragile nature of the collections.

THE BLACK AMERICAN WEST MUSEUM AND HERITAGE CENTER
3091 California St.
(720) 242-7428
blackamericanwestmuseum.org
The Black American West Museum is a small but fascinating place that sets a lot of

records straight and provides a long-buried picture of the role played by African Americans on the frontier. Among other topics, the museum depicts the stories of the Buffalo Soldiers, the Tuskegee Airmen, black cowboys, and countless others who came to the Western frontier. The museum is housed in the former home of Dr. Justina L. Ford, Colorado's first licensed African-American female doctor. It is closed Sunday and Monday.

BUFFALO BILL GRAVE AND MUSEUM
987 1/2 Lookout Mountain Rd., Golden
(303) 526-0744
buffalobill.org
Dramatically located on top of Lookout Mountain, this fascinating museum is filled with memorabilia honoring the famous frontier scout, showman, and Pony Express rider William F. Cody, colloquially known as Buffalo Bill. Included are gun collections, costumes, and posters from the Wild West show and a collection of dime novels. The grave site affords an expansive view of the plains to the east and mountains to the west. A kids' corral offers young visitors interactive opportunities. The museum is open daily May through October; Tuesday through Sunday the rest of the year.

THE CELL (COUNTERTERRORISM
  EDUCATION LEARNING LAB)
99 W. 12th Ave.
(303) 844-4000
thecell.org
Located next to the Denver Art Museum, the CELL exhibit is a high-tech, interactive experience that informs visitors about the threat of terrorism and addresses the issues that threaten community safety. The exhibit uses a blend of video clips, sound bites, and flash imagery to convey its dark and sometimes disturbing themes and messages.

CLYFFORD STILL MUSEUM
1250 Bannock St.
(720) 354-4880
clyffordstillmuseum.org
Containing around 94 percent of the artist's output—almost 2,400 paintings, drawings, and prints—the Clyfford Still Museum houses a beautifully displayed collection devoted to the life and works of this important abstract expressionist painter. Located next to the Denver Art Museum, it's open every day except Monday.

✳COLORADO RAILROAD MUSEUM
17155 W. 44th Ave., Golden
(303) 279-4591, (800) 365-6263
coloradorailroadmuseum.org
One of our personal favorites, this museum houses more than 70 historic locomotives and cars as well as additional exhibits in a 15-acre outdoor setting. Don't miss the D&RG Engine No. 346, the oldest operating locomotive in Colorado. The museum is open daily. To get to the museum, take exit 265 off I-70 West and follow the signs.

✳THE DENVER ART MUSEUM
100 W. 14th Ave. Pkwy.
(720) 865-5000 (recorded information)
denverartmuseum.org
The Denver Art Museum is the largest art museum between Kansas City and the West Coast and is especially noted for its superb collections of Native American, pre-Columbian, and Spanish colonial art. Its 7 floors also house impressive displays of American, Asian, and contemporary art and galleries devoted to design, graphics, and

architecture. See our The Arts chapter for more details.

DENVER FIREFIGHTERS MUSEUM
1326 Tremont Place
(303) 892-1436
denverfirefightersmuseum.org
Housed in old Station No. 1, which was built in 1909, the museum has a collection of original hand-drawn firefighting equipment, two engines from the 1920s, and various antique firefighting memorabilia, including helmets, uniforms, and trophies. The museum is open Monday through Saturday.

DENVER MUSEUM OF MINIATURES
DOLLS & TOYS
Pearce-McAllister Cottage
1880 Gaylord St.
(303) 322-1053
dmmdt.org
The 2-story Pearce-McAllister Cottage, built in 1899, is of interest for its architecture, original decor, and changing displays of vintage dolls, dollhouses, toys, and miniatures. The museum offers year-round workshops for adults and kids on doll-making, toys, and arts and crafts in miniature. A small gift shop sells toys, dolls, and dollhouse furniture. The museum is open Wednesday through Sunday (closed major holidays).

✳THE DENVER MUSEUM OF NATURE
AND SCIENCE
2001 Colorado Blvd. (in City Park, at Colorado Boulevard and Montview)
(303) 322-7009, (800) 925-2250, (303) 370-8257 (hearing-impaired TDD)
dmns.org
The Denver Museum of Nature and Science is the largest cultural attraction in the Rocky Mountain region, with an average of 1.5 million visitors annually. In addition to more than 90 dioramas depicting animals from around the world, the museum's permanent exhibitions include Expedition Health devoted to studying the human body and a fine gem and mineral collection that includes examples of Colorado gold and the largest rhodochrosite gem in the world. Other highlights include the Hall of Ancient Peoples, which deals with early man and early civilizations. Don't forget to take a look at the redesigned Egyptian Mummies exhibit. The museum also houses an award-winning dinosaur exhibit, the $7.7 million Prehistoric Journey. It includes walk-through "enviroramas" complete with controlled lighting and temperatures, sounds, vegetation, and even bugs!

The $50 million, 24,000-square-foot Space Odyssey provides an immersion experience in the wonders of space with interactive opportunities to learn about areas of the cosmos. Visitors can feel what it's like to dock a space shuttle, fly into deep space, and walk on the surface of Mars. The completely digital Gates Planetarium enables visitors to leave Earth's surface and fly through the solar system. It's one of the country's first all-digital planetariums and is equipped with surround sound. Although Space Odyssey is free to those who buy admission to the museum, the planetarium shows and some special exhibits cost extra. Watch for special exhibitions, which in the past have included artistic and archaeological blockbusters such as *Ramses II* and *Body Worlds 2,* and entertaining fare such as *Star Trek: Federation Science.*

The museum is open daily and has a cafeteria-style restaurant and the T-Rex cafeteria.

DOWNTOWN AQUARIUM
700 Water St. (in the Platte River Valley just west of downtown)
(303) 561-4450
aquariumrestaurants.com

Denver's most unusual attraction isn't exactly a museum, but it fits well under the category of other top-notch local and tourist spots in this chapter. Opened in the summer of 1999, this long-awaited addition to the Central Platte Valley was originally called Colorado Ocean Journey because it showcased water as it made its ways on two journeys from the Continental Divide to the Sea of Cortez and from an Indonesian rain forest to the depths of the Pacific. The 17-acre complex was purchased in 2003 by Landry's Restaurants and reopened in 2005 as an entertainment and dining complex. Downtown is open daily. Parking is extra, as are meals.

FORNEY TRANSPORTATION MUSEUM
4303 Brighton Blvd.
(303) 297-1113
forneymuseum.com

This longtime Denver favorite displays all kinds of old vehicles, including a number of one-of-a-kinds. Of special interest are the world's largest steam locomotive, Prince Aly Khan's Rolls Royce Phantom I, and an original McCormick reaper. The museum is open Monday through Saturday, but is closed on Christmas, Thanksgiving, and New Year's Day.

FORT VASQUEZ
13412 US Hwy. 85, Platteville
(970) 785-2832
historycolorado.org/museums

Forty miles downstream from Denver on the South Platte River lies Fort Vasquez, a reconstructed 1830s fur-trading post operated as a museum by the Colorado Historical Society.

The museum features exhibits and dioramas depicting the trading era. In summer "mountain men" entertain visitors with reenactments of Old West trading days. A buffalo tepee will interest youngsters. Admission is free; it is open daily Memorial Day to Labor Day and Wednesday through Sunday the rest of the year.

✳HISTORY COLORADO CENTER
1200 Broadway
(303) 447-8679
historycolorado.org

Opened in 2012, the History Colorado Center is an experiential museum with numerous interactive and digital exhibits. Even natives will find much they never knew about their home state. Blending technology, media, artifacts, and environment, the museum brings to life the state's history. Some of the high-tech highlights include taking a virtual ride across the plains in a Model T, soaring off a virtual ski jump, strapping on a headlamp and descending into a hard rock mine, and exploring state history with a virtual "time machine" on a 60-foot interactive floor map of Colorado. Open daily.

KIRKLAND MUSEUM OF FINE & DECORATIVE ART
1311 Pearl St.
(303) 832-8576
kirklandmuseum.org

Housed in one of the oldest commercial art buildings in Colorado, the Kirkland Museum contains an extensive collection of 20th-century decorative arts ranging from Art Nouveau and Bauhaus through modern and pop art. It's open Tuesday through Sunday. Children under 13 are not allowed due to the fragile nature of the collections.

MIZEL MUSEUM
400 S. Kearney St.
(303) 394-9993
mizelmuseum.org

The Rocky Mountain region's only museum of Judaica was established in 1982. Special programs, workshops, speakers, seminars, and films are designed to complement the museum's changing exhibitions, whether drawn from its own collection or borrowed from such prestigious institutions as the Israel Museum and the Smithsonian Institution. In 2001 it merged with the Mizel Family Cultural Arts Center and moved to the campus of the Jewish Community Center.

MUSEO DE LAS AMERICAS
861 Santa Fe Dr.
(303) 571-4401
museo.org

The Rocky Mountain region's first museum dedicated to Latin-American art, history, and culture, the Museo de las Americas showcases art from all the Americas, including the Caribbean, in changing exhibitions. (See our The Arts chapter for more information.)

ROCKY MOUNTAIN QUILT MUSEUM
1213 Washington Ave., Golden
(303) 277-0377
rmqm.org

The tiny Rocky Mountain Quilt Museum is as much a resource center for quilters as a museum, with more than 300 old and new quilts in its collection. Exhibits change five times a year. Quilts and other needlework are offered for sale at the museum, which also conducts classes and outreach programs. The museum is open daily.

US MINT
320 W. Colfax Ave.
(303) 405-4761
usmint.gov

One of Denver's most popular tourist attractions, the Mint produces 15 billion coins each year. Free tours are conducted Monday through Thursday. Reservations are required for the 30-minute tours, and the Mint strongly suggests that you make them online, since walk-up reservations are first-come, first-served and may not always be available. Go to usmint.gov/mint_tours, click on "Denver," and follow the instructions. The tours leave every 15 to 20 minutes from the Cherokee Street entrance. Expect a long line during the summer. Children younger than age 14 must be accompanied by an adult, and tours are not recommended for children under 7. Wheelchairs are allowed, but cameras are not. No photos can be taken inside the building. Hours for coin sales are the same as tour hours. The Mint is closed on all legal holidays and for one week in summer, usually in late June, for inventory.

WILDLIFE EXPERIENCE
10035 S. Peoria St., Parker
(720) 488-3300
wildlifeexperience.org

The $50 million Wildlife Experience opened in 2002 about 10 miles south of downtown Denver and 1 mile east of I-25. It's the brainchild of RE/MAX cofounders Dave and Gail Liniger, in which art and natural history are combined. They describe the museum as "where art and education lead to greater appreciation of animals in their natural habitats." The 101,000-square-foot facility has space for oil paintings, metal sculptures, traveling exhibits, art and photo galleries, and a 315-seat IWERKS theater for wildlife movies.

The museum also contains a cafe, a gift shop, and both indoor and outdoor facilities big enough for special parties and meetings. It's open every day except Thanksgiving and Christmas. To reach Wildlife Experience, travel south on I-25, take E-470 east, then exit at Peoria and follow it south to Lincoln Avenue.

WINGS OVER THE ROCKIES AIR & SPACE MUSEUM
7711 E. Academy Blvd.
(303) 360-5360
wingsmuseum.org
Perhaps the last remnant of Lowry Air Force Base in east Denver, this air and space museum on the site of the decommissioned base houses a wide range of aircraft and space memorabilia. Its permanent collection includes a B-18 Bolo, an RF-84K Thundercraft parasite, a B-1A Lancer, and an Apollo control module. It's open daily.

HISTORIC HOUSES & OTHER HISTORIC SITES

BYERS-EVANS HOUSE
1310 Bannock St.
(303) 620-4933
historycolorado.org/museums
John Evans was Colorado's second territorial governor. William Byers founded the *Rocky Mountain News*. Both men and their families were prominent during Denver's early years, and their names appear on avenues and mountain peaks. This house, built by Byers in 1883 and sold to Evans's son in 1889, has been restored to the 1912–24 period. The house is open Monday through Saturday and can be seen only on a guided tour. Combination tickets including entrance to the nearby History Colorado Center are available.

COLORADO GOVERNOR'S MANSION
400 E. 8th Ave.
(303) 866-5344, (303) 866-4686
colorado.gov/governor/residence
Completed in 1907, the governor's mansion was originally the private residence of the Walter Scott Cheesman family. In 1927 the house was sold to the Boettcher family, and in 1960 the Boettcher Foundation gave the property to the state to use as the governor's mansion. The colonial revival structure contains artwork from all around the world and a Waterford chandelier that once hung in the White House. The mansion can be visited on Tuesday afternoon between June and August. Tours start every quarter hour and last 45 minutes. The mansion is open to the public for a week during December, when it's decorated for Christmas. Call for dates, as they vary every year.

COLORADO STATE CAPITOL
Broadway and Colfax Avenue
(303) 866-2604
colorado.gov/capitoltour
The Colorado State Capitol stands exactly 1 mile above sea level. On the 13th step there's a carving stating the elevation as 5,280 feet, but a small brass plaque on the 18th step corrects the carving and proclaims itself the true mile-high marker. Inside the capitol building, free tours lasting about 45 minutes are given Monday through Friday. Due to heightened security, there is no public access to the gold-plated dome. Although the gold on the outside of the dome tends to receive more attention from the casual passersby, the real precious mineral is on the inside of the building, where rose-colored Colorado onyx was used as wainscoting. The onyx came from a small quarry in Beulah, Colorado, and has never been mined elsewhere.

CUSSLER MUSEUM
14959 W. 69th Ave., Arvada
(303) 420-2795
cusslermuseum.com

Author Clive Cussler lived in Metro Denver during his early years and, as his popularity grew, he diverted some of his financial proceeds into an extensive vintage automobile collection. Among the rarest are the foreign cars—a 1929 Isotta Fraschini and a 1936 Avions Voisins, for example. Cussler found ways to write many of the vehicles into his Dirk Pitt novels, and he often posed with them for the book jacket photos. Today the collection is tended by his daughter and open to the public Monday and Tuesday May through September.

FAIRMOUNT CEMETERY
430 S. Quebec St.
(303) 399-0692
fairmount-cemetery.com

This 320-acre privately owned cemetery dates from 1890 and is the final resting place for many former mayors, socialites, gunfighters, madams, and Civil War veterans. An infamous "resident" is Colonel John M. Chivington, responsible for the massacre of defenseless Indians at Sand Creek in 1864. The grounds contain more than 50 types of trees, and tours are given periodically by the Denver Botanic Gardens for those interested in this aspect of the cemetery. Self-guided tours are possible anytime (a guidebook can be purchased at the site), and free guided tours are available.

FOUR MILE HISTORIC PARK
715 S. Forest St.
(720) 865-0800
fourmilehistoricpark.org

Designated a Denver Landmark in 1968, Four Mile Historic Park commemorates the site of a former stage stop and contains the oldest home still standing in Denver. In addition to the 1859 log home, visitors can tour the living-history farmstead and, on nice days, have a picnic here. Special-events days are held about six times a year and include horse-drawn wagon rides and demonstrations of blacksmithing, butter churning, and other chores. There are reenactments of Civil War events during the spring and summer as well as a heritage program and evening concerts. It's open Wednesday through Sunday.

LAKEWOOD HERITAGE CENTER
801 S. Yarrow St., Lakewood
(303) 987-7850
lakewood.org/hca

A historic site and museum with several structures, including an 1880s farmhouse and a 1920s schoolhouse, Lakewood Heritage Center also has a barn gallery with changing exhibits. The visitor center has a permanent exhibit on May Bonfils, daughter of one of the founders of the *Denver Post,* and exhibits of work by local artists that change monthly. The visitor center is staffed Tuesday through Saturday. Call to ask about special children's programs. Groups of five or more should make reservations.

LITTLETON MUSEUM
6028 S. Gallup St., Littleton
(303) 795-3950
littletongov.org/museum

This living-history museum consists of a reconstructed 1860s homestead and a turn-of-the-20th-century farm that re-creates pioneer life. Among the original buildings on the 14-acre site are a 1910 icehouse, a sheep and goat shelter originally built as a settler's cabin in the 1860s, an 1890s farmhouse,

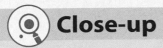 **Close-up**

Denver for Free

You don't need to spend money to have fun in Denver. Here are eight Denver activities that won't cost a dime!

Colorado State Capitol Building Tour: colorado.gov/capitoltour

Colorado Sports Hall of Fame Museum: coloradosports.org

Denver Public Library Western Art Collection: denverlibrary.org

First Friday Art Walks: visitdenver.com/artdistricts

Free Days for Colorado Residents at the Denver Art Museum: first Saturday of every month: denverartmuseum.org

Hammond's Candy Factory: hammondscandies.com

The **16th Street Mall** and shuttle: denver.com/16th-street-mall

US Mint Tour: usmint.gov/mint_tours

---

and the first schoolhouse in Littleton. The main museum underwent a 3-year, $8.5 million expansion and reopened in 2006 with expanded galleries and workshops and a lecture hall and research center. Outdoors, costumed staff and volunteers care for the chickens and livestock and go about the business of tending a 19th-century farm. They're not too busy to stop and explain things to visitors. Admission is free (large groups are charged a small fee and should call first). The museum is open Tuesday through Sunday; it's closed on Monday and major holidays.

✳MOLLY BROWN HOUSE MUSEUM
1340 Pennsylvania St.
(303) 832-4092
mollybrown.org
Only Baby Doe Tabor can match Molly Brown for name recognition among turn-of-the-20th-century Denver women. Each has had her life memorialized in song: Baby Doe, in the opera *The Ballad of Baby Doe,* and Molly

Brown, in the Broadway musical *The Unsinkable Molly Brown.* Molly was one of early Denver's more flamboyant characters and achieved true heroine status for her actions during the sinking of the *Titanic,* which she survived. Her Victorian home has been restored and furnished in period style with many personal mementos and possessions. Museum officials suggest arriving early as they do not take reservations. The museum is open Tuesday through Sunday, with the last tour starting daily at 3:30 p.m. A number of special dinners, teas, readings, and workshops are scheduled throughout the year; call for more information.

RIVERSIDE CEMETERY
5201 Brighton Blvd., Commerce City
(303) 293-2466
friendsofriversidecemetery.org
Denver's oldest cemetery, founded in 1876, contains the graves of three Civil War medal-of-honor winners; Augusta Tabor, the first wife of turn-of-the-20th-century silver baron

Horace Tabor; and Colorado's first African-American ballplayer, Oliver E. Marcel. Visitors can pick up a booklet and map for $2 during office hours, weekdays 8:30 a.m. to 4:30 p.m. The cemetery is on Brighton Boulevard about 2 miles north of I-70.

PARKS & GARDENS

*CONFLUENCE PARK
2250 15th St.
(303) 433-3676
Located along the South Platte River, Confluence Park is surrounded by attractions such as the REI flagship store, the Downtown Aquarium, and numerous restaurants, cafes, and shops in the nearby neighborhoods of Riverfront, LoHi, and Highland. The park lies along the 850-mile bike trail network, and a kayaking run next to REI provides free entertainment. The paved path here welcomes runners and walkers as well. On warm Sunday and Thursday nights, fire dancers and drummers often come to practice and play.

*DENVER BOTANIC GARDENS
1007 York St.
(720) 865-3500
botanicgardens.org
One of Metro Denver's most lovely refuges, the Botanic Gardens encompasses 23 acres and includes an herb garden and other specialty gardens. The 1-acre rock alpine garden is considered one of the finest in the country. Our personal favorite is the lovely Japanese Shofu-en (Garden of Pine Wind) designed by America's foremost Japanese landscaper, Koichi Kawana. It is complete with an authentic teahouse. Local residents look to the water-saving xeriscape demonstration garden and the home

demonstration garden for ideas they can put into use in their own yards. A tropical conservatory and pavilion houses orchids, bromeliads, and other warmth-loving species. Outdoor concerts are held here in the summer; come early and bring a picnic dinner. Schedules are available at the gate in early spring, but they sell out quickly. The Botanic Gardens are open daily.

*THE DENVER ZOO CITY PARK
East 23rd Avenue and Steele Street
(303) 376-4800
denverzoo.org
Easily combined with a trip to the Museum of Nature and Science, the Denver Zoo has the usual complement of lions and tigers and (polar) bears as well as monkeys and birds, in a mix of enclosed and open habitat areas. The new 10-acre Toyota Elephant Passage is the largest bull elephant habitat in the world. The $10 million Tropical Discovery exhibit is designed to re-create a rain forest habitat inside a glass-enclosed pyramid. More than 700 animal species live here, nearly double what the zoo had previously. There is a separate nursery area where new arrivals needing human help get their first taste of what it's like to be in the public eye. Primate Panorama, a 5-acre, all-natural habitat, is always a crowd-pleaser. For those who can't or don't feel like walking the zoo, a fun train circles the major outdoor exhibits frequently throughout the day. The zoo is open daily, including all holidays; Tropical Discovery and Bird World have slightly shortened hours. The zoo offers free admission on certain days through the winter. Call or visit the website for dates.

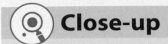 **Close-up**

Elitch Gardens Thrills Downtown Visitors

Elitch's started in 1890 when John and Mary Elitch turned a small apple orchard into picnic areas and ball fields open to the public. It later boasted Denver's first zoo. In 1891 the Elitch Theatre opened its first season and for 96 years hosted such luminaries as Sarah Bernhardt, Cecil B. DeMille, Grace Kelly, and Edward G. Robinson. In 1925 the treasured carousel with 67 hand-carved horses and chariots was installed. The restored carousel is a focal point of the new park.

Over the years, Elitch's became known for its signature gardens, a sprawling collection of impressive flowers, trees, and shrubs. It will take many years before the "gardens" in the new Elitch Gardens come anywhere close to the impressive foliage tenderly raised at the old site. In the meantime, efforts have been made to capture some of the nostalgia of the old Elitch's. A Victorian-style promenade with colorful storefronts and restaurants harkens to the old Elitch days. The Trocadero Theater, built in honor of Elitch's famed Trocadero Ballroom at the old park, seats 700 and features live shows. Although the park opens weekends in May, Memorial Day is the official launch of the season.

ELITCH GARDENS THEME & WATER PARK
I-25 and Speer Boulevard (exit 212A)
(303) 595-4386
elitchgardens.com

For more than 100 years, Elitch Gardens was a west Denver tradition. Opened in May 1890 as Elitch Zoological Gardens by John and Mary Elitch, it boasted three thrilling roller coasters: the Wildcat, the wooden Twister, and the Sidewinder. In 1995 Elitch Gardens reopened in a larger, 68-acre location in the Central Platte River Valley just off the Speer Boulevard exit from I-25. (At night, all lit up, it's a beautiful and memorable sight for anyone driving through Denver on the interstate.) A rebuilt 100-foot-high Twister II is one of the top attractions. There are 49 major rides in all, including several added in the past few years: The Flying Coaster (billed as the cure for the common coaster), an indescribable facedown ride that feels like you're flying

through the air; The Half-Pipe, a 100-foot-tall ride on a 40-foot-long snowboard; and the new Edge ride at the Island Kingdom Water Park, a 4-story near-vertical waterslide. For tamer pursuits there's a 300-foot-high observation tower with a panoramic view. The 1925 carousel made the move downtown. Open daily roughly Memorial Day through Labor Day.

LAKESIDE AMUSEMENT PARK
4601 Sheridan Blvd. (I-70 and Sheridan)
(303) 477-1621

An all-ages amusement park and one of the oldest in the nation, Lakeside has a merry-go-round, a Ferris wheel, a roller coaster, and other exciting rides. One of the best things to do at Lakeside is to ride the train around the lake after dark. The park is open May through Labor Day weekend. In May the park is open on weekends only. It is open 7 days a week June through Labor Day.

SUGGESTED OUTINGS

ONE-DAY FAMILY OUTING . . .

Visit the Denver Museum of Nature and Science and the Denver Zoo. Take in a show at the IMAX theater. Then, if you have time, the Denver Museum of Miniatures, Dolls & Toys isn't far away.

WITHIN WALKING DISTANCE DOWNTOWN . . .

The Denver Art Museum, the Museum of Western Art, the History Colorado Center, the US Mint, the Colorado State Capitol, the Molly Brown House, Clyfford Still Museum, Kirkland Museum, the Firefighters Museum, and the Byers-Evans House are all within walking distance of one another downtown. Don't try to see all these sights in one day, but pick the ones that interest you most; plot a route and save the rest for another afternoon.

FOR ART LOVERS . . .

The Denver Art Museum and the Western Art Museum can be visited in one day if you don't try to see the whole art museum. If you're at the Denver Art Museum at lunchtime, eat in its cafe.

TRAINS & AUTOMOBILES . . .

Metro Denver has three museums of special interest in this category: the Forney Transportation Museum, the Colorado Railroad Museum, and the Denver Firefighters Museum. With a car, all could be visited in one day.

ONE-DAY OUTING IN GOLDEN . . .

Start with a drive up to the Buffalo Bill Grave and Museum and the nearby Mother Cabrini Shrine, which honors the first American saint. For lunch take a picnic to Red Rocks Park if the weather's nice, or pick a spot in downtown Golden. In the afternoon visit the Colorado Railroad Museum or the Rocky Mountain Quilt Museum.

HISTORY BUFFS . . .

Don't miss the Black American West Museum. A visit there combines well with a visit to the History Colorado Center.

ETHNIC HERITAGE TOUR (HALF-DAY) . . .

Divide your time between the Black American West Museum and the Museo de las Americas. Afterward stop for lunch at one of the authentic Mexican restaurants along Santa Fe Drive. Try El Noa Noa or El Taco de Mexico (see our Restaurants chapter for full descriptions of these eateries).

ART & GARDEN TOUR . . .

Spend half the day at the Denver Art Museum and the rest at the Denver Botanic Gardens.

FAUNA & FLORA . . .

Spend half the day at the Denver Zoo and the rest at the Denver Botanic Gardens.

WALKING TOURS . . .

Suggestions for several walking tour itineraries are available at denver.org/what-to-do/itinerary. The information booth at Larimer Square can provide historical and architectural information about buildings in the 1400 block of Larimer Street.

CULINARY TOURS . . .

Two companies, Culinary Connectors (303-495-5487; culinaryconnectors.com) and Local Table Tours (303-909-5747;

localtabletours.com), lead participants to notable Colorado restaurants, foodie hot spots, bars, brewers, shops, chefs, farmers, producers, and food-related events.

PUBLIC ART TOUR . . .

A brochure identifying public art throughout the city is available at the Denver Visitors Information Center, 1600 California St., #6 (303-892-1505). The brochure contains a suggested walking tour and driving tour. Find suggestions for viewing public art by going to denver.org/what-to-do/itinerary and clicking the "Downtown Public Art Walking Tour" link under "Denver's Creative Side."

ART GALLERIES . . .

Art galleries are clustered in a variety of areas around Metro Denver. For printable maps and more information on First Fridays and touring 10 art districts, go to denver.org/galleryguide.

KIDSTUFF

We think of Denver as kids' country. Metro Denver offers a multitude of activities for the younger set—but we admit we like the outings, too. Best of all, Denver's laid-back attitude says kids are welcome just about anywhere—assuming they aren't totally unrestrained, of course.

One of the first places guests to Metro Denver should look for fun is outdoors: Take them out to play with Mother Nature. It doesn't matter what trail or mountainside you take them to; short hikes or climbs for smaller kids are found in the same places where adults and older kids go to get serious. There's an abundance of trails and natural beauty close to Denver. When hiking, make sure to protect yourself and your kids by using sunscreen and taking water bottles.

Mother Nature is only one of the kid-friendly attractions around Metro Denver. Check the other chapters of this book for ideas, especially Tours & Attractions, Spectator Sports, Annual Events & Festivals, Parks & Recreation, and Day Trips.

What follows is limited to a reasonable number of unique attractions aimed at the younger set, but there are others too numerous to mention. Take the kids fishing at any of the many reservoirs and rivers along the Front Range and in the nearby mountains. Go horseback riding at any of the stables around Metro Denver. Walk or ride bicycles on trails, usually along creeks, rivers, canals, and lakeshores that thread the greenbelts of the metro area.

Call nearby public libraries about story hours and other child-oriented activities. Call city and county departments of parks and recreation in your area to see about kid activities ranging from soccer and baseball to art classes. Local recreation centers are listed in our Parks & Recreation chapter.

One of your best local resources to kid activities is *Colorado Parent* magazine (303-320-1000; coloradoparent.com), a free monthly publication that can be found at 800 locations ranging from bookstores and libraries to doctors' offices and day-care centers.

WET 'N' WILD

There are swimming pools all over Metro Denver, and some of them go the extra mile to be kid-friendly.

CARPENTER RECREATION CENTER
11151 Colorado Blvd., Thornton
(303) 255-7800
The Carpenter Recreation Center is a fantastic indoor 15,000-square-foot aquatics

center, which includes artificially generated waves, lap swimming, a raindrop play area with waterfall and Jacuzzi, a lazy river, and a waterslide.

THE GOLDEN COMMUNITY CENTER
1470 10th St., Golden
(303) 384-8100
The Golden Community Center has an indoor pool that kids will love, with a raindrop play area, waterslide, and hot tub as well as a lap pool and leisure pool.

✳WATER WORLD
88th Avenue and Pecos Street, Federal Heights
(303) 427-7873
waterworldcolorado.com
Metro Denver's biggest outdoor water park, Water World offers more than 64 acres of aquatic fun. Float down a circular series of chutes and pools on an inner tube. Ride a huge rubber raft down a torrent. Sit on a plastic sled that plunges almost straight down and builds up enough speed to aquaplane across the pool at the bottom. Or try the newest attraction, the Zoomerang. Water World has it all. The park also added a Journey to the Center of the Earth ride, in which you cruise through caves where moving dinosaurs menace you. Water World is open from late May to the end of summer. If you're age 60 and older or age 3 and younger, it's free. Check the website for promotional discounts.

WESTMINSTER CITY PARK RECREATION CENTER
10455 Sheridan Blvd., Westminster
(303) 460-9690
This indoor facility has a large children's pool with a tile beach sloping gently at one end,

a fountain, and a slide just for kids. The main pool for lap swimmers bulges out at one side under a waterfall. You can go behind the waterfall and look through windows to get an underwater view of the next pool, one floor above and dedicated entirely to swinging out on and dropping from a rope fastened at the ceiling 3 stories up. Above the rope-swing pool is the beginning of a waterslide that ends with a splash in the main pool.

EATING OUT

Kids are welcome at just about any restaurant in town. Still, we've listed those that have true kid appeal.

CASA BONITA
6715 W. Colfax Ave., Lakewood
(303) 232-5115
casabonitadenver.com
Rising from the JCRS Shopping Center in Lakewood, the distinctive steeple of Casa Bonita has become a Metro Denver landmark. Although this is a decent Mexican restaurant with American dishes, too, people come here more for the play than for the food. It's like eating in a cave with huge chambers and a complex labyrinth of tunnels and hidden nooks. Strolling mariachis and cliff divers entertain while you eat. Kids love Black Bart's Cave, a series of creepy scares in tunnels sized for kids. There's a video arcade and other entertainment. The crowning glory is the 30-foot waterfall, where divers plunge into a pool below while performances at the top of the waterfall involve cowboy gunfights and explorers tangling with a gorilla. Every performance ends with somebody falling 30 feet into the pool. It's a popular place for kid birthday parties

and for parents who want to kick back while their kids run wild.

GUNTHER TOODY'S
4500 E. Alameda Ave., Glendale
(303) 399-1959

The staff at Gunther Toody's dress like characters from *Grease* at this 1950s concept restaurant, and they usually do such a good job of acting their sassy, gum-chewing parts that there must be a Gunther Toody's acting school somewhere. The only games are a few classic pinball machines, and it's not exclusively a kid restaurant. But that's why we're mentioning it here, because it deserves wider recognition as a great, non-arcade dining place for kids and their families. Additional locations include: 9220 E. Arapahoe Rd., Englewood (303-799-1958); 7355 Ralston Rd., Arvada (303-422-1954); 8266 W. Bowles Ave., Littleton (303-932-1957); and 301 W. 104th St., Northglenn (303-453-1956).

PLANES, TRAINS & BOATS

✳COLORADO RAILROAD MUSEUM
17155 W. 44th Ave., Golden
(303) 279-4591
coloradorailroadmuseum.org

A lot of Western city parks used to have trains that kids could climb around on, but now they're mostly surrounded by fences to keep the kids out. None of that nonsense here! The Colorado Railroad Museum is described in our Tours & Attractions chapter, but at 12.5 acres, with more than 50 pieces of "rolling stock," it's so fantastic for kids that it bears repeating. Kids can climb up and walk through the antique railway cars, climb into the cupolas of the cabooses to look out the windows, and scale the big engine right

outside the museum building and pull the rope and ring the awesome bell. You have to be a bit older to appreciate most of the two floors of memorabilia inside the museum building, but kids love the enormous model train set up in the basement, which you can run by plugging in a quarter. Several times a year the museum fires up and runs the state's oldest railway engine.

PIKES PEAK COG RAILWAY
US 24 West from Colorado Springs to the Manitou exit, west on Manitou Avenue, and left onto Ruxton Avenue, Colorado Springs
(719) 685-5401
cograilway.com

Adults become kids again when riding the world's highest cog train. We include more details about the 3.5-hour trip to the top of Pikes Peak in our Day Trips chapter, but here we'll mention just one thing. Kids who most enjoy the experience are those of an age and temperament to tolerate a long ride. Reservations are required.

PLATTE VALLEY TROLLEY
2785 N. Speer Blvd.
(303) 458-6255
denvertrolley.org

This turn-of-the-20th-century streetcar tour is for all ages, but those who grew up watching *Mister Rogers' Neighborhood* on television may recognize its near-exact resemblance to the streetcar on the TV show. You'll enjoy a narrated tour along the Platte River, with bits of history and expositions on features of this area such as Sports Authority Field at Mile High and Golda Meir's former residence. The hour tour goes up Lakewood Gulch, along the tracks where the interurban trolley used to run from Denver to Golden. Children 6 or younger may prefer the half-hour tour. The trolley closes during winter months, operating between April and October. To get to the trolley, park at the Children's Museum of Denver (see our listing in this chapter) and walk east to the Platte River.

WINGS OVER THE ROCKIES AIR & SPACE MUSEUM
7711 E. Academy Blvd.
(303) 360-5360
wingsmuseum.org

Wings Over the Rockies does for aviation what the Colorado Railroad Museum does for the railroads, putting the biggest and best of the historic hardware on very impressive display for the public. With the exception of the Space Station Module, you can't actually go inside the displays, but up-close and gargantuan, they have a tremendous, visceral impact. Among the three dozen aircraft on display in the museum are big bombers, racy fighter jets, and helicopters—a scan of aviation history. You've got civilian and military aircraft, models, simulations, photographs, and space-related objects so visitors can experience scientific discovery. It's all contained in the vast interior of Lowry's Hangar 1. Since it's all indoors, it's particularly nice on a winter day when outside activities are curtailed. There are also a variety of historic aviation artifacts and a museum store. Wings Over the Rockies is open daily. From I-225 take 6th Avenue west to Lowry Boulevard, turn left at the dead end, and proceed until you see the hangars. It's the first one to the west. Or you can take Alameda Street west to Fairmount Cemetery and turn right onto Fairmount Drive. Straight ahead you'll see the two hangars, and it's the first one to the east.

ℹ️ The Tattered Cover Book Store devote lots of shelf space to children's books. They also have kid-size tables and chairs where young ones can read or look at pictures.

NIGHTLIFE FOR THE YOUNGER CROWD

Rec & Rock

Held on different nights at three recreation centers, the Rec & Rock and Kids Night Out program features safe and supervised weekend nightlife for adolescents ages 9 to 14. They've turned out to be popular programs and take place during the school year. You'll typically find games, dancing, and music with a live DJ; activities such as basketball, dodgeball, wallyball, and volleyball; concessions for pizza and soft drinks; movies, contests, and special guests. There is one adult counselor for every 25 kids, a uniformed police officer on hand at all times, and parental check-in and checkout. Admission is $10. Find more information at ssprd.org.

BUCK RECREATION CENTER
2004 W. Powers Ave., Littleton
(303) 797-8787
Second Friday of the month
Ages 9–13

GOODSON RECREATION CENTER
6315 S. University Blvd., Littleton
(303) 798-2476
First and third Saturday of the month
Ages 10–14

LONE TREE RECREATION CENTER
10249 Ridgegate Circle, Lone Tree
(303) 780-3500
Second and fourth Saturday of the
month
Ages 10–14

THE PLANT & ANIMAL KINGDOMS

*BUTTERFLY PAVILION & INSECT CENTER
6252 W. 104th Ave., Westminster
(303) 469-5441
butterflies.org
If your child loves butterflies, this place is a perfect destination. More than 1,600 butterflies live in a 7,200-square-foot tropical forest. At the emergence viewing area, you can watch the last two stages of metamorphosis as butterflies emerge from their chrysalides. Outside is a butterfly garden, with flowers designed to attract butterflies. The center is also home to a variety of other insects, arachnids, aquatic invertebrates, and plants. The pavilion is open daily, but closes on Thanksgiving and Christmas Day.

*DENVER BOTANIC GARDENS
1007 York St.
(720) 865-3500
botanicgardens.org
Kids of all ages enjoy these lovely gardens and the tropical conservatory. We've described the gardens in detail in our Tours & Attractions chapter, but chances are good that children will be more interested in the changing menu of year-round kid activities, such as the Pumpkin Fest and the summer evening concerts listed in our Annual Events & Festivals chapter. It's also a pretty place to run around, with a couple of grassy knolls that small kids love to climb on and roll down. It's a nice place for a picnic. The gardens are open daily, with reduced winter hours.

*THE DENVER MUSEUM OF NATURE AND SCIENCE
2001 Colorado Blvd. (in City Park, at Colorado Boulevard and Montview Street)
(303) 322-7009
dmns.org
See our Tours & Attractions chapter for more details on this museum, but don't forget it's one of the greatest places around for kids. When you walk under the claws of the huge *Tyrannosaurus rex* skeleton as you enter the front door, you know you've entered a place of wonder. The museum has some great children's educational programs, but they fill up frighteningly fast once their scheduling becomes public knowledge. The museum is open daily.

*THE DENVER ZOO
City Park, East 23rd Avenue and Steele Street (near the Denver Museum of Nature and Science)
(303) 376-4800
denverzoo.org
You can't miss with a zoo, and the Denver Zoo may well be Metro Denver's most popular kid place of all. It's open daily, with some wonderful special events centered around the seasons. (See our Tours & Attractions and Annual Events & Festivals chapters for details).

ROCKY MOUNTAIN ARSENAL NATIONAL WILDLIFE REFUGE

72nd and Quebec Streets, Commerce City

(303) 289-0232

fws.gov/rockymountainarsenal

Take a 2-hour bus tour of one of the country's former toxic waste sites, now overrun with all kinds of wildlife. On this tour you hear the history of the area as well as its environmental cleanup. If you're lucky you'll also see eagles, hawks, mule deer, and prairie dogs. If the wildlife is out romping, this will be one of those "WOW!" experiences. Entrance is free. The refuge is open daily except for holidays.

THE WILD ANIMAL SANCTUARY

1946 County Rd. 53, Keensburg

(303) 536-0118

wildanimalsanctuary.org

Located northeast of Denver, this 720-acre refuge for large carnivores is a rescue center for animals that have been abandoned or subjected to neglect or cruelty. More than 200 animals, including tigers, leopards, bears, lions, wolves, and other animals, roam freely in any of 21 separate habitats. Overhead walkways provide a bird's-eye view of the animals.

MUSEUMS

CHILDREN'S MUSEUM OF DENVER

2121 Children's Museum Dr.

(303) 433-7444

mychildsmuseum.org

There are dozens of things to do here, all of them aimed specifically at kids and all educationally oriented. There's a miniature grocery store, where kids can shop or be the checkout person, an assembly plant for building things, and an art area where kids can get creative. There are laboratories where kids can work with earth sciences and natural phenomena and play educational games on computers. You'll find a light room and sound room, plant and animal exhibits, woodworking, and a traveling exhibit that changes every 3 months. Play Partners is a special toddler play area set up like the Three Bears' house.

It's a great museum, but a very busy one. The museum is open daily, but recommends coming between 2 and 5 p.m. on weekdays, when it's least crowded. Worthy of note is the museum's annual Halloween party, Trick-or-Treat Street, which runs for nearly a week, including Halloween. This is Denver's non-scary trick-or-treat alternative. The event includes pumpkin carving, performances, and other activities. The Parent Resource Center and the Center for the Young Child is a developmentally age-appropriate area for newborns to 4-year-olds. The museum can be a little tricky to reach, so here are some directions: It's right off 23rd Avenue and I-25. If you exit from I-25, go east on 23rd and take the first right onto 7th Street and then an immediate right onto Children's Museum Drive.

AMUSEMENT PARKS

ELITCH GARDENS THEME & WATER PARK

I-25 and Speer Boulevard (exit 212A)

(303) 595-4386

elitchgardens.com

Elitch Gardens is Denver's oldest fun park, dating from 1890 when it began as a botanical and zoological garden and had no mechanical rides. Since then it has become Denver's biggest and flashiest amusement

A Day in the Park

Thanks to the vision of Mayor Robert Speer (after whom Speer Boulevard is named), Denver has a system of parks and greenways that ranks among the nation's largest.

Speer was inspired to adorn Denver while visiting the 1893 Chicago Exposition, and formulated a "City Beautiful Plan" after he was elected mayor in 1904. It plotted tree-lined parkways and central Denver parks that form the framework for the city's open space (Civic Center Park, Washington Park, City Park, and Alamo Placita Park). Denver's first new park, Mestizo-Curtis Park, opened in 1968 at 31st and Curtis Streets, and it is still a vital part of this north Denver neighborhood.

More than a century after Speer was elected, the city and county of Denver now have 281 urban parks, 125 miles of hiking and biking paths, 100 miles of parkways, and 20,000 acres of mountain parks. Go to the suburbs and you'll find many more.

Though all the parks are soothing oases, the following are particularly beloved by kids.

Belleview Park
5001 S. Inca St., Englewood
Belleview is simply one of the region's most entertaining family parks. Often called Airplane Park, it has two playgrounds filled with space-related jungle gyms, slides, and swings. It also has a miniature train that takes visitors around the park and a petting zoo with cows, pigs, goats, and rabbits. If that's not quite enough, a clear shallow stream running through the park is perfect for wading.

Cheesman Park
East 12th Avenue and Humboldt Street
Cheesman Park has some terrific playground equipment (not to mention a pretty spectacular view of the mountains). Kids love the castle structure for climbing and hiding, and the jungle gym is one of the best around. Most striking is the Cheesman Park Pavilion, a Parthenonlike structure perfect for running around or watching the sunset.

City Park
17th Avenue and Colorado Boulevard
This park just east of downtown is full of possibilities, not the least of which are visits to the Denver Zoo and the Denver Museum of Natural History. A lake in the middle offers paddleboating. A rose garden close to the museum provides a great picnic site. Need more activity? The park has a public golf course and tennis courts. And in the summer there's a free concert each Sunday in the band shell near the lake.

Cushing Park
795 W. Eastman St., Englewood
This is the site of one of Metro Denver's first gold discoveries. Not surprisingly, its playground is reminiscent of the Old West, with a stagecoach, a tepee, a jail, and a horse and buggy—all of which keep active buckaroos busy while their parents relax under a tree. Cushing also has an area specifically for skateboarders.

Genesee Park
I-70 West to the Genesee exit, Genesee
How many cities boast a buffalo herd? The best reason to head to Genesee Park is to see the gentle giants roaming right off the highway. Once you see them, you won't care that all the other fancy trappings of city parks are lacking.

Ruby Hill Park
South Platte River Drive and West Florida Avenue
Recently completed renovations at this west Denver park include a walking trail, a new playground, and a pavilion on the hill overlooking Denver. The park is also home to the city's Urban Rail Yard, a ski and snowboard hill that opens only in the winter.

Washington Park
Louisiana Avenue and Downing Street
This is one of Denver's most popular park destinations. Originally a prairie, it has two lakes that allow fishing (don't forget your license) and a lawn bowling/croquet green. Best of all, most of the streets are closed to vehicular traffic, so your family can in-line skate, bike, or walk without fear of being mowed down.

park, expanding in 1995 onto 68 acres along the South Platte River. More details are available in our Tours & Attractions chapter. Getting to Elitch Gardens is no problem, since it has its own exit from the Speer Boulevard viaduct. There also is downtown access from 15th Street. Open May through October.

FUN CITY
9670 W. Coal Mine Ave., Littleton
(303) 972-4344
funcitycolorado.com
This is a 3.5-acre indoor fun center for all ages. Activities include bowling, Grand Prix racing, laser tag, an 18-hole miniature golf course, and a video arcade. It's open daily year-round.

HERITAGE SQUARE
18301 W. Colfax Ave., Golden
(303) 277-0040
heritagesquare.info
Heritage Square appears to be a small Western town wedged into the foothills, with porticoed boardwalks along the front of retail stores, restaurants, and entertainment options lining its streets. They include an alpine slide on the hillside, an operating train, amusement rides, miniature golf, and a variety of vendors. The Heritage Square Music Hall offers melodramas, a dinner theater, and a children's theater. Rides operate weekends in the spring and fall, and daily during the summer months.

JUMPSTREET
14500 W. Colfax, Lakewood (Colorado Mills)
(303) 590-1580
jump-street.com
Jumpstreet is an indoor trampoline park with more than 20,000 square feet of trampolines,

trampoline dodge ball, and a variety of other activities. Additional locations are at 7969 E. Arapahoe Rd., Greenwood Village (303-586-5530); and 10081 W. Bowles Ave., Littleton (303-339-3030).

LAKESIDE AMUSEMENT PARK
4601 Sheridan Ave.
Just south of I-70, Lakeside
(303) 477-1621
lakesideamusementpark.com
Lakeside is an old-fashioned park that has changed little since the 1940s. Little trains that run around the lake are sentimental favorites of past generations. The extensive kiddieland has 15 rides sized for the tots, while the Cyclone Roller Coaster and 39 other rides entertain the rest of the family. It opens weekends in May, goes full-time in June, and closes after Labor Day weekend.

SKYVENTURE COLORADO
9230 Park Meadows Dr., Lone Tree
(303) 768-9000
skyventurecolorado.com
A safe alternative to skydiving, SkyVenture offers the experience of free-falling without the risk. A vertical wind tunnel lets participants soar on a column of air above a trampoline-like floor. No experience is necessary, and anyone from the age of 3 is welcome.

SOMETHING DIFFERENT

COLORADO RENAISSANCE FESTIVAL
I-25 about 25 minutes south from Denver to Larkspur (exit 173), then follow the signs
(303) 688-6010
coloradorenaissance.com
See our Annual Events & Festivals chapter for more on the Renaissance Festival, but it's

such a kid-pleaser that it cannot be omitted from this section. It's a dizzying fantasy world full of battling knights, cavorting jesters, and associated monsters and grotesques, where hundreds of food vendors, craftspeople, and performers dress, act, and speak appropriately to their setting in this re-created 16th-century village. It's an event rather than a place, however, so remember it's only around for 8 weekends in June and July. Discount tickets are available at King Soopers supermarkets.

DENVER PUPPET THEATER
3156 W. 38th Ave.
(303) 458-6446
denverpuppettheater.com
The Denver Puppet Theater is a delightful experience for kids ages 3 and older. With six different plays performed each year—classics, world stories, new plays—kids can come back every 2 months for a new show. Marionettes and shadow puppets make up the characters, and visitors can see all the puppets after each performance. (No autographs, however.) Performances are on Thursday through Sunday from September to May, and Wednesday through Saturday during the summer.

TINY TOWN
6249 S. Turkey Creek Rd., Morrison
(303) 697-6829
tinytownrailroad.com
Hidden away in a mountain canyon southeast of Metro Denver, this is a curious and charming town of 110 miniature buildings constructed at one-sixth scale on 6 acres. Kids can actually go inside some of the buildings, but it's a place where families enjoy just walking around. You can ride a miniature train pulled by a real—but tiny—steam engine over a mile-long course. They have a snack bar, a gift shop, and puppet shows on weekends. Part of the magic of this place is that it looks rather ancient, and it is. It's the oldest miniature town in the US. George Turner was the owner of a Denver moving and storage business just after the turn of the 20th century, and this was his mountain property. His granddaughter was chronically ill, so he built a few miniature houses in the pasture for her to play in, then kept adding to the tiny town. Turkey Creek Road was dirt then, and people would stop their cars and delight their kids with the magical little town. By the 1920s and 1930s, it was one of Colorado's major tourist attractions. After World War II it went through several decades of decline, including a flood and a number of failed attempts to make it a profitable tourist business. Now it's operated by the Tiny Town Foundation, which donates 30 percent of the profits to charities and uses a lot of volunteers. Admission is low. It's open weekends only in May and September, and daily Memorial Day through Labor Day. Take C-470 to US 285, travel about 4 miles southwest on US 285, turn left onto Turkey Creek Road, and go about 0.25 mile. You'll see Tiny Town on the right.

ANNUAL EVENTS & FESTIVALS

L ove a lively parade or jumpin' jazz fest? Denver and its surrounding communities offer enough parades, concerts, rodeos, art shows, and ethnic celebrations—pick a reason, we've got a festival—to keep your calendar full year-round. And we've included as many as possible, from those with instantaneous name recognition, like the Cherry Creek Arts Festival, which draws more than a quarter-million people every July Fourth weekend, to the lesser-known ones like the Olde Golden Christmas, held in December in downtown Golden.

Our listings include events that happen every year. Some, such as the Bolder Boulder 10K run, are one-shot deals. Others, such as the World's Largest Christmas Lighting Display at the Denver City and County Building, may stretch out over weeks. For the most part these entries are confined to the Metro Denver area, but you'll notice that we've also covered events during the year at nearby ski areas and mountain communities. This list goes far afield: Cheyenne, Wyoming; Estes Park; and Colorado Springs—all easy day trips.

Our list should be viewed as a practical guide to those festivals and events with a designated date and location, but a few words of warning: Dates can change from year to year, so an event listed in September, for example, may actually turn out to be in October. A good source of last-minute information about special outdoor events is the calendar of events at denvergov.org (look for "Events & Attractions"). Also check the Friday weekend sections of the *Denver Post* and Boulder's *Daily Camera,* where the goings-on are listed in considerable detail, as well as *Westword,* Denver's leading weekly. Another reliable source for upcoming events is at visitdenver.org.

JANUARY

**ANNUAL COLORADO COWBOY
  POETRY GATHERING**
American Mountaineering Center
710 10th St., Golden
(303) 433-4949
coloradocowboygathering.com
Tales grow tall under a wide-open sky, and nobody spends more time under a wider sky than cowboys and cowgirls. Once a year in mid-January, the poetic cream of

the ranching and cowpunching community brings its Western oral tradition of tales and humor to Golden from Colorado and beyond. Expect about 40 poets, balladeers, and yodelers from 14 states and Australia to perform during the 4-day event. Guests can attend on-stage concerts as well as theme-poetry and Western music sessions.

COLORADO RV ADVENTURE TRAVEL SHOW

Colorado Convention Center
700 14th St.
(303) 892-6800, (800) 848-6247
gsevents.com

This is Metro Denver's version of hog heaven for the recreational vehicle enthusiast. Admire and wander through the 100 to 200 state-of-the-art recreational vehicles, see the latest in RV accessories, and meet exhibitors from lodges and resorts that cater to the RV crowd. This event is held in early January.

DENVER BOAT SHOW

Colorado Convention Center
700 14th St.
denverboatshow.com

This is boat-head heaven in early January. The year's biggest boat show usually lasts 4 days, spanning a weekend and jammed with aquatic craft, rubber rafts, and gear and accessories fore and aft. It's great fun to ogle at the huge luxury boats.

INTERNATIONAL SNOW SCULPTURE CHAMPIONSHIPS

Locations throughout Breckenridge
(970) 547-3100
gobreck.com/events/international-snow-sculpture-championships

In late January the city of Breckenridge lends its front-end loaders to fill wooden forms with 20-ton blocks of snow. Four-person sculpting teams from around the world climb on top and tromp and stomp until the snow is packed tight. The forms are removed, and what happens to each big block of snow is up to the contestants, who use only hand tools. Sculptures run the gamut from geometric to free-form to recognizable shapes and scenes. The sculptures

can last up to 10 days, depending on the weather. The event is free whether you participate or just watch.

INTERNATIONAL SPORTSMEN'S EXPOSITION

Colorado Convention Center
700 14th St.
(800) 545-6100
sportsexpos.com

This 4-day hunting and fishing show sometime in late January features products and services related to archery, firearms, and fishing. This is a how-to show with a lot of demonstrations designed to improve your hunting and fishing skills. You can sit in a U-shaped theater-seating section, for example, to watch a presenter onstage explain how he ties flies or wraps fishing rods. Video monitors allow you to see the small work. Top-name seminar speakers from magazines such as *Field and Stream* and *Outdoor Life* will be here. Expect around 350 exhibitors and crowds in the low 30,000s.

NATIONAL WESTERN STOCK SHOW & RODEO

National Western Complex
4655 Humboldt St. (Brighton Boulevard exit off I-70)
(303) 297-1166
nationalwestern.com

Founded in 1906, the National Western is the largest annual event in Denver—and it's growing. You'll be in the company of more than 600,000 people, but the event is spaced over 2 weeks in mid-January, so there's plenty of room and time to take in all the horses, sheep, cattle, chickens, and rabbits being exhibited by ranchers from miles around.

Rodeo events go on every day, with the nation's top horse and bull riders, calf ropers, you name it, competing for nearly $500,000 in prizes. Between the big events, you can see all kinds of oddball fun: rodeo clowns, Western battle recreations (cover the kids' ears if loud noises scare them), and a sheepdog herding sheep with a monkey in a cowboy suit riding on its back. Tickets to the Professional Bull Riders are the most expensive. The National Western begins with a colorful parade through downtown Denver.

Also check out what Denver calls the World's Largest Display of Christmas Lights at the City and County Building downtown. The lights are on from the first Thursday in December until January 1, but they're turned on at night during the stock show as well.

ULLR FEST
Locations throughout Breckenridge
(970) 453-5579, (800) 936-5573
gobreck.com/events/ullr-fest
Helmets with horns on them are the height of fashion at this free weeklong festival in honor of Ullr (pronounced "ooler"), the Norse god of snow. If you don't have a horned helmet, you will most certainly be able to find someone willing to sell you one. (They are also handed out free at the parade.) Ullr Fest starts on a Friday and runs for a week in early January. It includes a parade, kids' activities, and a variety of different events daily. Other activities include a version of The Dating Game, an ice-skating party, children's concert, and Ullympics competitions such as Broom Ball and volleyball with snowshoes.

FEBRUARY

BUFFALO BILL'S BIRTHDAY CELEBRATION
The Buffalo Bill Grave and Museum
987 1/2 Lookout Mountain Rd., Golden
(303) 526-0747
buffalobill.org
Each year, Colorado's most famous Wild West showman is celebrated on his birthday at the museum that bears his name. Buffalo Bill's remains are also buried on the Lookout Mountain site. Past celebrations have included bluegrass music, free ice cream and cake, and a birthday ceremony. Buffalo Bill lookalikes lend atmosphere, as does the buffalo chip–throwing contest. This party is held on a weekend close to Bill's February 26 birthday. Take I-70 west to exit 256, where the sign says Lookout Mountain and Buffalo Bill's Grave, and follow the well-placed signs to the top of Lookout Mountain. The celebration is free.

✳DENVER RESTAURANT WEEK
denver.org/denverrestaurant
For 2 weeks each winter from late February through early March, more than 300 area restaurants celebrate the local culinary scene. For a fixed "mile-high" price of $52.80 for two people, or, $26.40 for one (tax and tip not included), diners enjoy a special 3-course, prix-fixe dinner. It's a great way to try new restaurants or return to favorites.

REGISTRATION FOR RIDE THE ROCKIES
(303) 954-6700
ridetherockies.com
See the June entry, Ride the Rockies, for more on the largest and longest public group bicycling tour of the year, but right now is when you need to register if you're interested in taking part. It's a lottery, and you need to get on the stick if you want in.

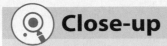 **Close-up**

Buffalo Bill

Buffalo Bill Cody died in January 1917. He lay in state in the Colorado State Capitol Building one weekend while 50,000 mourners and gawkers filed by. During the 6 months before he was buried, his body had to be embalmed six times. For his interment on June 3, next to what is now the Buffalo Bill Grave and Museum, 25,000 people walked or rode horses up the narrow Lookout Mountain Road. Bill had once said he wanted to be buried in Cody, Wyoming, a town he founded, and its residents thought that was a good idea. They threatened to steal the body, so Denver stationed a military tank at the grave. The plot was later covered with concrete, perhaps to seal Cody's final resting spot.

The *Denver Post,* sponsor of the ride, usually makes applications available in the first week of February, and they're due by the last week of February.

MARCH

DENVER AUTO SHOW
Colorado Convention Center
700 14th St.
(781) 237-5533
denverautoshow.com
Shop among, or just enjoy looking at, all the new cars under one roof. (No driving from lot to lot and being stalked by salespeople.) The show includes imports and domestics, sometimes exotics, futuristics, and prototypes. Attendance at this 5-day affair in late March or early April has exceeded 170,000.

DENVER HOME SHOW
National Western Complex
4655 Humboldt St. (take the Brighton Boulevard exit off I-70)
(800) 395-1350
homeshowdenver.com
There's nothing like a nice trade show in late March to get you ready for spring. This one showcases more than 500 experts willing to talk about home decor and home remodeling.

✴DENVER MARCH POW-WOW
Denver Coliseum
4600 Humboldt St. (take the Brighton Boulevard exit off I-70)
(303) 934-8045
denvermarchpowwow.org
Don't miss this one in mid- to late March. More than 1,000 Native Americans of tribes from most of the US as well as Canada dance simultaneously in full costume. At the edges of the dancing, groups of men surround huge drums and make the whole coliseum vibrate. The big en masse dancing and the Grand Entry happen all 3 days, with other activities scattered throughout. You'll get plenty of opportunities to see the costumes close up: The seats around you will be filled with Native American families related to the dancers. Costumed competitors will be sitting next to you and walking past you.

There's a modest Native American market downstairs. Expect between 40 and 50 drum groups to be at the powwow, along with representatives of 60 to 70 tribes and a total 3-day crowd in the neighborhood of 80,000. If you plan to bring a digital or video camera, you must purchase a permit.

ST. PATRICK'S DAY PARADE
Streets of downtown Denver
(303) 368-9861
denversaintpatricksdayparade.com
This is big, folks, the second-largest St. Patrick's Day parade in the country (New York City is first). The devil, you say. Yes, it's true. It never seems to end. Past parades have taken more than 4 hours for 250 floats, bands, and other colorful entrants to pass as clowns, leprechauns, and vendors ply the awesome crowds of spectators. There are ancillary events during the entire week, including the Running of the Green, a 5-kilometer race, and Irish entertainment at various pubs throughout town. Watch for complete details in the *Denver Post* or at denverpost.com.

WELLS FARGO SKI CUP
Winter Park Resort
Winter Park
(303) 293-5311
skifornscd.com
The Wells Fargo Ski Cup, the largest fundraiser of the year for the National Sports Center for the Disabled (NSCD), brings together world-class disabled ski racers, Denver Broncos alumni, and amateur skiers of all abilities. Teams of amateur skiers take to the slopes in the pro-am race, and a timing run enables casual skiers to compete against more aggressive skiers with racing experience. The *Denver Post* Celebrity Challenge brings together local media personalities, political leaders, and the occasional former football star, which team up with two racers from the NSCD's Winter Park Disabled Ski Team. The highlight of the weekend, the

World Disabled Invitational, is the only race in which disabled skiers compete head-to-head on parallel courses, a format used in professional racing events.

APRIL

EASTER SUNRISE SERVICE
Red Rocks Amphitheatre (north of Morrison on Hogback Road; take I-70 West to the Morrison exit, then go south), Morrison
redrocksonline.com
One of the most inspirational places you'll ever find for an Easter sunrise service is this gargantuan natural amphitheater of red sandstone facing east over the plains. The event is nondenominational, free, and open to the public, attracting upwards of 12,000 people. Gates open at 4:30 a.m., and music begins at 6 a.m. Dress warmly, because this is an outdoor service that has been cancelled only five times in six decades due to bad weather.

SPRING SPLASH/CLOSING DAY
Winter Park Resort, Winter Park
(970) 726-1564
winterparkresort.com
This is one of those events that public relations people love because they get to use the word "zany." In most years the sun is out, everybody wears sunglasses, and ski-babes in bikinis and ski-bozos in goofy costumes come barreling down the hill trying to hydroplane across a puddle of ice water. Most belly flop at the bottom with a big splash. The event is always held on the closing Sunday of the season (typically mid-April). It has become one of the quintessential Colorado outdoor spectacles, with viewers jockeying for position on the balconies of the base

lodge. Spectating is free; participating will cost you a lift ticket plus an entry fee.

MAY

✳**BOLDER BOULDER**
30th and Iris Streets, Boulder
(303) 444-7223
bolderboulder.com
Since 1979 the Bolder Boulder has been a Memorial Day tradition in this athletic college town. The 10K race that began with 2,700 participants has become one of the world's 10 largest road races. It now attracts more than 50,000 runners, walkers, and wheelchair racers, including professional racers who compete for the world's largest non-marathon prize purse. The largest group of entrants are the "citizens," who leave the starting line in 68 waves that take several hours to stage. Faster runners are assigned to the early waves and must qualify for them by proving they can run the course in 68 minutes or less. Slower participants, including walkers and walk/joggers, are assigned to the latter waves and tend to cover the 6.8-mile course at their own pace. The course winds its way through neighborhoods, around the downtown area, and into the University of Colorado's football stadium. Along the way, participants are cheered by more than 100,000 spectators who show their support by wearing costumes, belly dancing, spraying sweaty runners with a hose, and playing music of all types. (Don't be surprised to pass a formally dressed string quartet on one corner and a troupe of high-stepping grannies on the next.) The race starts at 30th Street and Walnut near the First National Bank of Boulder and finishes in Folsom Field. Registration fees start at about $48 for adults who preregister and

climb from there depending on how late you register and what kinds of race T-shirts or paraphernalia you'd like to include. Two things you should know: Baby strollers, pets, and in-line skates are not allowed, and local traffic slows to a standstill most of race day.

BOULDER CREEK FESTIVAL
Central Park and the Library-Municipal Building Complex, Canyon Boulevard (along the Boulder Creek Path), Boulder
(303) 449-3137
bouldercreekevents.com
In 1984 a group of volunteers agreed to meet along the banks of Boulder Creek over Memorial Day weekend to pick up trash along the 5.5-mile corridor from Eben G. Fine Park to the intersection of Pearl and 55th Streets. Their reward was an after-party that became so popular it turned into the Boulder Creek Festival. Now the trash cleanup is held the Saturday before Memorial Day weekend and is followed by a 3-day festival that attracts more than 400 exhibitors and 150,000 participants. Booths display arts and crafts, outdoor equipment and services, health alternatives, and technology. Performers dance and play music, and food and beverage vendors sell a wide range of edible treats. Admission and entertainment are free.

CINCO DE MAYO
Celebrate Culture Festival
Civic Center Park, between Colfax Avenue and 14th Street
(303) 534-8342
cincodemayodenver.com
This is Denver's celebration of its Hispanic heritage, the largest of its kind in the US, attracting more than 400,000 participants over 2 days in early May. Many confuse this with Mexican Independence Day, which is

on September 16. Cinco de Mayo is held in remembrance of La Batalla de Puebla, the Battle of Ciudad Puebla, which took place during the Mexican battle for independence from France. Mexicans, equipped with little more than farm implements, whipped one of the greatest armies on earth, although the French came back 5 days later and made up for it. Still, it's a spiritual moment for Mexico and has become a big holiday in Denver. It starts with the Celebrate Culture parade, intended to celebrate diversity, and a traditional mariachi mass in the park's Greek Amphitheater. Past celebrations included 250 exhibitors, a carnival, arts and foods, entertainment on six stages, ethnic-fashionwear showings, and Latin, jazz, rap, and contemporary music. Activities are also provided for children. The event is free.

DENVER BOTANIC GARDENS PLANT AND BOOK SALE
Denver Botanic Gardens
1007 York St.
(720) 865-3500
botanicgardens.org
The gardens' annual plant and book sale serves as the unofficial start of the gardening season for hundreds of Denver-area green thumbs. Held over 2 days, it's one of the facility's most popular fund-raisers, offering thousands of flowers, herbs, and vegetables that are especially suited to Colorado's climate. Among the most popular in recent drought years are the water-smart plants, although regulars plan their beds around the large stock of annuals, roses, water plants, and perennials. Crowds can be fierce, especially during the first few hours of the sale, and parking is limited. Additional parking is available at Cheesman Park. A fund-raiser plant sale preview party takes place the day before the sale begins, with a limited number of tickets available. Admission to the general sale is free.

FURRY SCURRY
Washington Park, East Louisiana Avenue and Downing Street
(303) 751-5772
ddfl.org
This annual 2-mile walk/run for humans and their canines benefits the Denver Dumb Friends League. Participants register for a fee and collect pledges as well. Dogs on leashes are welcome if they are at least 6 months old, have been spayed or neutered, and have current ID and rabies tags. Treats are available for people and their pets along the route and at the finish line. The event is usually held the first weekend in May.

i Find specifics on festivals and events each week by looking at the Friday sections of the *Denver Post,* and Boulder's *Daily Camera.* Also check the events listings in Denver's weekly, *Westword.*

JUNE

✳BRECKENRIDGE MUSIC FESTIVAL
Riverwalk Performing Arts Center
Park Avenue and Four O'Clock Road, Breckenridge
(970) 453-9142
breckenridgemusicfestival.com
Nearly every day from mid-June to mid-August, visitors can enjoy performances by the National Repertory Orchestra, the Breckenridge Music Festival Orchestra, and nationally know performers, such as the Glenn Miller Orchestra. More than 45 concerts showcase classical, jazz, show tunes, and children's music.

CAPITOL HILL PEOPLE'S FAIR
Civic Center Park
Between Colfax Avenue and 14th Street
(303) 830-1651
chundenver.org

Capitol Hill is one of Denver's most colorful and historic neighborhoods. The annual festival that raises money for its neighborhood organization has, for more than 30 years, been held on the first weekend in June. Organizers claim this event is Colorado's largest arts and crafts festival, with about 500 exhibitors as well as food, dance, and entertainment on six stages, and kids' activities such as minigolf, face painting, and more. In past years it has attracted crowds of 275,000; admission is free.

CHERRY BLOSSOM FESTIVAL
Sakura Square, Lawrence Street
(between 19th and 20th Streets)
(303) 295-1844
cherryblossomdenver.org

This celebration of Japanese culture is held at Sakura Square, the heart of Denver's Japanese community. If you love Japanese food, check out the food made by volunteers in the adjacent Denver Buddhist Temple. Also watch martial arts displays, bonsai demonstrations, taiko drumming, poetry singing, and traditional folk dancing. The festival, held in late June or early July, is free and open to the public. Food and beverages may be purchased.

COLORADO RENAISSANCE FESTIVAL
Off I-25 South, Larkspur
(303) 688-6010
coloradorenaissance.com

Renaissance festivals are ripping good fun, and this is truly one of the best. Spread out across a huge site beneath the trees, the festival re-creates a 16th-century marketplace filled with costumed characters and ruled by King Henry and Queen Anne. More than 200 costumed crafters sell handmade goods. One of the main attractions is the battling, strutting, and jousting by knights on foot and horseback. You'll also enjoy strolling minstrels, jesters, jugglers, medieval food, rides, and games galore for 8 weekends in June and July. From Metro Denver, take I-25 South to the Larkspur exit, then follow the signs to the festival.

*DENVER CHALK ART FESTIVAL
LoDo
(303) 534-2367
denverchalkart.com

More than 200 artists transform the streets of Larimer Square into a colorful museum of chalk art. Lasting 2 days, the festival gives attendees the opportunity to see art being created while they watch. Vivid pastel chalks bring the drawings to life and the end result is an amazing mix of old-master styles, modern, and the surreal. The festival is free of charge.

DENVER PRIDEFEST
Civic Center Park
(303) 733-7743
glbtcolorado.org/pridefest.aspx

The fourth-largest pride festival in the US, the 2-day Denver Pridefest celebrates Colorado's gay and lesbian community with a large parade, live entertainment, cultural programming, dancing, arts, crafts, food, and plenty of celebrating. Everyone is welcome.

ELEPHANT ROCK CYCLING FESTIVAL
Douglas County Fairgrounds
Castle Rock
(303) 282-9020
elephantrockride.com

With bike tours of various lengths—from the 8-mile family loop to the 25-mile fat-tire course to road bike routes of 32, 50, 65, and 100 miles—the Elephant Rock festival is a bicyclist's paradise. Held the first Sunday in June, the event begins and ends in the Douglas County Fairgrounds and sends participants down country roads and through rolling hills, across ranch lands, and through the Black Forest. The free Kids' Race is held on a special loop around the area. Entry fees vary by the length of the course. To reach the Fair Grounds, take I-25 south from Denver to exit 181 east.

ESTES PARK WOOL MARKET
Stanley Park Fair Grounds, Community
Drive off US Highway 36, Estes Park
(970) 586-6104
estesparkcvb.com

Sheep ranching is a big part of Colorado's history and economy. This event, held in mid-June, is dedicated to those who raise and shear them. You'll find spinning and weaving classes; dyeing classes; showings of sheep, llamas, and alpacas; spinning and weaving demonstrations and contests; spinning wheels for sale; and commercial exhibits related to the wool industry. All events are free, but you'll pay to park.

GREEK FESTIVAL
Assumption Greek Orthodox Cathedral
4610 E. Alameda Ave.
(303) 388-9314
assumptioncathedral.org

Assumption Greek Orthodox Cathedral, with its gold dome, is a familiar landmark. Denver's Greeks and Grecophiles convene on the church grounds each year in mid-June for "wonderful food prepared by the ladies of our church," live music, and Greek dance shows done by groups ranging in age from children to adults. Calamari, moussaka, baklava, Aegean beer, wine, and beverages are served, and there is usually a gift shop and a small carnival area for kids. All proceeds benefit the church and its charitable partners.

GREELEY STAMPEDE
Greeley
(800) 982-2855
greeleystampede.org

Held for 2 weeks in late June and early July (around July 4th), this long-running rodeo began in 1922. It features the usual events: bronc riding, bull riding, team roping, barrel racing, and a kid's rodeo, along with a demolition derby, entertainment, and food. There's also a Western art show, carnival midway, and other free stage entertainment.

RIDE THE ROCKIES
Statewide, a different route every year
(303) 954-6700
ridetherockies.com

If you have thighs like a *Tyrannosaurus rex*, Ride the Rockies is for you. At the very least, participants should be experienced bike riders who are comfortable covering at least 50 miles a day. To enjoy the event, they also should be accustomed to riding at high altitudes and climbing mountain passes that leave small cars choking for air. This event lasts 6 to 7 days, during which time a stream of about 2,000 bicyclists push their pedals for more than 400 miles. Past trips have taken them through such resort towns as Steamboat Springs, Telluride, Copper Mountain, and Vail and more "everyday" towns such as Walsenberg, Durango, Cortez, and Granby. At night they camp on high-school sports fields or in their gyms. Communities provide nightly low-cost meals and various forms of entertainment. This is a very popular event, and the number of participants is limited. The event's title sponsor, the *Denver Post*, holds a lottery in February. If you win, you're in. The registration fee includes camping space, restrooms and showers, transportation of one suitcase, a jersey, aid stations, and medical support.

SCANDINAVIAN MIDSUMMER FESTIVAL
Bond Park
Virginia Street and Elkhorn Avenue, Estes Park
estesmidsummer.com
June 24 is midsummer in the Scandinavian countries, which prompts their biggest celebration next to Christmas. Estes Park's version of the big, traditional Scandinavian festival features arts and crafts, ethnic foods, educational mini-seminars and demonstrations, and the raising of the maypole with appropriate Scandinavian folk dancers every hour. At least one dance group usually comes from Scandinavia. There's also a bonfire, which is how Norwegians celebrate midsummer. Not surprisingly, this free festival is held the Friday and Saturday closest to June 24. There's no phone number; so use the website listed or write to info@estesmidsummer.com for more information.

SUMMER CONCERT SERIES
Arvada Center for the Arts and Humanities
6901 Wadsworth Blvd., Arvada
(720) 898-7200 (box office)
arvadacenter.org/summer/events
For a mixture of country, Big Band, jazz, and Cajun music, come to the Arvada Center's outdoor amphitheater. You can picnic on the grounds before the shows and browse the art gallery. If you'd like, you may bring your picnic inside for the concert. The center also stages a musical every summer.

✳SUMMER CONCERT SERIES
Denver Botanic Gardens
1007 York St.
(720) 865-3500 (information recording)
(720) 865-3585 (information desk)
(866) 468-7624 (tickets)
concerts.botanicgardens.org
Sitting on the grass in the midst of the Denver Botanic Gardens on a summer evening is a great way to listen to world-class artists. Past performers have included Shawn Colvin, Al Green, Arlo Guthrie, k.d. lang, Diana Krall, Gipsy Kings, Los Lobos, Natalie Merchant, Nanci Griffith, and Keb Mo. This series of outdoor concerts is aimed at families in an informal setting. Bring an elegant picnic and a blanket and you're set for a fun evening. Tickets go early, so buy them in the spring if you intend to go.

YELLOW ROSE BALL: OPENING NIGHT
Central City Opera House
124 Eureka St., Central City
(303) 292-6500
centralcityopera.org
In late June or early July, the Central City Opera's season begins, usually with the annual presentation of debutantes

called the Central City Flower Girls, followed by a dinner at the Teller House and a performance.

JULY

BUFFALO BILL DAYS
Locations throughout Golden
(303) 279-3342
buffalobilldays.com
The city of Golden hosts this Western celebration, which started in Buffalo Bill's honor, on the last weekend of July. It includes a parade and other activities on Main Street and in Parfet Park, 10th Street and Washington Avenue, and Clear Creek Living History Park. Enjoy a variety of events such as a pancake breakfast, lots of musical entertainment, a golf tournament, a classic car show, living-history reenactments, Mutton Bustin', and a duck race. Admission is free.

✴CHERRY CREEK ARTS FESTIVAL
Cherry Creek North (on 2nd and 3rd Avenues between Clayton and Steele Streets)
(303) 355-2787
cherryarts.org
Pulling some 350,000 visitors for this event, Denver's upscale retail shopping area hosts a sidewalk festival during Fourth of July weekend that features fine arts and crafts. About 200 artists from around the nation and Mexico come for the juried show. National and international performers provide entertainment. Local chefs cook up their best for a block-long culinary arts extravaganza. Browsing is free, but prepare to pay top dollar for the artworks.

✴CHEYENNE FRONTIER DAYS
Frontier Park, Cheyenne, WY
(800) 227-6336 or (307) 778-7222
cfdrodeo.com
This is a 9-day Western extravaganza centered around rodeo events, but it also includes a carnival, evening shows by some of the biggest names in country-western music (in past years Toby Keith, Willie Nelson, Dwight Yoakam, Alan Jackson, Rascal Flatts, Lady Antebellum, and Chris LeDoux), parades, free pancake breakfasts, a chili cook-off, a performance by the Air Force Thunderbirds team, and a free entertainment area with music and other acts. Cheyenne is only 100 miles from Denver, so it makes an easy day trip. About 300,000 people show up during Frontier Days, but parking is generally no problem in the gravel lots around the stadium. The event starts on a Friday and runs through the last weekend in July. To get to Frontier Park, take I-25 North to Central Avenue (exit 12). Go east on 8th Avenue and turn right. After 0.25 mile, turn right onto Carey Avenue. The park is on your left.

COLORADO DRAGON BOAT FESTIVAL
Sloan's Lake Park, Lakewood
(303) 953-7277
cdbf.org
The only one of its kind in the US, this family-friendly festival highlights Colorado's Asian Pacific American heritage. Along with 2 days of intensely competitive dragon boat races across the lake, there are performing arts presentations, food, and arts and crafts. Folk and contemporary dance troupes, a variety of musical groups, the Denver Taiko drum ensemble, and other groups perform throughout the festival. Shop at the Asian Marketplace, and eat your way across Asia by sampling cuisine from China, Japan,

Korea, Thailand, Vietnam, Laos, and the Philippines. Dragonland is a separate kids' area with activities and performances geared toward the younger attendees. Admittance is free. Parking around the lake is congested; instead, park at Sports Authority Field for $5 and take the free shuttle buses that run every few minutes to the festival.

INDEPENDENCE DAY CELEBRATION
Four Mile Historic Park
715 S. Forest St.
(303) 399-1859
fourmilepark.org
Four Mile Historic Park, Denver's living-history park, throws a good old-fashioned, family-style Fourth of July party each year. This is a day of patriotic music, games, food, and visits from costumed actors such as Abraham Lincoln, Thomas Jefferson, and Uncle Sam who do historical reenactments. Past events also included historic and craft demonstrations such as blacksmithing, quilting, weaving, lace making, and butter churning.

INDEPENDENCE DAY EVE CELEBRATION
July 3
Civic Center Park
What do you get when you combine a free patriotic concert by the Colorado Symphony, a dazzling light show on the Denver City and County Building, and a spectacular fireworks show? A great preholiday kickoff to the July 4th celebration! Bring a blanket, low-rise beach chairs, and picnic before the show. Space is available on a first-come, first-served basis, so plan to arrive at least 2 to 3 hours early for a prime location. Food is also available. Park in one of many nearby downtown surface lots or parking garages just a few blocks from the park.

✳KAISER PERMANENTE MOONLIGHT CLASSIC
State Capitol
Broadway and Colfax Street
(720) 974-2457
moonlight-classic.com
Imagine cycling through the deserted streets of downtown Denver with the glow of the moon defining the course for you. Imagine doing so alongside thousands of other riders. The Moonlight Classic begins and ends at the State Capitol. The 10-mile course passes through the business district, LoDo, and by landmarks such as Coors Field and the Cherry Creek shopping district. The event benefits InnovAge Foundation and is followed by the Lunar Breakfast, a breakfast with music and prizes. The first wave of cyclists leaves at 8:30 p.m., and all must have helmets and front and back lights and reflectors. Note: The ride takes place in August on some years.

LAKEWOOD ON PARADE
Jefferson County Sports Stadium
500 Kipling St., at 6th Avenue, Lakewood
(303) 225-7680
The city of Lakewood's community festival, this free event is often centered on a theme such as Celebrating Our Troops. Although there's no longer a parade, the festival typically combines food, games, live music and other entertainment, a golf tournament, a beer garden, a car show, and an art show. End the day with a fireworks show.

PIKES PEAK INTERNATIONAL HILL CLIMB
Pikes Peak, outside Colorado Springs
(719) 685-4400
ppihc.com

You can enjoy this famous annual Pikes Peak hill climb even if you're not one of the top race-car drivers who come here to test their skills on one of Colorado's 14,000-foot peaks. But you do need tickets ($40) ahead of time to drive up, park, and watch the race from designated areas on the mountain. In preceding weeks other smaller races lead up to this big race, held the last week of June or first week of July.

☀NHRA MOPAR MILE-HIGH NATIONALS
Bandimere Speedway
3051 S. Rooney Rd., Morrison
(303) 697-6001, (800) 644-8946 (tickets)
bandimere.com
This is motorhead heaven. Between 600 and 700 cars and the nation's top racers gather for 3 days of competition in pro-stock dragsters, top fuel cars, motorcycles, and nitro funny cars in mid-July. All seats are reserved. Tickets can be purchased far in advance from the website, in person at the box office, or by phone at the number above.

ROOFTOP RODEO
Estes Park Fairgrounds
Community Drive off US 36,
Estes Park
(970) 586-6104
rooftoprodeo.com
Repeatedly voted Best Small Rodeo of the Year, this 6-day event in mid-July offers a rodeo parade and six Professional Rodeo Cowboy Association rodeos. These are joined on various days by music concerts, a golf benefit, and other activities. The Queen's Dance is held after the rodeo, hosted by the Rooftop Rodeo Queen and Royalty, and the entire community comes to celebrate Western heritage and practice the two-step.

Other past attractions include cowboy cartoonists and poets, and a dirt dance. The rodeo parade is free; admission is charged for the rodeo.

AUGUST

ADAMS COUNTY FAIR AND RODEO
Adams County Fairgrounds
9755 Henderson Rd., Brighton
(303) 637-8000
adamscountyfair.com
Adams County claims the largest county fair in Colorado, and it has included such attractions as rodeos, tractor pulls, more than 150 exhibits and livestock shows, 4-H events, a demolition derby, a children's pavilion, a petting zoo, a classic car show, a multicultural village, an artisans bazaar, free entertainment, and top-name concerts. Past entertainers include Alan Jackson and Mel Tillis. There's also a Mexican Cultural Day at the fair. Look for this event the first weekend in August. Admission to the fair is free; parking costs $5. There's an admission fee for the rodeo, truck pull, demolition derby, and Day of the Family entertainment event. To reach the fairgrounds, take I-76 north from Denver to US 85 (exit 12) and follow it north to Henderson Road. Turn left there.

CARNATION FESTIVAL
Albert E. Anderson Park
44th and Field Streets, Wheat Ridge
thecarnationfestival.com
Wheat Ridge was founded by farmers who supplied Denver with wheat, produce, and, in the 1940s, carnations. Still going strong after more than 40 years, the Carnation Festival celebrates that heritage with a jolly small-town parade along 38th Street from Harlan to Upham Streets on the third weekend in

August. Some floats are covered with carnations, but most just carry bigwigs and their families. The carnival in the park has rides for children, and the carnival midway has food and arts and crafts. There's also entertainment, a spaghetti dinner, a chili cook-off, a beer garden, a classic car show, and an art show. Enjoy a fireworks display on Friday night. Admission is free.

COLORADO SCOTTISH FESTIVAL AND HIGHLAND GAMES

Highlands Heritage Park
9651 S. Quebec St., Highlands Ranch
(303) 238-6524
scottishgames.org

Wake up and smell the heather early each August. Enjoy the competitions: bagpiping and drumming, highland athletic events, and highland dancing. You'll also find vendors selling merchandise from the British Isles, exhibitions of highland cattle and dogs, and Scottish food and beverages. Take C-470 east to Quebec Street and go south to the intersection with Lincoln Avenue. The park is on the southwest.

✳COLORADO STATE FAIR

State Fairgrounds
1001 Beulah Ave., Pueblo
(719) 561-8484, (800) 876-4567
coloradostatefair.com

The city of Pueblo is 2 hours south of Denver on I-25, but this is the state fair. It's one of the state's largest annual events and is well worth the drive. In addition to the full range of rodeo events, expect parades, art exhibitions, a Latin Fiesta Weekend, livestock sales, horse shows, cooking competitions, midway carnival rides, games, and lots of good food. Big-name entertainers in past years have included Pat Benatar, Tom Jones, Bob Dylan,

Chicago, and Julio Iglesias. The fair runs for 2 weeks, late August to early September.

DOUGLAS COUNTY FAIR

Douglas County Fairgrounds
500 Fairgrounds Dr., Castle Rock
(720) 733-6900
douglascountyfairandrodeo.com

This is an old-fashioned August shindig with a rodeo, carnival, and all the accoutrements. Simultaneously with the county fair, Castle Rock holds a community fair that includes a parade to celebrate the 4-H winners, with more than 100 parade entries and a barbecue in the Courthouse Square.

GENUINE JAZZ & WINE FESTIVAL

Copper Mountain Resort
(866) 837-2996 (ticket sales)
genuinejazz.com

Copper Mountain's 3-day jazz festival in late August features Colorado artists as well as national headliners such as Stanley Jordan. The ticketed music fills the Conference Center Ballroom and free music happens out on the deck of the center. Evening impromptu sessions take place at local bars. Along with listening to smooth jazz, fans also have the opportunity to taste excellent wines from around the world. Prices vary depending on which shows and wine tastings are attended.

GILPIN COUNTY HISTORICAL SOCIETY'S ANNUAL CEMETERY CRAWL

Various historic cemeteries in Central City
(303) 582-5283
gilpinhistory.org

Lend an ear to the living dead at this entertaining and educational event portraying the life of Gilpin County 100 years ago.

Members and friends of the Gilpin County Historical Society transform into "spirits" of former residents, leaders, and movers and shakers of the period. The spirits share their stories as visitors walk through a different historic cemetery each year in mid-August.

MOUNTAIN MELODIES MUSIC FESTIVAL
Buffalo Bill Grave and Museum
987 1/2 Lookout Mountain Rd., Golden
(303) 526-0744 or (303) 526-0747
buffalobill.org
Focusing on bluegrass and string bands, this annual festival highlights both established and new Colorado music groups. Bring a picnic and blankets or lawn chairs and bask in the warm summer air while enjoying spectacular views of the Continental Divide, Pikes Peak, and the Denver skyline. Food is also available at the full cafe located in the gift shop. While you're here, visit the museum and Buffalo Bill's grave. The event is free.

✳ROCKY MOUNTAIN FOLKS FESTIVAL
US Highway 36, Lyons (on the way to Estes Park)
(800) 624-2422
bluegrass.com/folks
This festival in mid-August features folk, bluegrass, blues, and Americana music performers, in the past including Warren Haynes, Indigo Girls, Jackson Browne, Taj Mahal, Norah Jones, and Rufus Wainwright. There is also the Song School, with workshops and activities geared toward future musicians, and a song seminar that includes sessions on songwriting, copyrighting, and bookkeeping. Situated along the idyllic St. Vrain River, this is one of Colorado's favorite musical festivals. Campsites are available for an additional fee.

SCULPTURE IN THE PARK
Benson Sculpture Garden
29th and Taft Streets, Loveland
(970) 663-2940
sculptureinthepark.org
Loveland bills this as one of the largest and finest outdoor juried exhibitions of sculpture in the US. The Benson Sculpture Garden ordinarily is home to about 40 pieces, but on this day during the second weekend in August, it attracts about 170 artists from around the world who show over 2,000 pieces and sell their work. The event features entertainment, demonstrations by artists, a silent auction, and speed-sculpting (artists who sculpt while you watch). Proceeds from this event buy new art for the garden.

USA PRO CYCLING CHALLENGE
usaprocyclingchallenge.com
Colorado is home to the USA Pro Cycling Challenge, the most demanding bike race ever held on American soil. Every August, after 7 days of riding through some of the most picturesque terrain in the world, professional riders sprint into Denver's Civic Center Park on the final stage for an epic finish and a day of parties for spectators.

WESTERN WELCOME WEEK
Various locations in Littleton
(303) 794-4870
westernwelcomeweek.com
This is Littleton's big yearly celebration, which runs for 10 days beginning the second Thursday in August. You'll find arts and crafts and continuous entertainment on Littleton's Main Street, with a circus, a parade, concerts, fireworks, a barbecue, pancake breakfasts, and used-book sales. Most events are free.

WINTER PARK FAMOUS FLAMETHROWERS HIGH ALTITUDE CHILI COOKOFF

The Village, Winter Park
(303) 316-1689
winterparkresort.com

Held toward the end of August, this 2-day event is an opportunity to sample different types of chili and salsa produced especially for the cook-off. Costumed chili chefs vie for the Flamethrower title. Guests can buy tickets to sample entries each day after they have been judged. The festival has been going for more than 30 years, and attendees can expect good music, wacky contests, and lots of wild slicing, dicing, and simmering. The event benefits the National Sports Center for the Disabled.

SEPTEMBER

✳AIDS WALK COLORADO

Cheesman Park, between 8th and 13th Avenues east of Lafayette Street
(303) 861-9255
aidswalkcolorado.org

Every year thousands of people converge on Cheesman Park in late August to raise money for the Colorado AIDS Project and other AIDS organizations throughout the state. From there they follow a 10-kilometer walking route that brings them back to the park for the Celebration of Life Festival. This after-walk party has live music and other entertainment, food, a beer garden, the Diva Dash Stiletto Fun Run, and a volleyball tournament.

BRECKENRIDGE FESTIVAL OF FILM

Various locations in Breckenridge
(970) 453-6200
breckfilmfest.com

This 4-day fest includes premieres of documentaries, feature films, and children's features as well as parties in local clubs and bars. Past years have seen visits by James Earl Jones, Mary Steenburgen, Elliott Gould, and Angie Dickinson. The Peak Ten Pass costs $199 and includes admission to all the films and events, plus a festival T-shirt.

CASTLE ROCK ARTFEST

Town Hall and Philip Miller Library parking lots
Castle Rock
(303) 688-4597
castlerockartfest.com

This arts festival is held in mid-September, with family entertainment, cultural activities, live music, and food. It features more than 170 artists displaying, selling, and working in a full range of media. There is an admission fee but parking is free. Pets are not allowed.

COLORADO BALLOON CLASSIC

Memorial Park, Pikes Peak Avenue and Union Boulevard, Colorado Springs
(719) 471-4833
balloonclassic.com

The Balloon Classic is a grand spectacle. Typically about 125 hot-air balloons from around the nation are invited to ascend en masse at 7 a.m. on Saturday, Sunday, and Monday of Labor Day weekend. They are preceded by the "dawn patrol," about five balloons going up at 5:30 a.m. and dangling strobe lights, just to let folks know that the big event is coming. About 50 balloons light up Saturday and Sunday nights in the "Balloon Glo." (Albuquerque trademarked the name "Balloon Glow," so the folks in the Springs had to drop the "w.") Other regular events include live entertainment, food vendors, balloon rides, photo contest, and evening concerts on Saturday and Sunday. Admission is free.

CORN MAZE
Denver Botanic Gardens at Chatfield
8500 W. Deer Creek Canyon Rd., Littleton
(720) 865-4336
botanicgardens.org/corn-maze
Each fall the Botanic Gardens folks create a winding maze through 8 acres of cornfield, providing kids and adults with a giant puzzle to figure out. Average time to navigate the tricky pathways and dead-ends and find the way out is approximately an hour. Hayrides and pony rides are available, and a variety of fall foods, including fresh-squeezed lemonade, funnel cakes, and kettle corn, are offered by vendors.

THE FESTIVAL OF MOUNTAIN AND PLAIN: A TASTE OF COLORADO
Civic Center Park, between Colfax
Avenue and 14th Street
(303) 295-6330
atasteofcolorado.com
One of Denver's largest annual gatherings, A Taste of Colorado runs 4 days over the Labor Day weekend and attracts more than 400,000 people. Organizers usually even block off a couple of streets. You can sample culinary delights from more than 50 Metro Denver restaurants, so it's a good way to find new restaurants. In addition to the food, the festival offers entertainment on seven stages, kids' activities, cooking demonstrations, arts and crafts booths, a carnival midway, stages with live entertainment, and a kaleidoscope of buskers and vendors. Entertainment is free; food can be purchased with tickets.

✳GREAT AMERICAN BEER FESTIVAL
Colorado Convention Center
700 14th St.
(303) 447-0816
greatamericanbeerfestival.com
This is the king of America's beer festivals and the largest commercial beer competition in the world. In 2012 the festival sold out months in advance, a mere 45 minutes after registration opened. It's usually held in late September or early October. Bring an ID that proves you are at least 21 and a designated driver because more than 2,700 festival beers will be available to taste, the product of some 580-plus American breweries, microbreweries, and brewpubs.

LONGS PEAK SCOTTISH-IRISH HIGHLAND FESTIVAL
In the Stanley Park area; evening events
at various locations in Estes Park
(970) 586-6308
scotfest.com
Held the weekend after Labor Day, the Highland Festival celebrates the Celtic tradition for 4 straight days—Thursday night through Sunday night—with performances and competitions by bagpipe bands, highland dancers, Irish step dancers, highland dogs herding sheep, and Scottish athletes throwing the hammer and the caber. There are parades, medieval reenactments and folk concerts, performances on the Celtic harp, and fiddle and tin-whistle contests. Each year organizers schedule a special seminar topic such as Scots and the military. Expect to pay a daily gate fee.

MINIATURE & DOLL FALL SHOW AND SALE

Doubletree Hotel Denver Tech Center
7801 E. Orchard Rd., Greenwood Village
(303) 651-6856 or (970) 224-3806
dmmdt.org
This is a benefit for the Denver Museum of Miniatures, Dolls & Toys, though the show and sale is never held at the tiny museum. It typically includes more than 100 national artists who specialize in making miniatures, dolls, teddy bears, and toys. They display and sell their wares during a 2-day weekend in mid-September. The sale is preceded by 3 days of workshops that are open to the public but require preregistration. Based on a different theme each year, the event also includes food, a banquet, seminars, an auction, workshops, and a theme brunch.

OKTOBERFEST

Larimer Square, Larimer Street (between 14th and 15th Streets)
(720) 255-1001
thedenveroktoberfest.com
Denver's main bow to the famous harvest festival of Munich (and the nation's second-largest Oktoberfest celebration, according to sponsors) is filled with polka bands and beer-drinking and sausage-eating fun. You'll see plenty of jolly Germanic costumes. One of the highlights of Larimer Square's festival year, this event is free unless you eat and drink. Oktoberfest includes Kinderplatz, a kids' area that has included Prince Ludwig's Castle, where kids can enjoy the Black Forest Maze and German storytellers, "the world's shortest parade," and more than 100 opportunities to do the Chicken Dance. The festival is usually held over 2 weekends in later September.

SPANISH COLONIAL & WESTERN ART MARKET AND 1830S RENDEZVOUS

The Fort Restaurant
19192 Colorado Hwy. 8, Morrison
(303) 697-4771
tesoroculturalcenter.org
Each September, Morrison's unique Fort Restaurant opens its gates to a quintessentially Western event. Fine Spanish artists from Colorado and New Mexico gather on the grounds to display and sell their creations. They're joined by reenactors dressed as 1830s-era mountain men, trappers, traders, and interpreters for a weekend of entertainment, storytelling, competition, and dancing. A patron preview party is held on Friday night, followed by the market on Saturday and Sunday. To get to the Fort from downtown Denver, take I-70 west to C-470 (exit 260). Follow C-470 south to US 285 south (Fairplay exit), then go 1.5 miles to the Highway 8 Morrison exit. The Fort is on the right.

Nature's Annual Events

Nature puts on her own annual events: the changing of the aspen in the fall, which draws Denverites out of the city to high-country roads; the ritual of elk bugling from mid-September to mid-October at Rocky Mountain National Park; and the blooming of a sea of irises at Long's Gardens, 3240 Broadway, Boulder, in late May/early June, where you can gaze at, photograph, or dig your own iris clumps for a reasonable price.

SUMMERSET FESTIVAL

Clement Park, Bowles Avenue and Pierce
Street, Littleton
(303) 973-9155
summersetfest.com

This end-of-summer (second weekend after Labor Day) outdoor celebration generally draws more than 40,000 people. Events include hot-air balloons, a muscle car show, three stages of entertainment, fireworks, a fishing derby, a pancake breakfast, a softball tournament, midway games, arts and crafts booths, and a skate festival. Admission is free.

OCTOBER

BOO AT THE ZOO

Denver Zoo in City Park
East 23rd Avenue and Steele Street
(303) 376-4800
denverzoo.org/event/boo-zoo

Celebrate Halloween at the zoo on the last weekend in October. More than 25 trick-or-treat stations are set up throughout the zoo, and kids get a food or toy item at each door. There is also a medieval village offering story-telling, creepy-crawly animal demonstrations, and face painting. The family-friendly event is free with paid admission to the zoo.

CIDER DAYS HARVEST FESTIVAL

Lakewood's Heritage Center
801 S. Yarrow St., Lakewood
(303) 987-7850
lakewood.org/ciderdays

In the early 20th century, apple trees were so common in Lakewood that the area was called Cider Hill. On the first weekend in October, the town celebrates its heritage with demonstrations of cider making, antique farm machinery, mule-drawn wagon and barrel train rides, a vintage tractor-pull

competition, food vendors, arts and crafts, and live music.

DENVER BEER FEST

Various Denver locations
denverbeerfest.com

Coinciding with the Great American Beer Festival, this 9-day event includes brewery tours, beer tastings, beer-paired dinners, and more than 140 other beer-related events. There's also a "Denver beer crawl," involving a dozen bars and breweries as well as prizes that include tickets for the Great American Beer Festival.

✳DENVER ZOMBIE CRAWL

Skyline Park to 16th Street Mall
Saturday closest to October 22
eyeheartbrains.com

Every October, thousands of the walking dead stagger and shuffle down the 16th Street Mall in this playfully macabre public parade. Zombie Crawls are held all over the world, but the Denver event is one of the largest. All ages are welcome and the event is free, but undead participants are asked to bring a nonperishable food item to donate to the Food Bank of the Rockies. Zombies don't attack their own kind, so you'll be safer if you come in costume. Maybe.

GREAT PUMPKIN HARVEST FESTIVAL

Four Mile Historic Park
715 S. Forest St.
(720) 865-0800
fourmilepark.org

Usually held in early October, this event takes place in the park's 12-acre historic farm. Activities include old-time music, games, dancing, hayrides, a pie-eating contest, and scarecrow making. The event is free, and pumpkins are available for sale.

PUMPKIN FESTIVAL AT CHATFIELD NATURE PRESERVE
8500 Deer Creek Canyon Rd., Littleton
(303) 973-3705
botanicgardens.org/pumpkin-festival
Bring a wheelbarrow and pick your own pumpkin(s) from the pumpkin patch. From tennis-ball size to behemoth, the sale of these orange globes raises money for the arboretum. There are also hay-rack rides, face painting, free amusement rides for kids, pumpkin-themed activities, and crafts and food booths. This event lasts from Friday through Sunday. Take C-470 to the Wadsworth exit, then follow Wadsworth south to Deer Creek Canyon Road. Turn right; the entrance is 0.25 mile down on the left.

NOVEMBER

BOTANIC GARDENS HOLIDAY SALE
Denver Botanic Gardens
1007 York St.
(720) 865-3500
botanicgardens.org
Plants are for sale as well as herbs, oils, and vinegars that volunteers have been producing all year long. Ornaments, handcrafted items, specialty foods, collectibles and seasonal items, and clothing are also available. You'll find books on gardening, tools, and other botany-related subjects. Usually held on a weekend before Thanksgiving, the sale costs $8 for adults, which includes admission to the gardens. A preview party the evening before the sale begins includes wine, hard cider, desserts, and holiday entertainment.

DENVER ARTS WEEK
(303) 892-1112 (Visit Denver)
denver.org/denverartsweek

Denver's vibrant arts scene is celebrated with more than 300 events in the city's galleries, museums, theaters, and performing arts venues. Admission is heavily discounted or free, and many local hotels offer special rates for the week. The week kicks off with the First Friday Artwalk held in several art districts around the city. Another highlight is Night at the Museums with free admission to more than a dozen museums. They stay open late, and a complimentary shuttle helps people "museum-hop" around town.

L'ESPRIT DE NOEL HOME TOUR & BOUTIQUE
Locations in Denver vary each year
(303) 292-6500
centralcityopera.org/lesprit
Each year the Central City Opera Guild stages this fund-raiser to support the opera's education and community programs. Local florists donate their time to decorate upscale homes for the holiday season, then open the finished products for 3 days of tours. It's held the weekend before Thanksgiving, featuring homes in high-end developments. The event is kicked off with a patron preview party, then is opened to the public.

LODO HOLIDAY LIGHTING OF UNION STATION
17th and Wynkoop Streets
(303) 628-5428
lodo.org
Join as many as 3,500 people as they gather to watch the lighting of Union Station around Thanksgiving. The LoDo district is seeking to expand coverage and promotion, making this a bigger event each year. Already it is a favorite among local residents.

STARLIGHTING
Old Courthouse Square
301 Wilcox St., Castle Rock
(866) 441-8508
castlerock.org

The annual lighting of the Christmas star on top of Castle Rock, the monolith that towers above the city of Castle Rock has been going on since 1936. It goes along with a ceremony in Courthouse Square, and includes carolers, Santa, reindeer, a fireworks show, ice-skating, entertainment, and hot chocolate. It is followed by a fire department–sponsored chili supper, all on the Saturday before Thanksgiving. Everything is free except the chili, which will only set you back a few dollars.

STARZ DENVER FILM FESTIVAL
Various Denver locations
(303) 595-3456
denverfilm.org

This 11-day festival showcases more than 200 top feature, documentary, and short films from around the world, screened at the SIE FilmCenter on East Colfax, UA Denver Pavillions, the Ellie Caulkins Opera House, and other locations. They're all located downtown. Usually held the second week in November, it draws a host of actors, directors, and producers. Previous festivals have drawn celebrities such as Robert Altman, Geena Davis, Sean Penn, and Shirley MacLaine. After some film showings, enjoy a question-and-answer session with the director, producer, actors, or others involved in the film's genesis. Call or visit the website for ticket information.

✳ZOO LIGHTS
The Denver Zoo in City Park
East 23rd Avenue and Steele Street
(303) 376-4800, (720) 337-1400
denverzoo.org/zoolights

This memorable family event begins at the end of November and runs evenings through December. Thousands of sparkling lights strung on trees create Christmas light sculptures of colored animals. There's nightly entertainment, storytelling, holiday refreshments, and an appearance by Santa Claus (until Christmas). Amid all the lights, it's fun to visit the animals and see what they do with their time on a winter night. Be aware that some of the animals are not out, but the seals and sea lions often make visitors laugh with their antics.

DECEMBER

✳BLOSSOMS OF LIGHTS
Denver Botanic Gardens
1007 York St.
(720) 865-3500
botanicgardens.com

During the month of December, the Denver Botanic Gardens does for plants what the Denver Zoo does for animals (see November listing). More than a million colored lights elegantly showcase the garden's winter beauty. There are giant flowers of Christmas lights and lights draped all over plants and other objects. There's nothing more invigorating than a stroll through a wonderland of lights on a frosty evening, and this event provides a different way of seeing Denver's beloved Botanic Gardens. Nightly entertainment is included, along with holiday refreshments.

CHRISTMAS EVE TORCHLIGHT PARADE
Winter Park Resort, Winter Park
(970) 726-1564
winterparkresort.com
On Christmas Eve guests begin by caroling around a bonfire at the base of the mountain. Santa Claus then leads a procession of torchbearers on skis as they make their way down Lower Hughes Trail. More color and motion come from snowcats decorated with Christmas lights. Their progress is punctuated with a fireworks display, followed by a nondenominational church service. Also on Christmas Eve, the mountaintop Lodge at Sunspot stays open for an elegant holiday dinner. Seating begins at 6 p.m., and reservations are required; call (970) 726-1446.

A COLORADO CHRISTMAS
Four Mile Historic Park
715 S. Forest St.
(720) 865-0800
fourmilepark.org
Find an old-fashioned Christmas atmosphere at Four Mile Historic Park during this 1-day affair in early December. St. Nick, or Father Christmas, will be there; Christmas music will be performed; and bobsled rides (if snow conditions permit) will be offered along with crafts, activities, food, and drink.

✳A COLORADO CHRISTMAS
Boettcher Concert Hall
14th and Curtis Streets
(303) 623-7876
coloradosymphony.org
This is a benchmark in our year, a favorite way to celebrate the Christmas season. The concert, usually held in late December, features the Colorado Symphony Orchestra, the Colorado Symphony Chorus, and the Colorado Children's Chorale.

✳HANDEL'S *MESSIAH*
Boettcher Concert Hall
14th and Curtis Streets
(303) 893-4100
coloradosymphony.org
Holiday music lovers adore this one: classic Christmas music with the Colorado Symphony Orchestra and the Colorado Symphony Chorus performing Handel's *Messiah*. This is typically held the first or second weekend in December. Call for ticket prices.

HOLIDAY HIGH TEAS
Molly Brown House
1340 Pennsylvania St.
(303) 832-4092
mollybrown.org
Held on select dates throughout December, the teas are traditional in their offerings of sandwiches, pastries, scones, and hot tea. Cost includes a tour of the home. Call for specific dates and reservations.

✳NEW YEAR'S EVE DOWNTOWN FIREWORKS
16th Street Mall
December 31
(303) 534-6161
denver.org/events
Each New Year's Eve the skies over the 16th Street Mall sparkle with a spectacular fireworks display. The event takes place twice, at 9 p.m. and again at midnight. Unless you're lucky enough to be invited to one of the lofts overlooking downtown 16th Street, the best views are from street level on the mall. Dress warm, be prepared for crowds, and ring in the New Year with a big bang. Arrive early to find a parking place. All the downtown parking lots and garages will be open.

ANNUAL EVENTS & FESTIVALS

*THE NUTCRACKER
Denver Performing Arts Complex
(303) 837-8888
coloradoballet.org
Another classic Christmas event, *The Nutcracker* has been entertaining audiences for more than 100 years. From those first glittering snowflakes until the final curtain, the dazzling costumes, elaborate theatrical sets, and unforgettable musical performances are on par with any ballet company in the US.

*OLDE GOLDEN CHRISTMAS
Throughout downtown Golden
(303) 279-3113
visitgolden.com
Golden may be growing, but it's still one of the last Metro Denver communities with a real small-town feel about it. And here's an old-fashioned, small-town Christmas festival. Holiday festivities begin in early December with candlelight walks through downtown Golden. Everybody carries a candle and files down to Clear Creek to see the tree lights ignited. Santa Claus shows up. In the past the event has featured a clogging dance troupe and dancing kids. The first three Saturdays of the month are celebrated with Christmas carolers, sleigh rides, carriage rides, reindeer, and cookie decorating as well as hot chocolate, cookies, and candy. At the Clear Creek Living History Ranch, folks serve up cowboy beans, doughnut holes, coffee, and great entertainment in restored cabins from the turn of the 20th century. At the Pioneer Museum, 923 10th St., there's live musical entertainment, hot cider, cookies, and a big bonfire.

*PARADE OF LIGHTS
Streets of downtown Denver
(303) 534-6161
denverparadeoflights.com
This is truly one of the great public events of Denver's calendar: a night parade that lasts more than an hour and features floats, clowns, marching bands, and giant balloon figures, all lit up or festooned with lights. The whole event is one big Roman candle of multicolored holiday illumination. The crowds are big enough that special shuttles run into downtown from select bus stations. Check with RTD for schedules. You might consider bringing extra wraps, blankets, and a thermos of something hot and comforting. And as with all parades, if you want to position a folding chair for a front-row seat, get there an hour or more before the show. The 2-mile parade is held the first Friday and Saturday night in December. The parade is free but grandstand seats are available for purchase.

*WORLD'S LARGEST CHRISTMAS LIGHTING DISPLAY
City and County Building, between Colfax Avenue and 14th Street (across from Civic Center Park)
(720) 913-4900
denvergov.org
If light were music, the Denver City and County Building would be the world's largest pipe organ. About 30,000 floodlights turn this huge government building into one big installation of colorful art. It has become a Denver holiday tradition to walk around and ogle on a frosty winter evening. Bundle up the kids. The display is up from the first Thursday in December until mid-January, after the National Western Stock Show has finished its run (see January entry).

THE ARTS

Denver's arts scene has exploded over the last two decades, in sync with the maturation of all the city's cultural attractions. A great deal of the credit goes to former mayor John Hickenlooper, now governor of Colorado, who built his campaign around the notion that healthy cities are fueled by a thriving creative environment. Artists of all types have felt the love, but business leaders also acknowledge that emerging neighborhoods attract artists, and artists attract the kind of attention that speeds their redevelopment. Core business leaders, members of the Downtown Denver Partnership, have worked hard to showcase the city's cultural attractions in a designated theater district, and city fathers support budding artists by funding studio and performances spaces.

Art lovers are the ultimate winners as galleries, theaters, concert halls, and literary cooperatives incubate throughout the city. In this chapter we've compiled a partial list of theaters and theater companies, art galleries, and art museums. Music venues, bars, movie houses, and restaurants with live entertainment can be found in our Nightlife chapter, and other kinds of museums are covered in the Tours & Attractions chapter. Given that one person's definition of culture may overlap with another person's idea of popular entertainment, expect to toggle between chapters to find the things that most appeal to your tastes. We begin by describing the Denver Performing Arts Complex, the historic hub of the city's cultural scene, then move through performing groups, theaters, theater companies, dinner theaters, popular music venues, art museums, community art centers, and art galleries. Finally, we detail the literary arts by describing the city's many writers' organizations.

PERFORMING ARTS

DENVER PERFORMING ARTS COMPLEX
Speer Boulevard and Arapahoe Street
(303) 893-4100, (800) 641-1222
denvercenter.org
The Denver Performing Arts Complex, a 4-block, 12-acre site, boasts more than 11,260 seats in nine performance venues and is the nation's largest in terms of the number and variety of performance spaces, the number and size of support facilities,

and the variety of activities taking place. It is second only to New York's Lincoln Center in terms of seating capacity.

Performances are offered by many tenants, the largest of which is the **Denver Center for the Performing Arts (DCPA).** In addition to Broadway touring shows and the region's largest resident professional theater company, the complex houses a state-of-the-art television, video, and recording production facility; offers the nation's only congressionally chartered graduate acting school; and conducts research with the world's only voice research laboratory associated with a performing arts center. Other tenants of the complex include the Colorado Symphony, Colorado Ballet, Colorado Children's Chorale, and Opera Colorado, all of which are described here. Tickets to all of the tenants' performances may be purchased by calling the numbers above.

The largest theater in the complex is the **Temple Hoyne Buell Theatre,** which opened in 1991 and has 2,830 seats. **Boettcher Concert Hall,** a unique 2,634-seat concert-hall-in-the-round, dates from 1978. The **Ellie Caulkins Opera House** is a grand old (1908) European-style theater with 2,268 seats. It was completely renovated in 2005.

The **Helen Bonfils Theatre Complex,** built in 1979, houses four smaller theaters. **The Stage** (770 seats) is a thrust stage; **The Space** is theater-in-the-round (well, it's actually more of a pentagon) with 427 seats; the **Ricketson Theatre** is a 250-seat informal proscenium; and the **Jones Theatre,** with 200 seats, is an intimate experimental thrust stage. The **Donald R. Seawell Grand Ballroom,** named for DCPA's chairman of the board, opened in 1998. The 10,000-square-foot glass-and-steel ballroom has a maximum capacity of 1,029 people, and it can accommodate a variety of functions with smaller configurations. Also in the complex is the **Garner Galleria Theatre,** which presents cabaret shows.

At intermission patrons spill out into the high, arched, glass-ceilinged galleria to stretch their legs and get some fresh air (or, conversely, to smoke a cigarette). The unique ceiling connects the diverse theaters.

DENVER CENTER ATTRACTIONS
Speer Boulevard and Arapahoe Street
(303) 893-4100, (800) 641-1222 (tickets and information)
(303) 893-4000 (information)
Broadway musical hits such as *Big River, Phantom of the Opera, Evita, Les Miserables,* and the pre-Broadway engagement of Disney's *Little Mermaid* make Denver Center Attractions a preferred stop on the touring circuit. The division is also known for its own productions of cabaret musicals including *Forever Plaid* and Denver's longest-running production, *Always . . . Patsy Cline.*

DENVER CENTER THEATRE COMPANY
Speer Boulevard and Arapahoe Street
(303) 893-4100, (800) 641-1222 (tickets)
(303) 893-4000 (information)
denvercenter.org
The Denver Center Theatre Company, recipient of the 1998 Tony Award for Outstanding Regional Theatre, is the region's largest resident professional theater company and features an 11-play season, including traditional and contemporary drama and world premieres. Its shows are performed in the Stage, Space, Ricketson and Jones theaters, all part of the overall Performing Arts Complex.

i Don't let the names confuse you. The Denver Performing Arts Complex is the city-owned facility that is rented by various performance companies. The complex comprises 10 performance spaces offering more than 10,000 seats. The Denver Center for the Performing Arts is an organization that presents and produces Broadway touring shows and live theater through its two companies: Denver Center Attractions and the Denver Center Theatre Company.

Music

COLORADO CHILDREN'S CHORALE
2420 W. 26th Ave., Ste. 350-D
(303) 892-5600
childrenschorale.org
Colorado Children's Chorale, a 400-member chorus that tours nationally and internationally, celebrated its 35th anniversary in 2009. It started with 50 members and now involves 20,000 children each year through its outreach program. Each year the chorale joins the Colorado Symphony Orchestra for a very popular holiday concert.

COLORADO SYMPHONY ORCHESTRA
821 17th St., Ste. 700
(303) 623-7876
coloradosymphony.org
The Colorado Symphony Orchestra, with 80 members, plays classical music and popular classics in Boettcher Concert Hall during its season, which lasts from September to May. Each season there are also several low-priced Sunday-afternoon concerts.

DENVER BRASS/DENVER BRASS5
2253 Downing St.
(303) 832-4676
denverbrass.org
Formed in 1981, the 14-member Denver Brass is one of very few symphonic brass ensembles in the country. Concerts feature something for everyone, from splendid brass fanfares to Big Band music. Performances, including an annual Christmas concert, are held at the Newman Center for the Performing Arts at the University of Denver and Bethany Lutheran Church, 4500 E. Hampden Avenue.

Also under the same management is the Denver Brass5. Founded in 1976, The Denver Brass5 has toured the US, Europe, and South America; performed its fresh and vibrant renditions of chamber music live on National Public Radio; and recorded several albums.

DENVER YOUNG ARTISTS ORCHESTRA
1245 E. Colfax Ave., Ste. 302
(303) 433-2420
dyao.org
The Denver Young Artists Orchestra was formed in 1977 as a means for Colorado's talented young musicians (ages 12 to 23) to rehearse and perform under professional standards. The orchestra plays four to six concerts each year in Boettcher Concert Hall and Gates Concert Hall, including one side-by-side concert with the Colorado Symphony Orchestra.

OPERA COLORADO
695 S. Colorado Blvd., Ste. 20
(303) 778-1500
operacolorado.org
Opera Colorado presents three grand operas each winter and spring, all performed at the Ellie Caulkins Opera House in downtown Denver. Performances are sung in the original language. Patrons are treated to seat-back titling at every seat in the house, in one of only three opera houses nationwide, nine worldwide, that provide such an amenity. Opera Colorado also performs at special holiday concerts and summer festivals throughout the state. The Opera Colorado for Children program includes children's opera workshops, matinee performances for students, and an in-school puppet opera.

Dance

CLEO PARKER ROBINSON DANCE
119 Park Ave. West
(303) 295-1759
cleoparkerdance.org

Cleo Parker Robinson Dance is a multi-cultural performing arts institution with a 12-person professional modern dance company and a dance school based in a historic African Methodist Episcopal Church. The ensemble performs regularly in Denver and extensively around the country and is one of the city's best-known exports in the arts field. Cleo Parker Robinson also sponsors a 4-week artist-in-residence program called the International Summer Dance Institute.

COLORADO BALLET
1278 Lincoln St.
(303) 837-8888 (office)
coloradoballet.org
The Colorado Ballet was established as the Colorado Concert Ballet in 1961, and has been molding dancers ever since. The resident company of 30 dancers is under the artistic direction of Gil Boggs and is the only dance company in the state to perform with a live orchestra. Its repertoire includes full-length classical and one-act ballets. Performances are held in either the Gates Concert Hall or Ellie Caulkins Opera House fall through spring.

DAWSON/WALLACE DANCE PROJECT
PO Box 140699, Edgewater 80214
(303) 789-2030
dawsonwallace.org
The Dawson/Wallace Dance Project is Denver's foremost professional contemporary ballet company. In addition, it's one of the region's major presenters of *The Nutcracker*, which is performed annually at the Lakewood Cultural Center and on tour throughout the state and the country. Although they perform classical dance, the main focus of the company is original contemporary

works. The performance of *A Children's Rainforest Odyssey* is one of its most popular productions. The company performs in different venues throughout Metro Denver from September through May.

KIM ROBARDS DANCE
1387 S. Santa Fe Dr.
(303) 825-4847
kimrobardsdance.org
Kim Robards Dance was established in 1987 as the Colorado Repertory Dance Company and is an important center for modern dance in Colorado. Its school and administrative offices are part of the emerging Platte River Drive South Cultural District, and the company recently secured a 24,000-square-foot permanent home. The company has a dynamic collection of works that include pieces by artistic director Kim Robards. The professional touring company has performed in New York and California, among other places. Locally the company presents a winter and spring season, a statewide educational outreach program, and classes for beginners age 4 to adult and professionals at its school.

Theaters & Theater Companies

AURORA FOX ARTS CENTER
9900 E. Colfax Ave., Aurora
(303) 739-1970
aurorafoxartscenter.org
From fall to spring, this historic landmark in the East End Arts District is home to the Aurora Fox Theatre Company and the Aurora Fox Children's Theatre Company. The adult theater company mounts six major productions each season, including musicals such as *A Christmas Carol* and dramatic classics such as *The Skin of Our Teeth*. The Little Foxes children's program offers classes

and workshops, and produces several shows each summer.

THE BUG THEATRE
Performance and Media Arts Center
3654 Navajo St.
(303) 477-9984
bugtheatre.org
The buzz is good on the Bug Theatre, a renovated movie house that's now an avant-garde showcase for emerging artists and their artwork, including poetry, music, film, and new media. Check out Freak Train, the open-mike talent show that takes place the last Monday night of each month. Perform-ers ranging from amateur to seasoned pros do pretty much whatever they want—for 5 minutes. Wild, uncensored, unpredictable, and occasionally off-key, the evening is any-thing but dull.

FESTIVAL PLAYHOUSE
5665 Old Wadsworth Blvd., Arvada
(303) 422-4090
festivalplayhouse.com
There's plenty of history behind the Festival Playhouse. The Denver Players Guild, formed in 1936, stages eight plays a year—primarily Broadway comedies—in this converted Grange building in Olde Town Arvada. The Players Guild believes it is the oldest com-munity theater group in the country under the same family management, and the playhouse is even older. Built in 1874, it's the second-oldest standing Grange hall in Colorado and the oldest building in the city of Arvada.

GERMINAL STAGE DENVER
2450 W. 44th Ave.
(303) 455-7108
germinalstage.com
Germinal Stage Denver was founded by four Denver actors in 1973, making it one of the longest-living small theaters in the region. Performances are held in an air-conditioned, 100-seat converted storefront, 5 blocks east of Federal Boulevard. The repertoire includes traditional works such as Tennessee Wil-liams's *The Eccentricities of a Nightingale* to more arcane and experimental plays. The Germinal has an excellent reputation for producing quality theater.

THE PHYSICALLY HANDICAPPED ACTORS AND MUSICAL ARTISTS LEAGUE
PO Box 44216, Denver 80201
(303) 575-0005
phamaly.org
PHAMALY was formed in 1989, when a group of Boettcher School alumni decided to organize a theater company for people living with disabilities. This group stages several plays each year, and a touring show that takes actors to businesses, senior cen-ters, festivals, and schools. Performances are always wheelchair-accessible, and arrange-ments are made to provide assistance to hearing-impaired and visually impaired audience members. Recent performances include *Little Shop of Horrors, Steel Magnolias,* and *One Flew Over the Cuckoo's Nest.*

SU TEATRO AT DENVER CIVIC THEATRE
721 Santa Fe Dr.
(303) 296-0219 (box office)
suteatro.net
Su Teatro was formed in 1971 by the stu-dents at the University of Colorado Denver as a forum for those interested in the Chi-cano civil rights movement. It has grown into a multidisciplinary cultural arts center that sponsors concerts, drama, performance

art, dance, festivals, film, poetry festivals, workshops, and art exhibitions. Theater performances emphasize original works by Chicano and Latino playwrights, including Rudolfo Anaya's classic, *Bless Me, Ultima*. The company has created more than 15 original productions that have toured widely around the country. The Denver Civic Theatre is the new home of Su Teatro.

Dinner Theaters

HERITAGE SQUARE MUSIC HALL
18301 W. Colfax Ave. (US Highway 40), Golden
(303) 279-7800
heritagesquare.info
Heritage Square Music Hall is a Victorian-style theater staging original comedies with melodramatic overtones and musical revues. A buffet dinner precedes the show, but it's possible to buy a ticket for the performance only. The performance earns better reviews than the buffet. Performances are Wednesday through Saturday evenings, with Sunday matinees year-round.

Music Venues

Outdoor rock and other popular music concerts are held at Comfort Dental Amphitheatre and Red Rocks Amphitheatre. Indoor venues include the Pepsi Center, the Fillmore Auditorium, the Ogden Theatre, and the Paramount Theatre. Tickets to all venues can be purchased online or by phone, but a trip to the box office can generally (though not always) save you from paying a service charge.

THE BLUEBIRD THEATER
3317 E. Colfax Ave.
(303) 377-1666
bluebirdtheater.net
The Bluebird Theater is one of three historic venues clustered along East Colfax that welcome music fans of all ilks to Denver's Capitol Hill neighborhood. Built in 1914 as a movie theater and originally used to show silent films, the Bluebird fell upon hard times and closed in the late 1980s. The restored theater reopened in fall 1994 as a performance hall for musicians of all kinds. Expect to see names such as Candlebox and Bonnie Prince Billy on the marquee.

COMFORT DENTAL AMPHITHEATRE
6350 Greenwood Plaza Blvd., Englewood
(303) 220-7000
ticketmaster.com
Originally named Fiddler's Green, this huge open-air amphitheater rocks during summer months. It holds 18,000 fans, which means only the performers who can draw a crowd are booked into this south Metro venue. Reserved seats are available, but you can also buy cheaper general admission tickets for the lawn area. In previous years, Fiddler's Green has hosted Rod Stewart, Aerosmith, Def Leppard, Tim McGraw, Nine Inch Nails, Toby Keith, Nickleback, and Bette Midler.

FILLMORE AUDITORIUM
1510 Clarkson St.
(303) 837-1482
fillmoreauditorium.org
This Capitol Hill landmark opened in 1907 as a skating rink but gradually fell into disrepair. It had a short but brilliant life at a concert hall called Mammoth Gardens in the late 1960s and early 1970s, hosting The Doors, The Who, and The Grateful Dead before closing its

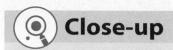

Close-up

Germinal Stage Denver

Ed Baierlein played to perfection the buffoon role of Major Petkoff in George Bernard Shaw's comedy *Arms and the Man,* scowling and bellowing, gaping and grinning, and lolling his tongue, his face a writhing parade of expressions so foolish that the audience sometimes laughed loudest when he was saying nothing at all.

"That's some play you're running," a fan told him over the telephone one night an hour before the curtain went up. "You're quite a comedian."

"Well, thanks," Baierlein said. "We're doing pretty well. You wanted how many reservations now? Would that be Visa or MasterCard?"

More than a comedian, Baierlein is also one of the Denver area's most respected serious actors, but that doesn't mean he is above taking reservations, cleaning the theater, maintaining the mailing lists, and doing the books at the Germinal Stage Denver theater in northwest Denver.

Since its founding in 1973, Germinal Stage has built a faithful audience with more than 130 plays including everything from experimental, first-run productions to Ibsen, Shaw, and Shakespeare. Those plays have earned the theater a reputation and influence all out of proportion to its 100-seat facility in an old 5,000-square-foot building.

While the large theaters of the Denver Performing Arts Complex are a point of pride and a focus of entertainment on Denver's cultural landscape, Germinal Stage and the more than a dozen other smaller local theaters perhaps provide a truer measure of that landscape's cultural depth.

"In the smaller theaters, the artists tend to be in primary control," Baierlein says. "They tend to be more eclectic, with a more specialized audience and repertoire. The problems today are fairly similar to what they were when we started out—on the one hand, maintaining the integrity of our repertoire, and on the other hand, being popular enough so that people will pay to see your next failure."

Baierlein and Sallie Diamond, his wife and partner in the nonprofit Germinal Stage and one of the area's most versatile and respected actresses, are among the many who came to Denver by chance and stayed by choice. "I was in the Air Force and was shipped here in 1968 and spent most of my time in the service at Lowry Air Force Base," Baierlein said. "My wife and I decided this was the nicest place we had ever lived. My philosophy is, find a place where you like to live and then make the work happen there."

It was the city that attracted them, Baierlein said. The city is where they and their son, Thaddeus, who was born here in 1980, spend most of their time. From their home just a block away from the theater, they take periodic trips to Glenwood Springs, a 3-hour drive to the west, to enjoy the world's largest outdoor hot pool.

"That's our favorite vacation, just to let the city seep out of us in the pools," Baierlein said. "We're not great outdoors people. We don't ski, and we don't camp."

Even so, Baierlein said they try to get to the mountains as much as possible, just to enjoy the beauty and solitude that is never far away from the lives and thoughts of even the most urbane of Metro Denverites.

"When you're away from here for any period of time, you really miss just the presence of the mountains," he said. "There's no other place I know where you can have the amenities of a big city and still, in a half hour, be absolutely isolated in a place where you feel nobody has ever been before."

doors. New owners reopened it in 1999 and named it for Bill Graham's Fillmore Ballroom in San Francisco, which provided the original inspiration. It now holds 3,600 people (it seats a whole lot less than that), and has become one of Denver's premier venues for groups such as KORN, Thievery Corporation, and Sound Tribe Sector 9.

THE OGDEN THEATRE
935 E. Colfax St.
(303) 832-1874
ogdentheater.net
A vaudeville-era theater that later became a movie house, the Ogden's newest incarnation is as a concert hall presenting a wide variety of local and national acts. It's located in the heart of Capitol Hill, along with the Bluebird Theater and the Fillmore. Some recent headliners included Brian Jonestown Massacre, Railroad Earth, and Lily Allen with Natalie Portman's Shaved Head.

PARAMOUNT THEATRE
1621 Glenarm Place
(303) 623-0106
paramountdenver.com
This historic art deco theater has more than once been on the verge of falling to the wrecker's ball. Built in 1930 by Temple Hoyne Buell, a prominent Denver architect, the theater is the epitome of art deco style and has one of only two Mighty Wurlitzer organs in the country (the other is at Radio City Music Hall in New York City). During the summer of 1994—under new management yet again—the Paramount underwent extensive remodeling. The Paramount seats 1,870 and presents a mixed bag of comedy, lectures, dance, film, and live music. Recent seasons have included jazz greats Chick Corea and John McLaughlin, Grateful Dead member

Bob Weir, and classic metal from Styx and Queensryche.

THE PEPSI CENTER
1000 Chopper Place
(303) 405-1100
pepsicenter.com
Home to the Denver Nuggets and the Colorado Avalanche, the Pepsi Center also hosts big-name shows. The arena seats up to 16,000, with a killer sound system and jumbo TV screens so everyone in the house has good views of the stage. In recent years, stars ranging from Eric Clapton, Paul McCartney, and Steve Winwood to country greats Keith Urban and Sugarland have made tour stops here.

RED ROCKS AMPHITHEATRE
I-70 West to the Morrison exit, Morrison
(720) 865-4220
redrocksonline.com
Red Rocks Amphitheatre is one of the most spectacular settings anywhere for a concert. About half the size of Comfort Dental Amphitheatre, Red Rocks is a natural red sandstone amphitheater set deep into the foothills on Hogback Road near Morrison (take I-70 west to the Morrison exit and follow the signs). It was renovated in 2003 to include a $16 million visitor center. Leonard Cohen, Neil Young, David Byrne, Tom Petty, Peter Gabriel, Mark Knopfler, James Taylor, Emmylou Harris, and the Mormon Tabernacle Choir are among the groups to have stopped here during recent tours.

✳SWALLOW HILL MUSIC ASSOCIATION
71 E. Yale Ave.
(303) 777-1003
swallowhill.com
The well-respected Swallow Hill Music Association is Denver's center for folk, roots, and

traditional acoustic music. Concerts are held at two theaters, the largest of which seats 300. Swallow Hill also presents concerts elsewhere in the city, including summer concerts at Four Mile Historical Park.

VISUAL ARTS

Art Museums

CLYFFORD STILL MUSEUM
1250 Bannock St.
(720) 354-4880
clyffordstillmuseum.org
The newest addition to Denver's burgeoning Cultural Arts District, the Clyfford Still Museum is devoted to the works of one of the most important painters of the 20th century. Representing around 94 percent of the artist's lifetime output—almost 2,400 paintings, drawings, and prints—the Clyfford Still Museum houses a beautifully displayed collection devoted to the life and works of this important abstract expressionist painter. Much of his work has been hidden from view for over 30 years and is now permanently displayed here. Located next to the Denver Art Museum, it's open every day except Monday.

THE DENVER ART MUSEUM
100 W. 14th Ave. Pkwy.
(720) 865-5000
denverartmuseum.org
The Denver Art Museum is the largest art museum between Kansas City and the West Coast and is especially noted for its superb collections of Native American, pre-Columbian, and Spanish colonial art. Its 7 floors also house impressive displays of American, Asian, African, and contemporary art and galleries devoted to design, graphics, and architecture.

The museum is nearly as well known for its buildings, the first of which was designed by Italian architect Gio Ponti in association with Denver architect James Sudler and the second of which was designed by architect Daniel Libeskind. The original building, completed in 1971, is a fortresslike 7-level structure with a 28-sided tiled exterior. The new 146,000-square-foot expansion was completed in 2006, almost doubling its size to house traveling exhibits and permanent modern, contemporary, African, Oceanic, and western American collections.

The museum is open Tuesday through Sunday, with extended hours on Friday evening. Family programs are held every Saturday, with free admission for Colorado residents the first Saturday of every month. The museum has a shop and full-service restaurant.

KIRKLAND MUSEUM OF FINE & DECORATIVE ART
1311 Pearl St.
(303) 832-8576
kirklandmuseum.org
Vance Kirkland may be Colorado's best-known painter. His work spans realism, surrealism, abstraction, abstract expressionism, and dot paintings, and his career stretched from 1926 to 1981. The museum showcases more than 600 of his paintings as well as housing a 2,000-object decorative arts collection and more than 300 works from Colorado artists. The building itself is worthy of note. Built in 1910–11, it's the second-oldest commercial art building in Colorado, designed in the Arts and Crafts style, and it served as Kirkland's studio. The museum is open Tuesday through Sunday. Children younger than age 13 are not admitted;

children age 13 to 17 must be accompanied by an adult. Tours are offered daily.

MUSEO DE LAS AMERICAS
861 Santa Fe Dr.
(303) 571-4401
museo.org

This museum is the only one in the Rocky Mountain region dedicated to Latin American art, history, and culture. Officially opened in July 1994, the Museo de las Americas showcases art from all the Americas, including the Caribbean, in changing exhibitions. The museum supplements its temporary exhibitions with lectures, workshops, and other educational programs and has built a small permanent collection. It has twice shown an exhibition jointly with the Denver Art Museum, with some of the material at the art museum and some at the Museo. The museum is open Tuesday through Sunday, and it's free on First Fridays 5 to 9 p.m.

MUSEUM OF OUTDOOR ARTS
1000 Englewood Pkwy., Englewood
(303) 806-0444
moaonline.org

Bringing art into everyday life, the Museum of Outdoor Arts (MOA) is located in and around the Englewood City Center and Greenwood Plaza. Their headquarters is at the Englewood Civic Center, but art at this "museum without walls" can be found in botanic gardens, office parks, city parks, and traditional sculpture gardens around the area. MOA is open to the public Tuesday through Friday during daylight hours. Details about their philosophy, location, and art tours can be found online.

Community Art Centers

ARVADA CENTER FOR THE ARTS AND HUMANITIES
6901 Wadsworth Blvd., Arvada
(720) 898-7200 (box office)
arvadacenter.org

The Arvada Center has two galleries, which display changing exhibits of contemporary art, folk art, design, and crafts. There's also a small historical museum. In addition, the center has both an indoor 500-seat auditorium and an outdoor amphitheater with 1,200 seats (600 covered, 600 on the lawn). It also maintains an impressive schedule of performing arts programming that includes children's and adult professional theater, dance, and music concerts. One resident company, the Arvada Center Chorale, calls the center home, but many groups perform here. It's the site each winter of a cowboy-poetry gathering. A highly regarded deaf-access program makes many programs accessible to the hearing-impaired. After 24 years the Arvada Center became a full-equity professional theater in 2000. It's open daily, with free admission to the gallery and museum.

THE FOOTHILLS ART CENTER
809 15th St., Golden
(303) 279-3922
foothillsartcenter.org

The Foothills Art Center is much smaller than the Arvada Center, but it is home to two prestigious national exhibitions—the biannual North American Sculpture Exhibition and Colorado Art Open and the annual Rocky Mountain National Watermedia Exhibition. It offers arts classes and hosts the statewide annual Colorado Clay exhibition. The center's schedule is composed of changing exhibits of national and regional arts and fine crafts.

Art Galleries

Downtown

Metro Denver's contemporary art galleries tend to be clustered around the city's historic core, although they are sprinkled throughout most of its neighborhoods. Working on the assumption that there's strength in numbers, galleries in Lower Downtown (LoDo), the Golden Triangle, Santa Fe Drive, Tennyson Street, and River North (RiNo) neighborhoods have banded together to coordinate openings and other special events, including First Friday events that are held the first Friday of each month. Especially in the summer, there's kind of a street festival atmosphere as patrons go from one gallery to the next, stopping to compare notes with friends on the sidewalk. Gallery openings are usually held on Friday and are, with rare exceptions, free and open to the public. Check *Westword* or the Friday edition of the *Denver Post* for a list of openings and current exhibit information. Most galleries close on Monday, but this varies so call ahead to be sure.

Think of art galleries as a wonderful free smorgasbord of exciting things to see. Of course, the bottom line is that galleries must sell art to stay in business, but unlike art dealers in some cities, Denver's are notably low-key and happy to educate browsers without pressuring them to buy. Dealers know that the best way to develop customers is to make people feel comfortable, and high-pressure sales tactics aren't going to do that.

The heart of Denver's avant-garde arts district is the 1700 block of Wazee Street. You'll find several galleries in the surrounding area. Many others have chosen the areas adjacent to downtown for their affordability and bohemian appeal.

CENTER FOR VISUAL ART
Metropolitan State College of Denver
1734 Wazee St.
(303) 294-5207
msudenver.edu/cva

Technically a college gallery, the Center for Visual Art seldom shows student work, but rather puts on some of the best and most provocative exhibitions in town. Traveling exhibits are booked years in advance for the purpose of art education. Past exhibitions have included contemporary Chinese painting, African-American quilts, and baseball paraphernalia from local collections.

DAVID COOK FINE ART
1637 Wazee St.
(303) 623-8181
davidcookfineart.com

David Cook offers a wide range of artists and styles, but its specialties are American regional art from the 19th and early 20th centuries, as well as historic American Indian art, from Navajo rugs to Pueblo pottery, from beadwork to baskets. You can also find antique jewelry and paintings of the Rockies by early Colorado artists.

KNOX GALLERIES
1512 Larimer St.
(303) 820-2324
knoxgalleries.com

Knox Gallery is one of the nation's premier bronze sculpture galleries. Located in Writer Square, the gallery represents local and regional painters and sculptors. Their sculpture garden is in Writer Square Plaza.

OLD MAP GALLERY
1550 Wynkoop St.
(303) 296-7725
oldmapgallery.com

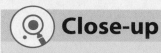
Close-up

First Friday Art Walks

On the first Friday of each month, galleries and studios around town open their doors for an evening of art viewing and socializing. Art aficionados and those out for a casual night of socializing hobnob with artists, chat, flirt, and network over wine and snacks, and occasionally art is sold. It's great fun, and it's free. From 6 to 9 p.m., First Fridays center around four Denver gallery areas:

Santa Fe Drive, between 5th and 10th Avenues; artdistrictonsantafe.com

Tennyson Street, between 38th and 44th Avenues; tennysonst.com

Lower Downtown (LoDo) district; (303) 628-5428; lodo.org

River North (RiNo) Art District, north of downtown; rivernorthart.com

If you're in the market for antique maps, this is the place. You'll find historic maps such as ones from the 16th century or maps of Louisiana before it was purchased. Maps range from $35 to several thousand dollars.

PLUS GALLERY
2501 Larimer St.
(303) 296-0927
plusgallery.com
Since 2001 Ivar Zeile has been showcasing the works of emerging as well as nationally known talents from his Ballpark neighborhood gallery. In 2009 he moved to a spiffier space just 5 blocks north of LoDo. Shows rotate every 6 weeks and include sculpture, photography, painting, video, paper, and installation art. The gallery is open Wednesday through Saturday and by appointment at other times.

ROBISCHON GALLERY
1740 Wazee St.
(303) 298-7788
robischongallery.com

Robischon Gallery has been open in Denver since 1976, providing a space for regional, national, and international artists that include Robert Motherwell, Manuel Neri, Christo, and Jeanne-Claude. It specializes in contemporary art of all kinds, as well as emerging young artists.

THE SLOANE GALLERY OF ART
1612 17th St.
(303) 595-4230
sloanegalleryofart.com
The Sloane Gallery of Art, located next to the Oxford Hotel in LoDo, is devoted exclusively to contemporary Russian art. It exhibits oils, acrylics, drawings, pastels, and sculpture.

Greater Downtown
THE CHICANO HUMANITIES AND ARTS
  COUNCIL
772 Santa Fe Dr.
(303) 571-0440
chacweb.org
CHAC, the Chicano Humanities and Arts Council, has a gallery that is open Wednesday through Saturday. It also sponsors a

number of special events and programs throughout the city, including a Day of the Dead exhibition, the annual Chile Harvest Festival held at Four Mile Historic Park in August, and Las Posadas at the gallery during December. CHAC is a consortium of artists, individuals, and organizations dedicated to the preservation and promotion of Chicano/Latino cultures.

CORE NEW ART SPACE
900 Santa Fe Dr.
(303) 297-8428
corenewartspace.com
Core New Art Space is a cutting-edge cooperative gallery that primarily features local artists who work in oil, photography, ceramics, and papermaking. It has two spaces, a main gallery and an annex that can be rented for 3-week runs.

i A funky collection of galleries in fast-changing northwest Denver is a fun and different way to spend a Friday or Saturday evening. Galleries such as Bug Theatre and Pirate are located in the 3600 block of Navajo Street. Have dinner at Patsy's Inn Italian Restaurant (3651 Navajo St.) and stroll through the galleries afterward.

GOODWIN FINE ART
1255 Delaware St.
(303) 573-1255
goodwinfineart.com
Located in the Golden Triangle Museum District, this gallery features painting, photography, sculpture, and limited edition prints, representing both regional and national artists. Shows rotate through the gallery every 6 to 8 weeks.

RULE GALLERY
3340 Walnut St.
(303) 777-9473
rulegallery.com
The peripatetic Rule Gallery opened in 1987 and was housed in several other places before landing at its present location. This gallery specializes in modern and contemporary painting, sculpture, and photography by regional and national artists.

SPARK GALLERY
900 Santa Fe Dr.
(720) 889-2200
sparkgallery.com
Spark Gallery is Denver's oldest artists' cooperative located in the vibrant Santa Fe Drive district. It features paintings, sculpture, and photographs sold directly by the artists and is open year-round Thursday through Sunday.

WILLIAM HAVU GALLERY
1040 Cherokee St.
(303) 893-2360
wiIIiamhavugallery.com
William Havu is located in Denver's Golden Triangle, a core neighborhood that gentrified during the 1990s and is now known for its high-rise lofts and trendy restaurants. The gallery's contemporary art blends well into the upscale surroundings. Hours are Tuesday through Saturday, by appointment Sunday and Monday.

Westside & River North Galleries
As LoDo has changed and rents have gone up, many artists have moved their studios from downtown to other transitional neighborhoods to the north and west.

EDGE GALLERY
3658 Navajo St.
(303) 477-7173
edgeart.org
Open Friday through Sunday, EDGE is an independent exhibition space that is run cooperatively by the artists who are shown there. It has nonprofit status, which means that it doesn't have to depend on sales for its survival. As a result, the contemporary art in the museum can be edgier and more contemporary than that seen in more traditional galleries. EDGE moved to its present site in Denver's historic Little Italy in 1992.

PIRATE: CONTEMPORARY ART
3655 Navajo St.
(303) 458-6058
pirateartonline.org
Pirate has what are generally regarded as the hippest openings in town. It is one of the most experimental galleries in Denver, showcasing stunning paintings and sculpture. Pirate is open Friday through Sunday, and shows change frequently.

Northeast of Downtown Denver
RIVER NORTH ART DISTRICT
rivernorthart.com
This emerging downtown arts district—roughly bounded by I-25, and I-70, Park Avenue West, and Lawrence Street—was once home to Denver's early-day foundries, smelters, ironworks, and the blue-collar families who made them run. For more than a decade it has drawn artists and real estate investors priced out of nearby LoDo and the Coors Field area. They banded together to form the informal River North Art District, called RiNo for short, and now sponsor district-wide studio tours and

individual events. The group's name comes from its location along the northern edge of the South Platte River. News is posted on the group's website, as are details about each of its more than 85 members.

LITERARY ARTS

If you love the written word—or the company of those who write—Denver has several writers' organizations that appeal to both beginning and advanced scribes as well as writers in a variety of genres.

COLORADO AUTHORS' LEAGUE
PO Box 24905, Denver 80224
coloradoauthors.org
Founded in 1931, the Colorado Authors' League is one of the oldest professional writers' organizations in the state. Counting such notables as Clive Cussler, Clarissa Pinkola Estes, and Joanne Greenberg among its ranks, this organization has monthly meetings with speakers on topics ranging from spotting trends to writing with a collaborator. Dues are $50 a year.

COLUMBINE POETS OF COLORADO, INC.
PO Box 6245, Broomfield 80021
(303) 431-6774
columbinepoetsofcolorado.com
Part of the National Federation of State Poetry Societies, this organization promotes poetry throughout the state by offering contests, workshops, and monthly critique groups. They have been active in Colorado for 30 years. The membership fee is $15, with a $35 fee to join the local Foothills chapter.

DENVER WOMAN'S PRESS CLUB
1325 Logan St.
(303) 839-1519
dwpconline.org

This club was formed in 1898 by 19 members whose mission included "functioning as a stimulating gathering place for people in literary journalism and media endeavors." Today the club meets regularly for lunch and dinner programs, offers Saturday seminars for the community at large, and has afternoon teas featuring authors in town on book tours. Housed in a charming historic landmark, this organization of women writers is the oldest in the state. Dues run $75 a year after a onetime $100 application fee.

MYSTERY WRITERS OF AMERICA
   (ROCKY MOUNTAIN CHAPTER)
(303) 665-3992
rmmwa.org

Monthly meetings and bimonthly programs keep the published and unpublished members of the regional chapter of Mystery Writers of America busy. Members get to attend all bimonthly programs for free. One of the highlights of each year is the annual meeting, where the featured speaker might be an FBI agent or a judge from a criminal court. National dues are $95, which allow membership locally.

ROCKY MOUNTAIN FICTION WRITERS
PO Box 735, Conifer 80433
(303) 331-2608
rmfw.org

This popular fiction-writing organization is geared to writers of commercial novels. Its 400 members are both published and unpublished and enjoy monthly meetings where speakers talk about anything related to writing and researching. Monthly newsletters offer market news, and critique groups are held all over Metro Denver. The annual conference in September is a much-awaited event; big-name writers, six or seven editors, and several New York agents attend. Dues are $45 a year.

WOMEN WRITING THE WEST
8547 E. Arapahoe Rd., Ste. J-541
Greenwood Village 80112-1436
(303) 773-8349
womenwritingthewest.org

This organization has 250 members from all over the US, Canada, and Australia. The motto here is "We don't do meetings, and we don't do T-shirts." What they do is work on marketing themselves—all of whom are interested in writing about "a new view of the women's west." Members get a quarterly newsletter, displays at booksellers associations, information on marketing their writing, and a major opportunity to network—all for $60.

PARKS & RECREATION

Greater Denver is a recreational heaven. Where else is it possible to ski on Saturday and play golf on Sunday—all on a sunny March weekend? It doesn't stop there. We've got biking trails, hiking trails, climbing spots, and picnicking galore. You can boat, swim, fish, snow ski, water-ski, or windsurf. You can hunt wildlife or simply admire it from afar. You name it, we've got it.

We have organizations, facilities, rental companies, and tour guides for bicycling, climbing, fishing, hunting, running, in-line skating, sailing, waterskiing, and horseback riding, to name a few. We even have ranges for skeet, trap, pistols, and rifles. Skiing, of course, is Colorado's most popular and famous form of winter recreation, which is why we've given it a chapter of its own called Ski Country.

Metro Denver's beautifully groomed urban parks are among its greatest assets, including those listed below. In general, Denver's parks are open from 5 a.m. until 11 p.m. and do not allow camping.

PARKS

Urban Parks

Metro Denver is laced with a network of city and county parks that provide everything from playing fields to playgrounds and trails for running, biking, and skating. In addition, Denver Parks and Recreation oversees the Denver Zoo, the city's golf courses, and 100 miles of foliated center strips on major streets.

Denver has about 250 parks, ranging from small triangles to enormous open spaces, as well as a trail system estimated at about 130 miles. The city also boasts 14,000 acres of mountain parkland and parcels preserved as natural areas.

CHEESMAN PARK
Between 8th and 13th Avenues
East of Lafayette Street
This vast urban oasis just east of downtown features a great 1.5-mile walking/jogging path, enormous trees, manicured flower gardens, and, at the eastern edge, an impressive pavilion with a stunning mountain view. It's one of the city's most popular sunset viewpoints. The compressed dirt jogging path is popular with nearby residents. The park was established in 1892 on the city's former first cemetery lot. It is adjacent to the Denver Botanic Gardens. To get there, take 14th Avenue east from downtown to Lafayette, then head south 1 block.

CITY PARK
17th Avenue Parkway and Colorado Boulevard

At 330 acres in size, City Park is Denver's largest park. The lake is ringed by acres of grass and mature trees that offer wonderful spots for picnicking. There is also an extensive path for biking, walking, and in-line skating. The historic City Park Pavilion has been restored, with a bandstand on the lake's west shore. During summer months, paddleboats can be rented for only $5 an hour. The Denver Zoo and the Museum of Nature and Science occupy the park's east end. To get there, take 17th Avenue east out of downtown to York Street. The park lies between York Street and Colorado Boulevard.

COMMONS PARK
Between 15th and 19th Streets on Little Raven Drive

Commons Park is Denver's most unusual urban park. It opened in 2001, reclaiming land that held Denver's earliest settlers from years of neglect. It was envisioned as the crown jewel in a string of riverfront parks that bisect the city. Forward-thinking city fathers (and mothers) spent more than 2 decades amassing the land, scraping away the rail yards and hobo shanties, and planning for redevelopment. First came the city park, a grassy knoll that offers people a place to stare at the eastern skyline and the mountains to the west or listen to a concert staged in the outdoor arena. Along one side, visitors can dabble their feet in the waters of the South Platte River. The pricey high-rises came next, attracting families and retirees, empty nesters, and urban professionals with their close proximity to Elitch Gardens amusement park, Coors Field, the Pepsi Center, and a free city-owned

50,000-square-foot skateboard park that attracts 200 to 300 skaters a day. Reach this rich cultural stew by riding the 16th Street shuttle west to its end point, then walking across the Millennium Bridge. By car, follow I-25 to Speer Boulevard, then exit south. Turn right at Elitch Circle, and keep turning right until you're on Little Raven Street. The park runs alongside Little Raven Street between 15th and 19th Streets.

DENVER BOTANIC GARDENS AT CHATFIELD
8500 Deer Creek Canyon Rd., Littleton
(303) 973-3705
botanicgardens.org

This little gem offers historic sites, trails, and naturalist guides. It's a great place for a picnic, and the traditional playground next to the historic schoolhouse is fun for kids. Each fall the gardens creates an 8-acre corn maze, with hayrides, pony rides, and food vendors providing more fun. Down the path along Deer Creek, you can see the foundation where the schoolhouse was before they moved it. Look for the piece of chain on one of the cottonwood branches above the path, the remnant of the swing where kids played more than 100 years ago. The nature preserve is just off Wadsworth Boulevard south of C-470 and is open daily 9 a.m. to 5 p.m. Admission is charged.

i The must-see view of Metro Denver and the Rocky Mountains can be had from the entrance to the Denver Museum of Nature and Science in City Park at Colorado Boulevard and Montview Street. The sweeping vista of treetops, skyscrapers, and snowcapped peaks is the best in town.

DINOSAUR RIDGE
16831 W. Alameda Pkwy., Morrison
(303) 697-DINO (3466)
dinoridge.org
This unexpected park is a treasure of exposed dinosaur bones and tracks, along with plant and animal fossils. In 1877, some of the nation's best preserved dinosaur bones were found on the slope of this ridgeline, and highway construction exposed dinosaur tracks in 1930. Life and science teachers treat this geologic treasure as an outdoor classroom, introducing their students to the place where the mountains meet the prairie, and where plant and animal life of all kinds has been fossilized in rock layers that have been uplifted over time until they pierced the ground.

A visitor center provides information about the discovery, but Dinosaur Ridge is essentially an outdoor experience. Reach it by traveling west on I-70 to the Morrison exit, then following Highway 26 south to West Alameda Parkway. Turn left and follow the road to the visitor center, which provides information about hours, tours, and displays, and also contains a small gift shop. Guided tours are offered of this wheelchair-accessible site. Admission is free, but donations are accepted.

SLOAN LAKE PARK
17th Avenue and Sheridan Boulevard
Sloan Lake is a Westside landmark, with acres of landscaped shoreline around a great boating lake. Dragon boat races are staged here each summer during the annual Dragon Boat Festival, joining a fleet of privately owned canoes and powerboats on the water. On dry land, children play in the large playground, joggers and strollers follow the trail that rings the lake, and others grab spots on the grass for picnics, Frisbee games, or summer naps. To get there, take Colfax Avenue west to Sheridan Boulevard, then right to 17th Avenue.

WASHINGTON PARK
Louisiana Avenue and Downing Street
Also designed around water, Washington Park is popular with sports enthusiasts of all types. Its lakeside paths are often used for organized races, but they're just as fun for bicycling, walking/jogging, and in-line skating. Two lakes in the middle provide fishing (especially for kids), and grassy lawns on all sides are used for impromptu soccer and volleyball games. The flower gardens along Downing Street are perfection, serving as the backdrop for many tourist photographs. But most of all, "Wash Park," as it's known, is a wonderful spot to relax and enjoy Denver's blue skies and sunny weather.

State Parks & Recreation Areas

County park and open-space systems extend the city's green space into Jefferson, Adams, Douglas, and Arapahoe Counties. The Denver Mountain Parks system includes 14,000 acres of land scattered through four counties. Red Rocks Park is one of these, as is the Winter Park ski area (see our Ski Country chapter for details). Colorado also oversees four state parks and two state recreation areas within driving distance of Denver. Expect to pay use fees in most of these parks.

BARR LAKE STATE PARK
13401 Picadilly Rd., Brighton
(303) 659-6005
parks.state.co.us/Parks/BarrLake
Barr Lake is a 2,700-acre state park surrounding a 1,900-acre prairie reservoir. Decades ago the reservoir used to be something of

a sewage dump, and people would roll up their car windows when they drove past it on I-76. But that was long ago. Today it's a charming and tranquil place with more than 300 species of birds. It's the area's best place to watch eagles that hunt around the lake and nest in the trees at the lake's southern half, which is designated as a wildlife refuge (no pets allowed in this area). It's also the biggest lake in the Denver area, where you can canoe, kayak, or otherwise go boating without being buzzed by personal watercraft, powerboats, and water-skiers. The only boats allowed on the lake are sailboats, hand-propelled craft, and boats with electric trolling motors or gas engines of 10 horsepower or less. Hiking here is pleasant because the lakeshore is lined with cottonwoods. There are plenty of aquatic plants and marshes, where it's always interesting to watch the big carp rooting and sucking. On both the north and south ends of the lake, you can walk out on wooden boardwalks extending into the water and watch wildlife from the gazebo at the end. Bring binoculars. Camping is not allowed at Barr Lake, but the park is open 5 a.m. to 10 p.m. daily year-round. To get there, take I-76 northeast out of Denver about 20 miles to exit 22, Bromley Lane, east to Picadilly Road, and south to the park entrance. There's also a nature center with displays and information and a bookstore.

CHATFIELD STATE RECREATION AREA
11500 N. Roxborough Park Rd., Littleton
(303) 791-7275
parks.state.co.us/Parks/Chatfield
Here you'll find Metro Denver's widest range of outdoor experiences, from powerboating to appreciating nature in remote surroundings. Along the southern end of the park, where the South Platte River empties into

Chatfield Reservoir, you'll find ample opportunities to enjoy heavily wooded areas that are tucked beneath a striking canopy of old-growth river-bottom cottonwoods. People bike, hike, watch birds, and ride horses along the river, stopping occasionally to cast a line into the stream. On the west side, between the river and US 75, you can walk along a wetlands area that contains ponds, waterfowl, animals, and flora. On the northern end, the reservoir is the star of the show. Its first-rate swimming beach is open Memorial Day through Labor Day. Boaters, water-skiers, and anglers share the water, with paddleboats, pontoon boats, water toys, and other vessels available to rent from the Chatfield Marina. Horseback rides are provided at Chatfield Stables. (More details are available in the Horseback Riding, Boating & Windsurfing sections of this chapter). The campgrounds have more than 150 sites with all the amenities, but we suggest reservations (303-470-1144). Note that dogs are allowed in Chatfield if they are leashed or are in an off-leash exercise area on the north side of the dam. To reach Chatfield, take I-25 or I-70 to C-470, then C-470 to the Wadsworth Boulevard exit. The park entrance is on the left.

CHERRY CREEK STATE PARK
4201 S. Parker Rd., Aurora
(303) 690-1166
parks.state.co.us/Parks/CherryCreek
Because it is centrally located, Cherry Creek State Park attracts so many visitors it's often at capacity on summer weekends. Water lovers are drawn to the reservoir, which has 880 surface acres of water, while nature lovers find solace in the natural prairie environment that surrounds it. In addition to camping, picnicking, trail riding, and guided nature walks, Cherry Creek offers model

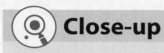

Close-up

A Stroll Along the South Platte River

Early pioneers deemed the South Platte River "too thick to drink, too thin to plow." As Denver grew, the local river became a dumping ground, polluted, abused, and neglected. In 1974 a major cleanup effort began, and today it's a 30-mile greenway of parks, trails, trees, and wildlife habitat. The South Platte River Greenway Trail is a paved riverside path shared by walkers, bicyclists, birders, skaters, and joggers. Whitewater boat chutes provide thrills for kayakers and fun for spectators during spring snowmelt. Any stretch is pleasant, but some favorites are the urban section heading upriver from the confluence with Cherry Creek (by the downtown REI flagship store), and the lower section from the crossing at Alameda Avenue to the trail end just north of Chatfield State Park. For more information, contact Visit Denver, the Convention and Visitors Bureau (303-892-1505; visitdenver.com/biketrails).

airplane flying, a shooting range, and a riding stable. Along the trail systems you may see mule deer and white-tailed deer, owls, coyotes, and foxes. Plan to make camping reservations well ahead of time. (More information about the marina is provided in the Boating & Windsurfing section of this chapter.) The recreation area is 1 mile south of I-225 on Parker Road, and is open daily 5 a.m. to 10 p.m.

GOLDEN GATE CANYON STATE PARK
92 Crawford Gulch Rd., Golden
(303) 582-3707
parks.state.co.us/Parks/
GoldenGateCanyon
This is the most mountainous of the six state parks closest to Metro Denver. It covers 14,000 acres with altitudes that range from 7,600 to 10,400 feet; has 275 picnic sites, 35 miles of trails for foot and hoof, and more than 130 campsites, as well as 20 backcountry shelters and tent sites. Two yurts and fire cabins are a recent addition to camping choices. (Reservations are recommended.) Stop at the visitor center on

the park's lower east end (open 9 a.m. to 4 p.m. daily) to get your bearings, browse through the museum, and watch the trout in a nearby pool. A nature trail designed for the physically impaired begins just outside the center. To reach the park, turn west off Highway 93 onto Golden Gate Canyon Road and follow it for about 15 miles.

ROXBOROUGH STATE PARK
4751 N. Roxborough Dr., Littleton
(303) 973-3959
parks.state.co.us/Parks/Roxborough
Roxborough was Colorado's first state park to be designated both a Colorado Natural Area and a National Natural Landmark. There is only one building, the visitor center, which serves as the gateway to a number of lovely hikes through dramatic terrain. The hikes are gentle, but the geology is spectacular, especially the Dakota Hogback and the red-rock moonscape of the Fountain Formation. There are no picnic sites, nor are camping, rock climbing, and pets allowed. Reach Roxborough by following US 85 (Santa Fe Drive) south from Denver to Titan Road. Take a right

onto Titan Road and go 3.5 miles. Follow Titan Road left onto Rampart Range Road. Go 3 miles and turn left onto Roxborough Park Road, then take an immediate right onto the park access road.

RECREATION

Bicycling

With more than 850 miles of biking, jogging, and walking trails, Metro Denver is one of the nation's most bike-friendly cities. Bike trails take riders to many local attractions, including the REI flagship store, Red Rocks Amphitheatre, the South Platte River, and Cherry Creek shopping district. For biking suggestions around the city, go to visitdenver.com/biketrails. Another good source for Colorado biking information is bikepaths.com. The city and county of Denver maintain good trail maps that can be downloaded or purchased (go to bikedenver.org/maps for details). The following are a few of our favorites.

BEAR CREEK BIKE TRAIL

You probably won't see any bears here, but this 20-mile trail from the South Platte River to the town of Morrison has great scenery and side trails connecting to Chatfield, Red Rocks, and Bear Creek Lake Parks. Stop in Morrison for ice cream and browse the antiques shops.

CHERRY CREEK BIKE PATH

Running east-west through Denver's urban core, the Cherry Creek Bike Path is one of a kind. It begins at Confluence Park, at the intersection of the South Platte River and Cherry Creek, and wanders through some of the ritziest areas of Cherry Creek before dumping riders out in Aurora. For much of the way, it follows the creek and is worlds away from the roadways above. Riders share the paved path with in-line skaters, joggers, and walkers, but in exchange they see everything from the Cherry Creek Country Club to beaver ponds.

CLEAR CREEK TRAIL

Running 20 miles from the Platte River Trail in Metro Denver through Wheat Ridge and on to Golden, this path parallels scenic Clear Creek for most of its length. It passes through the Wheat Ridge Greenbelt, skirts several reservoirs, and ends in Golden close to the Coors Brewery. The stretch from the greenbelt to Golden is popular with anglers, birders, and nature lovers.

EAST 7TH AVENUE BIKE ROUTE

This ride takes you through city streets, so watching for traffic is a must. But if you're more interested in sampling Denver's scenery and architecture than getting a real workout, this is a nice ride. Start just south of downtown at Broadway and East 7th Avenue, then head east on 7th and follow the bike route signs. You can take it for 4 miles before it dead-ends at Colorado Boulevard, through Denver's oldest neighborhoods, replete with mansions and stunning old trees.

THE HIGHLINE CANAL

This Denver-area highlight was built in the 1880s and is now lined by huge cottonwoods in what amounts to a river of ancient trees through the city. This favorite trail runs from Waterton Canyon in the west to Aurora's Environmental Park in the east. Depending on the time of year, the canal will either be swollen with spring runoff or bone dry. Watch for horses, as the dirt areas are popular with equestrians.

PARKS & RECREATION

i For a truly green tour of the Mile High City, explore Denver's 850 miles of off-road, paved and packed-earth bike paths through the city's bicycle sharing program, B-cycle (303-825-3325; denver.bcycle.com). Red B-cycles are available at more than 50 bike stations around Denver. For a small fee, anyone can pick one up and take it sightseeing, to lunch, or on errands before returning it to any B-station.

PLATTE RIVER GREENWAY TRAIL

This major bike trail in Metro Denver runs from Chatfield Reservoir in the southwest to the city of Thornton in the upper north metro region. The trail passes through more than a dozen parks. Access points are legion; consult trail maps for details. Two popular access points are Confluence Park at 15th and Platte Streets near Lower Downtown and Ruby Hill Park near Evans Street and Broadway.

Resources

Along with the bike trail suggestions we listed at the beginning of this section, the state of Colorado has urban trail maps for four different areas of the state. One of those is for the metropolitan Denver area: Urban Trails in Colorado, Denver Metro Area. The state also has a very useful Colorado Trails Resource Guide. These references are available free if you stop by or write Trails Guides, 1313 Sherman Ave., Room 618, Denver, CO 80203. Provide a self-addressed, stamped return envelope with six first-class stamps; the envelope should measure at least 6 by 9 inches. Some bike shops will have urban trail maps available as well.

Rentals

It's easy to rent a bike in Metro Denver. There are numerous rental shops in the area, but we've listed a few that have been around for a long time.

ADVENTURE CYCLING
4361 S. Parker Rd., Aurora
(303) 699-2514
adventurecycle.net

Adventure Cycling is convenient to those in the southeast part of Metro Denver.

THE BICYCLE DOCTOR
860 Broadway
(303) 831-7228
bicycledr.com

Located near downtown Denver, the Bicycle Doctor is a full-service shop that works on bicycles when it's not servicing skis. It also rents both.

SPORTS RENT
8761 Wadsworth Blvd., Arvada
(303) 467-0200
sportsrent.net

This shop specializes in dirt bike, boat, personal watercraft, and ATV rentals.

TREADS BICYCLE OUTFITTERS
3546 S. Logan, Lakewood
(303) 781-1162
treads.com

This shop rents everything from trail bikes for pavement to high-performance mountain bikes and has maps and brochures for sale. Additional locations are at 16701 E. Iliff Ave., Aurora (303-750-1671); and 10831 S. Crossroads Dr., Parker (303-690-2900).

Mountain Biking

If any outdoor sport could be said to define Colorado, mountain biking would probably run a close second to skiing. Hikers are still the primary users of Colorado backcountry, but increasingly they are sharing their trails with bikers. Mountain bikes have fat nubby tires, super-light frames, and gearing low enough to ride up the steepest hills.

A lot of great mountain-biking trails are located in Jefferson County on Denver's immediate west side. These are wonderful places for their terrain, scenery, and/or technical aspects. All are accessible to anyone with reasonably fit lungs and legs.

DEER CREEK PARK TRAIL

This area is about 4 miles up Deer Creek Canyon from Wadsworth Boulevard, in the Jefferson County Open Space. Its steep trails aren't for beginners or those who haven't been working out. Deer Creek Park has one hiker-only trail.

HAYDEN-GREEN MOUNTAIN PARK TRAILS

These intermediate trails also challenge riders. They wind through the park before climbing 1,200 feet to the Green Mountain summit. To get there, take 6th Avenue west to the Union Street exit, go south to Alameda Avenue, then right. The park is on the right side.

MOUNT FALCON

Several bike loops for riders with moderate technical skills can be accessed from the pavilion at Walker's Dream Shelter. To reach it, take US 285 west past C-470 to the Morrison exit, then right. Follow the clearly marked signs. From the Morrison trailhead,

you can head up the Castle Trail to the pavilion at Walker's Dream Shelter. Avoid the area's hiker-only trail.

> **i** The Sand Creek Regional Greenway Trail is a newly completed, 14-mile walking, horseback, and biking trail that even many residents still don't know about. The mostly unpaved trail connects the Platte River Greenway in Commerce City with the High Line Canal in Aurora and completes a 50-mile loop through wetlands, along creek beds, and beneath an old airport runway. Because much of the trail is soft-surface, bicyclists will probably want to ride a cross, hybrid, or mountain bike.

WATERTON CANYON

There are lovely, gentle trails around the Chatfield Recreation area, but up Waterton Canyon it gets a little more dramatic. No dogs are allowed because the canyon is home to a herd of bighorn sheep. A 6-mile dirt road heads up past Cottonwood Gulch, Mill Gulch, and Stevens Gulch to the Colorado Trail. To reach it, take Wadsworth Boulevard south from its junction with C-470, 4 miles to the Waterton Canyon Recreation Area sign, and turn left to park.

References

One of the best overall references for these and other rides is *The Best of Colorado Biking Trails* (revised edition), published by Outdoor Books & Maps, Inc. of Denver and available in many local bookstores, bike shops, and outing stores. Another is *Mountain Biking Denver and Boulder* by Bob D'Antonio (Globe Pequot Press).

Boating & Windsurfing

Boaters and windsurfers have a lot of lakes and reservoirs to choose from around Metro Denver, but if you're into powerboating, only a select few are large enough and allow enough horsepower to do more than putt from one fishing spot to the next. The most popular lakes for powerboating are the big boys: Cherry Creek and Chatfield Reservoir. Both are large reservoirs and, as part of state recreation areas, are nice environments in which to split the water. You can find more general descriptions of these areas in the State Parks & Recreation Areas section of this chapter, but boaters will be interested to know that both have extensive marinas offering a lot of rentals.

AURORA RESERVOIR MARINA
5800 S. Powhaton Rd., Aurora
(303) 690-1286
auroragov.org
This newer facility is 7 miles east of Quincy Reservoir in Arapahoe County. Powerboaters pay it little attention, since gas motors aren't allowed on the water, but the water is clean, and it's popular with sailors and windsurfers. There's a little marina with a general store where you can rent electric motorboats, rowboats, sailboats, sailboards, paddleboats, and canoes. It also features a paved bike path that stretches about 8 miles around the lake. You'll find the reservoir by driving about 2 miles east of Gun Club Road on East Quincy Avenue and turning right at Powhaton Road. Hours vary depending on sunrise and sunset, but generally run from dawn to dusk, and visitors will be charged a daily vehicle pass fee.

BEAR CREEK LAKE PARK
15600 W. Morrison Rd., Morrison
(303) 697-6159
lakewood.org/bclp
There are three water areas here: Bear Creek Lake, Little Soda Lake, and Big Soda Lake. Bear Creek is mainly for fishing as it allows no motors greater than 10 horsepower. There also is some sailing. An admission fee is charged, and there are no rentals. The access point is easy to see off Morrison Road, once you exit C-470. Big Soda Lake is open to the public for nonmotorized boats and has its own Soda Lake Marina (303-697-1522) where you can rent paddleboats, kayaks, sailboards, and canoe. Big Soda also has a swimming area. Little Soda Lake isn't open for public boating.

CHATFIELD MARINA
11500 N. Roxborough Park Rd., Littleton
(303) 791-5555
chatfieldmarina.com
This marina for the Chatfield Reservoir includes a store with boating and fishing supplies, groceries, and take-out food. It's Denver's only on-the-water grill and deli restaurant with a patio and an observation deck. The season runs April through October. Fishing boats, pontoon boats, and paddleboats can be rented by the hour or by the day. Call ahead for reservations.

CHERRY CREEK MARINA
4800 S. Dayton, Greenwood Village
(303) 779-6144, (303) 699-2501 (yacht club)
cherrycreekmarina.com
The marina is on the west side of the Cherry Creek reservoir; just follow the signs after entering. It has slips and rents pontoon boats, fishing boats, monohull dinghy

Public Recreation Centers and Programs

Public parks and recreation departments are your greatest resource for year-round exercise options. Public centers are prevalent throughout Metro Denver, most of which have indoor and outdoor swimming pools as well as fitness equipment, basketball courts, and other kinds of programming that can include youth team sports leagues. Because their offerings are too extensive to list here, we've just provided the contact numbers for you to call. Refer to other sections in this chapter for specifics about individual activities such as tennis or golf.

Denver

Denver Parks and Recreation Department
(720) 913-1311

Adams County

Adams County Parks and Community Resource
Aurora Parks and Open Space Department
(303) 739-7160

Brighton Recreation Center
(303) 655-2200

Commerce City Parks and Recreation Department
(303) 289-3789

Hyland Hills Park and Recreation District, Federal Heights
(303) 428-7488

Northglenn Parks and Recreation Department
(303) 450-8800

Thornton Recreation Center
(303) 255-7800

Arapahoe County

Aurora Parks and Recreation Department
(303) 739-7160

Englewood Parks Department
(303) 762-2680

South Suburban Park and Recreation District
(303) 798-5131

Douglas County

Castle Rock Recreation Center
(303) 660-1036

Parker Recreation Center
(303) 841-4500

Jefferson County

Arvada Parks and Recreation District
(303) 424-2739

Broomfield Community Center
(303) 464-5500

Foothills Park and Recreation District
(303) 409-2100

Golden Community Center
(303) 384-8100

Lakewood Recreation Department
(303) 987-7800

Westminster Parks and Recreation Department
(303) 460-9690

Wheat Ridge Recreation Center
(303) 231-1300

sailboats, Sunfish, paddleboats, kayaks, and canoes.

STANDLEY LAKE REGIONAL PARK
9805 W. 88th Ave., Westminster
(303) 425-1097
ci.westminster.co.us
Standley Lake, the big north Jefferson County lake bordered on the north and east by Westminster and on the south by Arvada, is a popular location for windsurfing, camping, fishing, bird watching, and ambling along the shore on trails. Motorboats are allowed there between May 1 and September 30, but you need a permit for boats with more than 20 horsepower, and the number of permits is limited. Call the number above for more information. There are no rental facilities at Standley.

Climbing

Climbing isn't a sport for beginners, but for anyone interested in getting the most from their workout, it can provide unparalleled challenges. Most of Colorado's best climbs are a drive away from the Denver area, but you can start by taking lessons and learning the ropes at local recreation centers with in-house climbing walls. Once you've mastered the basics, you can graduate to climbing areas just outside of Boulder, where the terrain is internationally known. Prefer to climb in groups? We've listed some that arrange excursions.

CITY PARK RECREATION CENTER
10455 Sheridan Blvd., Westminster
(303) 460-9690
ci.westminster.co.us
City Park has its own climbing wall in the gymnasium, where people can practice or take climbing lessons while the basketballs

bounce behind them. Classes are offered for beginner, intermediate, and advanced climbers. Or you can take a short orientation, then pay a low drop-in fee.

COLORADO MOUNTAIN CLUB
710 10th St., No. 200, Golden
(303) 279-3080
cmc.org
Technical climbing instruction is available from the grandfather of Colorado mountaineering organizations, the Colorado Mountain Club, but classes are offered only once a year. Basic rock climbing is offered in May and June, and the intermediate class is usually in August or September. Membership is required, but reduced rates for Friends of Colorado Mountain Club memberships are available for out-of-staters.

ELDORADO CANYON STATE PARK
9 Kneale Rd., Eldorado Springs
(303) 494-3943
parks.state.co.us/Parks/eldoradocanyon
No discussion of mountain climbing can occur without mentioning Eldorado Canyon State Park. It's where athletes from around the world gather to practice their skills, swap stories, and train for the really big mountains. The park is day-use only and boasts 500 routes that rise as much as 1,500 feet above the canyon floor. The easiest are used for climbing lessons; the most challenging are reserved for the experts. Because the area is a state park, expect to pay a use fee and then relax at picnic tables or by biking or fishing in the stream.

REI (RECREATIONAL EQUIPMENT, INC.)
1416 Platte St.
(303) 756-3100
rei.com

This gigantic store tempts visitors with its climbing wall at the entrance. REI offers a variety of classes for all levels. Kids climb free on Saturday, and free clinics are offered monthly. Call for details and times. REI's wall is designed for an introduction to climbing so it isn't equal to the rock gyms mentioned above. Beyond the wall, the store offers a full range of retail equipment for climbing and mountaineering. Walls and lessons also are available at REI stores at 1789 28th St., Boulder (303-583-9970); 9637 E. County Line Rd., Englewood (303-858-1726); and 5375 S. Wadsworth Blvd., Lakewood (303-932-0600).

THRILLSEEKERS
1912 S. Broadway
(303) 733-8810
thrillseekers.cc
This climbing gym offers more than 12,000 square feet of climbing space, including a 35-foot roof climb, 40 top ropes, five lead walls where climbers can get horizontal, and a separate "bouldering" area where you can free-climb. A complete lesson program is available for all levels, and a full retail section will fill your every climbing need. Lesson prices vary depending on level and number of people, so call ahead.

Fishing

One-third of the state's land area is open to public hunting and fishing, which is why Colorado is a national destination for these activities. People come from the Midwest and both coasts to cast a fly in rushing mountain streams.

Fishing in Colorado, of course, isn't just a matter of mountain trout streams. The state has flatland rivers, large lakes, and reservoirs aplenty. Colorado's 6,000-plus miles of streams and 2,000-plus lakes and reservoirs open to public fishing include high-country fishing for cutthroat, brook, brown, lake, and rainbow trout. There's also a lot of warm-water quarry such as walleye, largemouth and smallmouth bass, catfish, crappie, yellow perch, wiper, bluegill, and muskie. A lot of warm-water fishing is available right in Metro Denver. The state's record tiger muskie (40 pounds, 2 ounces) was caught in Quincy Reservoir, a half-mile east of Buckley Road on Quincy Avenue in Aurora.

The *Denver Post* publishes a weekly fishing and stocking report provided by the Colorado Division of Wildlife called "Colorado's Best Bets" that offers anglers up-to-the-minute scoops on hot fishing spots.

Recorded information about fishing (license fees, locations, limits, etc.) is available from the Division of Wildlife (303-291-7533); information on specific fishing conditions throughout the state is available mid-April through Labor Day weekend by calling (303) 291-7534. You can also visit the Colorado Division of Wildlife's website at wildlife.state.co.us/fishing.

Licenses
Fishing licenses are required; you can get yours at most major sports and outdoors stores or online at wildlife.state.co.us/fishing. The cost is $26 per year for Colorado residents, $56 for nonresidents. A day license costs $9 for residents and nonresidents, and a 5-day license is $21, nonresidents only. There are discounts for senior citizens and people with disabilities; children younger than age 16 do not need a license. Anglers receive a complete rules and regulations brochure when they purchase a license. Brochures are usually available where you buy your license. There are various size and

quantity limits as well as rules on allowable bait, depending on the waters and type of fish.

Fishing Spots

Although Colorado has been suffering through drought conditions that have affected reservoir levels and stream flows, the state remains world-famous for its Gold Medal trout waters. These lakes and streams have a high-quality aquatic habitat, a high percentage of trout 14 inches or longer, and a high potential for trophy fish. The Colorado Division of Wildlife has a booklet on the state's Gold Medal waters and other hot spots; find it online at wildlife.state.co.us/fishing/wheretogo.

The South Platte River is one of the best rainbow and brown trout fisheries in the nation and is world-famous among fly fishers. This Gold Medal river is for the serious fishing enthusiast and has it all: proximity to Denver, lots of big fish, consistent insect hatches, and incredible scenery. The Cheesman Canyon section of the South Platte holds approximately 5,200 trout per mile that average 15 inches in length (although some locals will tell you it also seems to have at least that many anglers).

The two best ways to reach Cheesman Canyon both involve traveling south to the Deckers area and then working your way back north along the river. Take US 285 west from Denver, then turn south onto County Road 126 at Pine Junction. Follow CR 126 for 20 miles toward Deckers; the Gill Trail parking lot is just off CR 126. The Gill trailhead is a 20-minute hike from the Gill Trail parking lot. If the hike to Gill Trail doesn't sound appealing, just continue on CR 126 into Deckers; parking and open fishing is plentiful right along the road north of town.

For those looking for an enjoyable but less rigorous fishing expedition, Denver-area reservoirs offer a wide range of opportunities.

Aurora Reservoir is home to some hefty rainbow and brown trout, with fish up to 17 inches not uncommon, and also contains many warm-water species such as largemouth bass, crappie, yellow perch, and walleye. The reservoir is open year-round from dawn until dusk. Take I-25 or I-225 to 6th Avenue and follow it until it turns south to become Gun Club Road. Quincy Avenue is about 2 miles past the BFI landfill. The reservoir is about a half-mile east at 5800 S. Powhaton Rd. and charges a daily access fee.

Chatfield Reservoir is one of the Denver area's most popular recreation spots. The 1,100-acre reservoir is an impoundment of the South Platte River described earlier in this section and offers fishing access to the river both above and below the reservoir itself. A daily Colorado State Parks permit is required. From Denver, take Wadsworth Boulevard (Highway 121) south past C-470, and turn left into the park at the Deer Creek entrance. As an alternate route, take Santa Fe Boulevard south to Titan Road and turn west. Go to Roxborough Park Road, and turn north to the Plum Creek entrance.

Golf

Metro Denver is a golfer's paradise, with more than 70 golf courses, 90 percent of them public. And if you want to make a day of it, there are another 20 or so spectacular mountain-area courses within a 1- to 2-hour drive from downtown Denver.

As with many major metropolitan areas, Denver's city courses are typically smaller, older tracts, but they often have more character than the treeless suburban courses that tend to show up in housing developments. While these inner-city layouts might not attract tournament golf, they almost always present more of a challenge than you would expect, the price is usually easier on the wallet, and you can get to most of them by cab, avoiding the freeways around Denver.

On the other hand, there is nothing, like teeing off in the Rocky Mountains at one of the nearby mountain courses. It's not unusual for a first-time player to return from a day of golf in Breckenridge or Winter Park only to find he can't remember how he played—he spent too much time looking around at the scenery!

Most courses require advance tee times but limit how far in advance you can call, usually not more than 7 days. This is only a problem if you need a weekend tee time, when courses are most crowded, or if you have no flexibility in your schedule. Otherwise, local experience reports that many courses can fit you in with a same-day call, and sometimes you can even "walk-on" without a tee-time reservation. Resorts typically allow you to make tee times when booking your vacation.

There are several excellent publications and websites that you can use to get course information in the Denver area, plus we're going to highlight some of the more exceptional courses in this chapter. *Colorado AvidGolfer Magazine* is available online at coloradoavidgolfer.com, by subscription at (720) 493-1729, or at local newsstands monthly. *Colorado Golf Magazine* is available online at coloradogolf.com or via quarterly subscription at (303) 688-5853. *DIVOT Magazine*, published in Littleton, is available online at divotmagazine.com or by phone at (303) 797-8700.

ARROWHEAD GOLF CLUB
10850 W. Sundown Trail, Littleton
(303) 973-9614
arrowheadcolorado.com

Designed by Robert Trent Jones Jr. in 1971, Arrowhead is a par-72, 18-hole course that winds 6,682 yards through a landscape of scrub oak and magnificent red sandstone rock formations. Arrowhead is regarded as one of the most beautiful and challenging courses in the state, and it regularly makes *Golf Digest*'s top 20 list of places to play in Colorado. Tee times can be made up to 7 days in advance, with greens fees ranging from $60 to $135 depending on day and time of year. No denim is allowed, and collared shirts are required. Take I-25 south to C-470 west, exit onto Santa Fe Drive, and go south 4 miles to Titan Parkway. Turn right onto Titan Parkway, follow it until it becomes Rampart Range Road, then follow the signs to Arrowhead.

BRECKENRIDGE GOLF CLUB
200 Clubhouse Dr., Breckenridge
(970) 453-9104
breckenridgegolfclub.com

Breckenridge Golf Club has the distinction of being the only municipally owned Jack Nicklaus–designed course in the world, and it is a masterpiece. Rated one of "America's Top 75 Upscale Golf Courses" by *Golf Digest*, Breckenridge features 27 holes that include some of the most beautiful valley vistas on any course anywhere. Like most mountain courses, the layout incorporates many of the surrounding area's natural settings, with tree-lined fairways, rock outcroppings, and hazard areas filled with mountain bushes and flowers. Greens fees are typical for mountain courses, between $65 and $114 depending on time of year for 18 holes plus

$18 per person for a cart. Tee-time reservations can be made 4 days in advance. Breckenridge is about 90 miles west of Denver. Take I-70 west to exit 203, and turn south onto Highway 9. Go 7 miles to Tiger Road. Turn left onto Tiger Road and proceed to your first right turn.

FOX HOLLOW GOLF COURSE
13410 W. Morrison Rd., Lakewood
(303) 986-7888
lakewood.org
Operated by the city of Lakewood, Fox Hollow is a 27-hole course you play by booking two of the three 9-hole venues, each of which offers a unique layout ranging from wide-open links to tree-lined river bottom to rugged canyon-lands. Part of the course is on a mesa with spectacular views of Denver and the plains beyond. Call for tee times up to 6 days in advance, wear appropriate golf attire to the course, and think about adding a third 9 holes to your round for an extra $25. Take C-470 south to the Morrison Road exit, then go east on Morrison Road for 3.5 miles. The course, which is well signed, will be on your right.

LEGACY RIDGE
10801 Legacy Ridge Pkwy., Westminster
(303) 438-8997
ci.westminster.co.us
Although parts of Legacy Ridge's 18-hole, par-72 course are laid out among housing developments, the majority of the holes either wind through protected wetlands or traverse a ridge that offers spectacular views of the Front Range of the Rockies. Renowned Ohio architect Arthur Hills designed this course in 1994, and it regularly makes the top 10 in player polls. If you play late in the day, be sure to enjoy a classic Colorado

sunset from the outdoor deck of the clubhouse bar and grill. From Denver take I-25 north to US 36 west, toward Boulder. Exit US 36 at the 104th Avenue exit, and head east on 104th Avenue to Legacy Ridge Parkway. Turn left and watch for the clubhouse on your left.

POLE CREEK GOLF CLUB
6827 County Rd. 51, Tabernash
(970) 887-9195, (800) 511-5076
polecreekgolf.com
When Pole Creek opened in 1985, it was named "Best New Public Course in the United States" by *Golf Digest*. Surrounded by 13,000-foot snowcapped peaks, at an elevation of 8,600 feet, Pole Creek is quintessential Colorado mountain golf. The original 18-hole layout, designed by Gary Player and Ron Kirby, has been expanded by Denis Griffiths to 27 holes that play up into the lodgepole pines, back down into the river-bottom meadows, and through some of the most beautiful scenery in the state. At this elevation golfers can expect an extra 15 percent distance on their shots, just one of the many benefits of making the drive up from Denver to play here. Tee times can be made 5 days in advance. Pole Creek is located 78 miles from Denver. Take I-70 west to exit 232, then follow US 40 to Winter Park. Pole Creek is 11 miles beyond the town of Winter Park. Turn left at the 220-mile marker and follow the signs to the course.

RED HAWK RIDGE
2156 Red Hawk Ridge Dr., Castle Rock
(720) 733-3500
redhawkridge.com
Red Hawk Ridge, south of Denver in Castle Rock, is a virtual cousin to nearby private Castle Pines, the country club famous for The

International pro-golf tournament. Designed by Jim Engh and opened in 1999, the par 72, 6,942-yard Red Hawk Ridge received immediate rave reviews in national golf publications for its dramatic setting and design, including the 15th hole, a 528-yard par 4 that shoots blind to a plateau, then downhill into a valley where the green lies at the bottom. Tee times can be made up to 7 days in advance. From I-25 take the Wolfensberger exit and turn west after approximately 0.5 miles. Turn right onto Red Hawk Drive and go about another 0.25 mile; the golf course is on the left.

RIVERDALE DUNES
13300 Riverdale Rd., Brighton
(303) 659-6700
riverdalegolf.com
Riverdale Dunes is a true hidden gem. Designed by Pete and Perry Dye in 1985, this course garners national praise every year from leading golf magazines. Rated as one of the "Top 75 Public Courses" in the country by *Golf Digest,* and the "#1 Public Course in Colorado" by *Colorado Golfer Newspaper,* the Dunes is an 18-hole, par-72 course that plays 6,398 yards in a Scottish-style links layout. Though hard to find, this reasonably priced, immaculately maintained course is worth the effort. From Denver go north on I-25 to the 120th Avenue exit, then east to Colorado Boulevard and turn left. Follow Colorado Boulevard to 128th Avenue and turn right. 128th Avenue ends at Riverdale Road, and you will feel as though you're in the middle of nowhere, but turn left onto Riverdale Road and follow it about 1.5 miles to the enormous clubhouse, which you will see on your right.

Hiking

Hiking is the most common way of enjoying Colorado's backcountry. For information on hiking safety and our favorite places to hike, see our Great Outdoors chapter.

Horseback Riding

What's more quintessentially Western than an outing on the back of a horse, especially when you're trotting along on the prairies or foothills? Riding in the Denver suburbs may not compare with the more remote horse experiences in the high country and points west, but it beats a canter through Midwestern cornfields.

A lot of people on the outskirts of Denver have their own horses, but those who don't can book rides at a variety of fine local stables. Those located in the two state recreation areas on Metro Denver's south side are nice, if for no other reason than that they're located in large and carefully cultivated natural areas that are filled with nature trails on which to ride.

CHATFIELD STABLES
11500 N. Roxborough Rd., Littleton
(303) 933-3636
chatfieldstables.com
The stables at the Chatfield State Recreation Area provide a serene riding setting with great foothill views. Rides can be available as early as March or April, depending on how wet the spring is, but regular summer hours begin May 15 and last through September 15. Reservations are required, and a State Park pass must be purchased to enter the park. Hayrack rides and pony rides also are available. To get there from C-470, take the Wadsworth exit south and turn left

at the third stoplight, into the park. From there, follow the signs.

PAINT HORSE STABLES
4201 S. Parker Rd., Aurora
(303) 690-8235
painthorsestables.net
With open meadows, natural grasslands, and wooded areas, Cherry Creek Reservoir State Recreation Area is a great spot for a ride. You need reservations to ride here, and a State Park pass must be purchased to enter the park. Paint Horse Stables also runs the Chatfield Stables; operating dates and programs are similar.

STOCKTON'S PLUM CREEK STABLES
7479 W. Titan Rd., Littleton
(303) 791-1966
stocktonsplumcreek.com
Stockton's has access to the 7,000 acres of Chatfield State Recreation Area via its own private entrance. The area is beautiful, with plenty of bird-watching opportunities on native prairie grasses. Find the stables by going about 4 miles south of C-470 on Santa Fe Drive and turning right on Titan Road. Call for information on hayrides and special events.

A WORTHY RANCH & STABLES
4241 W. Parker Rd., Parker
(303) 841-9405
aworthyranchandstables.com
On the south side of Metro Denver, A Worthy Ranch & Stables offers lessons as well as riding along miles of trails. Guided rides are available by reservation only, with a 2-hour minimum. Reach it by taking I-25 a little more than a mile south of its intersection with C-470, then traveling east about 2.5 miles on Lincoln Avenue (exit 193) before

turning right on a little dirt road called West Parker Road. A Worthy Ranch & Stables is about 2 miles down West Parker Road on the left.

> **i** If you want to hunt on private land, you have to ask the owner; it's legal in Colorado to hunt on private land with the owner's permission.

Hunting

Hunting and fishing pump $3 billion a year into Colorado's economy, second only to the ski industry in terms of economic impact. As vast as the numbers are, so are the locations and types of hunting that are available. It is legal on certain public lands as well as on private land with permission. The Colorado Division of Wildlife's website, wildlife.state.co.us/hunting, is the best place for information about licensing, game types and limits, seasons, and permissible locations. You can also reach them at (303) 297-1192, or you can use the following recorded information lines: big-game hunting, (303) 291-7529; small game, (303) 291-7546; game birds, (303) 291-7547; and waterfowl, (303) 291-7548.

All hunting, including on public land, requires licenses that can be purchased at any major sports and outdoors stores. The cost varies depending on the game hunted. For example, a resident deer license costs around $34; nonresidents pay $349. Rare game such as moose will cost much more to hunt—$254 for residents and $1,919 for nonresidents. There are limits on the number of licenses issued, with more reserved for residents. A lottery is held for some big-game hunting where numbers are kept to a minimum. Brochures for the various types of hunting are available from the DOW beginning in February and March, depending on the game, with yearly updates that spell out the rules and regulations. Most hunting is confined to specific seasons, whose dates vary from year to year.

Colorado is most famous for big game, including elk, mountain lion, black bear, mule deer, bighorn sheep, mountain goat, white-tailed deer, and pronghorn antelope. But 105 of the state's 113 species of sport game are small game, including ducks and geese, wild turkey, ring-necked pheasant, mourning dove, band-tailed pigeon, quail, grouse, rabbit, and coyote. During the winter, trappers hunt for beaver, muskrat, bobcat, weasel, marten, mink, badger, and fox.

Running

Runners are everywhere in Metro Denver: in the streets of downtown and the suburbs, in the city parks and greenbelts, and along the mountain paths. For those who prefer to run in parklike settings and on motorist-free trails, we will suggest a few popular locations.

Washington Park, between South Franklin and South Downing Streets just north of I-25, is one of the city's most popular running spots. That may be because it's one of Denver's biggest and most pleasant parks, or it may be because it's in an area with a lot of upscale empty-nesters who believe in exercise and don't have to get it by pushing their kids on the park's swings. Closer in, City Park, between Colorado Boulevard and York Street, 2 blocks north of East Colfax Avenue, is another popular running area where folks can get away from cars and run through some semblance of foliated quietude. Greenbelts, including the popular Highline Canal in Littleton, the Cherry Creek Bike Path, and the South Platte River trails at Chatfield Reservoir, are particularly nice because they

have the same aesthetic. If you like running on natural terrain, you may want to try some of the mountain-biking trails outlined in our Mountain Biking section.

For those who enjoy the group experience, there are plenty of events and clubs. Greater Denver's largest annual running events include the 5-mile Cherry Creek Sneak in April, the Drop Your Drawers and Run Wild 5K and Family Zoo Loop in May, the Race for the Cure 5K in October, and the 4-mile Turkey Trot on Thanksgiving morning.

Among the larger running clubs are the Colorado Masters, for the older-than-30 crowd (comastersrun.org), and the Rocky Mountain Road Runners (rmrr.org). Don't forget that walkers have found increasing acceptance in the area's big running events. The Front Range Walkers (303-377-0576; racewalk.com) is perhaps the area's biggest walking club.

Some running stores also serve as information clearinghouses on running clubs, events, and race series and are places where you can sign up for races. These include Runners Roost, 1685 S. Colorado Blvd. (303-759-8455) and 7878 W. Alameda Ave. (303-991-1851); check them out online too at runnersroost.com.

Skiing

You'd expect skiing to be the top entry in any guide to Metro Denver recreation, which is why we've given it its own Ski Country chapter. If you're a beginner, you may want to know about some ways to get into the sport.

Colorado Ski Country USA is a trade association for all the ski resorts in the state that publishes the *Colorado Ski Country Consumer Guide*. Within about 130 pages, it contains a lot of the information you may want to know about skiing in Colorado. Colorado

Ski Country USA will mail it to you free if you give them a call at (303) 837-0793.

ℹ️ **One of the best bargains in fitness is the Denver Parks and Recreation membership. Depending on the recreation center and the offerings chosen, Denver residents can lift weights, play basketball, and swim for between $190 and $369 a year. Single-visit, 15-visit, and 30-visit passes are also available. Check with your nearest rec center for details or visit denvergov .org and search "recreation."**

You may also want to know about Snia-grab (bargains spelled backward), and other big annual ski equipment and apparel sales staged every year by Metro Denver's largest sporting goods stores. They start on the Saturday before Labor Day and run through much of September.

Tennis

Metro Denver has plenty of tennis facilities, both private and public. You can find courts in just about any major city park. In Denver, try Washington Park, between South Franklin and South Downing Streets just north of I-25, and City Park, between Colorado Boulevard and York Street, 2 blocks north of East Colfax Avenue. Park play is free and usually runs on a first-come, first-served basis as long as there are no tournaments or lessons going on.

Beyond public courts, there are many organized centers and city recreation departments that offer players a chance to join group play, take lessons, and play in tournaments.

Metro Denver's central tennis resource is the Colorado Tennis Association (CTA)

(303-695-4116; coloradotennis.com). If you're looking for courts or are interested in finding out how to get into organized tennis leagues or sanctioned tournaments, the CTA can help steer you to the right place. It also has copies of tournament schedules for adults and juniors as well as general information brochures. It's the local branch of the US Tennis Association (USTA) as well, so you can get USTA memberships and publications through the CTA.

ARVADA TENNIS CENTER
Corner of 65th and Miller Streets, Arvada
(303) 420-1210
apexprd.org
This is a fine public facility with eight courts and sanctioned USTA play. If you want to take to the courts, we suggest making reservations in advance. It is open nightly and on Saturday and Sunday mornings.

AURORA PARKS AND RECREATION
Aurora-area parks
(303) 326-8700
Aurora has a good reputation for its public tennis program. Pros offer beginning, intermediate, and advanced lessons for 1-week or 2-week sessions as well as evening and Saturday lessons. Tournament play is available, too; check the summer brochure. Aurora maintains 72 courts on a first-come, first-served basis. Very few courts are lighted; one exception is Del Mar Park at 6th Avenue and Peoria Street.

DENVER PARKS AND RECREATION
Denver-area parks
(720) 913-1311
The city recreation district maintains a few dozen courts across the city for daytime play. There are junior programs and adult

lesson programs throughout the Denver area. The USTA youth tournament program runs 7 weeks of instruction in the summer and 1 week of tournaments beginning in early June. Adults age 18 and older can join the Congress Park (8th Avenue and York Street east of downtown) program or the Berkeley Park (46th Avenue and Sheridan Boulevard northwest of town) program in June and July. Call for information on other programs.

GATES TENNIS CENTER
3300 E. Bayaud Ave.
(303) 355-4461
gatestenniscenter.info
This popular facility is just south of the Cherry Creek Mall and consistently rated as one of the top public tennis facilities in the country. You don't need a membership, court times are reasonable, and lessons are competitively priced. It has one of the nation's largest tennis ladders, a challenge arrangement in which you sign up at a certain level and begin to play and move up and down the ladder. Gates has more than 1,000 people on its computerized ladder, enough to offer specialized ladders for singles, doubles, etc. There's even a coed ladder reputed to be a good place for singles to meet. It's a 20-court facility complete with clubhouse, locker room, and pro shop. Pros will teach you, and ball machines will test you.

HOLLY TENNIS CENTER
6651 S. Krameria Way, Englewood
(303) 771-3654
Holly offers the most USTA-sanctioned tournaments in Colorado. It offers programs on a total of 40 courts, including use of courts in the South Suburban Recreation District.

Six of Holly's courts are lighted. It also offers league play and group lessons.

KEN CARYL RANCH COMMUNITY CENTER
1 Club Dr., Littleton
(303) 979-2233
ken-carylranch.org
Ken Caryl has four indoor courts and six outdoor courts. You won't find prettier surroundings; the Ken Caryl Ranch community is in the red-rock moonscape of the valley hidden behind the Hogback Formation that runs north-south along C-470. The facility is actually owned by Jefferson County Open Space. Offered here are leagues, tournaments, and lessons for resident and nonresident youths and adults. You also can purchase a membership to the center. Cost varies depending on the program.

Wildlife Watching

While hunting wildlife is more traditional, a growing number of Colorado visitors and residents are interested in stalking wildlife either to photograph or just for the joy of getting an up-close look at the critters. There's something magical about watching a herd of elk feeding in a mountain meadow or catching a glimpse of a red fox as it darts amid trees. Colorado offers more than 100 places to view wildlife year-round. The best time to view is early morning and late evening (dawn and sunset).

As you travel Colorado's roads and highways, watch for signs that depict a pair of binoculars and say wildlife viewing area, then follow the signs. One such area is just outside Denver International Airport. Another is in the mountains along I-70 east of Georgetown (about an hour and a half from Denver). But there are dozens more. Contact the

Division of Wildlife at (303) 297-1192 for a list, or pick up a wildlife viewing book at any major bookstore. The *Colorado Wildlife Viewing Guide* is available through the Colorado Wildlife Heritage Foundation for $14.95 plus shipping/handling. Contact them at (303) 291-7212 or wordpress.cwhf.us.

Wildlife viewing has its own etiquette that keeps everyone involved as safe and healthy as possible. Never chase or spook animals; it's illegal.

In recent years bird watching has become an increasingly popular pastime. Reported as the nation's fastest-growing form of outdoor recreation, it attracts a well-educated and serious crowd in Colorado. Denver even boasts another kind of distinction—it's home to Christine Goff, a best-selling mystery writer whose lead character is a birder. Among the sinister plots she has written about are meadowlarks being ousted from their habitat by vintners (*Murdered by Merlot*). Anyone interested in joining Denver-area birders should contact the Audubon Society (303-973-9530; denver audubon.com).

THE GREAT OUTDOORS

Colorado's mountains offer unparalleled opportunity for adventure. You can venture deep into the Rockies for longs trips or drive less than a half-hour and be surrounded by great exploring territory.

Camping, hiking, and biking abound in Colorado's great outdoors, so we've compiled a few tips on how to enjoy them.

More than one-third of Colorado's land area is owned by and available to the public, including 8.3 million acres of Bureau of Land Management tracts and 14.3 million acres of national forest. There are 11 national forests in Colorado, covering major parts of the state. The national forests are basically undeveloped areas where you can hike, fish, hunt, ride, and camp just about anywhere. They are also where the vast majority of wilderness can be found, and if you want to hike to some remote and beautiful backcountry refuge anywhere in the US, the likelihood is that you'll do it in a national forest.

NATIONAL FORESTS

While national forests are generally open to timber sales, mining, and other activities that purists might find at odds with the idea of a natural setting, national wilderness areas allow no permanent roads, structures, timber sales, or mining other than those that already exist. These areas are wild country, accessible only by trail and closed to anything but foot transport. No bikes are allowed, but horses are.

Three of Colorado's national forests are located immediately to the west, northwest, and southwest of Metro Denver: Pike National Forest, Arapaho National Forest, and Roosevelt National Forest. You can seek information on these from the USDA Forest Service's Rocky Mountain Regional Office, (303) 275-5350, or call each national forest office individually.

Arapaho & Roosevelt National Forests

Arapaho and Roosevelt National Forests (970-295-6600) are combined into a jurisdiction that spans the Continental Divide from the Wyoming border to just south of I-70, west of Denver. Roughly speaking, the Roosevelt National Forest comprises that section east of the Continental Divide. The Arapaho National Forest lies west of the Continental Divide, although it comes east to cover the area south of I-70 to mid-Jefferson County.

Together they make up some 1.3 million acres in the Rocky Mountains and foothills, wrapping around Rocky Mountain National Park and including 47 national forest campgrounds and a number of wilderness areas such as the Rawah Wilderness on the Wyoming border, the Indian Peaks Wilderness west of Boulder, and the Cache La Poudre Wilderness around the Cache La Poudre

River that flows through Roosevelt National Forest and down to Fort Collins.

Pike & San Isabel National Forests

Another jurisdiction combines the 2.3 million acres that comprise the Pike and San Isabel National Forests (719-553-1400). At its northern end, the San Isabel is about 100 miles of winding, 2-lane US 285 away from Denver. At its southernmost end, it stretches almost to New Mexico. The 1.1 million-acre Pike National Forest is Metro Denver's southern neighbor, reaching southwest from I-70 and west from I-25 to Colorado Springs (Pikes Peak is part of this national forest). It contains several converging sources of Metro Denver's South Platte River as well as that river's most scenic stretches before it reaches the Flatlands. It has a half-dozen of the state's tallest peaks, sharing Mount Evans with Arapaho National Forest. Its vegetation is drier than Arapaho and Roosevelt National Forests, with more juniper, oak brush, and bristlecone pine. Its major wilderness area is the Lost Creek Wilderness, 106,000 acres on which Pikes Peak granite has been eroded into domes, spires, turrets, and crests, with a lot of big-boulder slopes. Lost Creek is less popular than Indian Peaks and the other big wilderness areas to the north, and it's a good place to backpack and find a bit of solitude. One unique feature of the Pike is a designated motorcycling area near Sedalia that has 118 miles of trails.

HIKING

Hiking—with backpack, daypack, or no pack—is the most common way to enjoy the backcountry. You can hike just about anywhere on national forest land as long as it isn't posted as off-limits. Before we get into the details of where to hike in the Denver area; however, it's important to emphasize safety and preparedness. Even a short hike up a seemingly innocent, well-groomed trail just outside the city can turn into a nightmare if you underestimate the power of nature. Having said that, there are a number of commonsense—and sometimes not so obvious—rules and guidelines. If you are careful to follow them, you will come away with memories of a wonderful, exhilarating experience.

The most important rule is to be prepared; even in the summer months, Rocky Mountain weather can be unpredictable and merciless. Wherever you hike, the scenery becomes more beautiful—and the necessity of preparedness more important—the higher you go. You will probably start out in the lower forests of aspen and ponderosa pines or in dark, moody groves of spruce and fir, but as you rise, the forest breaks open into the "krummholz," or crooked wood zone, where trees stunted by altitude and twisted by relentless winds make a border around the alpine meadows above. When you're above tree line, you're in the fragile alpine meadows, home to a stunningly beautiful landscape covered with wildflowers. You're also in the heights prone to drastic weather changes and a climate not unlike the arctic zones of the world.

Mountain-savvy folks dress in layers. When you start your hike during the warm months, you'll be inclined to wear T-shirts and shorts. But there are few things more miserable than reaching the high alpine meadows in them and watching a storm move in that drops temperatures into the 40s. Mountain storms also can bring high winds, cold rain or snow, and afternoon lightning. If you plan to hike in high altitudes, bring along a sizable backpack with a long-sleeved wool or flannel shirt, a sweater or sweatshirt to put over that, and a windbreaker/raincoat to put over that. A hood is always nice, but you should at least have a knit cap and warm gloves. Bring trousers, or at least sweatpants, to put on over the shorts.

During colder months, including the spring and fall, make certain that none of these clothes is made of cotton, especially your socks. Instead, choose wool or synthetic fibers specifically designed to wick moisture away from the body and to dry quickly. Cotton clothing retains moisture and will not dry quickly when wet, presenting the very real possibility of hypothermia.

Carry plenty of fresh water with you, and never drink stream or lake water without boiling it for at least 10 minutes, using disinfectant pills, or first passing it through a portable disinfectant pump. Drinking untreated water can lead to a nasty case of giardia, and your vacation will come to an abrupt end. You will need to pack a sizable water bottle, at least 32 ounces per person, and use the water disinfectant tablets or filtering pump as your backup for providing additional drinking water. Make sure you understand how to use the tablets or the disinfectant pump before leaving for the day.

As obvious as it might seem, don't forget your boots. Remember, you'll be on your feet most of the day, and good boots are a must. We don't recommend hiking in anything but hiking boots; sneakers, running shoes, and sandals might be attractive and look better with your shorts, but you'll be glad you left them behind if you encounter cold, wet weather, and your feet will thank you at the end of the day.

A good map is not only an essential emergency item, it adds to the enjoyment of planning your hike. Get a "quadrangle" map on a 1:24,000 scale, where 1 inch equals about 0.4 mile. You may need more than one to cover the area of your interest. Another great resource is the *Delorme Colorado Atlas & Gazetteer,* a road-atlas-size book that contains topographical maps of the entire state. Here the scale is more like 1 inch equals 2.5 miles, but you still get good detail, contour lines, and trail routes. You can find quadrangle maps and the *Delorme Colorado Atlas & Gazetteer* in well-stocked outdoor stores, bookstores, and even some gas stations. You can also get maps from the Bureau of Land Management in Lakewood (303-239-3600) or from the US Geological Survey at the Denver Federal Center in Lakewood, Map and Book Sales (303-202-4700).

Altitude sickness is another major killjoy that can be avoided. It can affect anyone coming from a lower altitude to Colorado's mile-high regions. Most people in good health will experience nothing more than a slight headache, light-headedness, and shortness of breath. Usually these symptoms are not severe and can be treated with aspirin and rest. More serious symptoms can include dizziness, nausea, and impaired mental abilities. Stopping and returning to lower elevation immediately often relieves these symptoms. Severe altitude sickness, called high altitude pulmonary edema, can lead to seizures, hallucinations, coma, brain damage, and death.

To avoid altitude sickness, refrain from strenuous activities for your first few days at a new altitude while your body acclimates. While it actually takes a few weeks for your body to fully acclimate, each passing day spent at a higher elevation helps your body create the extra red blood cells it needs to capture the limited oxygen where the air is thinner. Take the time to get used to the altitude here before you charge off in pursuit of the high country. Getting off the plane from sea level one day and going on a 6-mile hike to 10,000 feet the next is asking for big trouble.

Mounting most of Colorado's peaks won't require technical mountain climbing skills or gear such as ropes, carabiners, or ice axes. If that's the kind of climbing you're interested in, look for a guide or instructor, and practice at any of the gyms and recreation centers that have their own climbing walls. (See our Parks & Recreation chapter for more details.)

Most people just want to climb the mountains on any of the hundreds of trails that range in difficulty from easy to extremely hard. Unless you are an experienced hiker and are acclimated to our high elevations, avoid the 500 or so Colorado peaks that rise higher than 12,000 feet. An elite group of climbers like to "bag the 14ers," or climb to the summits of all 56 peaks that are 14,000 feet or higher. Doing so can be dangerous if attempted by novices.

We've listed a range of moderate day hikes that are within easy driving range of Denver. Find more trails in books such as *Hiking Colorado* by Maryann Gaug (Globe Pequot Press) and *Hiking Colorado's Front Range: Fort Collins to Colorado Springs* (Globe Pequot Press). Four books by Tracy Salcedo focus more closely on the Denver area: *Best Easy Day Hikes Denver* and *12 Short Hikes Denver Foothills North, Denver Foothills Central,* and *Denver Foothills South* (all Globe

Pequot Press). A good book for families is *Best Hikes with Children in Colorado* by Maureen Keilty (Mountaineers Books). And don't think just in terms of summertime hiking; the trails of summer become the snowshoe and cross-country ski trails of winter. Check out *Winter Trails Colorado: The Best Cross-Country Ski and Snowshoe Trails* by Andy and Tari Lightbody (Globe Pequot Press) or *Snowshoeing Colorado* by Claire Walter (Fulcrum Publishing).

GREEN MOUNTAIN TRAIL
About 4 miles north of Morrison
Jefferson County Open Space
Department
(303) 271-5925
Map: Jefferson County Open Space map for Hayden's Green Mountain Park
This easy trail in Denver's foothills wanders 3.5 miles one way (7.25 miles round-trip) and climbs 600 feet, from 6,200 to 6,800 feet. To reach it, drive west from Denver on 6th Avenue past I-70 and turn left onto US 40. After a short distance, turn left onto Rooney Road and drive south to the parking area to the east. Walk across C-470 on the pedestrian bridge to join the Green Mountain and Lonesome Trails. Take the Green Mountain Trail for the best nature experience. From the top of the mountain, you'll have panoramic views, and along the way you may see mule deer, foxes, coyotes, rabbits, and up to 150 species of birds. From May into July the area is good for viewing wildflowers. If you'd like to do a round-trip loop, take the Lonesome Trail back, but be aware that it follows Alameda Parkway much of the way back to the parking area.

HIGHLINE CANAL
Near Chatfield Reservoir, between Waterton and the Rocky Mountain Arsenal
Denver Water Department, Office of Community Relations, (303) 628-6000
Map: USGS Front Range Corridor map, sheet 2

Another easy trail south of Denver, this one runs a total of 71 miles along the irrigation ditch completed in 1883 by Scotsman James Duff. Only 58 of those miles are hikeable, but they can be traveled in segments long or short enough to suit any appetite. Most of the trail is wheelchair and stroller accessible, and it's open year-round to walkers, hikers, joggers, horseback riders, bikers, and in-line skaters. It can be reached in Englewood on South Santa Fe Drive, County Line Road, or Hampden Avenue, and in Aurora on Havana Street or Colfax Avenue.

WHITE RANCH PARK
Northwest of Golden and southwest of Boulder
Jefferson County Open Space
(303) 271-5925
Maps: USGS Ralston Buttes quad or White Ranch Park map (available at the park)

Ute and Arapahoe tribes camped and hunted on this land before Welsh immigrants James and Mary Bond settled on it. Originally on their way to California, they decided to stop here after a young son fell beneath the wagon's wheels and was killed. The land is now open space owned by Jefferson County. It is crisscrossed by trails of varying difficulty that range from 0.3 to 4.5 miles. Several are good for children, and the relatively easy 1.6-mile Sawmill Trail leads to a campground (an advance permit is required to stay there, available from the Jefferson County Open Space office). To get to White Ranch Park, drive north from Golden on Highway 93 to Jefferson County Road 70 (Golden Gate Canyon Road). After 4.1 miles, turn right onto Jefferson County Road 57 (Crawford Gulch Road) and drive another 4.1 miles. Turn right to enter the park.

CAMPING

Finding a location to camp on national forest land is simple once you've determined whether you want to "car camp" or backpack into a more remote location. The main distinction is simple: Car camping usually means you won't have to hike in, and will likely be at a designated campground with amenities such as outhouses and running water. If you car camp, you'll likely be near others—anywhere from 50 feet to a few hundred feet depending on the campground—and have a designated fire pit. You'll also pay a small daily fee for your site. If you backcountry camp, you can go virtually anywhere on national forest land and camp for free, but you won't have any amenities.

The rules for backcountry camping are fairly simple, but important: You must pick a spot at least 100 feet from a roadway, trail, or stream and at least a half-mile from standing water. Unless fire danger is high, as it has been for several years, fires are allowed for cooking and warming but must be in a contained pit. You must restore the fire area when you leave. Your car can be as much as 300 feet off the road but not parked in a bog; if you have a catalytic converter, do not park over grass as it can start a fire.

Making a reservation for car camping in designated campgrounds is highly recommended and nearly imperative on holiday weekends (see our list of phone numbers). Backcountry camping does not require a reservation and can be done anywhere as long as the rules are followed.

If you car camp, you can get to a campground early and take your chances at cruising around looking for an empty space or finding people who look like they are about to leave. Usually you need to show up by 7 p.m. or your reserved spot could be taken. The rules are somewhat loose and depend on individual campgrounds. The national forests have a toll-free number, and in any part of Colorado, a certain percentage of the forest service campgrounds are part of that reservation system. You can call (877) 444-6777 or go to recreation.gov. Make sure to have ready not only the name of the campground you want, but also a selection of other campgrounds in the vicinity. If the one you want is not open to reservations, you'll be able to ask for your second or third choice.

Following is a helpful list of national forest campgrounds in Colorado that are served by the centralized reservation system. Note that a road atlas or Colorado state map is likely to have a little tree symbol representing each campground but no name. The *Delorme Colorado Atlas & Gazetteer* often has the name of a lake or creek that coincides with the nearby tent symbol indicating a campground. One resource that names each campground on the map is the national forest visitor map, one for each national forest, produced by the USDA Forest Service itself and available from the USDA Forest Service's Denver Regional Office (740 Simms St., Lakewood; 303-275-5350).

Campgrounds

Following are just a few of the national forest campgrounds; there are many more. The daily fees average about $15. For a full list you can call the USDA Forest Service's Rocky Mountain Regional Office at (303) 275-5350. They'll mail you the free brochure, "Rocky Mountain Region Campgrounds," which lists all the campgrounds in Colorado, as well as in the national forest and national grasslands of Wyoming, Kansas, Nebraska, and South Dakota.

ARAPAHO/ROOSEVELT NATIONAL FOREST
(970) 295-6600

BOULDER RANGER DISTRICT, BOULDER
(303) 444-6600

CLEAR CREEK RANGER DISTRICT, IDAHO SPRINGS
(303) 567-3000

PIKE NATIONAL FOREST
(719) 553-1400

PIKES PEAK RANGER DISTRICT, COLORADO SPRINGS
(719) 636-1602

SOUTH PARK RANGER DISTRICT, FAIRPLAY
(719) 836-2031

SOUTH PLATTE RANGER DISTRICT, MORRISON
(303) 275-5610

SULPHUR RANGER DISTRICT, GRANBY
(970) 887-4100

You can find a lot of books about camping, but a good basic reference is *Camping Colorado* by Melinda Crow (Globe Pequot Press). For more information about recreation in other areas of Colorado, pick up copies of the *Insiders' Guide to Boulder and Rocky Mountain National Park* by Ann Alexander

Leggett, and the *Insiders' Guide to Colorado's Mountains* by Linda Castrone (both from Globe Pequot Press).

Resources

There are umpteen books on how to enjoy Colorado's recreational, scenic, and natural opportunities. A pass through a major bookstore will load you down with more than you need. Following are a few other informational resources.

BUREAU OF LAND MANAGEMENT
co.blm.gov

THE COLORADO DIRECTORY
(303) 499-9343
coloradodirectory.com

COLORADO DIVISION OF WILDLIFE HEADQUARTERS, DENVER
(303) 297-1192
wildlife.state.co.us

COLORADO MOUNTAIN CLUB
(303) 279-3080
cmc.org

COLORADO STATE PARKS (CAMPING, BOATING, AND RECREATION)
(303) 866-3437
parks.state.co.us

DENVER AUDUBON SOCIETY
(303) 973-9530
denveraudubon.org

DUDE RANCHERS ASSOCIATION (SERVING ALL WESTERN STATES INCLUDING COLORADO)
(866) 399-2339
duderanch.org

SKI COUNTRY

Although Denver is located on the plains, it's only about an hour away from some of the best skiing on the continent. Most ski areas are open from Thanksgiving to mid-April, but in good snow years (and with the help of snowmaking), the season can stretch from mid-October through June.

Colorado is home to 25 ski areas, ranging from down-home to world-famous, with seven major areas close enough to qualify as day trips from Denver. If downhill skiing isn't your thing, expect to find lots of things that can be done without skis. Ride the chairlift to Winter Park's Lodge at Sunspot, for example, just to have lunch and enjoy the view. Other options include ice-skating, snowmobiling, snowshoeing, dogsledding, or riding in horse-drawn sleighs. Cross-country skiing and snowshoeing also are popular, with groomed tracks and trails available at most downhill areas. Most ski areas also offer adult and child lessons, child care, and specialized lessons.

The mountain fun doesn't stop when the snow melts. Colorado's ski areas are really year-round resorts that offer as many things to do in summer as in winter. Mountain biking? How about an easy lift up with your bike on the gondola and a wild ride down. Music festivals? Ski slopes make great outdoor amphitheaters in the summer. Boating? Try it on a mountain lake or reservoir ringed in jagged peaks. Drift over the Vail Valley in a hot-air balloon, golf at a high-altitude course, or bike along more than 50 miles of paved paths that extend from Breckenridge to Vail.

It's crucial to take altitude into consideration when traveling to the mountains. Even folks accustomed to Denver's 5,280 feet above sea level can get dizzy at 10,000 feet unless they guard against altitude sickness. Drink plenty of water, avoid alcohol, give yourself time to adjust, and slow down or descend in altitude if you get a headache or feel nauseated. Also, no one should set out on backcountry trails without sound knowledge of avalanche awareness, direction-finding skills, and adequate clothing, food, and water. Even people going on day trips should be prepared to spend a night outside, as weather conditions in the mountains change in seconds. Local bookstores are filled with trail guides that offer basic safety information. And always let someone know where you're going and when you expect to be back. If you want to enjoy the great outdoors when the snow is gone, see our The Great Outdoors chapter for hiking and climbing information.

OVERVIEW

We've listed and described a few ski areas that make feasible day trips from Denver, with information about winter and summer activities, dining, shopping, and accommodations, should you decide to stay longer. For more information about all the state's ski resorts, contact Colorado Ski Country USA, a trade association (303-837-0793; coloradoski .com).

LOVELAND

Useful contact information:
(303) 569-3203
skiloveland.com
Loveland is the ski area closest to Denver, just 53 miles and an easy hour's drive west on I-70. It straddles the east face of the Eisenhower Tunnel but is accessed from exit 216, just before the east tunnel entrance. This area is strictly for skiing and snowboarding—Loveland offers no lodging, and its food service is limited to a traditional cafeteria serving deli fare, soups, baked goods, and specialty pizzas. A 5,000 square-foot retail area rents skis and snowboards, and sells clothing, gloves, and other outdoor essentials.

Loveland boasts the world's highest quad lift, at more than 12,600 feet above sea level, which serves 450 acres of expert terrain. With an average annual snowfall of 385 inches and prices that are lower than other close-in areas, there's plenty to pull you off the highway before you pass through the tunnel. One drawback: Loveland can get windy, especially on trails above the tree line.

WINTER PARK

WINTER PARK RESORT
(970) 726-5514
winterparkresort.com

WINTER PARK/FRASER VALLEY
CHAMBER OF COMMERCE
(970) 726-4221, (800) 903-7275
playwinterpark.com
This ski area is one of Denver's mountain parks, even though it is 70 miles away. Winter Park is a favorite with Front Range skiers because of its excellent terrain and casual ambience. Its ski terrain consists of three interconnected mountains, a high alpine bowl, and Vasquez Cirque, all accessible with one lift ticket. Winter Park and Vasquez Ridge offer a mix of beginner, intermediate, and advanced cruising runs. Mogul enthusiasts like the Mary Jane runs, and the high-alpine Parsenn Bowl, at 12,060 feet, is best known for its gladed tree skiing and above-timberline vistas.

Get there from Denver by driving west on I-70, take the US 40 West exit to Empire and continue over Berthoud Pass. There are two entrances to the ski area. Expert skiers turn off at Mary Jane, while beginners and intermediates continue to the main Winter Park base. The town of Winter Park is a few miles farther down the road, and Fraser is another 5 miles away. Both towns have grown up alongside the resort, and all remain casual. A free shuttle connects the ski resort with the towns of Winter Park and Fraser. Both have restaurants, shops, and places to stay, although Fraser is known as the place where locals also shop for necessities—it has a Safeway, for example.

Winter Activities

Eight high-speed quad lifts carry skiers and snowboarders to 2,886 acres of terrain. Winter Park is also home to the **National Sports Center for the Disabled** (970-726-1540; nscd.org). Its 39 full-time staff members and more than 1,000 volunteers can handle the needs of people with more than 40 different disabilities.

Down-valley from the ski resort is a top-notch cross-country and snowshoeing center called **Devil's Thumb Ranch** (970-726-5632 or 800-933-4339; devilsthumbranch.com). Skate-skiers and snowshoers love the 125 kilometers of groomed trails that fan out into the forest from an expansive meadow. To get there, drive west from Winter Park to the town of Fraser and turn right onto County Road 83. Lessons and equipment rental are available. Devil's Thumb Ranch is open year-round, with gourmet dining in the Ranch House Restaurant & Saloon and private or bunkhouse-style accommodations available. Ask about moonlight sleigh rides in the winter and horseback riding, trout fishing, rafting, and kayaking in the summer.

Backcountry skiers like the trails on top of Berthoud Pass and the Jim Creek Trail that begins directly across from the Winter Park ski area. No one should set out on these trails without knowledge of avalanche awareness, adequate clothing, food, water, and a trail guide or maps.

Dogsled rides are expensive, but if you're an Iditarod fan, there's nothing like them; contact **Dog Sled Rides of Winter Park** (970-726-8326; dogsledridesofwinterpark.com). If you'd rather be pulled by horses than dogs, go for a sleigh ride; contact **Grand Adventures** (970-726-9247; grandadventures.com). Ice-skaters can try the **Fraser Ice Rink** (601 Zerex Ave.; 970-726-4708).

The rink is free, but bring your own skates. It is outdoors and features bonfires at night.

Winter Park guides also offer Sno-Cat rides to the top of the ski mountain and snowshoe tours that start with a lift ride and conclude with a gentle descent through wooded terrain. Get information and reservations for both at (970) 726-1616.

Buy reduced-price lift tickets at Metro Denver locations including Safeway and King Soopers supermarkets, Total gas stations, and Sports Authority, Christy's, and REI sporting goods stores.

Summer Fun

Every summer the green slopes of Winter Park are the site of acclaimed musical events. If you plan to go, bring a lawn chair and rain gear. Other summer activities include an alpine slide, mountainside minigolf, a human maze, a climbing wall, and bungee and gyroscope rides. Winter Park also is known as Mountain Bike Capital USA. More than 600 miles of marked, mapped, and maintained trails wind through the Fraser Valley. At the ski area itself, riders can take the easy way up via the Zephyr Express chairlift to connect with another 45 miles of steep, exciting trails. Pick up a trail map at local bike stores or the Chamber of Commerce Visitor Center on the east side of US 40 downtown. Bike rentals are available at any number of local stores.

The Fraser River Trail is paved and the easiest, mellowest ride for families; it's good for in-line skaters, too. Valley trails go up from there, to rides even locals find frightening. Helmets, of course, are highly recommended. An all-day park pass for all activities, including the alpine slide, minigolf, and Zephyr lift for mountain biking, is $39. A one-ride Zephyr ticket for mountain biking costs $15.

Golfers will enjoy the beautiful 27-hole **Pole Creek Golf Club** (970-887-9195), about 10 miles northwest of Winter Park in the town of Tabernash. Pole Creek consistently rates as one of the top public courses in Colorado. Look for more details in our Parks & Recreation chapter. There also is the **Grand Lake Golf Course** (970-627-8008), about 40 miles farther west. It's not quite Pole Creek, but it's easier to get tee times.

Nongolfers can choose among fishing, hiking, horseback riding, Jeeping, and rafting. Much of the Fraser Valley that isn't privately owned falls within the boundaries of the Arapaho National Forest. The Winter Park/Fraser Valley Chamber of Commerce can provide more information.

Dining

Winter Park has traditionally been a day-use area for Denver families, but as it grows, so do the dining choices.

Gasthaus Eichler (970-726-5133), in downtown Winter Park on US 40, is noted for its Austrian and German specialties. Reservations are suggested. **Deno's Mountain Bistro** (970-726-5332) is also located in downtown Winter Park on US 40. Locals have been coming here since 1973 for steaks, pasta, pizza, and some of the best burgers in town. Its après-ski atmosphere is one of the town's mellowest. It's open for breakfast, lunch, and dinner.

Carvers Bakery & Cafe (970-726-8202) is a popular breakfast location. It can be hard to find, tucked behind Cooper Creek Square, but locals agree it's worth the search. Housed in a quaint log building, it's known for home-baked breads and pastries. Its lunches are just as good, featuring homemade soups, stews, and vegetarian dishes.

Lodge at Sunspot (970-726-1444) at the top of Winter Park mountain is a great experience if you're looking for something a little more memorable. Reservations are suggested. For more casual dining and night-life—it can get wild at times—there's the **Crooked Creek Saloon & Eatery** at 401 Zerex Ave. off US 40 in Fraser (970-726-9250), which serves Mexican and American food and no small amount of beer.

Accommodations

Accommodations in Winter Park range from mountainside condos to bed-and-breakfasts in town. **Winter Park Central Reservations** (800-979-0332) can arrange lodging in more than 50 condominiums, motels, hotels, lodges, inns, and bed-and-breakfasts.

If full-service hotels are what you're after, check into the **Vintage Hotel** (800-472-7017; vintagehotel.com). Its restaurant, Five Mountain Tavern, is a reasonably priced family place, featuring American home-style food, sandwiches, and pizzas. There's a pool on-site. **Arapahoe Ski Lodge** (970-726-8222; arapahoeskilodge.com) offers moderately priced lodging packages with breakfast and dinner or breakfast only.

The bulk of available lodgings are condominiums in larger complexes. **Beaver Village Resort** (800-666-0281; beavervillage.com) is well-run and centrally located, although not lavish. The **Viking Lodge** (800-421-4013) is great for small budgets, and it's clean and well maintained.

SUMMIT COUNTY

Summit County's four ski areas—Breckenridge, Keystone, Arapahoe Basin, and Copper Mountain—collectively attract more skiers than any other ski destination in North America. And why not? They offer tremendous variety, good shopping and restaurants, dependably fine snow, and easy access from Metro Denver.

Summit County is about 90 minutes west of Denver on I-70. We've treated each Summit County area separately, but things are close enough that it's possible to ski at Breckenridge, eat in Dillon, and stay overnight in Frisco. An excellent free public transportation system, the Summit Stage, makes it easy to get around without a car. Pick up a schedule at the visitor center in Frisco, 300 Main St., or in Dillon, on US 6 about 1 mile south of I-70 at the Dillon Dam Road. The visitor centers are open daily year-round.

Breckenridge

To reach Breckenridge, take the Frisco exit from I-70 and drive south on Highway 9 for 9 miles.

BRECKENRIDGE RESORT CHAMBER AND CENTRAL RESERVATIONS
(877) 864-0868
gobreck.com

BRECKENRIDGE SKI RESORT
General information: (970) 453-5000
breckenridge.snow.com

BRECKENRIDGE WELCOME CENTER
(970) 453-5579

TOWN OF BRECKENRIDGE TROLLEY
Information: (970) 547-3140

Winter Activities
The oldest and largest of the Summit County communities, Breckenridge is a former mining town that got its start when gold was discovered nearby in 1859. Its Main Street is a National Historic District lined with handsome Victorian buildings that now house great shops, art galleries, and restaurants. Breckenridge has 27 lifts and more than 2,208 skiable acres spread across four distinct peaks. There's close-in pay parking near Beaver Run and the Peak 8 base, but most skiers park in one of the town's public lots and take the free shuttle to the slopes. Cross-country skiers and snowshoers can find what they're looking for at the Nordic skiing center adjacent to the ski area (970-453-6855). Other winter activities in Breckenridge include sleigh rides, snowmobiling, ice-skating, and a variety of distinct winter festivals. Visit our Annual Events & Festivals chapter for more information. Ice-skating is available at the outdoor **Maggie Pond,** at the **Village at Breckenridge** (800-847-5445), and at the indoor **Breckenridge Ice Rink** (970-547-9974).

Escape the ski resort crowds at the **Frisco Nordic Center,** alongside Dillon Reservoir about 5 miles north of Breckenridge. Snowshoers and cross-country skiers find serenity among snow-covered evergreens and sloping trails. Stop at the horse barn and have lunch on the seat of a sleigh. Rentals and maps are available at the center's outpost (970-668-0866).

Good Times Adventures (970-453-7604; snowmobilecolorado.com) offers snowmobile rides and dogsledding. Sno-Cat tours are operated out of **Ski Cooper** (719-486-2277; skicooper.com), a small local ski area near Leadville. For disabled skiers, adaptive skiing with special seats and equipment is offered by the **Breckenridge Outdoor Education Center** (970-453-6422; boec.org).

Summer Fun
In summer there's hiking in the Arapaho National Forest and outstanding golf at the

Jack Nicklaus–designed municipal course, the **Breckenridge Golf Club** (970-453-9104). More information is included in our Parks & Recreation chapter.

The Pioneer Trail is an easy and popular trail for mountain bikers. Start at the top of the Colorado SuperChair and wind down the front side of Peak 8, through thick forests and wide-open ski runs. Breckenridge offers lift rides up for mountain bikers.

The **Breckenridge Recreation Center** at 880 Airport Rd. (970-453-1734) is open every day except Christmas and has indoor and outdoor tennis courts, a pool, racquetball courts, a steam room, a hot tub, and separate locker room facilities for men and women. Visitors can purchase a daily admission.

If you'd rather see the Ten Mile Range from the back of a horse, check out the gentle horses at **Breckenridge Stables** (970-453-4438; breckstables.com). Two 90-minute rides are available, one of which is a breakfast ride.

The Blue River, which runs through Breckenridge, is a favorite fly-fishing locale. Fishing licenses are required and can be purchased at sporting goods stores where fishing equipment and bait are sold. A water activity in Breckenridge that's fun for the whole family is paddleboating on Maggie Pond in the Village at Breckenridge.

The **Breckenridge Outdoor Education Center** (970-453-6422; boec.org) also offers disabled visitors summer recreation events such as kayaking and rope courses.

Dining

Breckenridge has superb dining options. Among our favorites are the **Briar Rose Chophouse & Saloon,** 109 Lincoln Ave. (970-453-9948); **Lucha Cantina,** 500 S. Main St. (970-453-1342), for homemade, healthy Mexican cuisine, burgers, and a nice tequila selection; **Clint's Bakery and Coffee House,** 131 S. Main St. (970-453-4022), the coolest coffeehouse in town with fresh pastries, bagels, and wraps; **Breckenridge Brewery,** 600 S. Main St. (970-453-1550), which is one of the state's first brewpubs; the **Blue Moose Restaurant,** 540 S. Main St. (970-453-4859), which has affordable natural food and a friendly atmosphere; and **Mi Casa Mexican Restaurant & Cantina,** 600 S. Park St. (970-453-2071), which serves Mexican lunches and dinners (no reservations) with daily specials.

Shopping

Breckenridge's shopping also gets rave reviews. A few hours spent walking up and down Main Street will acquaint you with the very best the town has to offer. In addition to the usual array of T-shirt and souvenir shops, there are galleries to check out. Get a complete list of them at the **Breckenridge Welcome Center,** 203 S. Main St. (970-453-5579; gobreck.com).

You won't want to miss **The Twisted Pine,** 505 S. Main St. and 100 S. Main St. It features fur and leather apparel and mountain home decor. For a free catalog call (970) 453-9588. **Goods,** at 105 S. Main St. (970-453-2880), is the most popular basic clothing shop in town.

Accommodations

Accommodations in Breckenridge range from luxury condominiums to Victorian-style bed-and-breakfasts in historic homes. The Breckenridge Central Reservations (877-593-5260) can help with listings and reservations. The **Village at Breckenridge** (970-453-5192; breckresorts.com) is a huge complex with athletic facilities. **Pine Ridge Condominiums** (800-333-8833; pineridge.com) has full kitchens and washer/dryers in the units. The complex has two common hot tubs and a pool. The **Lodge & Spa at Breckenridge** (970-453-9300; thelodgeandspaatbreck .com) has the distinction of being the world's highest athletic club and spa. The fitness center features individualized training for all levels. The **River Mountain Lodge** (970-453-4711) offers the convenience of being in town and is of high quality. **Allaire Timbers Inn** (970-453-7530; allairetimbers.com) is a high-end bed-and-breakfast with each room decorated individually. **Beaver Run Resort** (800-525-2253; beaverrun.com) is a ski-in/ski-out resort that's popular with visitors. **SkiWay Lodge** (970-453-7573; skiwaylodge .com) is a Bavarian-style chalet with 10 guest rooms and ski-in/ski-out access to the Breck Connect Gondola.

Keystone

To get there, exit onto US 6 at the Dillon-Silverthorne exit 205, turning left at the traffic light. Keystone is 6 miles down the road.

KEYSTONE RESORT
(970) 496-2316 (general information and reservations)
keystone.snow.com

SUMMIT CHAMBER OF COMMERCE
(970) 668-2051
summitchamber.org

Winter Activities
Keystone is known for its excellent beginner and intermediate slopes, as well as steep and bumpy terrain on North Peak, and powder-filled glades at Outback and the Outback Bowls. It excels at snowmaking, which often allows the ski runs to open earlier than its neighbors, and offers night skiing on some nights until 8:30 p.m. Keystone runs daily NASTAR races, including a self-timing system that allows skiers to improve with practice runs.

Keystone's Nordic Center (970-496-4275) is located in The River Course clubhouse on the west side of the resort. It has 16 kilometers of groomed trails and 57 kilometers of packed trails in the White River National Forest, and offers programs in cross-country skiing, snowshoeing, ski-skating, telemark skiing, and family tubing. If you'd rather strike out on your own, some of the best cross-country skiing in Summit County is found by continuing along the road to Montezuma past the Ski Tip Lodge. Peru Creek (for beginners) and St. Johns and Wild Irishman Mine (for intermediates) are favorite tours for Front Range skiers. Remember to take precautions: Don't go unless you are an experienced skier, and even then let someone know where you're going and when you expect to return.

As for other winter activities, Keystone is home to Keystone Lake, the largest maintained outdoor skating lake in the country. It's right in the center of the village, and skate rentals are available. Sleigh rides and snowmobiling can be arranged by calling the Keystone Activities Center.

Summer Fun
In summer Dillon Reservoir—locally known as Lake Dillon—provides landlocked Coloradans with one of the state's greatest recreational assets, a 3,000-acre reservoir ringed by mountains. The lake can accommodate sailboats, kayaks, and fishing boats; charters are available. Weather and water-level permitting, the marina is open from

the end of May through the last weekend in October. Swimming is allowed but only recommended for the hearty, as this mountain reservoir is ice-cold even in August. For information call the Dillon Marina at (970) 468-5100.

There's golf at the **Keystone Ranch Golf Club** (970-496-4250), designed by Robert Trent Jones Jr.; the **River Course at Keystone** (970-496-4444); and the **Raven Golf Club at Three Peaks** (970-262-3636).

The main fishing artery in Summit County is the Blue River, where anglers aim for trout. For more information, contact a local fishing shop or the Colorado Division of Wildlife (303-291-7533).

Mountain bikers can sign up for the resort's **Dirt Camp** weekends, in which elite-level coaching and training techniques are taught by world-class professionals. Hikers may want to try a Llama Lunch Trek, where you have fun hiking while the llama carries your lunch.

Dining

The award-winning **Alpenglow Stube,** atop Keystone's North Peak, serves Bavarian-accented contemporary cuisine for lunch and dinner and is reached via enclosed gondola chairlift. It is closed during the spring and autumn shoulder seasons, when the gondola doesn't operate. The rustic **Keystone Ranch,** rated among Colorado's best restaurants by the Zagat Survey, is a restored ranch with six-course dinners. It's open year-round. To make a reservation at either restaurant (required), call Keystone's Dining & Activities center at (970) 496-4386.

Cook your own steaks on the grill at **The Mint in Silverthorne,** 347 Blue River Pkwy. (970-468-5247). In one of the county's oldest buildings, The Mint is a fun-for-the-whole-family dining spot. For a hearty pre-ski or pre-sail breakfast, take your appetite to the **Arapahoe Cafe & Pub,** 626 Lake Dillon Dr. in Dillon (970-468-0873). **The Snake River Saloon,** 23074 US 6 in Keystone (970-468-2788), is locally famous for its spirited après-ski and late-night entertainment. **The Ski Tip Lodge** (970-496-4950) offers American regional cuisine, including several wild-game dishes, in a rustic atmosphere. This historic spot was Colorado's first skiers' lodge. Seating is limited so reservations are essential.

Keystone Resort has three fun options, all accessible at (970) 354-4386. **Der Fondue Chessel** entertains diners with Bavarian music while serving them a Swiss-style four-course fondue dinner. Dinner sleigh and wagon rides pull guests up to the **Soda Creek Homestead** and serve a Western-style meal while a cowboy performer leads the crowd in a sing-along. The **Bighorn Steakhouse** in Keystone's village is a good place to enjoy a Western meal while overlooking the lake.

Shopping

The factory outlet stores in Silverthorne are reason enough to drive up from Denver. Clustered in three malls just off I-70 at exit 205 are bargain outlets for 80 well-known manufacturers, including **Bass Shoes, Eddie Bauer, Nike, OshKosh B'Gosh, Great Outdoor Clothing,** and **Wilson's Leather.** The stores are open 7 days a week and claim a 40 percent average savings over retail. For information call (970) 468-5780.

Accommodations

Accommodations in Keystone are plentiful, with 1,600 lodging units available at the resort in seven neighborhoods. They include the luxurious Keystone Lodge and the truly deluxe Chateaux d'Mont. There are also condominiums of all sizes and private homes available for rent. Contact **Keystone Reservations** at (970) 496-4242. **The Ski Tip Lodge** (970-496-4950) offers good access to cross-country trails in a funky historic Colorado building.

Simpler but charming and comfortable lodging can be found in Frisco, Dillon, and Silverthorne. The **Frisco Inn on Galena,** 1st Avenue and Galena Street (970-668-3224 or 855-237-4726; friscoinnongalena.com), is a pretty, modern bed-and-breakfast in Frisco tucked a half-block back from Main Street and near the bike path. The **Best Western Ptarmigan Lodge** (970-468-2341; ptarmigan lodge.com) is on Lake Dillon at 652 Lake Dillon Dr. (take exit 205 off I-70). The lodge has deluxe motel accommodations, kitchenettes, and condominiums with fireplaces. The **Best Western Lake Dillon Lodge** at 1202 N. Summit Blvd. in Frisco (970-668-5094; lakedillonlodge.com) has some family rooms with three double beds, as well as an indoor pool, hot tub, restaurant, lounge, and ski shop. The 217-room **Holiday Inn** at 1129 N. Summit Blvd. in Frisco (970-668-5000; holidayinn.com) is more convenient than scenic. There's an indoor pool, sauna, hot tubs, restaurant, lounge, gift shop, and ski shop on the premises, and you are also within walking distance of Frisco shops and restaurants.

With ski traffic mounting every year, think about renting a condo for the weekend to avoid day-skiing hassles. On Saturday take a shuttle to the slopes. To avoid the heavy weekend traffic through Idaho Springs on Sunday, be the first on the slopes and the first to leave, or stay another night and drive down in the morning.

Arapahoe Basin

To reach Arapahoe Basin, take I-70 to exit 205, Dillon/Silverthorne, and follow US 6 for 12 miles. Arapahoe Basin is 5 miles past Keystone.

ARAPAHOE BASIN SKI & SNOWBOARD AREA
(970) 468-0718
arapahoebasin.com
At a base altitude of 10,800 feet above sea level, Arapahoe Basin is where Insiders head for unbeatable spring skiing. On years when late snows replenish its base, Arapahoe has welcomed skiers through the first week of August, but that's not its only claim to fame. Arapahoe Basin offers the highest lift-served terrain on the North American continent, with a summit at 13,050 feet. It is characterized by tough terrain and tough weather conditions—but a good day here is a great day. Don't forget the sunscreen.

Arapahoe Basin is a full-service resort, if not glamorous. The most important thing you'll find here is great skiing (490 acres; 40 percent expert), backed by a cafeteria, bar, ski school, rental shop, and retail store.

Copper Mountain

COPPER MOUNTAIN CHAMBER OF COMMERCE
(970) 968-6477
copperchamber.com

COPPER MOUNTAIN RESORT
General information, **(866) 841-2481**
coppercolorado.com

SUMMIT COUNTY CHAMBER OF COMMERCE
(970) 668-2051
summitchamber.org

Winter Activities

Copper Mountain was constructed in the early 1970s as a self-contained resort. It's still a very enticing place for experienced skiers, with 2,400 acres of skiable terrain and more than three-quarters of the trails ranked intermediate to expert.

Copper is Summit County's largest ski area. More than $500 million has been spent since 1998 to refurbish the base area. Among the additions were expanded base restaurants near the Super Bee lift, Commons, and Union Creek; additional snowmaking capacity; and a Super Pipe Dragon for carving out a larger half-pipe.

Copper has also put a great deal of effort into its ski school program, so beginners will feel comfortable here as well. In the past, Copper has even offered free skiing on its easiest lifts, K and L, which access 53 acres of terrain and have an easy grade just right for the first-time skier or boarder. The mountain is naturally divided between harder and easier skiing.

The cross-country skiing tracks begin near the Union Creek base area and branch off into the rolling, wooded valleys of the Arapaho National Forest. Dinner sleigh rides are offered nightly in winter and in summer (on wheels) and include a gourmet meal mid-mountain. Call the Copper Mountain Stables at (970) 968-2232.

Summer Fun

The **Copper Creek Golf Club** (866-388-9770) is the highest-altitude championship golf course in the US, at 9,650 feet, which means your ball will fly 15 percent farther than at sea level. Summer activities include an outdoor climbing wall, a quad-powered bungee jump and go-karts. Hikers, backpackers, and horseback riders enjoy challenging themselves on the Wheeler-Dillon Pack Trail, which begins across the highway from Copper Mountain and climbs rapidly into the rugged Gore Range in the Arapaho National Forest. The Colorado Trail, a 469-mile trail that extends from Denver to Durango, passes near Copper Mountain, too. You can also arrange a breakfast or dinner horseback ride out of Copper Mountain Stables.

From mid-June until about Labor Day you can ride the American Eagle lift free. Also free is the 18-hole Frisbee golf course through the base of the village. Mountain bikers can ride up the lift, for a fee, and ride down on either the mountain road or a twisty single-track. Bike rentals are easily found. Try **Gravitee Boardshop** (970-968-0171; gravitee.com) or **Peak Sports** (970-968-2372; coppersports.com). Intermediate riders might want to try the Ten Mile Canyon ride, which follows the old railroad grade along Ten Mile Creek.

Dining

Endo's Adrenaline Cafe (970-968-3070) is the place to chow down on huge sandwiches and specialty drinks. It's located in the Mountain Plaza Building. At **Double Diamond** in the Foxpine Inn (970-968-2880), you'll find a selection of steaks, sandwiches, pizza, and burgers. **Tucker's Tavern** (970-968-2033) features burgers, top sirloin sandwiches, pizza, and a full dinner menu. It is located in Snow-bridge Square. **Incline Bar & Grill** (970-968-6688) has salads and soups, sandwiches and burgers, and a variety of hearty ski resort entrees.

Accommodations

Copper Mountain is about 75 miles west of Denver. To get there, take I-70 west to exit 195. Virtually all the overnight lodging at Copper Mountain is in condominiums. Call **Copper Mountain Resort** for rental information.

VAIL & BEAVER CREEK

Vail is located on I-70 about 100 miles west of Denver; Beaver Creek is 11 miles farther west.

BEAVER CREEK RESORT
(970) 845-9090
beavercreek.com

VAIL/BEAVER CREEK RESERVATIONS
(877) 204-7881

VAIL RESORT
(970) 476-5601
vail.com

VAIL VALLEY PARTNERSHIP CHAMBER & TOURISM BUREAU
(970) 476-1000
visitvailvalley.com

Winter Activities

For as long as Vail has been a playground of plenty, Front Range residents have had a love-hate relationship with it. They love the skiing—acres and acres of varied, magnificently designed slopes—but hate the crowds, glitz, and high prices. Driving to Vail from Denver also means navigating Vail Pass, which can be treacherous in bad weather and an incentive to exit at Copper Mountain or sooner. Still, every self-respecting skier should try Vail at least once. It's the largest single ski-mountain complex in North America: three base areas, more high-speed quad chairlifts than any other ski area, and vast powder-filled back bowls that spread out across 5,200 acres of spectacular alpine terrain. China Bowl alone is as large as many ski areas. Intermediates especially can ski all day and never go down the same run twice. It attracts a diverse international crowd, so expect to hear a variety of foreign languages on the slopes and in the shops. The Eagle Bahn gondola is heated and lighted. The Adventure Ridge mountaintop activity center features an outdoor skating rink, snowmobile tours, and other winter activities. Chaos Canyon is for kids only, featuring an obstacle course and other kid-friendly attractions.

A ticket at Vail also is valid at Beaver Creek, Vail's little (but even richer and more exclusive) sister 11 miles farther west. First opened in 1980–81, elegant Beaver Creek attracts an international elite clientele as well as local skiers who praise the area for its spectacular natural beauty, lack of crowds, free parking, and intimate feel. About 65 percent of the runs at Beaver Creek are intermediate or advanced. Snowboarding is permitted at Vail and Beaver Creek.

Kids do not ski free here. There are, however, a total of 12 kids-only areas (in addition to the large Chaos Canyon) featuring historical Indian tepee villages, a mountain lion's den, ski-through mock gold mines, and a fort. Modeled after a Tyrolean village, Vail is a charming town that caters to pedestrians. Free buses link all the base areas and run from morning to late night. Vail is home to the **Colorado Ski Museum,** at the Vail Transportation Center (970-476-1876; ski museum.net), and is the frequent site of World Cup ski races. Vail and Beaver Creek have Nordic centers that offer lessons as well as equipment rentals and tours. Vail's Nordic Center is located at the Vail Golf Course (970-476-8366), with backcountry access to

Vail Mountain and the White River National Forest and the **Beaver Creek Nordic Sports Center** (970-754-5313), at the bottom of Strawberry Park lift (chair 12). At Beaver Creek skiers and snowshoers ride the lift up to McCoy Park, which is home to a system of groomed trails.

There are abundant opportunities for backcountry touring throughout the Vail Valley; the summit of Vail Pass itself is often the first ski tour of the year for many Denver backcountry enthusiasts, as it receives plentiful early snow. The town of Vail and Vail Pass are the starting or ending points for several overnight tours to huts that were built during World War II for soldiers from the 10th Mountain Division, including the (relatively) luxurious Shrine Mountain Inn. Reservations are essential; call the **10th Mountain Division Hut Association** (970-925-5775).

The bobsled run at Vail Is a thrilling ride. Snowmobile and sleigh rides can be booked through local companies, and Vail's world-class **John A. Dobson Ice Arena** is open for public skating (970-479-2271).

The **Adventure Ridge** mountaintop activity center (970-476-9090) features an outdoor skating rink, tubing hill, snowmobile tours, thrill sledding, ski biking, laser tag, snowshoeing, orienteering, and a free nature center. It's open in winter only until 10 p.m. and has three restaurants.

Summer Fun

Summer is glorious in the Vail Valley. In fact, many Denverites who avoid Vail's winter glitz look forward to its more laid-back summer style. Hikers and backpackers can explore a large network of trails, either on foot or on horseback. Most of these trails are fairly steep, but the many lakes and waterfalls provide lots of resting and picnic spots. Much of the land around Vail is part of the White River National Forest. For suggested routes and maps, call or visit the **Holy Cross Ranger District Office** (970-827-5715), located in Minturn at 24747 US 24.

Four chairlifts on Vail and Beaver Creek mountains make it easy to reach new mountain-biking heights and nearly 100 miles of world-class trails. Rentals are easy to find at any number of shops in town or at the Wildwood Shelter on top of Vail's Wilderness Express lift.

The Vail Valley has several public and private golf courses, the most touted of which is the **Beaver Creek Golf Club** (970-845-5775), a Robert Trent Jones Jr. course. Another option is the **Eagle-Vail Golf Club** (970-949-5267), located between Vail and Avon. **Vail Golf Club** (970-479-2260) is a par-71 public course with spectacular views of the Gore Range.

If you'd like to hike or ride a mountain bike in the Holy Cross Wilderness Area near Vail, Aspen, or Copper Mountain but aren't keen on sleeping in tents, the 10th Mountain Division Hut Association huts also are open in the summer July 1 through September 30. Call (970) 925-5775 for more information or to make reservations.

If you're looking for Vail glamour, book a treatment at the **Sonnenalp Resort**'s spa (970-479-5404). For the musically inclined, the **Bravo! Vail Valley Music Festival** (970-827-5700; vailmusicfestival.org) features an array of classical music and jazz.

Dining

Visitors to Vail will find no shortage of good restaurants. **Sweet Basil,** 193 E. Gore Creek Dr. (970-476-0125), serves inventive although expensive American cuisine in a pretty spot by Gore Creek. **Atwater at Vail**

Cascade, 1300 Westhaven Dr. (970-479-7014), serves creative American cuisine and specializes in craft beer and food/dessert pairings. **Left Bank,** 183 Gore Creek Dr. #4 (970-476-3696), serves authentic French cuisine and has been a Vail favorite for more than 40 years. Less expensive is **Los Amigos** (970-476-5847), at the top of Bridge Street, which serves standard Mexican fare in a bustling atmosphere. Also more for the budget-minded, **Blu's,** 193 E. Gore Creek Dr. (970-476-3113), is a longtime favorite serving breakfast, lunch, and dinner. The food is eclectic American cuisine, including soups, salads, pizzas, great desserts, and coffee.

Dining in Beaver Creek is even more heavily tilted toward the expensive than Vail, and reservations are de rigueur. **Mirabelle,** located in a former home at 55 Village Rd. (970-949-7728), receives high praise for its romantic ambience, excellent service, and French cuisine with a twist. It's closed briefly during the spring and fall, between ski season and summer. Up on the slopes of Beaver Creek, **Beano's Cabin** offers more than just a meal. Reached by sleigh ride, this elegant log-and-glass lodge offers six-course gourmet meals as well as entertainment for adults and children. In the summer you can get there via horseback or horse-drawn wagon (about a 1-hour trip) or by shuttle van (a 10-minute trip). Naturally, an experience like this does not come cheap. For reservations call (877) 354-0061. For a more casual meal, visit **Pazzo's Pizzeria,** 122 E. Meadow Dr. (970-476-9026), at the end of the Vail Village pedestrian mall.

Shopping

Vail and Beaver Creek are known for their fine selection of shops and galleries, but this is not bargain shopping. Sticker-shock is common, as are full-length furs, custom-designed jewelry, and designer labels. Vail and Beaver Creek offer resort-town shopping at its finest. **The Golden Bear,** 183 Gore Creek Dr. (970-476-4082), has ladies' clothing and men's and ladies' jewelry, including earrings, pendants, bracelets, and other accessories featuring its trademark golden bear (available in sterling silver, too). **Pepi Sports,** 231 Bridge St. (970-476-5206), is another longtime source for outerwear and sportswear as well as ski, bike, and in-line skate rentals. For colorful, contemporary regional art, visit **Vail Village Arts,** 122 E. Meadow Dr. (970-476-2070).

Accommodations

A reasonably priced room can be hard to come by in the Vail Valley. When money is no object, grand lodges and luxury hotels are happy to oblige. Try **The Lodge at Vail** (970-476-5011; lodgeatvail.rockresorts .com), **Beaver Creek Lodge** (800-525-7280; beavercreeklodge.net), and the truly special **Lodge & Spa at Cordillera** (800-877-3529; cordilleralodge.com). A bed-and-breakfast somewhat off the beaten path is the **Minturn Inn,** 422 Main St. in Minturn (970-827-9647; minturninn.com), a completely refurbished 1915 hewn-log home. **The Roost** (970-476-5451; roost-vail-lodging.com) touts itself as the least expensive lodging in Vail and offers continental breakfast.

SKI COUNTRY RESOURCES

ARAPAHO NATIONAL FOREST
Dillon Ranger District, 680 Blue River Parkway, Silverthorne
(970) 468-5400
fs.fed.us

**COLORADO CROSS COUNTRY SKI
  ASSOCIATION**
Information on cross-country centers
colorado-xc.org

COLORADO DIVISION OF WILDLIFE
Fishing information, (303) 291-7533
wildlife.state.co.us/fishing

**COLORADO SKI INFORMATION AND
  REPORTS**
(303) 825-7669
coloradoski.com (ski conditions)

NATIONAL WEATHER SERVICE
Denver and central mountains
(303) 494-4221
crh.noaa.gov/den

**ROAD CONDITIONS WITHIN 2 HOURS
  OF DENVER**
(303) 639-1111
cotrip.org

**10TH MOUNTAIN DIVISION HUT
  ASSOCIATION**
Aspen
(970) 925-5775
huts.org

USDA FOREST SERVICE
Denver Regional Office
740 Simms St., Lakewood
(303) 275-5350
fs.fed.us

US GEOLOGICAL SURVEY
Topographical maps
(303) 202-4700
usgs.gov

**WHITE RIVER NATIONAL FOREST
  OFFICE**
900 Grand Ave., Glenwood Springs
(970) 945-2521
fs.fed.us

SPECTATOR SPORTS

Spend a few days in Denver, and you're likely to think the term "sports town" was coined for the Mile High City. This town is rabid about its teams.

Denver is one of only a few cities that boast seven big-league sports teams: football's Denver Broncos, baseball's Colorado Rockies, hockey's Colorado Avalanche, basketball's Denver Nuggets, soccer's Colorado Rapids, and lacrosse's Colorado Mammoth and Denver Outlaws. When baseball's National League was looking for expansion cities, a majority of Metro Denver fans anted up with a tax hike to fund a stadium. "Build it and they will come" became the local mantra. We have Coors Field to show for our efforts.

The Pepsi Center opened as home to the Denver Nuggets and Colorado Avalanche in 1999. The 675,000-square-foot arena is also host to dozens of other events such as concerts, circuses, and ice shows. The Colorado Mammoth play here as well. It is located in the Central Platte Valley on the edge of downtown and is connected by a pedestrian walkway to Elitch Gardens amusement park. Inside are 17 concession stands, a 236-seat club restaurant, 95 luxury suites, and fully upholstered cast-iron armchairs throughout the arena. The Sports Authority Field at Mile High opened in fall 2001 to house the Denver Broncos. That year it hosted the first Monday-night game of the season when the Broncos met the New York Giants on September 10. The Denver Outlaws play here as well. The latest addition is Dick's Sporting Goods Park in Commerce City, the home field for the Rapids soccer team, which opened in 2007.

The National Western Complex and Coliseum in central Denver host periodic livestock events and rodeos, the largest of which is the National Western Stock Show & Rodeo in January. It's detailed in our Annual Events & Festivals chapter.

BASEBALL

COLORADO ROCKIES
Coors Field, 2001 Blake St.
(303) ROCKIES (762-5437)
rockies.mlb.com

The Colorado Rockies was one of two expansion teams added to the National League in 1993. Despite a losing inaugural season, they won the hearts of Coloradans and received national media attention for the record-breaking attendance they attracted.

After two seasons playing in Mile High Stadium, the Rockies began their 1995 season in their new home, Coors Field, at Blake and 20th Streets. Designed by Hellmuth, Obata & Kassabaum, a Kansas City firm, the 50,249-seat all-baseball stadium is an updated version of a classic ballpark. Its exterior is built of two shades of red brick, and its seats provide views of the Rocky Mountains. The nation got a good look at Coors Field when Denver hosted the 1998 All-Star Game. The game was a weeklong celebration of baseball and Lower Downtown fun for thousands of local and visiting fans.

Such an intense focus on baseball in Colorado once made the best game seats hard to come by, but things have since eased up, and good seats are available for almost every game. During the season, tickets can be purchased at the stadium at Gate C between 20th and 21st Streets and Blake Street or at Rockies Dugout Stores and King Soopers supermarkets. Wheelchair-accessible seating is available. Day-of-game "Rockpile" seats go on sale at the stadium 2 hours prior to game time at discounted prices. Coors Field has two "family sections" where alcohol is not served. Ask for sections 141 and 342.

RTD (Regional Transportation District) provides special buses to and from Rockies games from 16 suburban park-and-rides. Regular service to and from Market Street Station also brings you within walking distance of the stadium but may not be as conveniently timed for evening games. Schedules and fare information are available at (303) 299-6000, rtd-denver.com, or TDD (303) 299-6089.

BASKETBALL

DENVER NUGGETS
The Pepsi Center, 1000 Chopper Place
(303) 405-1100
nba.com/nuggets
Under the guidance of head coach George Karl, the Nuggets continue to pursue their playoff goals with a lineup mixture of seasoned veterans and top draft choices. Nuggets tickets are available by calling the number above or through Ticketmaster at (303) 830-TIXS. There are a number of special deals, such as family and youth nights and group discounts. Wheelchair seating is available on request. The Nuggets share the Pepsi Center, located in the Platte Valley next to Elitch Gardens, with the Colorado Avalanche.

i If you don't have tickets for a game but want to experience Bronco fever, stop by any of a number of sports bars to cheer on the team via television with other fans. Some popular spots: Sports Column at 1930 Blake St., Falling Rock Tap House at 1919 Blake St., Jackson's All American Sports Grill at 1520 20th St., Breckenridge Brewery at 2220 Blake St., Lodo's Bar & Grill at 1946 Market St., Giggling Grizzly at 1320 20th St., and Wynkoop Brewing Co. at 1634 18th St.

FOOTBALL

DENVER BRONCOS
Sports Authority Field at Mile High
1701 Bryant St.
(303) 649-9000
denverbroncos.com
After losing three Super Bowls (1986, 1987, and 1989), the Broncos finally granted fans their ultimate wish—the 1997 championship. And then they followed with the 1998 championship. Broncos fans were joined by legions of John Elway supporters across the country who wanted to see the veteran quarterback win a Super Bowl title. Although Elway has since retired, it's no surprise that virtually every home game is a sellout. If you want to attend, you'll have to call well in

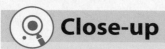

Close-up

Colorado Rockies Bring Baseball, Big Bucks, and Beer to LoDo

The time is the 1970s, the place is a small section of Denver—dirty, a little rough, and definitely seedy.

Brown bags and empty booze bottles litter the streets like bad reminders of the night before. Graffiti covers plywood, which covers shattered warehouse windows. The only signs of life are at night, and these aren't the signs of prosperity and possibility. If the place had a disclaimer, it would shout: "Danger: Go Away."

This is no place for America's favorite pastime.

Now fast-forward to the mid-1990s. Red brick surrounds gleaming windows in renovated warehouses. Litter is gone, replaced by bustling shops and streets and smiling pedestrians. Tourists lounge on the sunny patios of upscale joints and savor microbrewed beer. Above it all towers Coors Field, home of the Colorado Rockies.

This dramatic turnaround may sound like a scene from a developer's dream, but it's the reality of lower downtown Denver's revitalization. Much of the metamorphosis was prompted by the Colorado Rockies' new baseball stadium.

The Rockies have done wonders for Denver's economy and, specifically, the once-blighted area Insiders call "LoDo." An economic-impact study done in 1994 estimated the Rockies would bring nearly $200 million a year in new spending. That's a lot of beer and hot dogs.

Of course, there's more to LoDo than beer and dogs. In fact, unless the beer has a fancy name from one of more than a dozen local brewpubs (Sagebrush Stout, anyone?) and the dogs are dressed up with freshly crushed green chile salsa and served in the center of a dazzling food display, it probably isn't in LoDo. Indeed, LoDo (sort of like SoHo, only not quite) is home of the hip, cool, and happening.

Development around the stadium in the past few years is remarkable. More than 80 new restaurants and brewpubs have sprung up in LoDo since Coors Field opened.

advance for tickets and information or show up at the game and take your chances that someone in the parking lot has a ticket to sell. The Broncos played their first regular-season game in their new stadium, INVESCO field at Mile High, in the fall of 2001. The new stadium comes compliments of metro-area voters, who in November 1998 approved partial public funding for the old Mile High Stadium to be demolished and replaced with a state-of-the-art facility. The stadium has since been renamed Sports Authority Field at Mile High. Tickets, if you can get them, are available from the Broncos at (720) 258-3333 or through Ticketmaster at (303) 830-TIXS.

RTD's BroncoRide services all home games from a number of locations in Metro Denver, with special shuttles available for fans catching the BroncoRide along Federal Boulevard and from Market Street Station. Call RTD at (303) 299-6000 for schedules and current fare information.

High-rise residential buildings have also begun to spring up around Coors Field. Now that the abandoned warehouses have been revived into posh lofts, many of which advertised "Coors Field access," a new Ballpark neighborhood is emerging that is seen as an incubator for art studios, galleries, and other creative enterprises.

The city of Denver has done its part to build the area. Baseball-related infrastructure improvements include millions in road construction (at least $36 million for the city of Denver alone). Another $5 million has gone toward LoDo economic development projects and streetscaping.

In fairness to the LoDo area, much of the revival was launched pre-Rockies. But nearly everyone agrees the Rockies have stimulated business and interest in LoDo. The Rockies alone bring more than three million people to downtown during baseball season (of course, many of those are repeat customers). But the games lure people downtown who might not otherwise have made the trek—like suburbanites who in the '80s stayed away from the city. Those same people, having sampled the excitement and vibrancy of LoDo, return to eat, shop, and party. In a downtown Denver survey, 37 percent of metro respondents said baseball was the main reason they went downtown.

"It's turned LoDo into a year-round destination," says Ben Wright, chief economist for the Denver Metro Chamber of Commerce.

To some extent, the phenomenon happened out of luck—and lack of parking. A dearth of spaces near Coors Field (only 15,000 spaces for 50,000 fans) was once considered a drawback. But the paucity has forced fans to park in lots all over downtown and walk to the game—passing enticing restaurants and shops along the way.

A recent nationwide survey placed the Rockies and Coors Field 11th on the list of top tourist attractions. LoDo rose in popularity to seventh place. How does a neighborhood achieve that kind of success while balancing the quality-of-life issues that having a major-league team in your backyard brings?

If you're Coors Field and lower downtown Denver, you do it with a little luck and a lot of style.

HOCKEY

COLORADO AVALANCHE
The Pepsi Center
1000 Chopper Place
(303) 405-1100
coloradoavalanche.com

In mid-1995 Denver boasted about having four major-league teams when it announced that the Quebec Nordiques were coming to town, renamed as the Colorado Avalanche. In 1996 the boasting continued when its new team won the Stanley Cup. They repeated that win in 2001 against the New Jersey Devils in Game 7 of the series. The Avs remain an annual playoff contender, and they boast a legion of devoted followers. Single-game tickets go on sale in early fall at the number above, or at Ticketmaster, (303) 830-TIXS. Ask about group discounts if you plan to bring a crowd.

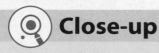 # Close-up

Sports Authority Field at Mile High

Nearly 3 years and $400 million after the proposed design of the new Denver Broncos stadium was unveiled, INVESCO Field at Mile High opened on August 11, 2001, with a concert featuring the Eagles. A pyrotechnics extravaganza followed, rivaling the millennium festivities in downtown Denver.

Throughout the development process, efforts were made to retain ties to the history of Mile High Stadium while creating a first-class, state-of-the-art facility. To that end, the new stadium logo incorporated the recognizable standing horse silhouette. And "Bucky" the bronco was reconditioned and moved to a perch atop the new south scoreboard. The "Mile High" moniker was negotiated into the naming rights agreement.

The differences, however, are more striking than the similarities, particularly in terms of amenities. While the seating capacity has remained nearly identical, the stadium's total square footage was doubled from 850,000 square feet to 1.7 million square feet. Approximately 8,500 club seats have been included, as well as 762 pairs of *Americans with Disabilities Act*–compliant seating. All seats have expanded in both width and length. Each seat now has a cup holder—a change welcomed by most but decried by a few for taking up precious leg room. Televisions, escalators, and a greater number of elevators have been added. The number of restrooms has

LACROSSE

COLORADO MAMMOTH
The Pepsi Center
1000 Chopper Place
(303) 405-1111 (box office)
coloradomammoth.com
The Colorado Mammoth are a member of the National Lacrosse League. Moving to Denver in 2003, the team soon took a position among the league leaders in attendance numbers. In 2006 the Mammoth won the league's Champion's Cup.

DENVER OUTLAWS
Sports Authority Field at Mile High
1701 Bryant St.
(303) 688-5297
denveroutlaws.com
The Denver Outlaws play in the Major League Lacrosse field lacrosse league. Their inaugural game was in May 2006. They won the Western Conference championship in their first season.

RACETRACKS

ARAPAHOE PARK RACETRACK
26000 E. Quincy Ave., Aurora
(303) 690-2400
mihiracing.com
Pari-mutuel thoroughbred, quarter horse, and other races are held here from June through early August, and other races from throughout the country are simulcast in the park. Call for dates and event details.

BANDIMERE SPEEDWAY
3051 S. Rooney Rd., Morrison
(303) 697-6001, (303) 697-4870 (recording)
bandimere.com

doubled, and the number of concession stands has more than quadrupled. Finally, video boards have been added to each end of the field and increased in size over the one video board present in Mile High Stadium.

The naming of the stadium proved to be an emotionally charged issue for fans who had filled every seat in Mile High Stadium for every regular season game since 1970. Torn between reducing the public's debt load and retaining the historic "Mile High" name, the Metropolitan Football Stadium District was able to negotiate a naming rights agreement that incorporated "Mile High." INVESCO, a company that has had ties in the community for more than 70 years, wanted to prevent shortening of the name to "Mile High," but in agreeing to retain those words in the stadium name, they satisfied at least part of the public's desire.

In 2011 the Metropolitan Football Stadium District announced that it would transfer the naming rights to Englewood, Colorado–based Sports Authority. The words Mile High remain in the official stadium name.

The September 10 game between the Broncos and the New York Giants kicked off the 2001 Monday-night football season, while simultaneously being the first regular-season game in the new stadium. In addition to the Broncos, Sports Authority Field at Mile High hosts the Denver Outlaws professional lacrosse team, community events, and festivities.

Championship drag racing events are held from April to October at Bandimere Speedway in Morrison (off C-470 between Alameda Avenue and Morrison Road). Events aren't limited to drag racing; they include motorcycle and snowmobile events as well as such unusual shows as "most unique vehicle" and "stereo wars."

COLORADO NATIONAL SPEEDWAY
4281 Weld County Rd. 10, Erie
(303) 665-4173
coloradospeedway.com
Colorado National Speedway is in Erie, 20 minutes north of Denver, off I-25 at exit 232. It hosts NASCAR and a variety of other races on a paved three-eights-of-a-mile oval track on Saturday from April through September.

SOCCER

COLORADO RAPIDS
Dick's Sporting Goods Park
6000 Victory Way, Commerce City
(303) 727-3500
coloradorapids.com
The Colorado Rapids kicked off their first home game in April 1996 and have been gaining momentum ever since. In 1997 the team captured the western conference championship. In 1998 four of its star players made the All-Star lineup: Marcelo Balboa, Chris Henderson, Paul Bravo, and Adrian Paz. Along with the 1997 title, the team also has the distinction of raising its win/loss record from "worst" in 1996 to "first" in 1997. The Rapids moved to their new home in 2007, Dick's Sporting Goods Park in Commerce City. Tickets can be purchased at the number above or from Ticketmaster, (303) 830-TIXS.

DAY TRIPS

Measure 100 miles from Denver in any direction and you'll have defined more than 3,000 square miles from which to plan day trips. We've recommended a few that will take you north and south along the Front Range as well as west into the mountains. That's not to say that the Great Plains to the east aren't worth visiting. Few landscapes are more tranquilizing than the endless rolling prairie, and few things are more magnificent than 180 degrees of sky, but the majority of Colorado's visitors come with mountain scenery in mind. Bear in mind that snowstorms can render high mountain roads treacherous, if not impassable, from September through May. Consider calling (303) 639-1111 for the Colorado State Highway Patrol's report on road conditions before taking off on a mountain jaunt during these months. If conditions are bad, make sure your vehicle has good snow tires or carry chains. If the chain law is in effect at a particular pass, those without chains will be turned back, no matter how good their tires are. And sometimes the road will close to all traffic until the weather improves. It's really a pain to pull out of Vail heading east up I-70 and discover that they've swung the gates closed across the interstate.

BOULDER

There's so much to do in this college town that a day trip won't do it justice. That said, we've outlined a few of the best things about Boulder. When approaching it on US 36, watch for the Louisville/Superior exit and watch for a sign that says Scenic Overlook. From that turnoff you'll get a stunning view of the town and its mountainside setting. During the warmer months, the Boulder Convention and Visitors Bureau operates an information kiosk on Davidson Mesa, as this hill is known.

Boulder is contained within the scenic bowl of Boulder Valley by the foothills of the Rocky Mountains. The most identifiable rock formation is the Flatirons, enormous sandstone monoliths that lean against the slopes like a row of fossilized aircraft carriers.

i When opening carbonated beverages in the car during high-altitude drives, remember that they have been bottled at a lower altitude and pressure. They can squirt in your face and all over the interior of your vehicle if you are not careful.

Detractors still call it "the people's republic of Boulder," a nickname from the Vietnam era protest days that stuck. Today Boulder is a national mecca for alternative medicine, natural foods, spirituality, and outdoor sports such as bicycle racing, mountain biking, and technical climbing.

Naropa University, a national center for Buddhist studies based in Boulder, is the only fully accredited, Buddhist-inspired institution of higher education in North America, offering bachelor's and master's degrees. Tours of its main campus are offered weekdays at 2 p.m. when school is in session. Tours of the Paramita and Nalanda campuses are by reservation only. Call (303) 444-0202 or visit naropa.edu for more information.

Celestial Seasonings Herbal Tea, 4600 Sleepytime Dr., was founded here and still manufactures teas at its headquarters in the Gunbarrel neighborhood. Tour the facility for an up-close look (and sniff) of the fragrant herbs that find their way into the tea bags. Call (303) 581-1202 or visit celestialseasonings .com for more details.

Boulder is filled with other examples of the innovation that has led to national recognition. Many are spin-offs started by scientists originally affiliated with the University of Colorado and federal government laboratories such as the National Center for Atmospheric Research and the National Institute of Standards and Technologies. CU is nationally prominent in fields ranging from molecular biology to telecommunications and works closely with that community.

Start your visit on the **Pearl Street Mall,** which serves as the center of the city. Formerly Boulder's main street, it's now a pedestrian mall lined with unique shops, restaurants, art galleries, flower gardens, and street performers. It makes for a delightful stroll in any but the worst weather, except for the occasional panhandler. Next try **University Hill,** south on Broadway from Pearl Street and up the hill, where you can enjoy a walk around the graceful CU campus.

Go farther south on Broadway past the campus to Baseline Road, turn right onto Baseline, and go up a long hill. Just past 9th Street you'll find the entrance to **Chautauqua Park & Auditorium** on the left. Its auditorium is a lovely venue for a summer evening concert. For information, call the Chautauqua box office at (303) 440-7666. If possible, stay for breakfast, lunch, or dinner at the **Chautauqua Dining Hall,** built in 1898, where you can gaze out at the mountains as you eat; call (303) 440-3776.

Chautauqua serves as the gateway to **Boulder Mountain Parks,** some 8,000 acres of trails and rough climbing through terrain that includes Bear Peak, Green Mountain, Flagstaff Mountain, and, of course, the Flatirons.

i It's always cool in the mountains at night, even in the summer. Take a sweater.

Another entrance to the park, and an attraction in its own right, is the **National Center for Atmospheric Research,** commonly referred to around Boulder simply as NCAR (say it EN-car). The agency works with universities to study the atmosphere, but its building, designed by the renowned architect I. M. Pei, may be its best-known asset. It perches like an Italian hill fortress on a mesa to the south of Chautauqua, providing views of the mountains and plains and the weather fronts that move across them. You find it by going still farther south on Broadway from Baseline to Table Mesa Drive. Turn right, and keep going until you run into the facility. You may see deer on the way. You can pick up a map in the lobby and take the self guided tour daily, including holidays. Guided tours take place daily at noon. The

Science Store stocks a great selection of books and activities for children. And best of all, admission is free. More information is available at ncar.ucar.edu or (303) 497-1174. Outside NCAR, you can hike on 400 acres of the mesa top on a nature trail that is wheelchair-accessible. Just west of the mesa, you can access Boulder Mountain Park trails.

Climbers scaling the Flatirons are a common sight, but the best place for close-up watching of technical climbers is **Eldorado Canyon.** Keep going south on Broadway from Table Mesa Drive until Broadway becomes Highway 93. Watch for the Eldorado Springs Drive turnoff on the right or Highway 170, just more than 5 miles south of Boulder. **Eldorado Springs** is about 8 miles down that road. Around the turn of the 20th century this resort town was called "the Coney Island of Colorado" because of the people who flocked here for resort hotels and 76-degree hot springs. Pass through the town to reach **Eldorado Canyon State Park,** where you'll find a magnificent cut between high cliffs. The little smudges of white on the rocks are chalk from climbers' hands. In good weather you'll see people dangling from the canyon walls.

COLORADO SPRINGS

"The Springs," as locals call it, is 67 miles or an hour's drive south of Denver. It has the largest single cluster of tourist attractions within day trip range. **Pikes Peak** is the biggest show in town. You can drive to the top by taking US 24 west to Cascade and turning left on the same road driven by international auto racers to the summit during the annual Pikes Peak Hill Climb. Or you can do the dizzying trip on the **Pikes Peak Cog Railway.** Reach its terminal by driving west from Colorado Springs on US 24 to the Manitou exit, west on Manitou Avenue, and left onto Ruxton Avenue. This is the highest cog railway in the world. Established in 1889, it's a historical as well as a sensory experience. During the 3.5-hour round-trip, you get more panoramas than you can stuff into your brain, including Manitou Springs and the Garden of the Gods below. On a clear day you can see north to Denver and south to New Mexico. Take care not to exert yourself too much at the 14,115-foot summit; oxygen is scarce up there, and altitude sickness is not a pleasant experience. Also on the summit are an information center, gewgaw shop, and concession area. The railway is open daily from April to October, and reservations are required. Information is available at cograilway.com or (719) 685-5401.

Garden of the Gods is another of Colorado Springs's most famous sights. A drive through the park reveals one of the most spectacular displays of dramatic red sandstone formations in Colorado. It's just northwest of downtown at 1805 N. 30th St. (719-634-6666; gardenofgods.com). **Cave of the Winds,** in Manitou Springs on Highway 24 West, is the biggest commercial underground cave in Colorado, and well worth touring. More information is available at (719) 685-5444 or caveofthewinds.com.

If you want to go a bit beyond the 100-mile limit of our day trip definition, you will certainly enjoy the **Cripple Creek & Victor Narrow Gauge Railroad** (719-689-2640; cripplecreekrailroad.com). **Cripple Creek,** one of Colorado's most famous old mining towns and a National Historic District, is worth visiting too. Since limited-stakes gambling was legalized here in 1991, the town's ambience has changed, but it still provides a peek into the state's rough and tumble ancestry. About an hour's drive from Colorado Springs on Highway 115 is the Royal Gorge, where you can drive or walk across the world's highest suspension bridge 1,178 feet above the Arkansas River. The accompanying theme park includes an aerial tram, a minitrain, a carousel, a wildlife park, and an incline railway, a cagelike ride that takes you down to the bottom of the canyon to the river's edge. Information is available at royalgorgebridge.com or (719) 275-7507.

Other things do in the Colorado Springs area include the Victorian town of **Manitou Springs** and its natural hot springs; the **Cliff Dwellings Museum** on US 24 (719-685-5242); the historic **Broadmoor Hotel** (719-634-7711) and its spa and 18-hole golf courses; **Santa's Workshop at the North Pole** (719-684-9432), a funland open mid-May through Christmas Eve; and the **ProRodeo Hall of Fame,** which shares space with the **Museum of the American Cowboy,** both at (719) 528-4764.

Of all Colorado Springs's attractions, the busiest is the **US Air Force Academy.** Although it covers 18,000 acres, visitor access is limited for security reasons. You can stop at the visitor center from 9 a.m. to 5 p.m. daily, take a self-guided driving tour around the grounds daily between 8 a.m. and 6 p.m., or walk the 0.3-mile nature trail to the cadet chapel, which is architecturally striking. Perhaps the best way to experience the academy is at a football game or by attending the spring graduation ceremony, where you can watch cadets tossing their caps in the air and enjoy a performance by the Thunderbirds, the Air Force's famed jet-acrobatics team. You do need advance tickets for commencement, which is always held on the first Wednesday after Memorial Day. Call the academy's

visitor center at (719) 333-2025 for tickets and other information.

Directly across I-25 from the north gate of the Air Force Academy is the **Western Museum of Mining and Industry.** It's a nice place for a picnic, with 27 acres of rolling hills, trees, meadows, streams, beaver ponds, and picnic tables. The museum itself has more than 15,000 square feet of exhibits in four buildings, along with outdoor displays. It's a treat to watch employees fire up the 1895 Corliss steam engine, which drives a 17-tone flywheel. You can see mining and milling demonstrations and even pan for gold. The museum is open 9 a.m. to 4 p.m. Monday through Saturday year-round, and until 5 p.m. June through August. More information is available at wmmi.org or (719) 488-0880. To reach the museum get off I-25 at exit 156A, Gleneagle Drive.

FORT COLLINS

We go to Fort Collins when we need a small-town fix, although this college town (home of Colorado State University) has seen tremendous growth in the last few years. Reach it by driving about an hour north of Denver on I-25, then taking the Harmony Road exit. Go right for a quarter of a mile until you see a farm with 150 shiny sculptures. This is the **Swetsville Zoo,** a menagerie of dinosaurs and mythical creatures made by owner Bill Swets. This self-styled artist makes his creatures out of car parts and farm equipment. Open every day year-round, the zoo is free, though donations are appreciated.

Once you're ready to head into town, get back on I-25 and go north to the Mulberry Street exit. Follow it past downtown and to Roosevelt Street. Here you'll find City Park and the **Fort Collins Municipal Railway,** a fancy term for a restored trolley car that travels downtown along Mountain Avenue. Powered by 600 volts of electricity, the trolley runs on tracks that line the grassy median of one of the city's major thoroughfares. Don't be surprised if the conductor gets out when you reach downtown and smokes a pipe before returning to City Park. Remember, this is small-town living, not a New York subway. It operates weekend afternoons and holidays May through September.

Fort Collins offers shopping that transcends the typical mall experience. **Historic Old Town Square** at College and Mountain Avenues is a trove of art galleries, shops, and outdoor cafes all housed in historic buildings. Like the Pearl Street Mall in Boulder, this is a pedestrian-only area with places to sit and watch people when you're tired of shopping.

For beer drinkers, a visit to Fort Collins wouldn't be complete without a free tour of the **Anheuser Busch Brewery,** off of I-25 at exit 271. Opened in 1988 and one of the world's largest breweries, it offers free tours daily. The 75-minute tour shows high-tech brewing processes as well as a chance to see the famous Clydesdale horses. Best of all, at the end, you can visit the Hospitality Center to taste a few brews. Information is available at budweisertours.com or (970) 490-4691.

While you're here, don't overlook two smaller but equally worthwhile local breweries. Actually, in the world of craft beer, they're both big. **New Belgium Brewing** (500 Linden St.; 970-221-0524; newbelgium .com) and **Odell Brewing** (800 E. Lincoln St.; 970-482-2881; odellbrewing.com) are two of the most successful microbreweries in Colorado. Both companies make excellent beer, and both offer tours. Some beer aficionados

consider the New Belgium tour one of the best brewery tours in the country.

If you want to explore Colorado craft beers even further, **Funkwerks Brewing** (1900 E. Lincoln Ave.; 970-482-3865; funk werks.com) was awarded the Small Brewing Company of the Year at the 2012 Great American Beer Festival. **Choice City Butcher and Deli** (104 W. Olive St.; 970-490-2489; choicecitybutcher.com), along with an outstanding menu of deli fare (try the buffalo Reuben), offers a great selection of rare beers.

To visit **Colorado State University** (CSU), stop at the visitor center just south of College Avenue and Laurel Street for a map of the campus and a current schedule of events.

GEORGETOWN

Georgetown is a historic mining town that has been lovingly maintained and restored, with a turn-of-the-20th-century style that makes it resemble the miniature towns that adorn model railroads. It's a National Historic District that nestles deep into a valley that is overshadowed by the steep slopes of several 12,000-foot mountains.

The biggest single attraction is the **Georgetown Loop,** an old Western railroad train that hauls tourists and train history buffs on a 3-mile loop between Georgetown and **Silver Plume.** The train ride includes passage over a 100-foot trestle known as Devils Gate Bridge. We can't recommend this trip highly enough, not just for the scenery or the fun of riding but for the historic element and the bits of cinder that fly from the engine stack and settle on the passengers behind. It's one of the few great antique train rides in Colorado, by far the closest one to Denver. For a special treat, do it in the fall when the aspens are at high color. The train operates from May through October, and reservations are suggested. For reservations and information call (888) 456-6777.

ℹ Layering is the key for dressing in Colorado, especially in the mountains. Temperature changes often take visitors off-guard, but if you're prepared, it's not a problem. An inexpensive rain poncho for mountain showers can be a trip-saver.

Georgetown was founded in 1859, but transformed itself into "the Silver Queen of the Rockies" by the 1870s. Now it's just a fun place to stroll past shops, restaurants, museums, galleries, and National Historic Register sites. The museums include the **Hotel de Paris,** the **Hamill House,** and the **Energy Museum,** which was renovated with help from the State Historic Fund. The Hamill House was built in the 1870s in the Gothic Revival style and has been restored to that period. The Hotel de Paris, owned by Louis Dupuy, included a fine dining room and is open for tours, as are all the museums. Reach Georgetown by taking I-70 exit 228, about 50 miles west of Denver. You can also drive south from Georgetown on the **Guanella Pass Scenic Byway,** which goes all the way to the town of Grant on US 285. The byway tops out at Guanella Pass, elevation 11,669 feet, where you have wonderful views that include Mount Bierstadt. The summit is a good place to get out of the car and look around, but don't stand up too fast in the thin air at this altitude. Find a big rock and have a picnic.

Georgetown has another neat little element. The state of Colorado chose a spot near the lake east of Georgetown for its first **Watchable Wildlife Viewing Station.** Stop and see if you can spot a herd of bighorn sheep on the mountainsides. Sometimes you can seem them while whizzing by on I-70. Georgetown visitor information is available at (303) 569-2405 or georgetown-colorado.org.

GRAND LAKE/GRANBY LOOP

We call this the Grand Lake/Granby loop drive because the sightseeing trip is anchored by those two towns on the western side of the Continental Divide. Reach it by driving from Denver to Estes Park and over Trail Ridge Road (closed in winter), through Rocky Mountain National Park and down to Granby. To return to Denver, take US 40 from Granby south through Winter Park, over Berthoud Pass through Empire to I-70 east. The loop is almost 200 miles and takes a full day to drive, especially if you stop along the way. If that's too much of a commitment, consider dividing it in two, with the Boulder, Estes Park, and Rocky Mountain National Park trip one day and the Denver to Grand Lake trip on another.

Grand Lake is the name of the city as well as the lake on which it perches. Lake Granby sits to the west of Grand Lake. You'll travel along their western edges, enjoying scenery reminiscent of Switzerland. The lakes are huge, clear, and deep blue in color, lined with small resorts and usually decorated with sailboats. Grand Lake is the state's largest glacier-fed lake; the town is a quaint historic village with boardwalks along the main street. Walk around and catch a bite to eat, or buy something and head out for a picnic at **Arapahoe Bay,** on the far southeastern end of Lake Granby. It's a favorite fishing spot in June, when the Mackinaw, or lake trout, are at their peak. Reach it by taking the first left turn off US 34 at the southwestern tip of Lake Granby. A long gravel road passes over Granby Dam and skirts the southern edge of the lake. At the end of the bay, you'll find campgrounds and some nice short hiking trails. You can follow the trail east past Monarch Lake and go as far as you want toward the Indian Peaks Wilderness. Return to civilization by heading out to meet US 40 just west of Granby. You may want to take an added excursion west, or right, on US 40 along the scenic highway toward Steamboat Springs. If not, return to Denver by taking a left onto US 40 and follow it through Granby, Tabernash, Fraser, Winter Park, Berthoud Pass, and Empire on to I-70.

Most people just hustle through **Empire,** but there are some nice places to stop for refreshments. Its most famous is **The Peck House** (303-569-9870), Colorado's oldest operating hotel. You can see it from the highway to the east, a big white building with red trim. It's a moderately priced hotel with a nice restaurant.

HOT SULPHUR SPRINGS

This quaint town of about 375 residents came alive again when the Hot Sulphur Springs Resort was renovated in 1997. To reach this town located 90 miles northwest of Denver, take I-70 to US 40, heading west. Follow the road through Winter Park and Granby before heading west toward Kremmling. Once you're in Hot Sulphur Springs, cross the Colorado River and you'll see the **Hot Sulphur Springs Resort & Spa** on the right, nestled against 70 acres of sagebrush.

The Ute Indians once "took the waters" here to heal and relax. Today people come for the same reasons. You can soak in any of the 22 pools where 200,000 gallons of hot mineral waters flow at temperatures of 95 to 112 degrees F year-round. Too darn hot? Go to the kid's pool that runs around 85 degrees.

This casual resort has private pools, pools with views, and cavelike pools. And if you're feeling particularly luxurious, you can book a massage and facial. If you're feeling invigorated, you may want to hike and picnic in the beautiful surroundings. The pools are open year-round 8 a.m. to 10 p.m. More information is available at (970) 725-3306 or hotsulphursprings.com.

IDAHO SPRINGS

Idaho Springs, 32 miles west of Denver, is the first mining town you'll hit on your way west on I-70. Thanks to the yellow tailings piles that spill from holes dotting the mountainside, the town's historic roots are obvious. If you want a closer look at this phenomenon, take the "Oh My God Road" from Idaho Springs to Central City, a narrow and scary road with even more holes and tailings dotting the hillsides.

Prospector George Jackson launched Idaho Springs in early 1859 when he pulled out nearly $2,000 worth of gold in one week. Miners flocked in, and the town was off. Two of your best choices for a look into the town's mining past are the Argo Gold Mill and the Phoenix Mine. The **Argo Gold Mill** is the biggest structure on the north side of the valley, and the name is printed in large letters on its front. Where much of the local ore was processed is now a museum and National Historic Site that can be toured May to October; for information, call (303)

567-2421 or go to historicargotours.com. The **Phoenix Mine,** sunk in 1872, is once again a working mine, although it can be toured year-round, weather permitting, with an experienced miner as the guide. Learn about the history, geology, and art of gold mining; dig your own ore; and pan your own gold. Call (303) 567-0422 or visit phoenix goldmine.com.

Idaho Springs also has natural hot mineral springs. The **Indian Springs Resort and Spa,** a National Historic Site, offers hot baths and a covered mineral-water swimming pool. It's east of downtown at 302 Soda Creek Rd. Call (303) 989-6666 or visit indianhotsprings.com for details. For more information on these and other attractions, call the Idaho Springs Visitor Center at (303) 567-4382.

MOUNT EVANS

If you love mountains, this is the fastest route to the region's greatest vistas. For out-of-town visitors with only a morning or afternoon to see the mountains, this is the best recommendation we can make. Highway 5 to the top of Mount Evans is the highest paved road in the world, providing the opportunity to visit the summit of a Colorado "14er" without having to huff and puff up thousands of feet. You can park at about 14,260 feet, wander around, and look down and out 100 miles in every direction. The view is absolutely magnificent. To reach it from Denver, take I-70 west to Idaho Springs, a 30-minute drive. Get off at exit 240, and follow Highway 103 uphill to its intersection with Highway 5 at **Echo Lake.** This is where rangers will collect a daily visitors' fee. The lake is a nice place for a picnic and some fishing. Head uphill on Highway 5 for

another 14-mile trip to the top. Acrophobics should be warned that this stretch may produce whiter knuckles than any paved road in Colorado. The road is very narrow, especially on the ride down. Looking out from the passenger seat, you can easily imagine the car slipping off the side and cartwheeling into the abyss. Instead, keep an eye out for the mountain goats and marmots often seen along the road.

Once at the parking lot, you can climb a short trail to the highest point and look down to the west on the Continental Divide, east over Denver and the Great Plains, north over the Roosevelt National Forest, and south over the Pike National Forest. Bring along a state map; it's fun to identify some of the major peaks. If you like boulder fields, there are plenty to scramble around on. If you're a flatlander who hasn't been in Denver for at least 3 days, bear in mind that there's only about half as much oxygen up here as there is at sea level. Altitude sickness can hit you right away, or it can hammer you after you've been back in Denver for hours. Take it easy, drink lots of water, and you should do fine. The road to Mount Evans is open only in the warmer months, and even then, weather can turn bad. To check on road conditions or ask other questions, call the Clear Creek Ranger District of Arapaho National Forest at (303) 567-3000.

THE PEAK-TO-PEAK

The Peak-to-Peak Highway is so called because it follows the eastern slopes of more peaks than you can shake a stick at. It's basically the road that follows the Continental Divide between the tourist mecca of Estes Park on the north to the historic towns and gambling meccas of Black Hawk and Central

City on the south. Along the way there are plenty of westerly turnoffs that will get you closer to Longs Peak, Mount Meeker, Chiefs Head Peak, Isolation Peak, Ouzel Peak, Mount Alice, Mount Orton, Mahana Peak, and Copeland Mountain—and those are just some of the peaks along the first 10 miles. The highway is about 60 miles long and actually consists of Highways 7, 72, and 119.

Take the Peak-to-Peak in either direction. The entire route is a winding road of beautiful vistas and lovely mountainsides. It's a worthwhile tour anytime but an especially great place to take in the views of autumn's golden aspens, generally in September. Ten miles south of Estes Park, you find the well-traveled turnoff for the Longs Peak trailhead. This may be the most popular ascent of a Colorado "14er," but it's rigorous. Don't try it without consulting an expert for tips about how to prepare.

Another 4 miles or so along, you'll find on the right the turnoff for the **Ouzel Falls Trail at Wild Basin.** If you want to get out of your car for a pleasant walk to a gemlike waterfall in the cool forest, this is the opportunity. The falls are only about 3 miles up the trail.

All along the Peak-to-Peak, turnoffs to the west lead to scenic areas and other attractions, while turnoffs to the east take you back to the flatlands in case you decide to bail out midway. At one of these points, the historic mining town of Ward, you can head downhill via **Lefthand Canyon** or head west up to **Brainard Lake.** This crystalline, high-mountain lake is a beautiful place to absorb spectacular views without walking more than a few steps from your vehicle.

Pass on south to Nederland and Rollinsville. A drive west from here on a gravel road

will bring you to the Moffat Tunnel, which connects Denver by railroad with points west. A trail to the east of the tunnel makes a nice hike and is popular in winter with cross-country skiers.

More tourist attractions await you in **Black Hawk** and **Central City,** where it has been legal to gamble since 1991. Black Hawk was one of the first mining camps near Gregory Gulch, where gold was discovered in 1859. Nearby Central City, in the middle of Gregory Gulch, became the prominent population center because of its location, which claims the "richest square mile on Earth." It is a great old mining town, but some feel that its historic authenticity has been obliterated by the casinos. The **Central City Opera House** is still one of Colorado's reigning opera performance centers during its summer season. In 1878 it was built on the site of the Montana Theatre, which had burned to the ground in 1874. Closed when the silver boom ended, it has been operating again since 1932. Call the Denver business office at (303) 292-6700 for opera information.

The **Teller House,** next to the opera, is Central City's historic hotel, perhaps best known for the "Face on the Barroom Floor." Although painted in 1932, the faded image of a woman has intrigued visitors with its mysterious expression. The **Gilpin County Historical Museum** has preserved the history on this gold and silver town, (303) 582-5283.

Your Peak-to-Peak Highway tour is likely to run into heavy gambler traffic here, bumper-to-bumper on busy gambling nights. Also be warned that this area is well patrolled by police. If you decide to linger in either Central City or Black Hawk, you'll find plenty of casinos and restaurants to occupy

Special Summer Events

Denverites don't mind the 45-minute trip to Central City or Boulder for the following summer performing arts events.

The **Central City Opera** (303-292-6700) is a favorite summer tradition. Begun in 1932, the opera holds its performances in the historic Opera House, which was built in 1878 and ceased operations in 1927. The Central City Opera Association took over the building in 1932, and began restoration and performances. Such notables as Edwin Booth, Mae West, Helen Hayes, and Beverly Sills have performed here. Three operas are staged each summer.

The summer concerts at Boulder's **Chautauqua Auditorium** are another reason to head west. Boulder's Chautauqua dates from 1898, when a national movement brought the arts to numerous Chautauqua summer camps throughout the country. Before the evening concerts in the wonderful wooden auditorium, concertgoers can enjoy a picnic dinner under the big shady trees at the base of the foothills or a sit-down dinner at the Chautauqua Dining Hall (303-440-3776). Chautauqua concerts include both a popular music series (303-440-7666, box office) and the Colorado Music Festival (303-449-1397; coloradomusicfest.org), which emphasizes classical music.

The **Colorado Shakespeare Festival** (303-492-0554; coloradoshakes.org) is another summer-only event in Boulder that draws audiences from Denver and beyond. Held at the outdoor Mary Rippon Theatre and indoor University Theatre on the University of Colorado-Boulder campus, the annual event features both traditional and modern renditions of Shakespeare's plays and non-Shakespearean classics. Falstaff's Fare, a box dinner, can be ordered and eaten on the lawn before the show begins. There are evening and matinee performances.

your time. A short ride down the road will take you to I-70, if you're in a rush to get back home. But if you're here for the scenic route, you're well-advised to take a left on US 6 down scenic Clear Creek Canyon to Golden.

ROCKY MOUNTAIN NATIONAL PARK

With the possible exception of Yellowstone in Wyoming, Rocky Mountain National Park (970-586-1206) is the nation's most famous. It provides the full spectrum of Rocky Mountain nature in one gulp. You can roam from the darkest subalpine forests below to the sun-sprinkled meadows and granite grandeur of the continent's roof—265,000 acres of which are well connected by roads and trails.

The best way to do the park by auto is on Trail Ridge Road, 48 miles of US 34 that vault over the park from Estes Park on the east to Grand Lake on the west. The drive over the top is one of the nation's great scenic routes, although its two lanes are jammed in the summer season. The opening of Trail Ridge Road by snowplow some time around Memorial Day is an annual Colorado event. The road closes again in late October, but you can access the park year-round. The east side has plenty of lovely drives and hiking opportunities. To reach the west side in winter, take I-70 west from Denver to US 40 at Empire, then US 40 north to Granby, where you go right on US 34 to the park. Autumn and spring visits are particularly enjoyable. We love to visit on late-summer or early-autumn evenings when the elk are bugling, particularly in the Kawuneeche Valley on the western side.

Appendix

LIVING HERE

In this section we feature specific information for residents or those planning to relocate here. Topics include real estate, education, health care, and much more.

RELOCATION

Colorado has always been a popular place to live, and population experts predict it will continue to be, regardless of the financial vagaries of its major industries. Starting with 19th-century gold mining, then continuing through the oil boom of the 1970s and the telecommunications explosion of the 1990s, Colorado has always attracted newcomers looking to make a fortune. These boom cycles are always followed by a bust, but they do little to stop the state's rampant growth. In 2000 the US Census found Colorado to be the country's third-fastest growing state, adding new residents at a rate of 2.2 percent per year, while the US average was just 1.2 percent. After the dot-com bust of 2001, however, growth cooled. By 2004 migration had flattened considerably, and the net population gain was nearly zero. Since then population growth has grown steadily, and by 2009 Colorado was the seventh-fastest growing state in that decade.

The same things attract newcomers today as attracted them in the 1880s—breathtaking mountains, blue skies, sunny days, and the opportunity to live the kind of outdoor lifestyle so many Americans crave. Some Colorado transplants were hooked during college, coming to the University of Colorado or Colorado State University and falling in love with the state's beauty. Others were among the 26.2 million tourists who come here on vacation each year and leave with an appreciation of Denver's charm. It also appeals to entrepreneurs looking to locate in beautiful surroundings without compromising their business edge. Denver is the largest city between San Francisco and St. Louis, which makes it an excellent place to headquarter businesses serving the western half of the country. And Denver International Airport makes it easy for globally oriented businesses to connect with transportation hubs on the East Coast and in Europe.

HOUSING

Housing prices are among the nation's highest, however, which can be discouraging for transplants from cities other than urban hubs like Boston and San Francisco. Bargains can be found, but it takes some research and legwork to find them. The Neighborhoods and Real Estate Resources sections in this chapter have information about housing prices and the region's largest real estate firms, respectively.

Public schools in Metro Denver are among the nation's best, and private-school options abound, from those with religious connections to those specializing in college preparatory programs. Colleges also abound. Colorado's state-financed junior college and university system offers a wide range of program and location options.

Metro Denver also has one of the nation's highest percentages of baby boomers (not to be confused with retirees), which may explain the broad support for public recreation centers, parks and open-space areas, arts and entertainment complexes, shopping centers, and fine restaurants. Younger families can also find the amenities they are looking for, from parks to child-friendly destinations (see our Kidstuff chapter for some places to get started) to good, dependable child care.

Like other cities, Denver has plenty of day-care homes and centers but lacks enough infant care. If you find yourself in the market for child care, we suggest a couple of good places to get started. Metro Denver Child Care Resource and Referral Partners 2-1-1 Child Care Options (303-561-2244, or dial 211) can refer callers to child-care providers in their neighborhoods. Qualistar Colorado (303-339-6800; qualistar.org) provides information, assistance, and referrals for parents seeking quality child care. If you'd like to check the background of a day-care provider before hiring him or her, you can do so at the Colorado Division of Child Care, 1575 Sherman St., Denver (303-866-5958). With the correct name and/or street address of the provider, this office can tell you if the person's license is current. If you want to know about complaints that may have been filed against your candidate, ask to speak to a counselor who can help you view the case file (72-hour advance notice is required).

Colorado does have its growing pains. The number of students in its public and private schools has grown steadily every year since 1989, according to the state's Department of Education. And traffic problems have kept pace with the population. Major thoroughfares are being widened and light-rail routes are being expanded as quickly as possible, but that means construction projects will inconvenience drivers in the meantime.

Newcomers to Metro Denver needn't feel like they're alone, however. More than one in four residents has arrived within the past decade, and many remember what it feels like. Two groups are designed to help transplants settle in. The Newcomers Club (newcomersclub.com/co.html) arranges social events for people throughout the metro area. After the Boxes Are Unpacked faith-based workshops are offered in Highlands Ranch, Englewood, Castle Rock, and Colorado Springs; visit just-moved.org for details.

A line charting Denver home sales over the years looks like a wave—up, down, up, down, up, down. Denver's housing market historically mirrors the state's "boom/bust" economy. Even so, while housing values fell as much as 35 percent in some states in the wake of the mortgage meltdown, Colorado's homes on average lost only about 5 percent.

For a cursory look at Denver's real estate market, turn to the Internet, where you can find information on prices, neighborhoods, agents, and photos of properties. It's an easy way to scan listings. If what you seek is the offbeat, then "cohousing" might be for you. Specially planned communities that house residents in individual homes but bring them together in jointly owned kitchens, greenhouses, nursery schools, gardens, and workshops can be found in at least eight Colorado locations. Closest to the city are two near Boulder and one in Golden.

Some of Denver's neighborhoods are hotter and more expensive than others.

Cherry Creek North, in the shadow of Denver's No. 1 tourist attraction, Cherry Creek Shopping Center, is booming. Tiny crackerbox houses once occupied by working-class families are being bought, demolished, and replaced with expensive townhomes and row houses fashioned in the old, East Coast style. Price tags easily climb as high as $1.2 million. (Walking distance to Saks Fifth Avenue has its price.)

Loft living is another hotter-than-hot trend. In the late 1980s developers began transforming run-down warehouses into empty, but very stylish, loft shells for a reasonable price. You supply the walls, kitchen, etc. Today's urban palaces can cost more than $1 million, but most are much less.

New-home sales have cooled a bit. The vast majority of that market is in the suburbs, where land is plentiful and opposition to development is minimal. New development inside Denver's city limits tends to be small, exclusive infill projects on vacant lots. Two major redevelopment projects are the exception: at the former site of Stapleton Airport, which was replaced by Denver International Airport, and at Lowry Air Force Base, which was closed by the federal government. Both have been redeveloped to include a "new urbanism" mix of residential homes, parks, open spaces, and retail. The 1999 redevelopment of the historic Elitch Gardens site in northwest Denver also incorporated new urbanism concepts.

A full picture of Denver's residential scene would require a book much larger than our entire guide, since Denver alone has more than 70 officially designated neighborhoods, and hundreds more are contained in surrounding counties. Nonetheless, we've scanned several to give you an idea of Metro Denver's residential fabric.

The most important factor to remember is that prices within neighborhoods can vary greatly. In Capitol Hill, for instance, a lovely Victorian condo can be a mere 3 blocks from a mansion that commands ten times as much. Because no centralized data exists about housing prices, we've resisted the urge to speculate. If that's what interests you, turn to the Internet for a little comparison shopping. Online listings can provide you with the latest data about specific neighborhoods that attract you.

NEIGHBORHOODS

Denver

As Metro Denver's urban center, the city and county of Denver covers the widest range of neighborhood types and home prices, from humble to haughty. Downtown includes the Union Station area on the north, the Auraria neighborhood to the west, and the Civic Center area on the southwest. It reaches east to Broadway, where it borders the North Capitol Hill and Capitol Hill neighborhoods. This is where you live if you like the downtown lifestyle, and here you almost certainly live in a condo.

Lower Downtown, the redbrick historic area between the central business district, Union Station, and the Central Platte Valley, is particularly popular of late. LoDo has been hot since Coors Field was built, and stays hot because so much revitalization is in progress.

Downtown Denver is just as chic, but is an anomaly as far as residential opportunities. Condo prices are high, and single-family homes are virtually nonexistent.

After an exodus of families from Denver to the suburbs in the 1980s, the inner city is experiencing a resurgence of popularity. The Denver Public Schools have done their part to improve test scores and the overall quality of education. In fact, in 1998 voters approved a bond to upgrade and build new schools in the core city to accommodate growth.

The **Uptown** neighborhood, just east of downtown and centered around 17th Avenue, is experiencing a revival that includes several new infill projects. Most notable here are 3-story, statuesque row houses, mixed with grand mansions that have been turned into law offices, graphic arts studios, and single-family homes. The feel is urban elegance. Prices haven't skyrocketed because of the neighborhood's proximity to East Colfax Avenue, formerly known for sleaze and crime, but things have been improving there in recent years.

Just east of downtown Denver, you'll find historic neighborhoods untouched by the revitalization boom shaking Lower Downtown. **North Capitol Hill** and **Capitol Hill,** bounded roughly by 20th and 6th Avenues, Clarkson Street, and Broadway, were among the first of Denver's housing developments in the 1800s. While those in the working class were making their homes down by the river and in other outlying sections, the aristocrats were populating this area east and upslope from the business district. Here you find most of the historic mansions and a stretch of Grant Street once known as "Millionaires Row." In recent years people have come to appreciate the historic charm of the area and its accessibility to downtown. Many of Capitol Hill's mansions have been converted to condominiums, offices, and bed-and-breakfast inns, and there are a lot of cultural and fine-dining opportunities close by. Because of Capitol Hill's reputation for crime, many prefer to live farther east in the Cheesman Park or City Park West neighborhoods. The **Cheesman Park** neighborhood, bounded by University Boulevard, Clarkson Street, and Colfax and 6th Avenues, surrounds one of Denver's finer parks, Cheesman Park, and borders one of the city's finest amenities, the Denver Botanic Gardens. The Cheesman Park neighborhood contains two historic districts and has a feel of urban gentility with lots of pedestrians, coffee shops, and neighborhood gathering spots.

Things start to get more expensive as you move south of Cheesman. Still relatively reasonable, however, is **City Park West,** an urban treasure trove of historic homes going back to Denver's silver boom of 1880–93. Bounded by Clarkson Street, University Boulevard, and Colfax and 23rd Avenues, it's located between North Capitol Hill and City Park, Denver's largest central park, containing the Denver Zoo and the Denver Museum of Nature and Science. It's a moderate walk to the Botanic Gardens and a reasonable walk to downtown, and it has a hospital complex on its northern edge. The 17th Avenue strip of fine restaurants and entertainment runs right through it.

Washington Park is Denver's other big, well-known public green space, and the Washington Park neighborhood is one of Denver's most popular living areas. It has a lot of homes built in the early to mid-1900s. It's convenient to transportation, bordering on I-25 to the south and Colorado Boulevard to the east. The Denver Country Club is just north of it, where home prices climb to more than $1 million.

Just east of the Denver Country Club is fashionable **Cherry Creek.** Bounded by University Avenue, Colorado Boulevard, and 6th and Alameda Avenues, it's an area of large- to moderate-size homes, expensive condos, and shopping nirvana. It's Metro Denver's premier retail and arts area. It has a gracious ambience, one reason its residences are highly sought after.

Directly east of Cherry Creek is **Hilltop,** another prestigious living area of well-cared-for streets adjacent to the major north-south corridor of Colorado Boulevard. **Park Hill,** to the north and just west of City Park, is an area of handsome old homes and large mature trees. Prices climb the farther south you go.

One area that has become particularly interesting of late is the area known as **Far Northeast Denver.** These neighborhoods stand out not only geographically but also as a focus of growth expected as a result of the new airport. **Montbello** and **Green Valley Ranch** are established, quiet neighborhoods, although some complaints about noise have been filed since Denver International Airport opened. The oldest homes in Montbello were built in the 1970s, while the oldest in Green Valley Ranch were built in the 1990s. These are low-crime areas with panoramic views of the mountains, room for another 9,400 dwellings, and a lot of open space. They're still the extreme edge of Denver's urban fabric, places where residents can take a walk and see a deer or an eagle in flight and maybe even hear coyotes howling at night.

Gateway, between Montbello and Green Valley Ranch and directly bordering the airport on the north, is where Denver planners envision big-time development. Already launched are the beginning stages of a planned $1 billion Denver International Business Center just a few miles from the terminal. The local media has referred to Gateway as "our first 21st Century neighborhood" and represented it as a future community of 65,000 people with strong economic links to the airport. Although it was annexed by Denver to link the city with the airport, it's not yet officially a neighborhood. Denver planners envision it as a new employment area on the level of the Denver Tech Center, which is only one-sixth the size of Gateway.

Southeast Denver is a popular area with a variety of housing options. In general, houses tend to be more expensive and newer than their northwest counterparts. However, that doesn't necessarily mean homes are bigger. Southeast Denver offers anything from tiny frame two-bedroom homes on up. Neighborhoods such as Southmoor Park offer quiet residential living with plenty of trees and nearby parks. There also are plenty of upscale apartment, condo, and townhome choices.

We've given a lot of mention here to the central and eastern parts of Denver, perhaps more than is fair. But this is where the oldest neighborhoods, the big-name neighborhoods, and the well-known neighborhoods are. A lot of people, however, prefer the west side of the city. It's the smaller part, is closer to the mountains, and generally has a feeling of being near to its country roots.

Northwestern Denver is the city's smallest quadrant, bounded by West Colfax Avenue on the south, 52nd Avenue on the north, Sheridan Boulevard on the west, and the South Platte River on the east. The **Highland** and **Jefferson Park** neighborhoods, stretching west from the high ground above the South Platte, were where Denver put its first residential neighborhoods west of the South Platte. Around the turn of the 20th century, there was a large Italian neighborhood here. Descendants of truck farmers in what are now the western suburbs still tell of taking their produce downtown for delivery to Italian produce salesmen who would sell their wares in the streets. These neighborhoods now have a rich ethnic mix and some fine restaurants, including Latin American and Vietnamese establishments. Here, as elsewhere, prices are on the rise.

Sloan Lake, West Highland, Berkeley, and **Regis** are some of the neighborhoods to the west that are pleasantly equipped with quiet streets and the greenery of lawns and parks around small lakes. These northwestern neighborhoods are as old as a lot of east Denver neighborhoods between downtown and Colorado Boulevard, but they're across the river, up the hill, and over the ridge from the central city. The feeling here is apart from the urban bustle.

Southwest Denver is larger, more extensive, and more dynamic than the west side of the city. Certainly it has its older neighborhoods close in, such as **Val Verde** and **Sun Valley.** Val Verde, Spanish for "green valley," was a separate town established in 1873 and annexed into Denver in 1902. Bordered by 6th and Alameda Avenues, the South Platte River, and Federal Boulevard, it is today an ethnically diverse neighborhood with a large industrial and warehousing base. As you move southwest toward southern Lakewood, however, you get a sensation of increasingly newer urban landscape. Not that there haven't been homes in this area since the 1800s, of course, but the neighborhood wasn't developed as early and extensively as the northwest.

One of Denver's few areas where major new development is taking place is the **Marston** neighborhood that juts down into unincorporated Jefferson County on Denver's farthest southwestern point. Near Marston Reservoir you'll find particularly high-quality residential living. Generally, however, southwest Denver vies with northwest Denver for the city's lowest overall housing prices, and

a much larger percentage of its population consists of married couples and families.

Adams County

Adams County is often viewed as the area's most blue-collar, working-class county, and that has a lot to do with the heavy industry and warehousing around **Commerce City,** northeastern Denver, and the I-76 corridor leading northeast. Commerce City, Adams County's industrial-warehousing heartland, where twice as many people work as live, certainly has some of the county's lowest housing prices.

One of the first things you may notice in driving north on I-25 to Thornton, Westminster, and Northglenn is a sensation of climbing to higher ground. **Federal Heights,** a community between Westminster and Thornton, is well named. From here you're actually looking down at the tops of downtown Denver's highest buildings. Much of this northern area seems to be on high ground, and since there is little in the way of high-rise buildings, Denver's northern suburbs have some of the grandest views of the Rockies.

Westminster is the northside suburb that is closest to the mountains. Westminster spreads all over the place, so it isn't easily categorized. It's roughly centered around the area off US 36 at 88th Avenue, but the newest parts of the city stretch north to 120th Avenue. To the west, 88th Avenue contains extensive shopping complexes. To the north there are attractive housing developments clustered and scattered through a lot of open country with big-sky views. Another arm of Westminster protrudes west and wraps around two sides of Standley Lake, one of Metro Denver's best water recreation resources. Westminster has lots of upscale townhomes and middle-class neighborhoods as well as established areas with mature trees and big lots.

Westminster's eastern half, near **Northglenn** and **Thornton,** is where you'll find the most building, with the newest developments ringing the well-respected Legacy Ridge Golf Course.

The **North Suburban Central** area, bordered by I-25 on the west, the South Platte River on the east, Denver on the south, and 144th Avenue on the north, contains the bulk of the city of Thornton, which has a moderate- to lower-income population and a suburban feel. Some newer developments, such as **Hunter's Glen** and **Thorncreek,** surround a golf course and are more upscale, but the mid-1970s 2-story homes still dominate Thornton. Because of its outlying location, prices here haven't climbed as much as elsewhere.

Brighton, the Adams County seat to the northeast, is seeing a lot of growth but still has the benefit of a small-town, rural atmosphere within an easy 15-mile commuting distance to Denver. Here you'll find homes with acreage and space for horses. Some new developments have a minimum 35-acre requirement. Home prices are moderate.

Southeast of Commerce City, the city of **Aurora** has its industrial centers in its northern Adams County side, along the I-70 corridor near Denver International Airport.

Arapahoe County

Most of Aurora lies in Arapahoe County. This is where the bulk of the city's office and research/development centers are found. It's also where the homes are higher priced. A typical, moderately priced Aurora development is **Tollgate,** where the homes are new,

the neighborhood is clean, and the lawns are well manicured. The area is close to the Denver Tech Center business area on the south and is well-connected north-south by I-225 to both I-70 and I-25.

Aurora's population is young, with a median age of 31. The city has always suffered from a lack of identity, due primarily to its proximity to Denver. It's known for its flat landscape and lack of mature trees, prompting the nickname "Saudi Aurora." But with a good supply of affordable housing, Aurora is popular with young families looking for starter homes or wanting more room for less money.

The region known among Realtors as the **Suburban Southeast,** roughly defined by the Arapahoe County line, County Line Road on the south, and Aurora on the north, contains most of the region's most expensive properties. The northwestern segment contains about half of Greenwood Village and most of Cherry Hills Village.

The bulk of this area lies in unincorporated Arapahoe County east, west, and north of Centennial Airport. It includes the Denver Tech Center. Home prices here tend to be skewed rather dramatically upward by prestige pockets such as **Cherry Hills Village,** one of Greater Denver's most upscale communities, with residences averaging $1.5 million Cherry Hills Village, for example, has virtually no commercial base, and the only nonresidential features are two private schools and the Cherry Hills and Glenmoor country clubs. **Greenwood Village,** just south of Cherry Hills, wrapping under the Denver Tech Center and up its eastern side, is another highly desired living area with distinctive custom homes. Many are on large lots and are tucked away from the street. Greenwood Village has some condominiums, but single-family homes in some neighborhoods can exceed $4 million.

Move a little to the west, and you'll find the area directly below the city of Denver known as the **South Suburban Central** region, which includes the cities of Littleton, Englewood, about half of Greenwood Village, and a substantial patch of unincorporated Jefferson County between Greenwood Village and County Line Road, Littleton, and I-25.

The unincorporated part of South Suburban Central is generally an area of clean, new neighborhoods with the kind of convoluted street patterns that make life confusing for pizza deliverers but peaceful for residents. It has a country feel, being the last neighborhood south of Denver before you arrive at Douglas County. There are some good shopping complexes along County Line Road, including Park Meadows; the Denver Tech Center is just up I-25; and C-470 provides fast access west and up to I-70 near Golden.

The city of **Littleton** grew from an old downtown established in 1890 on what is now its northwestern edge along the South Platte River. It still has that old, traditional community atmosphere, with ranch homes on big lots, but the city also has its newer areas reaching south to Douglas County and C-470. The South Platte River runs north-south through nearly the entire length of the city, and the extra green spaces make Littleton a particularly pleasant place to live.

Englewood, like Littleton, is one of the southern suburbs with an old downtown established in the 1800s along Broadway. Also like Littleton, it has a small-town appeal. But it's closer to Denver, and its business corridor along South Santa Fe Drive on the city's west side is home to hundreds of manufacturing, industrial, and service companies.

Homes are smaller frame structures. On the east side, the city borders Cherry Hills Village.

Broomfield County

The city of **Broomfield** is just north of Westminster, mostly in Boulder County but with a good quarter of its population in the newly recognized Broomfield County. Originally a residential community, it's fast becoming a business-development area thanks to its strategic position between Boulder and Metro Denver and the rampant development of business and industrial parks along US 36. Broomfield is popular because it still retains its own identity, separate from Greater Denver, with enduring, solid 1950s brick ranches. This is attractive to people who work in Denver and Boulder and want more affordable living. Broomfield's home prices are climbing along with closer-in locales.

Douglas County

Anyone who has lived in Metro Denver for 10 years or more is likely to be struck by the number of new residences in Douglas County, set well apart like estates, speckling the landscape from I-25 south. It's an area of rolling hills and open spaces, with views of the mountains and the feel of the Great Plains—at least for now. Douglas County in January 1999 lost its designation as the fastest-growing county in the nation, but with a 62.4 percent increase from 2000 to 2011, it still ranks as one of the fastest-growing counties in the US.

Douglas County certainly is the metro area's fastest-growing county, although figures can sometimes be misleading. Because the area had so few residents, the influx of several thousand new residents meant three-figure growth rates. It is a huge area with just a few old and well-established towns such as **Larkspur, Franktown,** and the county seat of **Castle Rock.** Otherwise you'll find very little in the way of residential buildings that aren't either ranches, farm structures, or the large expensive homes that are popping up like crazy in exclusive planned communities with names such as **Castle Pines Village, Deer Creek Farm,** and **The Meadows.** These are among the 20 to 30 planned communities along the Denver/ Colorado Springs corridor that are expected to bring Douglas County's population as high as a half-million by 2030.

Highlands Ranch is the Douglas County community best known by Denverites, partly because it now represents a continuum of the Metro Denver urban fabric. It lies on the northern edge of Douglas County directly south from the city and county of Denver. The population surpassed 96,000 in 2010. No one will be too surprised if at some point it is incorporated as a city. It's already starting to look like one, with well-established schools and community centers; a huge central green space, Northwest Community Park that branches through the main, western cluster of the community; and the large Highland Heritage Regional Park on the growing eastern cluster.

Jefferson County

Here is where home buyers can choose from the widest variety of landscapes, simply because Jefferson County has both the bulk of Metro Denver's mountain communities and a large percentage of the area's flatland communities. The mountain communities are a big attraction. After a hot summer day at work in Denver, residents retreat to cool mountain evenings among the pines.

Of course, the drive can be less appealing in the winter, when commuters are faced with severe mountain snowstorms. Sport utility vehicles tend to be popular among mountain-community commuters.

Jefferson County's flatland communities, however, still offer the attraction of being near the mountains, and the county in general has a good reputation for quality-of-life factors such as good schools, relatively low crime, and nice neighborhoods. Actually, flatland is a bit of a misnomer here, because Jefferson County's eastern half is close to the mountains and tends to include lots of ridges and valleys. On average, Jefferson County's population is moderately well-to-do and well educated.

Jefferson County South is the county's most expensive housing region, bordering directly on Denver. The vast majority of residences here are in the area bounded roughly by US 285 on the north, Sheridan Avenue on the east, and C-470 on the south and west. Bulging into that area on the northeast corner is the city and county of Denver's Marston neighborhood, which surrounds Marston Lake. It's an unincorporated area, but one that envisions itself as a unique community on the edge of the mountains. It has rejected efforts at incorporation as a city, but it holds its own community festivals and has its own organization of homeowners associations known as the Council of Homeowners Organizations for Planned Environment.

South Jeffco also has some nice housing south and west of C-470; for example, in Ken Caryl Valley on the other side of the Dakota Hogback, where there's a mix of everything from townhomes to million-dollar mansions. **Ken Caryl Ranch** is a stable area with lots of horse property, surrounded by the foothills and tucked away from the big city. North from Ken Caryl is **Green Mountain,** with stunning city views and moderate prices.

The city of **Lakewood** is the giant of Denver's southwest side and the third-most populous city in Metro Denver after Denver and Aurora. Unlike many suburbs, Lakewood is a major employment center, with the Denver Federal Center, strong retail communities, and substantial light industry. At the same time, it also has a lot of semirural areas inside the city limits. Lakewood's older neighborhoods lie to the east, where the city shares about half the western border of Denver. On the west it reaches into the foothills, where its 6,000 acres of parks include Green Mountain and the surrounding William Frederick Hayden Park. Lakewood touches the city of **Morrison,** a small town hidden in one of the red rock-rimmed valleys in the Rocky Mountains' first folds.

North of Lakewood is the city of **Wheat Ridge,** also bordering Denver. It has developed largely since World War II. Before then it was a farming area known for fruits, vegetables, and carnations. Wheat Ridge also has that uniquely rural flavor characteristic of many suburbs here, with older homes on larger lots. Foxes come into the neighborhoods at night from the Clear Creek greenbelt. Deer sometimes blunder into busy Wadsworth Boulevard at morning rush hour. Walkers in serene suburban neighborhoods sometimes see people riding horses.

Driving west on 32nd Avenue and passing out of Wheat Ridge as you go under I-70, you are on the way to the city of **Golden,** on the other side of South Table Mountain. Between I-70 and South Table Mountain, however, you notice nicely groomed new neighborhoods primarily on the left. You are on the north side of a loosely defined

area known as **Applewood,** which includes bits of Lakewood, Golden, and Wheat Ridge but is mostly in unincorporated Jefferson County. Applewood is a name often heard on the lips of westsiders considering a move to a new home, but it also includes older, established homes with mature trees.

Keep going west on 32nd Avenue, around South Table Mountain, past a row of Adolph Coors Co. subsidiary companies, and finally past the brewery itself, and you'll enter Golden through the back door. Largely hidden from Denver by South Table Mountain and scrunched into the foothills on its western side, Golden has kept an identity apart from the rest of the metro area. It has an Old West downtown, and it is a charming small town. Once a Coors company town, it's now mainly a high-technology and university town, largely influenced by the culture of the Colorado School of Mines just up the hill from Washington Avenue. New neighborhoods have been climbing up the side of South Table Mountain, growing south toward Heritage Square and Morrison and spreading east toward Lakewood. The level of education among Golden's population is one of the highest in the Metro Denver area.

Northeast of Golden and north of Wheat Ridge is one of the larger cities of Denver's west side, **Arvada.** Looking north from the top of the ridge that is the center of Wheat Ridge, you can see the historic center of Arvada, now known as **Olde Town Arvada.** But Arvada has spread considerably from that historic beginning, out to the "horse country" of the far west side. Arvada's central area consists largely of homes typically built in the 1950s and 1960s, but a rapidly growing high-end development called **West Woods Ranch** offers new homes centered around a golf course. Arvada is known for its family-oriented lifestyle and its easy access to Boulder and Denver.

Arvada and Westminster define the residential majority of the area known as **Jefferson County North.** The parts of the two cities in this area—north, east, and south of Standley Lake—are more like each other than they are like their respective city centers. A lot of new homes have gone in here in the last 5 or 10 years, primarily tract homes with some high-end custom homes and some of the patio homes preferred by empty-nesters. The area has a country feel because you're looking west across the last prairie before the mountains. It's a short shot north on Wadsworth Boulevard to Broomfield and on US 36 to Boulder.

West beyond Rocky Flats and Golden, off Highway 93, there are growing mountain developments up side roads such as **Coal Creek Canyon, Golden Gate Canyon,** and **Crawford Gulch.**

Metro Denver's big mountain communities, though, tend to be off I-70 and US 285. Communities such as **Genesee, Evergreen, Conifer, Aspen Park, Indian Hills, Kittredge,** and **Hidden Valley** offer a lot of new, high-end living across ridgetops with fantastic vistas and in hidden, pine-covered valleys and hillsides. The only drawback is the sometimes hazardous 30-minute commute from Evergreen to Denver, 45 minutes to an hour from areas farther out. The bulk of housing opportunities are in burgeoning, although tasteful, developments. Genesee homes are more in the foothills, with better access to Denver.

Evergreen is probably the largest, most-established community near I-70, about 8 miles south of it, actually, on Highway 74. There are more than 9,000 people in the city of Evergreen—45,000 including the nearby communities of **Kittredge** and **Bergen Park**—and there's even a downtown, just below the dam that holds back Evergreen Lake. Evergreen also has shops, restaurants, and the Little Bear bar, which pulls people up from Denver for its great musical evenings and singles scene. Housing here is among the most expensive in the region, ranging well into the millions.

Mountain communities down US 285, in the **Conifer** and **Aspen Park** area, have Denver commuting times closer to an hour, but here you'll find properties in all price ranges, with some horse properties and more available space.

REAL ESTATE RESOURCES

You can get more information on the local real estate market, Realtor licensing and ethics, and other information involving the sale or purchase of homes by contacting the following agencies.

COLORADO ASSOCIATION OF REALTORS
(303) 790-7099
coloradorealtors.com

DENVER METRO ASSOCIATION OF REALTORS
(303) 756-0553
dmarealtors.com

DOUGLAS/ELBERT REALTOR ASSOCIATION
(303) 688-0941
derarealtors.com

SOUTH METRO DENVER REALTOR ASSOCIATION
(303) 797-3700
smdra.com

HOME BUILDERS

Colorado's home-building business thrived during the 1990s and early 2000s before being stalled by the mortgage meltdown of 2008. Based on available space, most new-home construction—master-planned communities and tract-housing developments—occurred in the suburbs. Single units and smaller townhome or condo developments make up the bulk of city infill projects. Perhaps the biggest trends are the growing number of upscale townhomes and row homes being built on vacant city lots and the pop-top phenomenon in older core neighborhoods, in which new owners remodel small homes into larger modern ones with all the amenities of the suburbs.

On a larger scale, redevelopment of both Lowry Air Force Base, a few miles east of downtown, and the old Stapleton Airport site were major projects that included residential, retail, and parks. Work on Lowry is nearly completed, while Stapleton construction will extend well into the future.

Another trend hitting Metro Denver is the revival of new urbanism, in which communities are built to look like the days of old, with "vintage" housing and neighborhood amenities just down the street. The Lowry and Stapleton sites include new urbanism, as does development in the Central Platte Valley, just west of downtown.

For more information on the hundreds of home builders, call the Home Builders Association of Metropolitan Denver at (303) 778-1400.

REAL ESTATE FIRMS

The following are among Metro Denver's more well-known real estate brokerages.

CENTURY 21 PROFESSIONALS, INC.
century21.com

Century 21 is a worldwide company operating in 30 countries and territories. Each of the Denver/Front Range's 25 offices is independently owned. The general website contains links to a complete list of addresses and phone numbers.

i In the central Denver real estate market, homes frequently sell at or above the asking price. At best, bargaining is reserved for the overpriced or run-down homes. In general, your dollar buys a lot more square footage, and often lot size, in the suburbs.

COLDWELL BANKER DEVONSHIRE
105 Fillmore St.
(303) 758-7611
Coldwell Banker Devonshire frequently produces several of the top 10 agents in the Denver area. The awards say a lot not only about the agency's expertise but also about the high-end homes in which it specializes. "Cottages to Castles" is its slogan.

COLDWELL BANKER RESIDENTIAL SERVICES
8490 E. Crescent Pkwy., Greenwood Village
(303) 409-1500
After a merger in 1999, Coldwell Banker became the largest real estate services firm in Colorado, with more than 900 associates. Each office is staffed by experts who know their area or can help you anywhere across Colorado. This busy Greenwood Village office is in South Suburban Central—an area known for its mountain views and mix of suburban living amid open space. Coldwell

Banker is active all over the Denver area, listing new homes as well as resales.

THE KENTWOOD CO.
5690 DTC Blvd., #600W, Greenwood Village
(303) 773-3399
denverrealestate.com
Based in the Denver Tech Center but with offices in Cherry Creek and downtown, The Kentwood Co. is Denver's largest independent brokerage. They specialize in upper-price homes, properties, condos, and townhomes throughout the metro area. The company offers a complete range of real estate services, including corporate relocations, condo conversions, and new-home sales. The company's 190 sales associates average 20 years of experience and more than $13 million in annual personal sales volume. Additional area locations are at 44 Cook St., Cherry Creek (303-331-1400) and 1660 17th St., Ste. 100 (303-820-2489).

LEONARD LEONARD
420 Downing St.
(303) 744-6200
leonardleonard.com
Founded in 1983, Leonard Leonard is known for specializing in the heart of Denver. Owner Sonja Leonard Leonard has built a staff of agents whose attention to detail shows in their high-quality properties. And their open-house tours, which often feature champagne and munchies at every stop, are a fun way to spend a few hours.

METRO BROKERS INC.
4 Inverness Court East, #200, Englewood
(303) 843-0100
metrobrokersonline.com
Metro Brokers Inc. is a trade association of independent brokers that operate all over the state. With more than 60 offices and 1,800 agents, they have been working in Colorado for almost 30 years.

RE/MAX
8390 E. Crescent Pkwy., Ste. 500, Greenwood Village
(303) 770-5531
remax.com
RE/MAX began in Denver in 1973 as a locally owned real estate office and has grown to become a global franchise network. RE/MAX offices are now open in more than 60 countries on six continents, with more than 114,000 sales agents working from 4,400 offices. Corporate headquarters are located in Greenwood Village, but to find an office near you, it's best to visit the website.

EDUCATION

Choices, choices, and more choices. That best describes the educational scene in Metro Denver. Your child loves music and dancing? Denver Public Schools offer the Denver School of the Arts. You have a child who's goofing off and not living up to his or her potential? Numerous private schools offer a low pupil-teacher ratio and individualized instruction. You want your child to have rigorous college-prep courses? Several public schools offer the International Baccalaureate program. No matter what you're looking for, chances are good that you'll find it here.

Better yet, Colorado's public schools were made more accessible in 1994 by legislation creating open enrollment statewide, meaning you can enroll your kids in any public school at no extra cost. Got your eye on a school with some real nice programs but live outside the traditional enrollment area? That problem has been eliminated by open enrollment. Of course, local children have priority, so it depends on whether space is available.

OVERVIEW

The state stands at the educational forefront in many ways. In 1993, for example, Colorado became the third state after Minnesota and California to enact charter schools, which are publicly funded but run by groups of parents, teachers, and other individuals who want to devise their own curriculum. Metro Denver now has charter schools in operation in every one of its counties. Many schools are governed by cooperative decision-making teams, made up of parents, teachers, administrators, students, and local businesspeople. And, not surprisingly, the end of 25 years of court-ordered busing in Denver Public Schools in 1997 has already brought a tremendous amount of community support for what will now, once again, be neighborhood schools.

The state of Colorado maintains lots of data about its public schools; it's available through the Department of Education's Communications Center at 201 E. Colfax in Denver (303-866-6600; cde.state.co.us).

Colorado's colleges and universities in many ways stand among the nation's best, and its residents are some of the best educated. Higher education is available in a wide variety of forms in Metro Denver, the most obvious choices being the major institutions such as the University of Colorado at Boulder and Denver, or the Metropolitan State College of Denver. Private colleges and universities are generally smaller but are numerous and diverse. In many ways the most important part of Metro Denver's higher-education establishment is the community college system.

EDUCATION

At any one time about 40,000 students are attending the area's five community colleges. These are public colleges so well distributed around Metro Denver that no resident is very far from one of them. They tend toward curricula that are career oriented and designed for accessibility by working students.

Our list of colleges and universities is by no means a full account of local adult educational opportunities. Colorado has nearly 200 private occupational schools, ranging from the A-Plus Real Estate School to the Xenon International School of Hair Design. The bulk of these are in the Metro Denver area. Contact the state of Colorado's Department of Higher Education, Division of Private Occupational Schools at highered.colorado .gov for more information.

Whatever educational needs and interests you may have, Metro Denver has an abundance of opportunities to offer. We'll begin with the public school systems.

i Regis University's College for Professional Studies (SPS) has new campuses in Aurora and Longmont. The Longmont campus, at 2101 Ken Pratt Blvd., offers undergraduate classes in business, accounting, teacher education, and liberal arts. The Aurora campus is at 6 Abilene St., located near Lockheed Martin, Raytheon, and Buckley Air Force Base. It offers undergraduate courses in business, accounting, liberal arts, and teacher education, as well as graduate degrees in business and education. For information about the SPS programs, call (303) 458-4300.

PUBLIC SCHOOLS

ADAMS COUNTY SCHOOL DISTRICT NO. 1
Mapleton Public Schools
591 E. 80th Ave.
(303) 853-1000
mapleton.us

Adams County School District No. 1, more familiar to most as Mapleton Public Schools, lies just north of Denver and includes part of the city of Thornton and some of unincorporated Adams County. With the third-smallest total enrollment in Metro Denver, the system has an early learning center, a Montessori preschool/elementary school, three elementary schools, six combination elementary/middle schools, two combination middle/high schools, and four high schools. Although this system has Metro Denver's lowest percentage of teachers with postgraduate (master's or higher) degrees and one of the highest pupil-teacher ratios, it has one of the area's lower high-school dropout rates.

The district provides a lot of special opportunities for its diverse student body, including programs in back-to-basics, learning enrichment, accelerated classes, bilingual and multicultural education, Native American education, and open enrollment for all schools based on availability.

ADAMS COUNTY SCHOOL DISTRICT NO. 14
5291 E. 60th Ave., Commerce City
(303) 853-3333
adams14.org

One of Metro Denver's smaller school systems, District No. 14 has seven elementary schools, two middle schools, two high schools, and one alternative high school. It also has a full-time preschool. This district pulls students from Commerce City and areas in Thornton and unincorporated Adams County. It's solidly in the midrange of Metro Denver school districts as far as the education and salaries of its teachers and its spending per pupil. Its high-school dropout rate is considerably higher than the state average, and it has one of Metro Denver's lowest graduation rate and lowest composite ACT scores in recent rankings.

At the same time, District 14 has a gung-ho attitude about the future, with a commitment to improving its schools under a basic "Reading + Writing x Math" CSAP-driven base curriculum. Adams City Middle School has a personalized alternative instructional program for students at risk of dropping out. Since it was established in 1991, the program has grown to serve more than 10,000 students and families. With more than 83 percent of its students Hispanic, Adams 14 puts a lot of effort into bilingual education and accommodating cultural diversity.

ADAMS COUNTY SCHOOL DISTRICT NO. 50
6933 Raleigh St., Westminster
(303) 428-3511
adams50.org
School District No. 50 serves the city of Westminster and parts of Arvada and unincorporated Adams County with one early-childhood program, 15 elementary schools, four middle schools, three high schools, and a career enrichment park. Its average teacher salary is competitive in the metro area, and its revenue per pupil is the lowest. Its mission statement is "Push to excel; prepare to succeed."

In 1993 the district began the Graphics Communication Cluster, a prototype for a new method of integrating academic and

technical education. Today there are four cluster programs: Graphics Communication, Business Cluster, Engineering Cluster, and Health Studies Cluster. Through these, students are afforded the opportunity to succeed in an applied setting, where they can see the relevance of academics in a real-world environment.

Adams County 50 pushes for technological innovation and offers such features as comprehensive networked computer labs and a computer in every classroom that provides the teacher with classroom management.

ADAMS 12 FIVE STAR SCHOOLS
1500 E. 128th Ave., Thornton
(720) 972-4000
adams12.org
The Five Star Schools, Adams County's largest school district and the seventh-largest in the state, includes more than 36,000 students attending 48 schools in a 62-square-mile area serving Northglenn, Federal Heights, and parts of Thornton, Broomfield, Westminster, and unincorporated Adams County. In addition to 29 elementary schools, it includes nine middle schools and six high schools as well as the Bollman Technical Education Center, Vantage Point Alternative School, and four charter schools—Stargate, for the gifted and talented; the Academy of Charter Schools, a basic school; Colorado Virtual Academy; and the Pinnacle Learning Center.

Per-pupil spending at Five Star Schools is in the midrange in Greater Denver, as are the graduation and dropout rates. Principals work in conjunction with school improvement teams to further student achievement at each school. The district reviewed and approved a strategic plan that sets goals for improved graduation rate and a lower dropout rate. Another district goal is an increase in proficiencies for all students. The district honors the diversity of individuals and believes a student's success is linked to a "responsive school community."

ℹ️ **Colorado high-school seniors have the opportunity to take college courses at community colleges and state universities and colleges. Not only does this provide a challenging academic experience, but it also reduces the duration and expense of college.**

AURORA PUBLIC SCHOOLS
15701 E. 1st Ave., Aurora
(303) 344-8060
aurorak12.org
Aurora Public Schools covers most of Aurora, which is Metro Denver's second-largest city. The district's mission is to develop its kids into "lifelong learners who value themselves, contribute to their community, and succeed in a changing world."

Strong emphasis is placed on student achievement in basic subjects. The district is committed to preparing students for life in the 21st century by helping them become self-directed learners, collaborative workers, complex thinkers, community contributors, and quality producers. Special services and classes are offered for gifted and talented students, special-education students, and non-English-speaking young parents, pre-schoolers, and adults.

The Aurora district has a total of 34 elementary schools, seven middle schools, and eight high schools, three of which are alternative high schools. There are also three charter schools, a vocational school, and several specialty alternative schools.

Special classes in 50 skill areas are offered within the district at the T. H. Pickens Technical Center, 500 Airport Blvd., Aurora. Some programs offer credit toward an associate degree from the Community College of Aurora.

The district has been designated by School Match, an international business relocation firm, as one of 50 in Colorado to provide "what parents want."

BRIGHTON PUBLIC SCHOOLS
18551 E. 160th Ave., Brighton
(303) 655-2900
sd27j.org/
The closest thing to a small-town, country-school district in Metro Denver, Brighton Public Schools (District 27J) serves about 240 square miles of farmland around the 21,000 population of Brighton, the Adams County seat. As a school district, Brighton's enrollment is the second-smallest in Metro Denver. The district has five elementary schools, two middle schools, one high school, one charter school, and one alternative school. Just about half of Brighton's teaching staff has master's degrees. The dropout rate is the Denver area's second highest. In accordance with state law, District 27J is developing content standards for all academic areas. Included in this effort toward Standards Based Education is the improvement of instructional techniques as well as the assessment of skills and knowledge learned. The average composite ACT score for Brighton students is 17.5. The district's schools offer enrichment programs including bilingual education, programs in basic skills, and accelerated education.

CHERRY CREEK SCHOOL DISTRICT 5
4700 S. Yosemite St., Englewood
(303) 773-1184
cherrycreekschools.org

Covering Metro Denver's southeastern corner, District 5 encompasses Cherry Hills Village, Glendale, parts of Aurora, Englewood, Greenwood Village, and some of unincorporated Arapahoe County. It includes the rapidly growing and well-to-do communities along the northern edge

District 5 has some impressive statistics, including the state's highest average teacher salary. It has 39 elementary schools, 11 middle schools, six high schools, and one alternative high school. Thirteen Cherry Creek schools have received the John Irwin Award, given to the state's highest-performing schools. In 1996 West Middle School also became a Blue Ribbon School. Smoky Hill High has one of Colorado's International Baccalaureate programs, in which advanced studies give students a jump on college. Every elementary and middle school in the district makes special accommodations for gifted and talented students.

i Metro Denver's largest student populations are not in the city and county of Denver but in Arapahoe and Jefferson Counties.

DENVER PUBLIC SCHOOLS
900 Grant St.
(720) 423-3200
dpsk12.org

The Denver Public Schools is the second-largest district in the state, serving 72,000 students. It is home to many high-performing schools and programs that serve a diverse population. The district routinely produces graduates bound for

the country's top colleges and universities, and it boasts the 2006 Kinder Excellence in Teaching national award-winner, Linda Alston, a kindergarten teacher at Fairview Elementary. The no-strings-attached, $100,000 grant recognizes an outstanding public-school teacher who teaches in a low-income community.

The district's George Washington and East High Schools were ranked among the nation's top by *Newsweek* for promoting Advanced Placement and International Baccalaureate classes. They ranked 50th and 84th out of 450, respectively. The district is also home to an array of magnet schools, including the Center for International Students, two high-school computer magnet programs, and the Denver School of the Arts, the only one of its kind in the region. With the assistance of Collaborative Decision-Making Teams (school staff, parents, and community representatives) at each school, the district's neighborhood schools are constantly adapting and reshaping themselves to meet the unique needs of the city's many neighborhoods.

DOUGLAS COUNTY SCHOOL DISTRICT
620 Wilcox St., Castle Rock
(303) 387-0100
dcsdk12.org

This district's 42 elementary schools, four charter schools, seven middle schools, eight high schools, and three alternative schools cover a far-flung area ranging from the southern edges of Jefferson and Arapahoe Counties much of the way to Colorado Springs. Douglas is one of the fastest-growing counties in the US. The district currently has 48,000 students.

The majority of the county's elementary students go to school on a four-track,

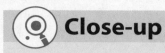 **Close-up**

The Teacher of the Century and Her School of Unlimited Opportunity

Emily Griffith is still Denver's best-known educator, even though she died in 1947. As a Denver public school teacher who taught 8th grade at the Twenty-Fourth Street School during the day, Griffith volunteered at night teaching adults, many of them immigrants, to read and write and acquire basic math skills. But her true goal was to start a school where the age limit was lifted and the hours were flexible so that a working adult who could spare an hour could come for some job training or self-improvement.

In 1916 Denver Public Schools converted the Longfellow School at 13th and Welton Streets into the Opportunity School. (It didn't become Emily Griffith Opportunity School until 1934, a year after Emily retired. In 2011, the school became Emily Griffith Technical College.) Her eponymous school, which has touched more than 1.5 million lives since it opened, had a dream to help people help themselves. On the first day Emily sat near the front door and personally greeted each student. By the end of the first week, 1,400 students had registered. School was open 13 hours a day, five days a week. Tuition was free. Emily's goal was to provide training wherever it was needed.

One day a man came to look at course offerings. When he started to leave without registering, Emily asked why he hadn't signed up. "There are no courses for sign painters," he told her. Shortly thereafter, the school offered a course in sign painting. Over the years the course offerings have continued to meet students'—and society's—needs. From radio communications and ambulance driving during World War I to victory gardening and defense work during World War II, the Opportunity School has stayed current with a changing marketplace.

A few years ago, local grocery stores, including King Soopers, Safeway, and Cub Foods, approached the school's administration with a request for a program designed

year-round calendar, a rotation of nine weeks in school followed by a three-week break, throughout the year.

Douglas County has one of the highest graduation rates and the lowest dropout rate. How do they do it? The system overall places a high value on educational excellence. Cherokee Trail Elementary School in Parker was named by *Child* magazine as one of the 10 best schools in the nation. Metro Denver's first charter school, Academy Charter School, is in Castle Rock. Beginning in the 1994–95 school year, the county approved a

teacher-compensation plan linked to performance rather than longevity.

Douglas County is one of four school districts partnering in the Renaissance Expeditionary Learning Outward Bound School, which is located in Parker. The K through 12 school has won national grants and acclaim for its challenging learning program.

ENGLEWOOD SCHOOLS
4101 S. Bannock St., Englewood
(303) 761-7050
englewoodschools.org

to train workers for bakery and deli work, an area that would continue to grow as more people turned to prepared foods for their meals. Thus was born the food-services department, which operates a bistro and restaurant where students can practice their craft.

Though many courses lean heavily toward technology, the school still offers classes in areas such as cake decorating, creative sewing, floral design, dental anatomy—even aircraft-accident investigation. In fact, just scanning course offerings can be enjoyable in and of itself.

What has remained constant since 1916 are the high-school and continuing education courses for adults who never finished high school and immigrants who wish to become citizens. Each year the school enrolls between 11,000 and 15,000 students and graduates over 8,000. While the list of graduates isn't exactly filled with household names, their stories are the stuff of the American dream: a college dropout who took transportation courses at EGOS, went back to college, then law school, and is now a transportation lawyer; a man who took automotive mechanics classes and today owns his own transmission shop; a woman who took typing classes, which launched her into the business world, and eventually became a state senator; a former mayor's sister-in-law who dropped out of high school 24 years earlier and graduated with a GED from EGOS in June of 1997, armed with a certificate in Early Child Care Professions.

Today almost 15,000 students train in more than 500 classes. Since its inception, the school has assisted more than 1.6 million students. Students range from age 17 to 94. Though tuition is no longer free (it was until several years ago), it now costs $1.55 an hour—still a bargain by anyone's standards. Better yet, the school and its students provide a wide range of services to the community at discount prices. Want a filling, inexpensive lunch? Twelfth Street Deli, which trains the food-service students, offers meals for $4 to $6.25. Need a haircut? A barber student will cut your locks for $3. How about a manicure for $4? Having dinner guests but don't have a table decoration? Floral centerpieces are $8 to $15.

Also known as Arapahoe County School District No. 1, this district educates approximately 4,300 students in 10 schools spanning pre-K through 12th grade.

Englewood was not shy about its educational ambitions when it adopted a student-created name for its only alternative high school: Colorado's Finest Alternative High School. The school was devised by the Englewood School District for kids at risk of dropping out. It received the John Irwin Excellence In Education Award the first six years it was given, and the school was twice named one of the top 50 in the US by *Redbook* magazine.

The Board of Education has adopted 10 core beliefs; among them are emphasizing high student achievement, honoring diversity, and valuing every student and family.

JEFFERSON COUNTY PUBLIC SCHOOLS
1829 Denver West Dr., Golden
(303) 982-6500
jeffcopublicschools.org
Jefferson County makes up Colorado's largest school district, with more than 84,000

students and a total general fund budget of $922 million. Many people seem to want to get their kids into Jefferson County schools.

What is it about Jeffco that makes it so desirable? Well, it's a nice place to live, right up against the mountains with a lot of upscale neighborhoods and light-industry, white-collar employment. Also, the school system has one of Greater Denver's highest percentages of teachers with master's degrees or higher and the second-highest average teacher salary.

Jeffco has a "least-restrictive environment" policy for special-education students that gives primary responsibility for a special-needs student's education to the neighborhood school. The school district also has a Multicultural Learning Center that provides multicultural resources for teachers across the district.

Jeffco pursues these lofty goals in neighborhood schools—93 elementary schools, 19 middle schools, and 17 high schools—as well as a wide range of educational-choice programs. These include open enrollment where space is available, schools within a school, alternative schools, and self-governing charter schools.

LITTLETON PUBLIC SCHOOLS
5776 S. Crocker St., Littleton
(303) 347-3300
littletonpublicschools.net
Pulling students from the city of Littleton and the city of Centennial, Littleton Public Schools is another one of those districts that does a good job with its money. The district serves more than 16,000 students in Littleton and Centennial, including 15 elementary schools, four middle schools, three senior high schools, three alternative schools, two charter schools, and three preschool programs.

LPS students consistently rank above state and national averages on standardized tests. Littleton has one of Metro Denver's highest composite ACT scores in recent rankings, the third-highest average teacher salaries, and the third-lowest high-school dropout rate. Of the district's more than 1,000 full-time teachers, more than 64 percent hold master's or doctorate degrees, and they average 12 years of teaching experience.

The district places a high value on small class sizes, which range from 17 to 23 for elementary and 28 to 32 for middle- and high-school classes. School choice is available to all district residents through an open enrollment/transfer policy. LPS also enjoys a high level of community involvement and support.

SHERIDAN SCHOOL DISTRICT NO. 2
4000 S. Lowell Blvd.
(720) 833-6991
ssd2.org
Metro Denver's smallest school district, Sheridan has a total enrollment of 1,750 in two elementary schools, one middle school, and one high school. It serves the city of Sheridan, which surrounds the Englewood Municipal Golf Course and pieces of Englewood. The district's graduation rate is the fourth highest in Denver. Not surprisingly, it also has the lowest student-teacher ratio.

PRIVATE SCHOOLS

Not every private school in the area is included here, of course, but you will find the larger, as well as many smaller, schools that come to us by word-of-mouth recommendation. Some accept only boys or girls, and many of them are religion-based private schools. None of the religious schools profess to turn away students on the basis of their religion or lack of religious commitment. Actually, however, religious schools require students to take religious instruction, and lack of adequate preparation can in some cases disqualify a student. At Yeshiva Toras Chaim School, for example, students need to have a sufficient grounding in the Hebrew language, since the school focuses heavily on the Talmud and Torah.

ACCELERATED SCHOOLS
2160 S. Cook St.
(303) 758-2003
acceleratedschools.org
Students, including the gifted and the learning disabled, study independently through individually prescribed instructional and motivational systems. The school offers a low student-teacher ratio. Heavy use of computer instructional programs increases time spent on prescribed learning tasks and gives immediate feedback with an emphasis on practical business applications. Students can attend part-time or full-time in morning, afternoon, and evening classes. The school offers accelerated reading and college classes for extra credit as well as field trips and other activities. Transportation to and from home is included in tuition. Housing is available for students who need it. The school serves students from preschool through college level.

ALEXANDER DAWSON SCHOOL
10455 Dawson Dr., Lafayette
(303) 665-6679
dawsonschool.org

This college-prep school is on a 107-acre campus, 35 miles north of Denver. The school has a need-based financial aid program with more than $1.25 million in grants, which go to 20 percent of the student body. Though the school has historically had boarding students, it has been strictly a day school since 1998. The rigorous academic program includes a keen interest in the arts. Alexander Dawson takes part in interscholastic athletic competitions, including canoeing, skiing, and horsemanship. Soccer and lacrosse fields, tennis courts, two gyms, an outdoor swimming pool, and certified ropes course are on campus. The school has a new library as well as a $3 million gym and a $2.7 million arts center. It offers grades K through 12.

BEACON COUNTRY DAY SCHOOL
6100 E. Belleview Ave., Greenwood Village
(303) 771-3990
beaconcountrydayschool.com
Beacon Country Day School is a private, non-profit school on a large acreage in Greenwood Village. The programs use each child's interests to promote learning in classrooms designed for small learning groups. The grounds include a pond and wetlands area for eco-studies. The school offers a variety of extracurricular activities as well. Offering pre-K through 8th grade, the school has approximately 125 students and is coed.

BETHLEHEM LUTHERAN SCHOOL
2100 N. Wadsworth Blvd., Lakewood
(303) 233-0401
bethlehemschool.org
Bethlehem Lutheran, a coed school, is part of the national network of Lutheran schools, the largest Protestant school group in the

country. It offers quality education in a Christian environment and has received National Lutheran School Accreditation. It has a good music program, computer lab instruction, and interscholastic athletics as well as an advanced reading program for students in 3rd through 6th grades. The school's students are in grades pre-K through 8.

BISHOP MACHEBEUF HIGH SCHOOL
458 Unita Way
(303) 344-0082
machebeuf.org
Formerly Machebeuf Catholic High School, this school emphasizes the students' "responsibility as children of God in a democratic society" as well as preparing them for college. The school boasts that more than 95 percent of its graduates enrolled in college by graduation, and it employs a full-time college admissions counselor. It has received high honors for excellence in education. More than 480 students are in grades 9 through 12.

CHRIST THE KING ROMAN CATHOLIC SCHOOL
860 Elm St.
(303) 321-2123
christthekingdenver.org
This school, where boys and girls in grades K through 8 wear uniforms, places a high premium on top-quality academic skills along with developing a sense of responsibility all within the framework of the Catholic faith. Along with religion, students are exposed to a core curriculum enhanced by music and art. Extracurricular activities include Junior Great Books, volleyball, basketball, and baseball. The school's enrollment is approximately 250.

COLORADO ACADEMY
3800 S. Pierce St.
(303) 986-1501
coloradoacademy.org
Founded in 1906, Colorado Academy is in southwest Denver on a lovely 94-acre campus. It's a college-prep program emphasizing a well-rounded education in academics, fine arts, and athletics with a 10-to-1 ratio of students to teachers. Bus transportation is available. About 875 students are in grades pre-K through 12.

DENVER ACADEMY
4400 E. Iliff Ave.
(303) 777-5870
denveracademy.org
The Denver Academy applies a structured, closely supervised, and highly personalized approach to educating students with learning differences. This school has a 7-to-1 student-teacher ratio. About 420 boys and girls fill grades 1 through 12. Extracurricular activities on this 22-acre campus include drama and sports.

DENVER CHRISTIAN SCHOOLS
2135 S. Pearl St.
(303) 733-2421
denver-christian.org
Denver Christian Schools was established by a small group that settled here before World War I, many of whom were from the Netherlands and ill with tuberculosis. Since the first classes in 1917, DCS has grown to four schools at three Denver locations: Denver Christian High School at 2135 S. Pearl St.; Van Dellen Preschool and K-8 Campus at 4200 E. Warren Ave.; and Highlands Ranch Preschool and K-8 Campus at 1733 Dad Clark Dr. More than 1,000 students study in grades K through 12.

DENVER MONTCLAIR INTERNATIONAL SCHOOL
206 Red Cross Way
(303) 340-3647
dmischool.com

Denver Montclair International School is a multicultural school that attracts students committed to studying in two languages, choosing between French, Spanish, and Mandarin Chinese. Founded in 1977, it offers grades pre-K through 5 and prepares its students to thrive in a global society. Their middle school is an International Baccalaureate Candidate School for students in grades 6 through 8. Students study the usual round of subjects in bilingual instruction with an intensive immersion program. Child care is offered before and after school. Language courses and clubs are offered to nonstudents as well.

THE DENVER WALDORF SCHOOL
940 Fillmore St.
(303) 777-0531
denverwaldorf.org

The Waldorf movement emphasizes working with the whole child—teaching to the hands, the head, and the heart, according to the school's administration. Contrary to the popular belief that it is an arts program, the Waldorf curriculum is academically rigorous, and by 8th grade, most students have had exposure to chemistry, biology, geometry, and algebra. The arts, both visual and performance, are integral to the program as well and permeate every aspect of learning in this integrated curriculum.

The school seeks to meet the needs of the child at each developmental age and works to establish a balance and rhythm throughout each day, week, month, and year. The school offers pre-K through 12 and serves approximately 300 students.

FAITH CHRISTIAN ACADEMY
6210 Ward Rd. (elementary/middle school), Arvada
(303) 424-7310
4890 Carr St. (high school), Arvada
(303) 424-7310
fca-schools.org

A unique, charismatic Christian school, Faith is open to anyone interested in a Christian education. The curriculum includes the full range of traditional subjects. About 1,250 students study in grades K through 12. The Ward Road address is for grades K through 5, with grades 6, 7, and 8 just across the street. The Carr Street address is for grades 9 through 12.

GOOD SHEPHERD CATHOLIC SCHOOL
620 Elizabeth St.
(303) 321-6231
goodshepherddenver.org

Good Shepherd is between 6th Avenue and East Colfax Avenue, York Street and Colorado Boulevard. It offers a Catholic education along with a core educational curriculum. The enrichment program is a before- and after-school program, between 6:30 a.m. and 6 p.m., which includes guided study time, structured playtime, and extracurricular activities. A Montessori program is also available for age 3 through grade 3. The school offers grades pre-K through 8 to approximately 280 boys and girls.

GRALAND COUNTRY DAY SCHOOL
30 Birch St.
(303) 399-0390
graland.org

Among Denver's premier private schools, Graland has a history of fostering academic and personal growth. Its enrollment is limited to maintain small classes and close interaction between teachers and students. Graland is in a residential neighborhood 5 miles south of downtown Denver. About 645 boys and girls study in grades K through 8.

HAVERN SCHOOL
4000 S. Wadsworth Blvd., Littleton
(303) 986-4587
haverncenter.org
This is one of the best and oldest schools in the area for students with average IQs who have been diagnosed as learning disabled. With a 4-to-1 student-teacher ratio, the school offers kids with learning disabilities individualized instruction and occupational, speech, and language therapy as well as self-esteem groups. The goal of Havern is to ultimately reintroduce the child into mainstream education. The school currently has around 90 students.

HOLY FAMILY HIGH SCHOOL
5195 W. 144 Ave., Broomfield
(303) 410-1411
holyfamilyhs.com
Founded in 1922 as a parish high school, Holy Family's mission statement proclaims a Catholic-Christian learning environment that "stresses academic excellence, fosters mutual respect, demands responsibility, and encourages self-growth." Besides the standard high-school core curriculum, there are also courses in subjects such as theology, journalism, advanced computer applications, law, and drama. About 480 students study in grades 9 through 12.

HUMANEX ACADEMY
2700 S. Zuni St.
(303) 783-0137
humanexacademy.com
This alternative high school is for students in grades 9 through 12 who may not have been successful in other schools. Humanex is dedicated to the idea that every student can succeed in the proper environment. The school has a student-teacher ratio of 7 to 1, a closed campus, progress reports to parents every two weeks, and parent notification within 20 minutes after school starts if the student does not show up. It is oriented to pupils who have been diagnosed with or thought to have learning disabilities, ADD, ADHD, HFA, Asperger's disorder, twice-exceptional learning, bipolar disorder, and many other unique needs. Enrollment is at around 60 students, male and female.

KENT DENVER SCHOOL
4000 E. Quincy Ave., Englewood
(303) 770-7660
kentdenver.org
Kent Denver has roots going back to the founding of the Kent School for girls in 1922 and the founding of the Denver Country Day School for boys. The two schools merged to create the present institution in 1974. Its challenging, college-preparatory curriculum produced an average SAT score of 1,246 and an average SAT II score of 1,304 in the graduating class of 2004. Kent Denver has a campus of 200 acres with five academic buildings that include more than 40 classrooms and laboratories; six studios for music, dance, and art; two gymnasiums; six tennis courts; and 20 acres of playing fields. In grades 6 through 12, there are 672 students.

THE LOGAN SCHOOL FOR CREATIVE LEARNING
1005 Yosemite St.
(303) 340-2444
theloganschool.org
A school for gifted and creative children grades K through 8, the Logan School boasts a stimulating academic program with hands-on learning experiences for its 190 boys and girls. To be considered for admission, students must complete educational-assessment and intelligence testing and make an observation visit to a Logan classroom.

MILE HIGH ADVENTIST ACADEMY
711 E. Yale Ave.
(303) 744-1069
milehighacademy.org
This school dates from a one-room school established by Seventh-Day Adventists in Denver in 1913. The themes here are academic excellence, individual resourcefulness and responsibility, Christian philosophy, and making the world a better place within the student's sphere of influence. About 250 students attend grades K through 12.

MONTESSORI SCHOOL OF DENVER
1460 S. Holly St.
(303) 756-9441
montessoridenver.org
The oldest Montessori in Denver (there are other independent Montessori schools in Metro Denver), this school has about 275 boys and girls, ages 3 through 12. Like all Montessori schools, this one adheres to a philosophy that allows students "the opportunity to achieve individually, creatively, and successfully." The school has a wide parent volunteer base and offers a Montessori

curriculum including botany, zoology, language, math, art, physical education, and Spanish.

MOST PRECIOUS BLOOD PARISH SCHOOL
3959 E. Iliff Ave.
(303) 757-1279
mpbdenver.org
Students get a standard curriculum here along with religious instruction, including morning prayer and mass once a month. The school also features geography and spelling bees, science and art fairs, speech meets, and a "super citizens" program in which grades 3 through 5 choose a super citizen from their class each month to be honored by the Colorado Optimists Club. Grades pre-K through 8.

MULLEN HIGH SCHOOL
3601 S. Lowell Blvd.
(303) 761-1764
mullenhigh.com
One of Denver's more well-known Catholic private high schools, Mullen was founded in 1931 as a home for orphaned boys. In 1965 it became J. K. Mullen Prep, a college-prep school for boys. It has been coeducational since 1989. It's run by the Christian Brothers of St. John the Baptist de LaSalle, a religious teaching order. Today it has a population of more than 1,000 students.

OUR LADY OF FATIMA
10530 W. 20th Ave., Lakewood
(303) 233-2500
olfcs.com
At this Catholic school, religious instruction is offered in addition to the academic courses. The school has an extensive athletic program as well as special features including

a science lab, a reading lab, and a computer lab. About 305 students are in grades pre-K through 8.

REGIS JESUIT HIGH SCHOOL
6400 S. Lewiston Way, Aurora
(303) 269-8000 (boys division)
(303) 269-8100 (girls division)
regisjesuit.com
Regis has the Jesuit-school mystique of quality education with a public-service mentality. It has earned a US Department of Education School of Excellence designation. Special senior projects, volunteerism, student retreats, counseling, and peer tutoring are among the additions to regular curriculum here, as well as college credit earned from Regis University. Its population is currently at about 1,350, including 500 girls.

RICKS CENTER FOR GIFTED CHILDREN
2040 S. York St.
(303) 871-2982
du.edu/ricks
As the name implies, Ricks Center is for children who've demonstrated "educational needs in the gifted range." A strong academic curriculum is enhanced with extracurricular activities such as chess, student council, yearbook, and Odyssey of the Mind. The school serves approximately 250 students, grades pre-K through 8, and is part of the University of Denver.

ST. FRANCIS DE SALES SCHOOL
235 S. Sherman St.
(303) 744-7231
sfdsdenver.com
Since 1906 this Catholic school has been serving the same neighborhood south of downtown Denver, combining religious instruction and experiences with a strong basic curriculum and small classes for its 210 students in grades pre-K through 8.

ST. JAMES CATHOLIC SCHOOL
1250 Newport St.
(303) 333-8275
stjamesdenver.org/school
On Denver's eastern side, just northwest of the former Lowry Air Force Base, St. James provides a values-based education that emphasizes academic excellence, self-direction, responsibility, a genuine love of learning, and the wherewithal to become solid Catholic citizens. The school teaches 200 boys and girls in preschool through 8th grade.

ST. LOUIS CATHOLIC SCHOOL
3301 S. Sherman, Englewood
(303) 762-8307
stlouiscatholicschool.org
Mastery of the basics is the focus at St. Louis, along with art, music, computer training, and programs such as Junior Achievement, Great Books, and Community Resource. It's a Catholic-sponsored school, but non-Catholics are welcome. There's religious instruction, student-prepared masses, and special sacramental instruction for 175 students in grades K through 8. Extracurricular activities include spelling and geography bees, competitive speech, and competitive sports.

ST. MARY'S ACADEMY
4545 S. University Blvd., Englewood
(303) 762-8300
smanet.org
St. Mary's Academy is a Catholic, independent school founded in 1864 by the Sisters of Loretto. In 1875 it awarded the first high-school diploma in the Colorado Territory.

Among its features are its Early Learning Center at the Denver Tech Center and the all-girls' high school. St. Mary's emphasizes values-based education, small classes, strong curriculum, personalized attention, and community service. Coed through 8th grade, girls only in high school, St. Mary's serves a total of over 700 students.

ST. THERESE SCHOOL
1200 Kenton St., Aurora
(303) 364-7494
stthereseschool.com
St. Therese School includes Catholic teaching with its conventional curriculum. It's staffed by Sisters of Charity as well as lay teachers. It has a reading specialist and full-time teachers in physical education, computer science, and music education for around 225 students in grades preschool through 8.

ST. VINCENT DE PAUL SCHOOL
1164 S. Josephine St.
(303) 777-3812
svdpk8.com
A Catholic parish school, St. Vincent was founded to instruct children in the Catholic faith while also providing them with all the standard core academic subjects. Special features include a technology program and full-time teachers for computer education, art, music, and physical education. The student-teacher ratio is 20 to 1. St. Vincent's starts at preschool and goes up through 8th grade. It serves 485 students.

STS. PETER AND PAUL CATHOLIC ELEMENTARY SCHOOL
3920 Pierce St., Wheat Ridge
(303) 424-0402
sppscatholic.com

One of the west side's better-known Catholic schools, Sts. Peter and Paul provides sound academics and Catholic values and traditions to 425 students from pre-K through 8th grade. Features of its integrated curriculum include a literature program, computers, art, music, speech and drama, math, and physical education.

SHRINE OF ST. ANNE CATHOLIC SCHOOL
7320 Grant Place, Arvada
(303) 422-1800
stannescatholic.com
A high-quality, well-rounded curriculum in basic academics is accompanied by daily classes in religion. The school describes itself as a "Christian community witnessing to the gospel message of Jesus Christ." Special features include an education fair, a science fair, and a life education program, which tackles real-world issues that students face and will face in life. The school offers a computer lab, science lab, and library to its 473 students in grades K through 8.

SILVER STATE CHRISTIAN SCHOOL
14711 W. Morrison Rd., Morrison
(303) 922-8850
silverstateschool.org
Strong in music and orchestra, with daily Bible classes, Silver State has its own mix of standard educational curricula in a Christian environment. The school also participates in interscholastic sports governed by the Colorado High School Sports Athletic Association. Silver State has 195 students in grades K through 12.

STANLEY BRITISH PRIMARY SCHOOL
350 Quebec St.
(303) 360-0803
stanleybps.org

Stanley British Primary School (or B.P.S. as it's called locally) teaches 340 students in grades K through 8. Its philosophy is that education should be experiential, and to that end, students study where they are developmentally, rather than strictly by age or grade. The curriculum revolves around core subjects, with the inclusion of study skills. This school relies heavily on parental involvement, both in the classroom and in fund-raising.

YESHIVA TORAS CHAIM SCHOOL
1555 Stuart St.
(303) 629-8200
This private orthodox Jewish high school would be one of many in New York, but here in the Rocky Mountain area it has been unique since its founding in 1967. Half of each day is spent in studying the Talmud and Torah, and the other half is spent in secular studies. About half of the 65 male students board at the school.

COLLEGES & UNIVERSITIES

COLORADO CHRISTIAN UNIVERSITY
8787 W. Alameda Ave., Lakewood
(303) 963-3000
ccu.edu
As the only major evangelical Christian university in the Rocky Mountain region, Colorado Christian University offers fully accredited undergraduate and graduate courses with 21 undergraduate majors. CCU also offers programs designed to serve the social and spiritual needs of all students. The university has an enrollment of more than 4,000 students in all programs. The Adult Studies program offers accelerated evening, weekend, and on-site corporate classes (on-site training to company personnel) for adult learners, with centers at Lakewood's main campus and in Colorado Springs, Loveland, and Grand Junction. It offers undergraduate and graduate degrees and a teacher-recertification program, as well as an online MBA program. CCU is a Division II member of the NCAA, competing in men's and women's basketball, soccer, cross-country, and tennis in addition to women's volleyball and men's golf.

COLORADO SCHOOL OF MINES
1500 Illinois St., Golden
(303) 273-3000
mines.edu
"Mines," as it's called, is a school of engineering, energy, environment, and economics nationally known for academic rigor. It was founded in Golden in 1874 because that city was the gateway to Colorado's booming minerals mining industry. A public school, Mines now has about 4,300 students who focus on areas such as engineering, engineering systems, chemical engineering, petroleum engineering, mining engineering, economics, geology, and geological engineering. Degrees are also available in chemistry, geochemistry, petroleum engineering, and physics. Its metallurgical, materials science, environmental science, and engineering programs are among the best in the nation. Not surprisingly, Mines is strong in math and computer science.

Mines also has the benefit of a beautiful location. Golden is nestled against the foothills behind (from Denver) South Table Mountain and retains a small-town atmosphere. The school is a short walk from downtown. Golden is connected by I-70 and US 6 directly into Denver, by I-70 into the mountains, and by US 6 West through scenic Clear Creek Canyon into the Gilpin

County/Clear Creek County historic mining areas and mountain communities. Golden claims a higher per-capita concentration of PhDs than Boulder, home of the University of Colorado.

COLORADO STATE UNIVERSITY— DENVER CENTER (CSU)
410 17th St., Ste. 1400
(303) 376-2624
colostate.edu/denver

Colorado State University in Fort Collins is one of the state's most highly esteemed public schools. It offers a significant number of majors that are not available anywhere else in the state. It's nationally famous for its College of Natural Resources and its School of Veterinary Medicine. CSU is the state's only land-grant university; its Agricultural Experiment Station and Cooperative Extension form the education/research backbone of Colorado's agriculture industry.

CSU's Denver-area educational and technical services are found in a single location, the Colorado State University—Denver Center. Located downtown on Tremont Avenue between 16th and 17th Streets are services aimed heavily toward downtown Denver's working population. Among the degree programs offered are the executive MBA program, communication management, organizational performance and change, and construction management. Certification programs are offered in construction management, process management, and project management. Offerings include courses in education, vocational education, business and professional services, and personal advancement. This campus specializes in customized training for businesses.

COLUMBIA COLLEGE
6892 S. Yosemite Ct., Ste. 3-100, Centennial
(303) 771-0176
ccis.edu/aurora

This is actually one of 30 extension centers of the Columbia College campus in Columbia, Missouri, but it's a sizable operation. Some 700 students attend evening and weekend classes here, working toward associate and baccalaureate degrees in the liberal arts, sciences, business administration, computer information systems, psychology, criminal justice, history, government, and other subjects. It's primarily adult education, with an average student age of 34.

> **i** The Colorado Free University (which isn't really free, but very affordable) offers a vast array of fun, interesting, and informative classes for busy people. Whether it's computers, yoga, or wine tasting, CFU has something for everyone. Pick up class schedules at grocery and convenience stores.

THE METROPOLITAN STATE COLLEGE OF DENVER
Speer Boulevard and Colfax Avenue (Auraria Campus)
(303) 556-2400
mscd.edu

Founded in 1965, Metro, Colorado's third-largest college with more than 20,000 students, is a cosmopolitan city college on a 175-acre oasis on the edge of Denver's downtown business district. Half of its student body is of traditional college age (18 to 25), and nearly half consists of nontraditional students—those older than age 25 who have already been in the workforce. This, of course, can be a delight to professors who find they are dealing not only with students fresh out of high school but also with professional adults as well. And it's great for students because they can learn from their peers as well as their professors. Metro has a reputation as the working student's college, with an emphasis on applied education, and takes pains to accommodate that student with a lot of weekend and evening classes.

The main campus, the Auraria Higher Education Center, is unique. Metropolitan State College of Denver shares the campus with two other institutions, the Community College of Denver and the University of Colorado Denver. The three schools together offer a more potent education package than any one could alone because they allow students to cross-register for classes in all three schools and enjoy a combined menu of lectures, concerts, plays, and student programs.

Metro offers a full lineup of NCAA Division II intercollegiate athletic competitions in men's and women's sports. The teams use one of the region's best athletic facilities, the Auraria Events Center, which seats more than 2,300 and is used for a variety of campus-wide events. Metro's basketball team has gone to nine consecutive NCAA tournaments.

Metro has all the elements of a traditional university, such as extensive physical education facilities, one of Metro Denver's best libraries, and a quiet, tree-lined campus. The historic 19th-century Bavarian-style brewery, the Tivoli, which until recently was an independent shopping center, has been transformed into one of the country's most picturesque student unions. The Tivoli houses shops, the campus bookstore, restaurants, an arcade, recreation rooms, and nightclubs as well as student offices and services.

Although there are no on-campus dormitories, many students get assistance from the campus housing office to live on their own in surrounding apartments. Plus, Metro is an easy walk from downtown Denver, the Denver Center for the Performing Arts, Elitch Gardens, Coors Field, the nightlife and restaurants of Lower Downtown, and Sports Authority Field at Mile High.

Oh yes, and Metro has classes, too, 2,400 of them each fall and spring. The emphasis at Metro is on individual attention, with an average class size of just 22 students. Each class is taught by a master teacher; no student teaching assistants here. Summer offerings are also available.

Metro has 50 majors, in addition to the individual degree program. Degree offerings cover business, performing and visual arts, liberal arts, natural and social sciences, and specialty areas such as criminology, aerospace, journalism, and aviation and engineering technology.

Metro also operates two other campuses that offer degree programs and specialty classes. Metro South, in Greenwood Village, offers evening and weekend classes to more than 1,500 students from southeast Denver. Metro North, in Northglenn, serves the northern suburbs.

NATIONAL AMERICAN UNIVERSITY
1325 S. Colorado Blvd.
(303) 876-7100
national.edu

Aimed at the career interests of the nontraditional adult student, National's average student is age 32. The university offers bachelor's degrees in accounting, applied management, business administration, and computer information systems; associate degrees in accounting, applied management, business administration, nursing, and computer information systems.

REGIS UNIVERSITY
3333 Regis Blvd.
(303) 458-4100
regis.edu
Regis University got a nice big public relations boost in the summer of 1993 when it was chosen as the spot where President Bill Clinton met with Pope John Paul II on the pope's historic visit to Denver. Secret Service helicopters buzzed like flies over the surrounding residential neighborhoods. Regis has been around for a long time, founded in 1877, and it has a pretty 90-acre main campus, about 11,000 students, and a sterling reputation as an educational institution. It's a Colorado Jesuit university, centered around the Ignatius Loyola philosophy of leaders in service of others. Regis pursues that philosophy in three colleges: Regis College, the School for Professional Studies, and the Rueckert-Hartman School for Health Professions. Regis College itself is a relatively small school, with about 1,400 undergraduate students studying liberal arts, sciences, business, and education. The student-faculty ratio is 16 to 1.

The School for Professional Studies has undergraduate and graduate programs in business, education, and computer sciences and offers classes in Denver, Colorado Springs, Fort Collins, Broomfield, and Boulder.

The Rueckert-Hartman School for Health Professions is particularly well-known among the Metro Denver nursing community. Its graduate and undergraduate programs include nursing, physical therapy, and health care administration and management.

UNIVERSITY OF COLORADO AT BOULDER
Broadway between Baseline Road and Colorado Avenue, Boulder
(303) 492-1411
colorado.edu
Known in the vernacular as CU, this flagship institution of higher education in Colorado was founded in 1876, the year in which Colorado became a state. Today it is a university of international prominence. The university's campus in Boulder has 29,000 students, 75 percent of whom are undergraduates.

The University of Colorado at Boulder, or CU-Boulder, is where the university started, and it's still the state's largest and most important campus. Placed in the beautiful setting of Boulder's University Hill, its 786 acres of rural Italian-style buildings and complexes of Colorado sandstone make it one of the nation's most aesthetically pleasing campuses. A 1991 book, *The Campus as a Work of Art* by Thomas Gaines, ranked CU-Boulder fourth among 50 of the "most artistically successful campuses in the country." Because of nearby skiing and the many outdoor activities available, and because it's often the campus of choice for wealthy students who want an excellent place in which to spend their campus years, some people think of CU as a "party school." But CU-Boulder is far more than the place where actor and director Robert Redford played on the baseball team and waited tables in a local bar.

CU-Boulder excels as both a teaching and a research university. In 2005, *US News & World Report* ranked CU 34th among the nation's top 50 public universities offering doctoral programs. CU-Boulder's leading programs include telecommunications, aerospace engineering, and atmospheric and space physics. The department of molecular, cellular, and developmental biology is ranked among the top 10 national doctoral programs by the National Research Council. The chemistry and biochemistry department boasts 1989 Nobel Laureate Thomas Cech among its teaching faculty. Two CU professors won the Nobel Prize in Physics in 2001 for their work on Bose-Einstein condensate: Eric A. Cornell and Carl E. Wieman. And the 2005 Nobel Prize in Physics was awarded to John L. Hall, a fellow and senior research associate at JILA (a joint research institute of CU and the National Institute of Standards and Technology). CU-Boulder has a separate 147-acre research park nearby that is home to some of its many research institutes.

Programs include the schools of law, business and administration, education, journalism and mass communications, arts and sciences, music, and architecture and planning. The schools offer more than 3,400 courses in more than 170 fields of study to some 29,000 students.

Part of the Big 12, the school's sports program is impressive, too. Between 1988 and 2007 the football team went to 16 bowl games. Its women's basketball team has also made big news, making it as far as the regional semifinals in 2003 for the sixth time in eight years.

i The Auraria Campus—shared by the Metropolitan State College of Denver, the University of Colorado Denver, and the Community College of Denver—is a jewel of the metro region not only for its outstanding educational offerings but also for its accessibility to nontraditional students. Night classes have long been a mainstay for working students, and online classes are increasingly popular.

UNIVERSITY OF COLORADO DENVER
1250 14th St. (physical address, no mail delivery)
(303) 556-5600
ucdenver.edu

UNIVERSITY OF COLORADO ANSCHUTZ MEDICAL CAMPUS
13001 E. 17th Place, Aurora
(303) 724-5000
ucdenver.edu/anschutz

In 2004, the University of Colorado Denver consolidated with the CU Health Sciences Center, creating a new university with its main campus at the 175-acre Auraria Higher Education Center, shared with the Metropolitan State College and the Community College of Denver. The University of Colorado Hospital is located at 9th Avenue and Colorado Boulevard, and the Anschutz Medical Campus is located at the 217-acre decommissioned Fitzsimons Army Medical Center in Aurora.

UC-Denver, as it's commonly referred to, has more than 80 undergraduate and graduate programs, and students can cross-register at all three schools. The more than 12,000 undergraduate students at UC-Denver are therefore part of a much larger student body and enjoy more academic and extracurricular opportunities than those provided by UC-Denver alone.

A 5-minute walk from downtown, UC-Denver makes the opportunities of a state university available to working students in an urban environment. Strong programs include liberal arts and sciences, business and administration, engineering and applied science, architecture and planning, arts and media, and education.

The Anschutz Medical Campus is home to Colorado's only academic health center and the seat of medical research in the region. The main 46-acre campus offers baccalaureate and graduate programs in medicine, nursing, dentistry, pharmacy, and health-related fields. The center is as prominent nationally in research as it is regionally in medical education and is renowned in numerous fields including transplants, cancer, neuroscience, molecular biology, prenatal care, and cardiovascular services.

UNIVERSITY OF DENVER
2199 S. University Blvd.
(303) 871-2000
du.edu
Founded in 1864, this is the oldest independent university in the Rocky Mountain region and the reason why one of Denver's main north-south thoroughfares is named University Boulevard. In a residential area 8 miles southeast of downtown, the University of Denver, called "DU" by locals, is a good combination of big-university experience and small-liberal-arts-college atmosphere. The campus includes 100 buildings on 125 acres. Its Lamont School of Music and its College of Law are on the university's Park Hill campus, formerly Colorado Women's College. The student body counts about 11,000 students. About 4,500 of those are graduate students, and plenty of faculty members are at the forefront of research in their fields. The student-faculty ratio is 16 to 1 for undergraduates. Class sizes average 20 students. Undergraduate degrees are available in arts, fine arts, music, music education, science, business administration, accounting, chemistry, electrical engineering, and mechanical engineering. Campus Connection, a mentoring program, joins each new freshman with a faculty adviser in his or her major area of study.

UNIVERSITY OF PHOENIX
10004 Park Meadows Dr., Lone Tree
(303) 755-9090
phoenix.edu
This is the Colorado campus of the University of Phoenix, which is based, of course, in Phoenix, Arizona, but has more than 100 campuses in the US and Puerto Rico. It has four in the Metro Denver area, plus campuses in Fort Collins, Pueblo, and Colorado Springs. To attend you have to be a high-school graduate or GED certificate holder and be employed. This university focuses on degree programs and services for working adults. Degrees range from nursing and business administration to educational administration, computer information systems, and technology management. The University of Phoenix has about 4,000 students in Colorado.

WEBSTER UNIVERSITY
9250 E. Costilla Ave., Ste. 310,
Greenwood Village
(303) 708-8305
webster.edu
Webster University is based in St. Louis, Missouri, and has about 15,000 students worldwide; about two-thirds of them are graduate students. The Denver campus in Aurora offers graduate courses in business administration, business, computer resources and information management, human resources development, and human resources management. All programs are designed for working adults and offered in the evening format. The university has two other Colorado locations in Colorado Springs, one of which is at Peterson Air Force Base.

COMMUNITY COLLEGES

ARAPAHOE COMMUNITY COLLEGE
5900 S. Santa Fe Dr., Littleton
(303) 797-4222
arapahoe.edu

Arapahoe Community College's 7,500-plus students attend classes on a 51-acre campus adjacent to Littleton's downtown and just east of the South Platte River, which affords great mountain views to the west. It was established as Arapahoe Junior College in 1965, the first 2-year college in Metro Denver. It joined the Colorado State System of Community Colleges in 1970 as Arapahoe Community College.

Arapahoe leans toward 2-year associate degrees that help students enhance their careers with a degree or certificate, often while working. Some 50 percent of its students are working students. But courses can also transfer to a 4-year college or university. The college has more than 70 degree and certificate programs in both academic and vocational areas, with more than 2,400 classes per year. ACC also offers community education classes for the lifelong learner. The average cost of education here is 10 to 50 percent less than most Colorado four-year schools. The college also operates satellite classrooms at the Denver Tech Center and in Parker.

COMMUNITY COLLEGE OF AURORA
16000 E. Centre Tech Pkwy., Aurora
(303) 360-4700
ccaurora.edu

Community College of Aurora has been the community college of Greater Denver's east side since its founding in 1983. It moved to a 35-acre campus just west of Buckley Air National Guard Base in 1991 and, with the closing of Lowry Air Force Base, opened a second campus there in the fall of 1994, the Higher Education and Advancement Technology Center. Residence halls are available on the Lowry campus. Like other community colleges, it accommodates adult learners. About 60 percent of the students are older than age 25.

Community College of Aurora offers the full range of courses needed by students planning to transfer to 4-year institutions with associate of arts and associate of science degrees. It has vocational programs that focus on an associate of applied science degree and training for employment certification. And it provides a menu of courses that serves a wide variety of interests. The college's faculty development program, which trains faculty in better methods of teaching, has won several national awards and has been used as a model for schools across the country.

COMMUNITY COLLEGE OF DENVER
1111 W. Colfax Ave.
(303) 556-2600
ccd.edu

With about 6,600 full-time and part-time students, this is Metro Denver's "inner-city" community college. It shares the Auraria Higher Education Center's 175-acre campus with the Metropolitan State College of Denver and the University of Colorado Denver. About 37,000 students can cross-register in the courses of all three schools.

The college offers degree programs in the full range of college subjects, as well as transfer courses for the baccalaureate degree, occupational programs for job entry skills or upgrading, remedial instruction and GED prep, continuing education, community services, and cooperative programs with the other schools.

FRONT RANGE COMMUNITY COLLEGE
3645 W. 112th Ave., Westminster
(303) 404-5000
frontrange.edu

The community college of Greater Denver's north side, Front Range is Colorado's largest community college. It has about 13,000 students at its Fort Collins, Longmont, Brighton, and Westminster campuses. Front Range has more than 100 degree and certificate programs, including associate degrees in arts, sciences, and general studies as well as degrees and certificates in applied sciences.

Front Range offers classes for GED, English as a second language, and literacy and classes for students with learning disabilities. It is the leader among local community colleges in delivering courses at business and industry work sites, including companies such as AT&T in Westminster, Geneva Pharmaceuticals in Broomfield, and Rocky Flats in Jefferson County, where Front Range has 600 employee-students. It is also one of the few places in the West that teaches hearing people to interpret for the deaf. Its nursing program won acclaim as a 1994 program of excellence, and in addition to its vocational programs, it has 60 courses that transfer to 4-year schools. Locals can also take a lot of fun lifelong-learning courses such as handwriting analysis and garden management.

RED ROCKS COMMUNITY COLLEGE
13300 W. 6th Ave., Lakewood
(303) 914-6600
rrcc.edu

Red Rocks is among the fastest-growing institutions of higher learning in the state, and given its location, that's not hard to understand. Its 140-acre main campus perches on the western edge of Lakewood, in some of Jefferson County's most beautiful natural settings. Since 1969, when Red Rocks Community College was established, its annual student body has grown to 14,000 students on two campuses.

Red Rocks was founded in 1969 as a 2-year institution. It also serves northwest metro suburbanites with an Arvada campus. Its largest enrollments are in math, followed by the sciences, computer information systems, English, multimedia, fire science technology, and criminal justice. More than half of the students say they attend for job-related reasons. The college has special programs in construction technology, film and video technology, medical assisting, and biotechnology. The Red Rocks' Rocks Institute does customized training for businesses. The Red Rocks OSHA Training Institute began in 1992 as one of four sites in the nation designated by the US Department of Labor for OSHA training. A Computer Access Center trains individuals with disabilities to use adaptive computer technologies.

HEALTH CARE

The past 15 years have brought significant change to Denver's health care scene, due to hospital mergers and major new construction projects. Several of the city's largest facilities have been rebuilt on the Aurora campus that holds the University of Colorado Denver's health care programs. A few more have invested millions to upgrade their buildings.

Metro Denver residents are now well served, with three Level I trauma centers, with two emergency helicopter companies (AirLife and Flight for Life), as well as facilities such as Craig Hospital and National Jewish Health that have earned national and international acclaim for outstanding care and research developments.

In all, Metro Denver has 18 acute-care hospitals and three rehabilitation centers. Two operations, Centura Health and HealthONE, own and operate several facilities. The largest of Denver's hospitals, Presbyterian/St. Luke's, just east of downtown, has 680 licensed beds and nearly 1,600 employees. The smallest, Platte Valley Medical Center, north of Denver in Brighton, has 78 licensed beds.

Because of the city's attractive setting, Denver is able to lure high-quality professionals to staff its facilities. Hospitals and physicians work with university researchers and high-technology companies. The University of Colorado Hospital has been ranked as one of the 25 best hospitals in the country.

Pulmonary medicine is one example of a field in which Metro Denver enjoys renown. Many of the city's major hospitals, including National Jewish Health and the Swedish and Exempla Lutheran medical centers, originally began as tuberculosis treatment centers back in the days when tuberculosis patients came to Colorado for the healthy air. Research and expertise at institutions such as National Jewish and the Web-Waring Lung Institute are among the reasons why some of the world's most advanced pulmonary-technology manufacturers make their homes in the Denver area.

Denver's other research and medical advancement highlights include the Belle Bonfils Blood Center, the Eleanor Roosevelt Institute, the Barbara Davis Child Diabetes Center, and the C. Henry Kempe National Center for the Prevention and Treatment of Child Abuse.

To insure their health, Denverites, like others across the nation, have turned to managed-care companies that appeal to residents' sense of health and outdoor living through advertisements and policies that stress preventive care and healthy lifestyles.

PHYSICIAN & HOSPITAL REFERRALS

Clearly, health care choices abound in Denver. To find what's right for you, you can go to research extremes and get a desk directory of Colorado hospitals from the **Colorado Hospital Association** (720-489-1630; cha.com). The agency maintains a free directory of hospitals on its website. Other publications include issue papers on such topics as violence, teen pregnancy, and smoking. **Mile High United Way** is a great place to start when seeking all kinds of community-service information, and medical service is no exception. You can call their HelpLine at (303) 433-8900.

Metro Denver has more than 100 nursing homes and more than a dozen hospices, some operated in association with hospitals. A good number to keep on the telephone if you have kids is the Rocky Mountain Poison Center (303-739-1123).

Among the referral services to start with:

ANSWER LINE AT EXEMPLA GOOD SAMARITAN MEDICAL CENTER
(303) 425-2929

CENTURA ASK-A-NURSE
(303) 777-6877

HEALTHONE
(877) 432-5846

PHYSICIAN REFERRAL LINE
(800) 362-8677

ROSE MEDICAL CENTER
(303) 320-7673

HOSPITALS

Denver

CHILDREN'S HOSPITAL COLORADO
13123 E. 16th Ave., Aurora
(720) 777-1234
thechildrenshospital.org

The name says it all. Children's Hospital is a health care system caring for kids with the full spectrum of needs from wellness and prevention through the most complex care. Serving a 12-state region, Children's has been an innovator in medicine since it was founded in 1908, with firsts including the largest and most successful pediatric heart transplant program, the nation's first pediatric transport system, and the discovery of toxic shock syndrome. In 1997 it was designated as a Level I pediatric trauma center, the only one in the region devoted solely to children. In 2007 a new 1.44-million-square-foot facility was built adjacent to the University of Colorado Denver School of Medicine in Aurora to enhance treatment and research opportunities with faculty and students. The new campus has 270 beds and medical equipment especially designed for children, but its mission remains the same—clinical care, research, education, and advocacy.

Beyond the walls of the hospital, Children's offers pediatric services throughout the metropolitan area, the state, and the 12-state Rocky Mountain region through partnerships with other health care institutions and clinics. Children's also operates three specialty physician satellite offices, four community-based urgent and emergency care sites, and three specialty care centers. The hospital itself handles more than 10,000 inpatient and almost 350,000 outpatient visits yearly.

DENVER HEALTH MEDICAL CENTER (DHMC)
777 Bannock St.
(303) 436-6000
denverhealth.org

This is Colorado's largest public hospital, operated by Denver Health, which also runs Community Health Services, the Rocky Mountain Poison Center, and Denver CARES Community Detoxification. The medical center includes 398 staffed beds for a range of inpatient medical and behavioral health services. The center runs the Rocky Mountain Regional Trauma Center—the region's only Level I trauma center certified for both children and adults. It also operates Denver's 911 emergency system, paramedic services, . and one of the nation's most competitive emergency medicine residency programs.

To a large extent, DHMC is the safety net for Denver residents regardless of their social or economic status. Nearly half of all charges for inpatient and outpatient services come from people without health insurance, and more than a third are from people covered by Medicaid and Medicare. DHMC also emphasizes adolescent and adult inpatient psychiatry and handles some 3,000 childbirths a year. DHMC's Rocky Mountain Regional Trauma Center serves the entire Rocky Mountain region. With more than 3,000 trauma patients annually, it is the busiest Level I trauma center in the area. Denver Health also operates 10 health centers throughout Denver and 10 student health clinics in Denver Public Schools. Denver Public Health monitors communicable diseases such as AIDS, tuberculosis, measles, and hepatitis. It operates several outpatient clinics for diagnosis and treatment of these and many other diseases. Through its Environmental Health Division, Public Health provides a wide range of nonclinical services such as air and water pollution monitoring, restaurant inspections, licensing for day-care facilities and personal boarding-care homes, and operation of the Denver Municipal Animal Shelter.

DENVER VA MEDICAL CENTER
1055 Clermont St.
(303) 399-8020
visn19.va.gov

Through the VA Eastern Colorado Health Care System, the federal government delivers health services to people who have previously served in the military. With 128 beds in use, it provides medical, surgical, neurological, rehabilitation, and psychiatric care. The center also has a 100-bed Nursing Home Care Unit and reaches out to other parts of Front Range Colorado through outlying clinics and a mobile MEDIVAN program. Among their special programs are care and treatment for aging veterans, female veterans, homeless veterans, ex-POWs, and Vietnam-era veterans and issues relating to Agent Orange and the Persian Gulf. The center is also a major research site, the 14th largest in the Veterans Administration, with projects including a Schizophrenia Center, a VA Alcohol Research Center, and an AIDS Clinical Trial Unit. A new and long-awaited facility is scheduled to open in 2015 on the Aurora medical campus; it's being built on the former site of the Fitzsimons Army Hospital.

EXEMPLA SAINT JOSEPH HOSPITAL
1835 Franklin St.
(303) 837-7111
exempla.org/stjoes

Denver's oldest private hospital, Saint Joseph was founded in 1873 by the Sisters of Charity of Leavenworth, Kansas, and they still sponsor it. It has been designated as one of the top 100 hospitals in the US by the Solucient 100 Top Hospitals: Cardiovascular Benchmarks for Success survey, and it has a national reputation for the quality of its heart care. There are 565 licensed beds and 1,300 physicians. It has the busiest childbirth center in Colorado: With more than 5,000 births per year, Saint Joseph is the birthplace of 10 percent of Colorado's babies. The hospital's Maternal/Fetal Medicine program and Level III Neonatal Intensive Care Nursery ensure that babies needing extra help get the best care available before and after birth. Saint Joseph excels in other services including oncology, orthopedics, gastroenterology, and pulmonology. It also serves as the downtown emergency center for Children's Hospital and Kaiser Permanente.

HCA/HEALTHONE SPALDING REHABILITATION HOSPITAL
900 Potomac St., Aurora
(303) 367-1166
spaldingrehab.com
Although Spalding is officially in Denver, it actually has patients throughout the metro area. Its 169 licensed beds are located at other hospitals, in wings or units that specialize in the treatment of stroke, brain injury, chronic pain, neck/back injuries, neurological disorders, multiple sclerosis, and orthopedic problems. Spalding's history dates back to the Episcopal Church's Convalescent Home, which opened in 1914 to serve poor women and children. It was sold, with proceeds going toward a new 80-bed facility that was opened in 1965. In 1988 it opened a hospital-within-a-hospital at Swedish Medical Center, providing rehabilitation services in a hospital setting. That model continues

today with 100 beds and specialization in treatment for a wide variety of injuries and medical conditions. Inpatient and outpatient specialty care is offered at the main Aurora facility as well as at Presbyterian/St. Luke's Medical Center. Spalding is a joint venture of HealthONE and Columbia/HCA Healthcare Corporation.

NATIONAL JEWISH HEALTH
1400 Jackson St.
(303) 388-4461
njc.org
People with asthma and other chronic respiratory diseases come here from all over the world because National Jewish has an international reputation as a leading—if not the leading—medical center for the study and treatment of chronic respiratory diseases, allergic diseases, and immune system disorders.

National Jewish's pedigree is impressive. It is ranked among the top 10 independent biomedical research facilities in the world and is the No. 1 private institution in the world for immunology research. One of those Denver medical centers that originated to serve tuberculosis patients, it started in 1899 with the opening of the National Jewish Hospital for Consumptives. Today this nonsectarian medical center's staff of 1,100 serves patients on a sort of modified outpatient basis, in which patients usually stay in hotels or in some cases at another hospital. One out of every five pediatric allergists in the US was trained here.

National Jewish operates a free telephone information service, Lung Line, to answer questions and forward literature on such subjects as acute bronchitis, asthma, emphysema, and pneumonia. Call (303) 355-LUNG (5864) if you're in Colorado or (800)

222-LUNG (5864) if you're not for the 8 a.m. to 4:30 p.m. service.

PORTER ADVENTIST HOSPITAL
2525 S. Downing St.
(303) 778-1955
porterhospital.org
This hospital on Denver's southern border is a 369-bed, acute-care hospital that boasts more than 1,200 physicians. A division of Centura Health and a nonprofit organization, it's one of four—along with Parker Adventist in Parker, Littleton Adventist Hospital, and Avista Adventist Hospital in Boulder County—affiliated under Rocky Mountain Adventist Healthcare. It was founded in 1930 by Denver pioneer and businessman Henry M. Porter after he was impressed by his treatment at California hospitals that were owned by the Seventh-Day Adventist Church. He and his daughter gave the church $315,000 and 40 acres to start a hospital in Denver. The hospital's mission is "to serve as a continuation of the healing ministry of Christ." Its specialties include cancer care and cancer support, heart care and healthy heart programs, the Clyde G. Kissinger Center for Sight, the Porter Birthplace, Porter Breastcare, a center for treatment of substance abuse and eating disorders, transplant services, and education programs in areas such as stress management, weight control, nutrition counseling, smoking cessation, and alcohol education. Independence Square helps cardiac rehabilitation patients return to normal activities by simulating situations patients will encounter when discharged from the hospital.

PRESBYTERIAN/ST. LUKE'S MEDICAL CENTER
1719 E. 19th Ave.
(303) 839-6000
pslmc.com
A division of HealthONE, this huge medical center has more than 1,000 affiliated physicians and more beds (680) and staff than any hospital in Metro Denver. It would be hard to dispute its claim to being the most comprehensive health care provider in the Rocky Mountain West, given its amazing range of services. Among them are the Mother and Child Hospital, the Mothers' Milk Bank, the Sleep Disorders Center, the Colorado Gynecology and Continence Center, the Institute for Limb Preservation, the Senior Citizen's Health Center, the Hyperbaric Medicine Center, psychiatric services, organ and tissue transplants, Addictions Recovery Centers, and a wide variety of women's and pediatric services. The list goes on and on.

The Family Birth Place has been named as one of the top 10 maternity units in the US by *Child* magazine. More than two dozen nearby hotels offer discounted rates for patients who are being treated at the medical center. Call the welcome center Monday through Friday at (303) 839-6000 or visit the website at pslmc.com/patient_resources/hotel-discounts.htm for more information.

i Need specialized medical attention for your pet? Colorado State University in Fort Collins is one of the leading veterinary schools in the nation, and Metro Denverites often take their pets there for chemotherapy or other advanced veterinary needs. Call (970) 297-4477 for information.

ROSE MEDICAL CENTER
4567 E. 9th Ave.
(303) 320-2121
rosemed.com
Rose Medical Center, also a division of HealthONE, is well-known to many Metro Denverites as the place where their children, grandchildren, nieces, and nephews were born. That's not surprising considering its emphasis on women's health services, parent education classes, infertility, and high-risk pregnancies. The Rose Breast Center performs more mammograms than any other facility in the Denver area. And the Rose Children's Center is strong on inpatient, ambulatory, and emergency services for infants, children, and adolescents. All this is not to say that Rose is just for women and children. Opened in 1949 and named after Denver World War II hero General Maurice Rose, the Medical Center provided the first comprehensive, primary care–oriented health program designed especially for men. The special Suites at Rose continue to provide a distinctive level of care, including private chefs. Among the general list of hospital services provided by Rose's 1,100 affiliated physicians is advanced oncology research and Colorado's first coronary-care unit.

With 420 licensed beds, it was also the first adult acute-care metro medical center to formally affiliate with the nearby University of Colorado Health Sciences Center. Rose is also a teaching hospital. Other special features include a surgical treatment of emphysema program and sports medicine orthopedists, who provide care for professional and weekend athletes alike. In 1994 Rose created what it calls an orthopedic center of excellence, the Rose Institute for Joint Replacement, which is recognized for its model of full-service care. At the new Elaine and Melvin Wolf Ambulatory Surgery Building, Rose offers cosmetic and laser surgery services and a minimally invasive breast biopsy technology that is taught to physicians from around the world.

ST. ANTHONY HOSPITAL AND MEDICAL CAMPUS
11600 W. 2nd Place, Lakewood
(720) 321-0000
stanthonycentral.org
Replacing St. Anthony Hospital Central, St. Anthony Hospital and Medical Campus is the newest hospital in the region, with 8 floors and 560,000 square feet. It is home to a Level 1 trauma center, two new medical office plazas, a primary stroke center, and the region's only orthopedic specialty hospital. St. Anthony Hospital is treating heart attacks 38 minutes faster than the national average. There are 222 private inpatient rooms, including 76 intensive care and 128 medical/surgical. The hospital offers some of the most advanced technology and smart building features available. Specialties include trauma, cardiology, orthopedics, neurosciences, and oncology. The hospital also operates Flight for Life Colorado, providing emergency air transport throughout the Rocky Mountain region.

UNIVERSITY OF COLORADO HOSPITAL
12605 E. 16th Ave., Aurora
(720) 848-0000
uch.edu
University Hospital moved from its old, cramped inner-city location in 2007 to the shiny new Anschutz Medical Campus in Aurora. On the site of the former Fitzsimons Army Medical Center, it joined the University of Colorado's medical schools, a state-of-the-art cancer center, an eye institute, a

research library, the Center for Bioethics and Humanities, Children's Hospital, and a growing bioscience research park. Its first phase, the Anschutz Inpatient Pavilion, opened in 2004 as a family-focused community hospital. Those portions of the hospital that provide highly specialized care came next, joining the Anschutz Outpatient Pavilion and the Anschutz Cancer Pavilion on a campus that will consist of more than 3 million square feet of educational, research, clinical, and support space once it is completed. University Hospital was founded in 1921, performed the nation's first successful liver transplant, and consistently ranks among top hospitals in *US News & World Report* and many other rating agencies. Pushing the medical frontiers, the hospital has developed special expertise in areas ranging from heart surgery to cancer. All the providers at the hospital are faculty members at University of Colorado Denver School of Medicine, one of the country's premier academic research institutions. It's one of two public hospitals that serve Metro Denver residents.

Adams County

NORTH SUBURBAN MEDICAL CENTER
9191 Grant St., Thornton
(303) 451-7800
northsuburban.com
Since 1985 North Suburban has served the north metro communities of Westminster, Northglenn, and Thornton. It now has 157 beds, and offers women's diagnostic and treatment services at its Women's Center as well as diagnostic, intervention, and rehab treatment through its Cardiovascular Services department. The 26-bed emergency department is rated a Level IV trauma center with heliport facilities and has six beds dedicated to pediatric treatment.

PLATTE VALLEY MEDICAL CENTER
1600 Prairie Center Pkwy., Brighton
(303) 498-1600
pvmc.org
Platte Valley stays busy partly because of its proximity to US 85 and I-76. It's also the closest hospital to Denver International Airport. Founded as Brighton Community Hospital in 1960, it came under the management of Rocky Mountain Adventist Health Care in 1980. Although it's one of Metro Denver's smallest acute-care hospitals, it provides a solid spectrum of general hospital care ranging from coronary care and cardiac rehabilitation to perinatal and pediatric services. Its new building more than tripled its size, and its 50-acre campus allows for future expansion. Once completed, the planned build-out will include three 6-story buildings and more than 300 beds, transforming Platte Valley into a full-scale regional medical center.

ST. ANTHONY NORTH HOSPITAL
2551 W. 84th Ave., Westminster
(303) 426-2151
stanthonynorth.org
One of several major hospitals operated by Centura Health (see St. Anthony in Lakewood), St. Anthony North was built in 1971 to serve the northern suburbs. This 196-bed hospital is oriented toward the needs of young families in a growing community. The emergency room is one of the state's busiest. Major medical specialties include diabetes management, family practice, pediatrics, cardiology, and obstetrics, with advanced intermediate and intensive-care nurseries. It also plays an educational role, offering parent education classes, wellness seminars, obstetrics classes, sick child day care, and health-promotion activities for businesses.

VIBRA HOSPITAL
8451 Pearl St., Thornton
(303) 288-3000
northvalleyrehab.com
This is a comprehensive, long-term medical rehabilitation facility for adult inpatients and outpatients with traumatic brain injury, stroke, amputation, orthopedic conditions, arthritis, neurological disorders, pulmonary conditions, psychiatric disorders, or other disabling conditions. It's a 117-bed facility near I-25 just off the 84th Avenue exit. Comprehensive brain injury services include coma rehabilitation, acute brain injury rehabilitation, and neurobehavioral rehabilitation. Comprehensive rehab includes multiple trauma, neurological, stroke, orthopedic, amputee, arthritic, and neuromuscular rehabilitation. Pulmonary rehab includes ventilator rehab, ventilator management, and pulmonary restoration. There's a substance-abuse program for people with disabilities.

Arapahoe County

CRAIG HOSPITAL
3425 S. Clarkson St., Englewood
(303) 789-8000
craighospital.org
Craig Hospital dates from 1907, when it was started as a tuberculosis colony by Frank Craig, who himself suffered from the disease. Today Craig Hospital is dedicated exclusively to patients with spinal cord and brain injuries. It has been rated in the *US News & World Report* compilation of top hospitals every year since the ratings began. In 2011 it was ranked as the #1 Rehabilitation Hospital in the US by the American Nurses Association. Some 29,000 patients have been treated and rehabilitated since Craig converted to a rehabilitation facility in 1956. Another of those Metro Denver hospitals with an international

reputation in a specialized niche, Craig pulls the majority of its patients from outside Colorado. It supports that widespread patient base with an air-transport team that flies an average of 200,000 miles a year in a specially equipped air-ambulance, a Lear jet, and other aircraft. About a mile south of the Denver border in Englewood, Craig tries to maintain a casual, home-away-from-home atmosphere because it's a long-stay hospital that encourages family involvement in a patient's progress. In addition, there is a Transitional Care Facility, an outpatient and family housing facility, and an in-house cell center for clinical research trials. In these apartmentlike units, patients during the last phase of their inpatient stay can work on adjusting to independent life. The units are designed to hold the patient's family members as well, so family can help with the adjustment. Acute-care patients can be managed almost immediately after injury by Craig physicians and therapists in neurotrauma units at adjacent Swedish Medical Center and at St. Anthony Hospital and Medical Campus in Denver. The hospital is licensed for 93 beds.

LITTLETON ADVENTIST HOSPITAL
7700 S. Broadway, Littleton
(303) 730-8900
mylittletonhospital.org
A division of Centura Health, Littleton Adventist was opened in 1989 in response to growing development in south Metro Denver, from Littleton and Englewood to Highlands Ranch and Castle Rock. It's affiliated under Rocky Mountain Adventist Healthcare, and is located just north of C-470, near the intersection of Broadway and Mineral Avenue. Littleton features services including obstetrics and gynecology, pediatrics, surgical,

radiology, cardiopulmonary, rehabilitation, a Level II trauma center, and 24-hour emergency care. All of its rooms are private. The hospital's Family Life Center offers a wide selection of classes and programs. This 139-licensed-bed hospital represents an extension of the Adventist healing mission. In 2003 the hospital completed a $38 million expansion that added about 100,000 square feet to its original 210,000-square-foot structure, most in its emergency room area, but also adding a neonatal intensive care unit.

THE MEDICAL CENTER OF AURORA
1501 S. Potomac St., Aurora
(303) 695-2600
auroramed.com

Aurora's only full-service hospital, this facility consists of three campuses: the Main campus, the North campus, and the Centennial Medical Plaza. The center as a whole employs nearly 1,200 people and is licensed for 346 beds. The Main campus hosts among other things a Level II trauma center, the Women's Center, and the Colorado Spine Center. A new 84-bed tower for cardiovascular patients was added in 2009. The North campus includes the Sleep Disorders Center and the Geriatric Psychiatry/Senior Care Center. The Centennial campus has day-surgery services, and imaging and lab services.

SKY RIDGE MEDICAL CENTER
10101 Ridgegate Pkwy., Lone Tree
(720) 225-1000
skyridgemedcenter.com

Sky Ridge covers 57 acres and serves residents of Highlands Ranch, Lone Tree, Parker, Castle Rock, and Littleton. The facility has 156 beds and maintains a Level III trauma center, with 24-hour emergency care and orthopedic surgeons. It also provides cardiac

services, has a cancer center and a sports medicine and rehabilitation center, and provides women's and children's services. Sky Ridge also advertises its sleep disorders, bariatric surgery, and complementary/alternative medicine services.

SWEDISH MEDICAL CENTER
501 E. Hampden Ave., Englewood
(303) 788-5000
swedishhospital.com

A division of HealthONE, Swedish serves as a regional center for the most complex trauma, neurological, and infertility cases. Swedish received the Consumer-Choice Quality-Leader Award 4 years in a row between 1996 and 2000, and in 2002 it was ranked among Solucient's Top 100 Hospitals. Because it shares its campus with two major regional rehab hospitals, Craig Hospital and Spalding Hospital, it is well positioned to provide continuum care for victims of spinal cord injury, stroke, neurological disorders, and complex orthopedic problems. Critical health care includes cardiovascular and pulmonary services, oncology services, and an emergency and Level I trauma center. Special facilities include the Women's Center and the Oncology Center. The Laser Clinic offers state-of-the-art treatment for removing port-wine stains, spider veins, birthmarks, moles, tattoos, etc.

Jefferson County

EXEMPLA LUTHERAN MEDICAL CENTER
8300 W. 38th Ave., Wheat Ridge
(303) 425-4500
exempla.org/lutheran

This community-owned nonprofit health system was founded in 1905. In recent years it has rated among the top 100 hospitals in the nation. Lutheran offers a variety of outpatient and community outreach programs in addition to a 400-bed hospital, inpatient and outpatient psychiatric services, a rehabilitation center, a skilled nursing unit, a residence for seniors, and a full-service home-care and hospice division. It employs 2,500, with 800 physicians, and has a Level III trauma center.

MENTAL HEALTH

AURORA COMMUNITY MENTAL
HEALTH CENTER
14301 E. Hampden Ave., Aurora
(303) 617-2300
aumhc.org
Thousands of people a year receive help from Aurora Community Mental Health's six counseling centers and six residential facilities and through the Aurora and Cherry Creek school districts. Services include counseling for depression, older adults, divorce, parenting, drugs and alcohol, and group therapies. Also offered are residential services from overnight to long-term adjustments.

COLORADO MENTAL HEALTH
INSTITUTE AT FORT LOGAN
3520 W. Oxford Ave.
(303) 866-7066
colorado.gov
This is one of two state psychiatric hospitals, charged with providing treatment and services for the mentally ill. It was founded in 1961 and has 410 staff members. Fort Logan houses the statewide program for all deaf and hearing-impaired clients with mental illness. Areas of specialty fall in three treatment divisions: children and adolescents, adult psychiatry, and geriatrics. An inpatient-only facility with 153 inpatient and 20 residential

beds, this hospital is based on a treatment team approach—a patient's team consists of a psychiatrist, a psychologist, a social worker, psychiatric nurses, and mental-health clinicians. The team also has special-education teachers for children and adolescents.

COMITIS CRISIS CENTER
2178 Victor St., Aurora
(303) 343-9890 (helpline)
(303) 341-9160 (office)
comitis.org
This privately owned nonprofit has been serving youth awaiting placement into permanent residential homes since 1971. Comitis is a short-term residential care facility with a small emergency housing area for homeless kids. It helps get people off the streets and into low-income housing. Its main mission is to care for runaway and throwaway kids.

COMMUNITY REACH CENTER
8931 Huron St., Thornton
(303) 853-3500
communityreachcenter.org
Founded In 1957, this center has been serving Adams County residents with emergency and outpatient mental-health needs. About 4,000 people a year receive treatment for such things as anxiety disorders, substance abuse, and family issues. It also has five outpatient offices, in Brighton, Commerce City, Thornton, Northglenn, and Westminster.

DEVEREUX/CLEO WALLACE CENTER
8405 Church Ranch Blvd., Westminster
(303) 466-7391
devereux.org
Devereux/Cleo Wallace Center is Colorado's largest and most comprehensive behavioral health care organization dedicated to

the treatment of psychiatric, emotional, and behavioral problems in children and adolescents. Cleo Spurlock Wallace was a local schoolteacher who saw a need for special services for troubled youth, which was why she started the center in 1943. The center provides an inpatient hospital, residential facilities, day treatment, and outpatient services for children and adolescents with behavioral health concerns and for their families. In all, the center has 112 beds. It runs a school certified by the Colorado Department of Education, each classroom having both a teacher and a paraprofessional to integrate treatment into education. Devereux/Cleo Wallace is accredited by the Joint Commission on the Accreditation of Health Care Organizations. John Wayne used to come here for fund-raising events; he was a member of the Sigma Chi fraternity, which selected Cleo's hospital and school as its special charity.

JEFFERSON CENTER FOR MENTAL HEALTH
4581 Independence St., Wheat Ridge
(303) 425-0300
jeffersonmentalhealth.org
A wide variety of mental-health services are offered, including counselors in schools, an older adult program, several residential areas for inpatient services, and 24-hour emergency services. In all, Jefferson Center operates 16 satellite locations in Jefferson, Gilpin, and Clear Creek Counties.

ALTERNATIVE & HOLISTIC HEALTH

The alternative health scene is growing and gaining notice—and credibility—in Metro Denver. In fact, Denver has more professionals than most comparably sized cities. And nearby Boulder is well-known for its array of alternative healers.

Colorado's alternative health doctors got a boost in 1997 when the state legislature passed a law protecting the ability of MDs to do business by prohibiting the state medical board from disciplining doctors merely for practicing alternative medicine. The stamp of credibility was seen as a sign from lawmakers that alternative medicine is a viable option for thousands of people across the state.

Alternative medicine is generally defined as anything outside the mainstream of Western medicine. Services generally include herbology, acupuncture, massage, counseling, hypnotherapy, nutrition, hydrotherapy, reflexology, homeopathy, and chiropractics. Holistic is an approach to healing that views the patient as a whole being with a diverse life and range of reasons for ill-health. Holistic practitioners look for the interconnections of a person's health—not just the source of one given problem.

i As with many states, Colorado has varying requirements for alternative practitioners. Depending on the specialty, one may be required to be licensed, certified, or registered. The following listings are recommended as organizations committed to professionalism and overall health.

BRIDGES INTEGRATIVE HEALTH AND WELLNESS
8098 W. 38th Ave., Wheat Ridge
(303) 425-2262
exempla.org/bridges

Bridges is the only hospital-based center of its kind in the Denver metro area. It is a joint project of Exempla Healthcare and Lutheran Medical Center Community Foundation. Services range from massage and acupuncture to nutrition counseling, holistic counseling, and a wellness nurse consultation. Its mission is to offer complementary therapies that can be combined with traditional medicine, offering patients the best of both worlds and nourishing the mind, body, and soul. All practitioners meet the professional credential standards for their specialties.

Bridges also offers classes and workshops to the public, including yoga and meditation, as well as lectures on complementary healing topics.

EAST WEST HEALTH CENTERS
Central Tower
8200 E. Belleview, Ste. 202C, Greenwood Village
(303) 694-5757
east-west-health.com
This center includes more than 20 practitioners, including an internist and family physician, with both Eastern and Western specialties. Western services include family and sports medicine, preventive medicine, geriatric care, physical therapy, counseling, and OB/GYN. Eastern offerings include acupuncture, herbology, naturopathy, chiropractics, massage, Rolfing, nutrition education, exercise prescription, and stress management.

PROGRESSIVE HEALTH CENTER
701 Hampden Ave., #225, Englewood
(303) 788-9399
progressivehealthcenter.org
Integrating both nontraditional (Eastern) and traditional (Western) approaches to health and healing, this center offers a wide variety of therapies and treatments, including craniosacral therapy, acupuncture, reflexology, yoga, therapeutic massage, ayurveda, personal training, and meditation. Their Cancer Care Initiative, in conjunction with Swedish Medical Center, combines traditional therapies with nutrition, fitness, massage, acupuncture, pain management, and other comprehensive services. Through their various areas of expertise, the 16 practitioners here provide an integrative approach to wellness and health.

RETIREMENT

Forget Wednesday-night bingo and mashed potatoes in a dingy dining room. Metro Denver's retirement homes are called communities for a reason: They offer residents a place to recreate, socialize, and thrive. Auditoriums, fitness centers, restaurants, and swimming pools are only a few of the amenities. And with the older generation getting stronger and more prevalent—over the next five years the area will see a 30 percent increase in the number of people over 60 living here—housing options are getting better.

Metro Denver isn't exactly a retirement mecca on par with Arizona or Florida, but its sunny, mild climate (belied by our rare but news-making blizzards) has lured thousands over the years, including seniors who want to be closer to relatives or who end their careers in colorful Colorado.

The city and county of Denver has by far the greatest number of independent and assisted-living facilities for seniors in the area, but when you seek word-of-mouth recommendations, Denver's outlying areas, and especially the suburban counties, tend to get the most praise. That may not be fair to Denver's senior communities. It may simply say more about life being more difficult for the elderly in an urban setting.

DECIDING WHERE IN METRO DENVER TO RETIRE?

There are a variety of information sources to aid your decision. Referral agencies, such as **Community Housing Services** (303-831-4046; chsico.org), are a good place to start. Community Housing Services provides free housing referrals to use as a start in comparing costs, availability, and other factors. Another good one is **Senior Housing Options** (303-595-4464; seniorhousingoptions.org), a nonprofit corporation that owns and manages assisted-living properties and HUD-subsidized properties.

You can do your own word-of-mouth research by asking other seniors you meet in groups, such as the **American Association**

of Retired Persons Colorado (866-554-5376; states.aarp.org/category/colorado) and the **Senior Assistance Center** (303-455-9642; seniorassistancecenter.org). The **Area Agency on Aging at the Denver Regional Council of Governments** (303-480-6734; drcog.org) offers information and referral services for seniors, as well as a Nursing Home Ombudsman Program. You can socialize with seniors at any of Metro Denver's numerous senior centers. You might also get a copy of *The Denver Business Journal Book of Lists,* an annual publication of the *Denver Business Journal* (303-837-3500). We've mentioned it before as a great resource for all kinds of area information. One of its lists ranks the top 25 retirement communities.

The *Seniors Blue Book* is another source of information for seniors in the Denver metro area. Call (303) 393-1971, or try their website at seniorsresourceguide.com.

Once you know what part of Metro Denver you'd like to live in and have some communities in mind, call their sales offices for brochures and information packages. Then check them out in person. Arriving around mealtime gives you a sense of the staff and how well it relates to residents. Of course, most communities have marketing representatives eager to give guided tours.

Vital to picking the right place is the surrounding neighborhood: whether it's clean, pleasant, and quiet; whether there are parks and shopping within walking distance; and whether the surroundings are congenial to the elderly. Metro Denver's 4-lane traffic arteries such as Wadsworth Boulevard can be tough to negotiate, even for speed-walking teenagers. A more docile setting might be best for those with difficulties moving around.

The following entries represent the more-talked-about examples of retirement communities in Metro Denver. But by no means is the list comprehensive or meant to suggest other places aren't equally good. We have tended to look specifically at places with independent and assisted living in which seniors have their own homes or apartments. These are the midrange of a spectrum of senior living and care options ranging from nursing homes to prestigious single-family developments. Assisted living simply means that assistance is available for such needs as medication reminders; help with dressing, grooming, and bathing;

close-by medical and health monitoring; laundry; in-apartment meal services; and rehabilitation programs. Typically, both independent and assisted-living units have call buttons at strategic locations so that residents can summon help if needed.

Overall, these senior living communities resemble moderate to upscale apartments or condominiums. The difference is in the community feel, which places more emphasis on communal dining and gathering areas, shared activities, and services. Typically, at least one meal is included in rent, although this may vary. Housekeeping is a fairly standard service. Virtually every community listed here offers a calendar of social activities, many have their own newsletters, and all of them have their own transportation services to area shopping and other attractions. Residents are likely to have their own garage or carport space and storage lockers. Perhaps best of all, someone else cleans the bathroom and does the dishes!

RETIREMENT COMMUNITIES

CHERRY CREEK RETIREMENT VILLAGE
14555 E. Hampden Ave., Aurora
(303) 693-0200
cherrycreekretirement.com
Cherry Creek has a nice location in a residential neighborhood, across the street from Aurora's public Meadow Hills Golf Course. The village is in a 3-story, buff-colored building with a large circular drive and two atriums for relaxing and entertaining.

Some apartments have patios or balconies. Every unit has a window over the kitchen sink that looks out into one of the halls. They have 30 assisted-living and 185 retirement apartments. Monthly rent covers amenities ranging from continental breakfast and weekly housekeeping to excursions. Meals and other amenities are available at a nominal charge. The village has card and game rooms, an exercise room, library, country store, billiards, an arts and crafts area, restaurant-style dining, and a private dining room. Independent and assisted living are provided. Cherry Creek Retirement Village is part of the Century Park family of senior living communities, headquartered in Chattanooga, Tennessee.

THE COTTAGES AT DAYTON PLACE
1950 S. Dayton St.
(303) 751-5150
morningstarseniorliving.com/
daytoncottages

Dayton Place is on the western edge of the city of Aurora's south side, just off Parker Road, a major thoroughfare that runs northwest to Denver and southeast past the Cherry Creek Reservoir State Recreation Area. It is a 3-story complex with an open feel, in part due to its suburban location and perhaps in part due to its setback on large grounds with meandering walkways, gardens, and outdoor patios. Dayton has a general store, chapel, beauty and barber shop, TV lounges, a billiards room, and a cards and activities room. The facility has 96 assisted-living and 104 independent-living units called "cottages."

i Check the fine print when looking for a retirement home. Some communities require long-term leases and large down payments, while others are month-to-month. Decide what's best for you, then take the time to ask good questions.

THE COURTYARD AT LAKEWOOD
7100 W. 13th Ave., Lakewood
(303) 239-0740
thecourtyardatlakewood.com

Three blocks east of Wadsworth Boulevard and a couple blocks south of Colfax Avenue in Lakewood, the Courtyard is in a quiet residential neighborhood. Every apartment in the 3-story building has a view of the center courtyard, where there are flowers, rock gardens, and a pond. The Courtyard is managed by two husband-and-wife teams who live on the premises.

Beyond the living quarters, the Courtyard's amenities include a giant-screen TV room, a large kitchen for group activities, a beauty shop, a library, billiards areas, and a spa. They have 122 apartments. The Courtyard is owned by Holiday Retirement Corporation.

HARVARD SQUARE RETIREMENT COMMUNITY
10200 E. Harvard Ave.
(303) 696-0622
leisurecare.com/harvardsquare

Harvard Square's interiors are bright and open yet reminiscent of the club spaces in an Ivy League university, with dark wood and formal, old-world style. They maintain 189 private, unfurnished rooms. The exterior and grounds—overlooked by a second-story deck—also exude a country club air. Harvard Square is in the northwest corner of Denver's Hampden Heights neighborhood, just west of Aurora near the pleasant green spaces of Babi Yar Park and the private Los Verdes Golf Club. Although it's basically an independent-living community, it has a formal Assisted Living Program managed by a professional social worker with nursing support. Under the same roof, Harvard

Square also includes a dining room, beauty and barber shop, game room, library, and multipurpose room.

HERITAGE CLUB
2020 S. Monroe St.
(303) 756-0025
brookdaleliving.com/heritage-club-denver.aspx

Heritage Club has a good reputation for elegant living at affordable prices. The apartments are luxurious. The dining room looks like something in an upscale downtown restaurant with a menu to match, and there's a private dining room for special occasions. Heritage Club has a private library, exercise room with whirlpool and spa, country store and ice-cream parlor, billiards room, cards and games room, arts and crafts studio, and a beauty and barber shop plus shuffleboard, a putting green, and horseshoes pit. The bay windows and balconies are nice features, and the community is in the University Park neighborhood, a pleasant part of the city southwest of Colorado Boulevard's intersection with I-25.

MERIDIAN
10695 W. 17th Ave., Lakewood
(303) 232-7100
brookdaleliving.com

Denver's western suburbs in Jefferson County have the largest number of retirement communities. One of the most extensive retirement-residence organizations that gets mentioned in a positive light is Meridian, which has four retirement communities in Metro Denver. All are owned by Brookdale Senior Living, the nation's largest owner and operator of senior living communities. They also own a Meridian in Boulder and the Village at Lowry, 150 Quebec St. (303-364-7149).

Each is managed independently, but all are essentially the same: nicely appointed buildings on campuslike settings, with elegant interiors and formal furniture. The Lakewood and Englewood Meridians have nursing-home sections, while the others have independent and assisted living only. Besides the Lakewood location listed above, other area Meridians are located at 1805 S. Balsam St., Lakewood (303-980-5500); 9555 W. 59th Ave., Arvada (303-425-1900); and 3455 S. Corona St., Englewood (303-761-0300).

PARKPLACE
111 Emerson St.
(303) 744-0400
brookdaleliving.com/parkplace.aspx

In the heart of Denver, this 18-story independent- and assisted-living facility resembles one of those quiet, elegant hotels that get known by word-of-mouth. Its elegance is immediately apparent in the dark wood and rich upholstery of the lobby, lounge, and formal dining room, and the atmosphere is maintained throughout. It's next to Hungarian Freedom Park on the south side of Speer Boulevard, south of Denver's downtown and not far from the Cherry Creek shopping area. The Cherry Creek greenbelt and its pedestrian/bicycle path run along Speer Boulevard out front. Parkplace has an indoor swimming pool with a hot tub, exercise room, convenience store, beauty and barber shop, library, card lounge, patio dining area, and auditorium. Parkplace is owned and managed by Brookdale Senior Living Inc., Brentwood, Tennessee.

PORTER PLACE
1001 E. Yale Ave., Englewood
(303) 765-6800
centuraseniors.org/porterplace

Porter Place is on the campus of Porter Adventist Hospital in Denver's University Park neighborhood on the northernmost edge of Englewood. In addition to independent and assisted living (with studio, one-bedroom, and two-bedroom apartments), it offers small studio apartments for visiting family and friends of residents, and the facility offers respite care. Porter Place is affiliated with Centura Health and Porter Adventist Hospital, but that doesn't mean it looks like a medical facility. The interiors are lovely, from the grand piano and high ceilings of the lobby to the pleasant tranquility of the library. There are flower gardens and outdoor patios, activity rooms, a chapel, gift shop, beauty and barber shop, big-screen TV room, parlor, card room, and craft room. Plus residents have access to the hospital's Porter Health Club. A recently completed addition provides assisted living in a secure environment, called Memory Care, in the Elizabeth Rose Wing.

SHALOM PARK SENIOR RESIDENCES
14800 E. Bellevue Dr., Aurora
(303) 680-5000
shalompark.org

One of Metro Denver's newer retirement additions is Shalom Park Senior Residences. The 41-acre community offers residents lovely grounds as well as an in-house activity department to keep them entertained. There are a total of 104 units, including 44 patio homes and 60 apartments. Any of the 104 units can be assisted or independent living, depending on the needs of the occupants.

SPRINGWOOD RETIREMENT CAMPUS
6550 Yank Way, Arvada
(303) 424-6550
springwoodretirement.com

The Springwood Retirement Campus is just off Yankee Doodle Park in a nice residential section of Arvada. Facilities and services include a full-time social director, dining room, maid service, laundry and dry cleaning, general store, library, chapel, hair salon, game room, and exercise facility. They offer three different lifestyle possibilities based on individual needs, including independent living, assisted living, and memory care. Lutheran Medical Center provides input to Springwood's health care and health-promoting activities.

Springwood offers a variety of one- and two-bedroom apartments, with two-way intercom and emergency buzzers; it also offers assisted living at its Nightingale Suites. The cottages at Springwood are 1,100-square-foot residences built on a private cul-de-sac. Each includes a foyer, living room, dining room, covered patio, master bedroom with its own bath and oversize walk-in closet, guest bedroom, second bathroom, laundry and utility room, and attached garage.

i If you're in the market for a retirement community, start early. Allow yourself up to a year to compare and visit locations, especially if you need a large space. Many communities have waiting lists for two-bedroom units, which are tougher to come by.

THE VILLAS AT SUNNY ACRES
2501 E. 104th Ave., Thornton
(303) 255-4100
centuraseniors.org/villassunnyacres
Perhaps the most oft-recommended retirement community by word-of-mouth, Sunny Acres is a large facility on a campuslike setting just south of Stonehocker Park in Thornton. The northern suburbs are quiet areas with good mountain views and a lot of remaining open space, and the landscaped grounds include two fishing lakes as well as gardening areas for residents. To that Sunny Acres adds amenities including home health care, 10 libraries, a 3,000-square-foot fitness center, a whirlpool, pool tables, a woodworking and carpentry shop, lounges, dining rooms including a restaurant, a convenience store, and beauty and barber shops.

MEDIA

Greater Denver is not exactly a media center, at least not in the sense of New York or Los Angeles. It doesn't produce a lot of television programs or magazines, though it does occasionally show up in movies. Still, as the largest city between California and Missouri, Denver has a wealth of respected print, television, and radio broadcast media outlets.

NEWSPAPERS

Denver was among the last US cities to have two independent newspapers. That changed in 2009, when the *Rocky Mountain News* published its last edition. The *Denver Post* remains as the city's only daily newspaper. *Westword*, the city's free arts and entertainment publication, comes out weekly. There are also many community papers, too numerous to list here. Specialized publications are always coming into and going out of existence to serve a particular region (downtown) or interest (art).

Dailies

THE DENVER POST
1560 Broadway
(303) 954-1010
denverpost.com

The *Denver Post* has a long and colorful history. It was founded in 1895 by Harry Heye Tammen and Frederick Gilmer Bonfils. The early *Post* was a prime example of sensational journalism, relying on stunts and gossip to attract readership. In the 1920s Tammen and Bonfils got themselves entangled in one fine mess, the Teapot Dome scandal. Originally vehemently opposed to

questionable oil leases in Wyoming, the *Post* dropped the issue when paid to do so. Tammen died of cancer in 1924, and Bonfils resigned in 1926.

After Bonfils died in 1933, ownership passed largely to his daughters. In the 1960s May Bonfils sold her stock to S. I. Newhouse, head of a chain of newspapers and magazines. Helen Bonfils contested the sale, and after years of litigation, Newhouse finally dropped his bid to gain control of the *Post* in 1973. The *Post* was sold to the Times Mirror Company, owners of the *Los Angeles Times,* in 1980, and sold again to William Dean Singleton of the Denver-based MediaNews Group in 1987.

The *Post* switched from evening to morning distribution in 1982. Daily circulation for the *Post* is about 353,000; Sunday sales average around 538,000 including digital editions.

Weeklies

In addition to the following non-dailies, weekly newspapers are published for residents of Englewood, Highlands Ranch, Littleton, Evergreen, Golden, Greenwood

Village, and Westminster. If you live there or are interested in news about those communities, check for these papers at local newsstands.

BROOMFIELD ENTERPRISE
1006 Depot Hill Rd., Ste. G, Broomfield
(303) 448-9898
broomfieldenterprise.com
This community paper is a subsidiary of the *Daily Camera*, Boulder's daily newspaper. It is delivered free to Broomfield residences and businesses and carries news of Broomfield, Metro Denver's most northwestern community. Regular offerings include news and feature stories, editorials, and classified ads. Coverage is strong on government, business, schools, and sports. The paper also publishes special sections ranging from homes and gardens to election issues.

COMMUNITY MEDIA OF COLORADO
110 N. Rubey Dr., Ste. 120
(303) 279-5541
ourcoloradonews.com
This company publishes 18 different weekly newspapers for residents of Metro Denver communities and beyond, as well as an online edition. The papers focus on news relevant to these suburbs and include quarterly education sections and a yearly garden insert. The website lists publications covering specific areas.

DENVER BUSINESS JOURNAL
1700 Broadway, #515
(303) 803-9200
bizjournals.com/denver
The weekly *Denver Business Journal* covers local business news in depth and includes a small-business strategy section, along with specialized sections that relate to a variety of topics from health care to personal finance. The paper comes out on Friday and is available by subscription or throughout Metro Denver by single copy.

WESTWORD
969 Broadway
(303) 296-7744
westword.com
Owned by Village Voice Media, a national publisher of "alternative" papers, *Westword* is known for its muckraking investigative stories and is depended upon for its arts and entertainment coverage. Not everyone admires the weekly paper's zeal in pursuing stories, as is evidenced by heated letters to the editor. But many of its articles, such as an investigation of the Rocky Flats grand jury proceedings that examined who should be held responsible for environmental crimes, have won awards and national media attention.

Westword is distributed free throughout Metro Denver and hits the streets late Wednesday afternoon. You can find it in boxes on street corners all over town. Its arts/dining/entertainment listings are superb.

MAGAZINES & SPECIAL INTEREST PUBLICATIONS

COLORADO EXPRESSION
New West Publishing
3600 S. Beeler St., Ste. 100
(303) 694-1289
coloradoexpression.com
Colorado Expression is the flagship of New West's three magazines. The others are *Confetti* and *Architecture & Design of the West*.

COLORADO HOMES & LIFESTYLES
1780 S. Bellaire St., Ste. 505
(303) 248-2060
coloradohomesmag.com
Colorado Homes & Lifestyles, which is published nine times a year, not only includes a wealth of information about home and garden design, but also personality profiles of Colorado residents.

COLORADO PARENT
5460 S. Quebec St., Ste. 130
Greenwood Village
(303) 320-1000
coloradoparent.com
This magazine includes a comprehensive calendar of events and lists classes of interest to parents in the Metro Denver area. The free paper comes out the first of each month and can be picked up in about 800 different locations around town, including libraries and bookstores. The folks at Colorado Parent also publish an annual A-to-Z directory of local resources for parents each January.

5280
1514 Curtis St., Ste. 300
(303) 832-5280
5280.com
5280, "Denver's Mile-High Magazine," debuted in 1993, named for Denver's altitude at 5,280 feet above sea level. It's fresh and independent and has a lively design like any city magazine. It covers things of interest to locals—restaurants, getaways, and interesting people.

HIGH COUNTRY NEWS
119 Grand Ave., Paonia
(970) 527-4898
hcn.org

An environmentally oriented newspaper, High Country News is published in Paonia, Colorado. The much-praised paper focuses on issues intrinsic to the West, such as use of public lands and water and grazing rights. This sharp biweekly is highly recommended to Metro Denver newcomers who would like to know more about the region they now call home. It's available at the Tattered Cover Book Store (see our Shopping chapter) and other locations throughout the city, or call for a subscription.

OUT FRONT COLORADO
3535 Walnut St.
(303) 778-7900
outfrontonline.com
A gay and lesbian newspaper, Out Front Colorado is published every 2 weeks (with a break at Christmas). The paper is free and is available at local bars, restaurants, gay businesses, and bookstores. It's noted for its entertainment and nightlife listings.

RADIO

Nothing but the Rocky Mountain weather changes as much as Denver radio stations. One day you're listening to jazz; the next day the station has gone country-western. Consider that caveat when tuning in to the stations listed below. For an up-to-date list, check the TV section in the Sunday Denver Post.

Adult Contemporary
KYSL 93.9 FM
KOSI 101.1 FM

Christian
KLDV 91.1 FM

TJRN 107.9 FM
KLTT 670 AM
KPOF 910 AM
KRKS 990 AM and 94.7 FM

Classical

KVOD 88.1 FM

Country

KYGO 98.5 FM

Hip-Hop

KQKS 107.5 FM

Jazz

KUVO 89.3 FM
KJCD 104.3 FM

Mexican/Spanish

KJMN 92.1 FM
KXPK 96.5 FM
KMXA 1090 AM
KLVZ 1220 AM
KBNO 1280 AM

National Public Radio

KGNU 88.5 FM
KUNC 91.5 FM
KCFR 1340 AM
KCFC 1490 AM

News/Talk/Sports

MMAZ 87.5 FM
KLZ 560 AM
KHOW 630 AM
KKZN 760 AM
KNUS 710 AM
KOA 850 AM
KBJD 1650 AM

Oldies

KDJM 92.5 FM
KRFX 103.5 FM (classic rock)
KXKL 105.1 FM (1960s–1970s)
KEZW 1430 AM

Rock, Alternative & Progressive

KTCL 93.3 FM
KBCO 97.3 FM
KQMT 99.5 FM
KBPI 106.7 FM

Sports Only

KCKK 93.7 FM and 1510 AM
KLZ 560 AM (ESPN)
KKFN 950 AM
KEPN 1600 AM

TELEVISION

With all the recent mergers and acquisitions in the cable industry, Denver is down to one main cable TV supplier for most of the metropolitan area. Call Comcast at (303) 266-2278 for service information for your area. An alternative to cable is satellite TV. DirecTV (directv.com) operates its national direct-satellite service out of Castle Rock, about a half hour south of Denver. The area's other provider is Echo Star, in Englewood (303-706-4000).

Major Local TV Stations & Network Affiliates

KWGN Channel 2 (Independent/WB)
KCNC Channel 4 (CBS)
KRMA Channel 6 (PBS)
KMGH Channel 7 (ABC)
KUSA Channel 9 (NBC)
KBDI Channel 12 (PBS)

MEDIA

KTVD Channel 20 (Independent/UPN)
KDEN Channel 25 (NBC Telemundo)
KDVR Channel 31 (Fox)
KRMT Channel 41 (Independent)
KCEC Channel 50 (Entravision)
KETD Channel 53 (Independent)

INDEX